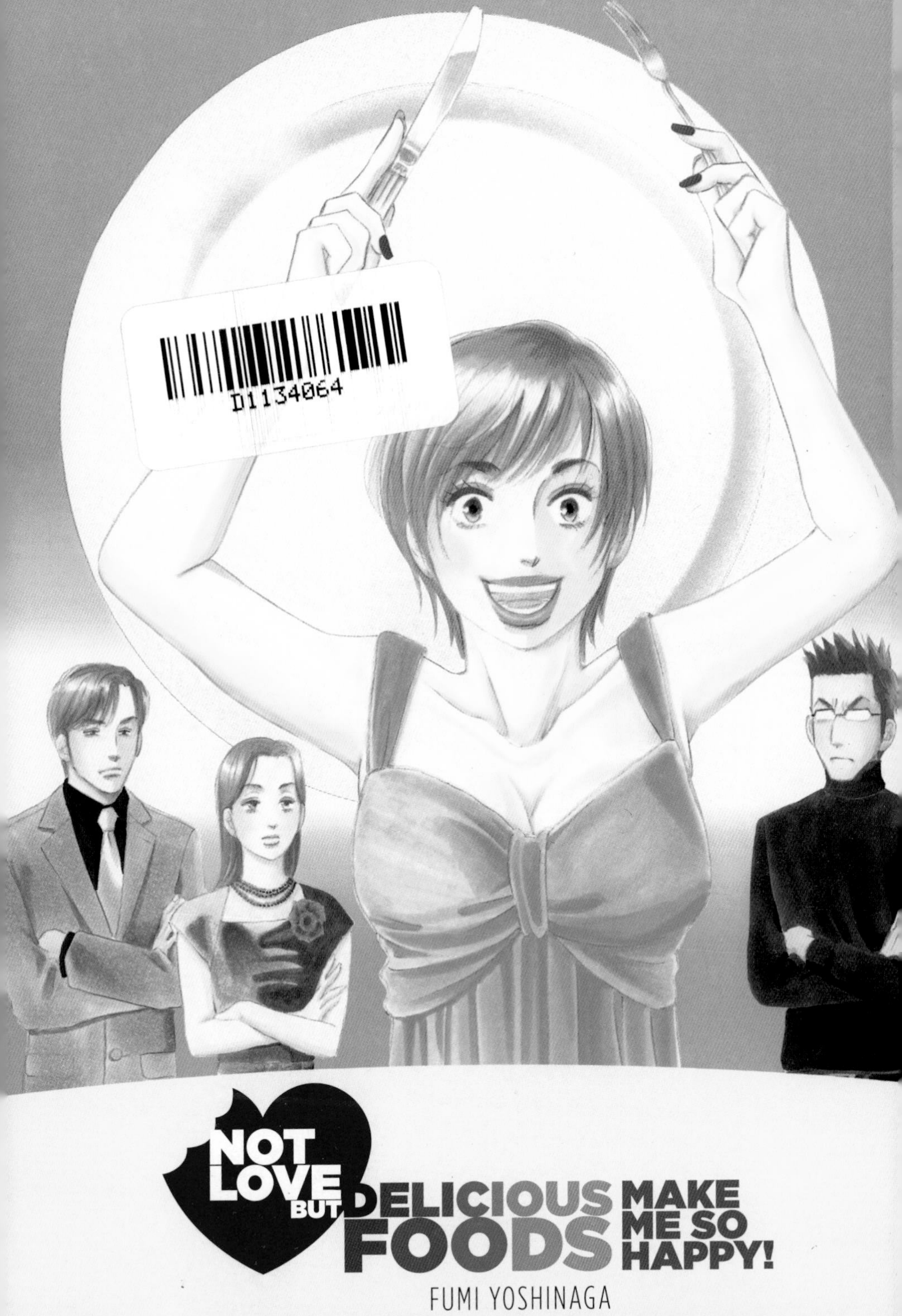

NOT LOVE BUT DELICIOUS FOODS MAKE ME SO HAPPY!

FUMI YOSHINAGA

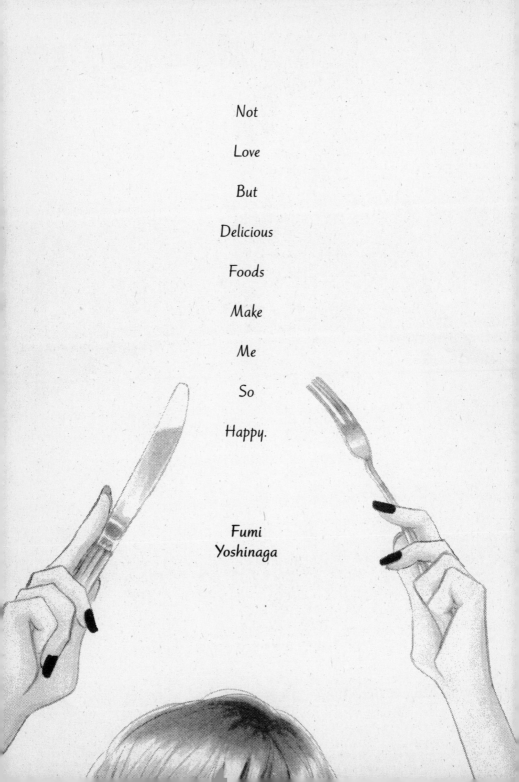

Not

Love

But

Delicious

Foods

Make

Me

So

Happy.

Fumi
Yoshinaga

menu
contents

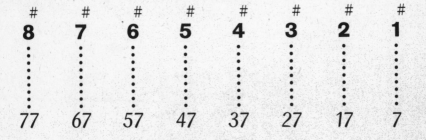

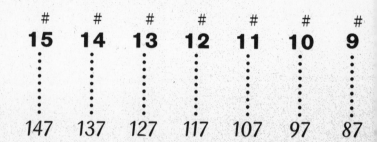

NOT LOVE BUT DELICIOUS FOODS MAKE ME SO HAPPY!

This story is a work of fiction. Any similarities to actual persons is purely coincidental. But all of the restaurants in this book are real.

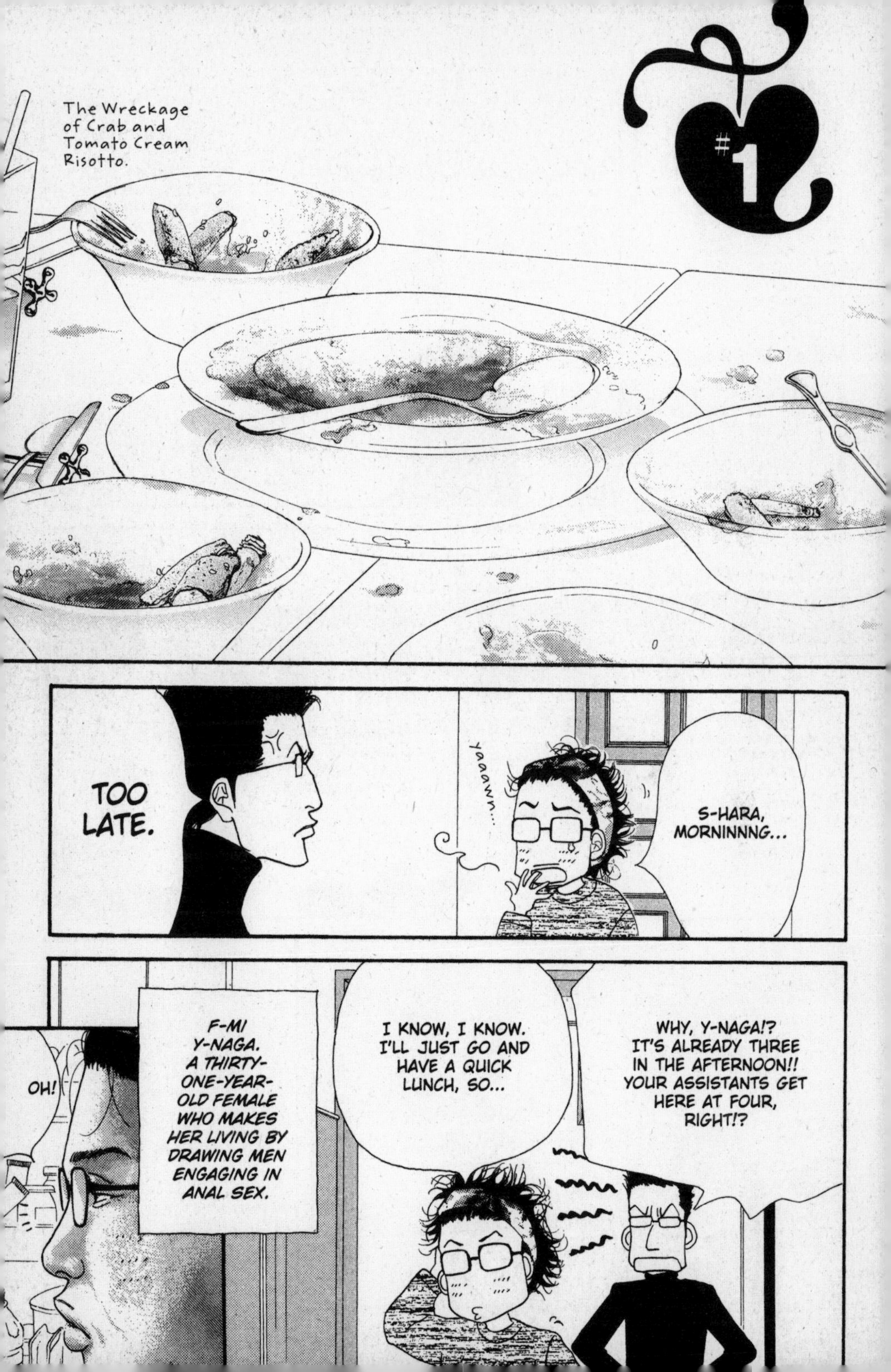
#1
The Wreckage of Crab and Tomato Cream Risotto.
S-HARA, MORNINNNG...
Yaaawn...
TOO LATE.
WHY, Y-NAGA!? IT'S ALREADY THREE IN THE AFTERNOON!! YOUR ASSISTANTS GET HERE AT FOUR, RIGHT!?
I KNOW, I KNOW. I'LL JUST GO AND HAVE A QUICK LUNCH, SO...
F-MI Y-NAGA. A THIRTY-ONE-YEAR-OLD FEMALE WHO MAKES HER LIVING BY DRAWING MEN ENGAGING IN ANAL SEX.
OH!

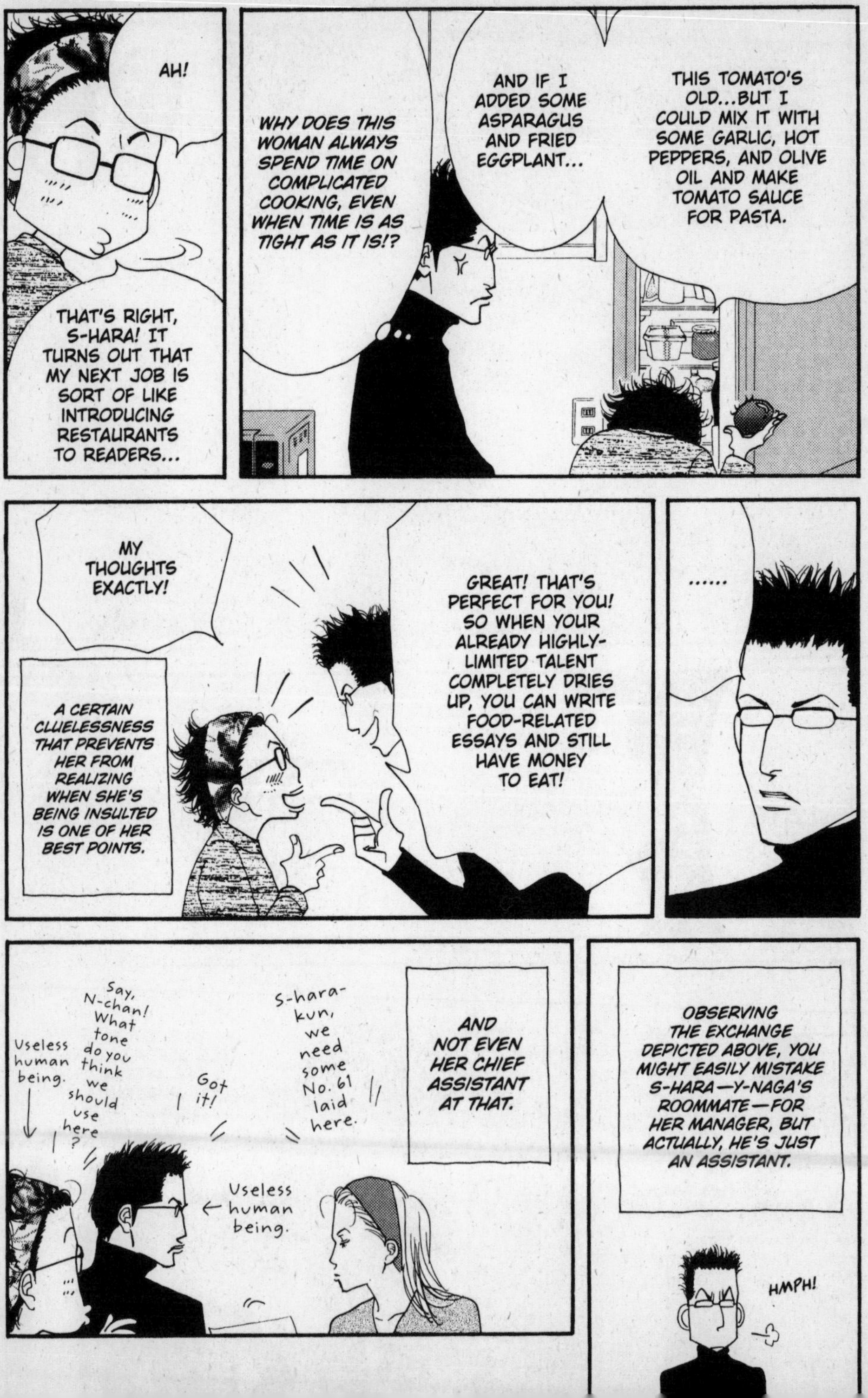
THIS TOMATO'S OLD...BUT I COULD MIX IT WITH SOME GARLIC, HOT PEPPERS, AND OLIVE OIL AND MAKE TOMATO SAUCE FOR PASTA.
AND IF I ADDED SOME ASPARAGUS AND FRIED EGGPLANT...
WHY DOES THIS WOMAN ALWAYS SPEND TIME ON COMPLICATED COOKING, EVEN WHEN TIME IS AS TIGHT AS IT IS!?
AH!
THAT'S RIGHT, S-HARA! IT TURNS OUT THAT MY NEXT JOB IS SORT OF LIKE INTRODUCING RESTAURANTS TO READERS...
......
GREAT! THAT'S PERFECT FOR YOU! SO WHEN YOUR ALREADY HIGHLY-LIMITED TALENT COMPLETELY DRIES UP, YOU CAN WRITE FOOD-RELATED ESSAYS AND STILL HAVE MONEY TO EAT!
MY THOUGHTS EXACTLY!
A CERTAIN CLUELESSNESS THAT PREVENTS HER FROM REALIZING WHEN SHE'S BEING INSULTED IS ONE OF HER BEST POINTS.
OBSERVING THE EXCHANGE DEPICTED ABOVE, YOU MIGHT EASILY MISTAKE S-HARA—Y-NAGA'S ROOMMATE—FOR HER MANAGER, BUT ACTUALLY, HE'S JUST AN ASSISTANT.
HMPH!
AND NOT EVEN HER CHIEF ASSISTANT AT THAT.
S-hara-kun, we need some No. 61 laid here.
Got it!
Say, N-chan! What tone do you think we should use here?
Useless human being.
Useless human being.

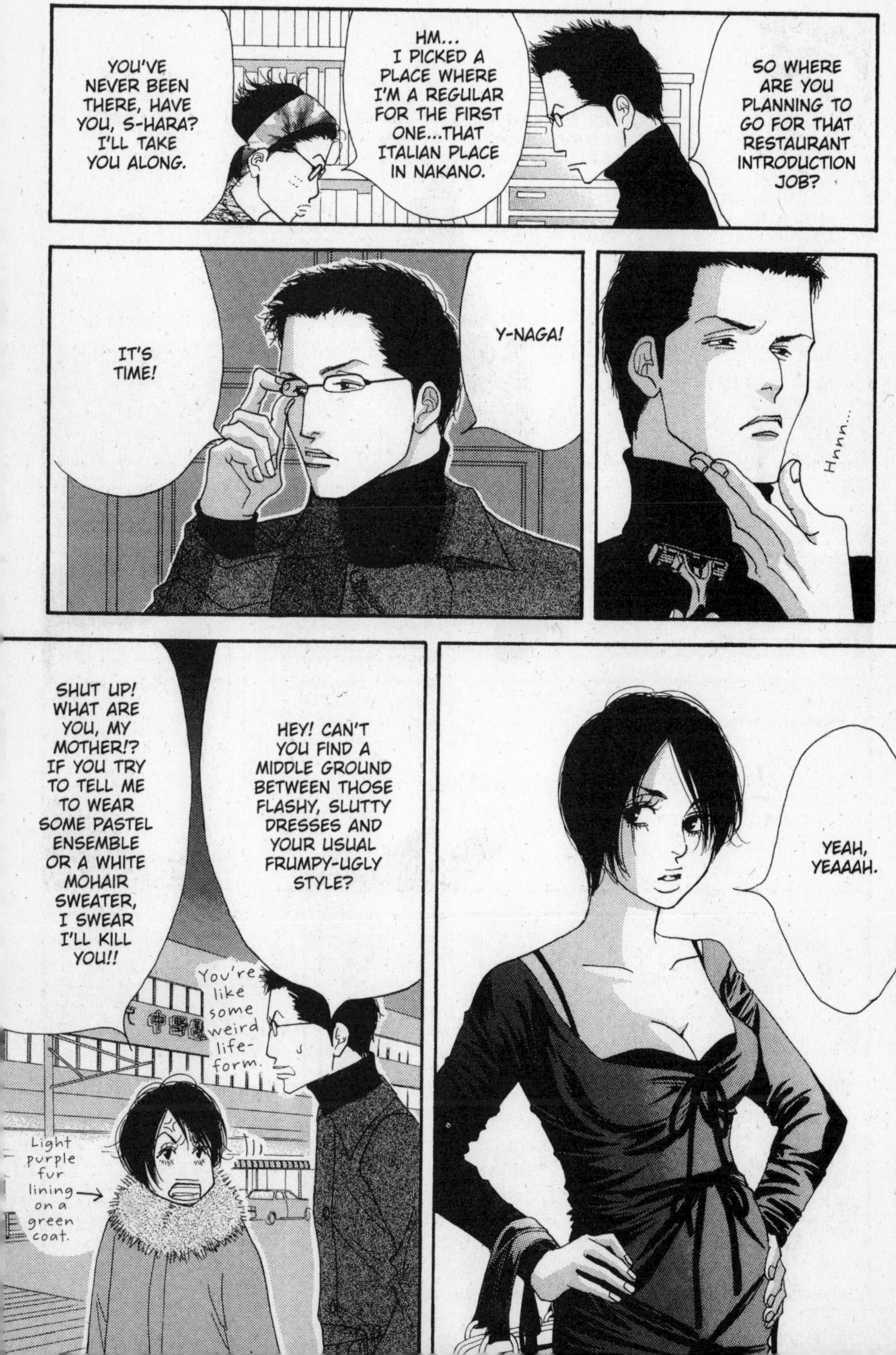

SO WHERE ARE YOU PLANNING TO GO FOR THAT RESTAURANT INTRODUCTION JOB?
HM... I PICKED A PLACE WHERE I'M A REGULAR FOR THE FIRST ONE...THAT ITALIAN PLACE IN NAKANO.
YOU'VE NEVER BEEN THERE, HAVE YOU, S-HARA? I'LL TAKE YOU ALONG.
Hnnn...
Y-NAGA!
IT'S TIME!
YEAH, YEAAAH.
HEY! CAN'T YOU FIND A MIDDLE GROUND BETWEEN THOSE FLASHY, SLUTTY DRESSES AND YOUR USUAL FRUMPY-UGLY STYLE?
SHUT UP! WHAT ARE YOU, MY MOTHER!? IF YOU TRY TO TELL ME TO WEAR SOME PASTEL ENSEMBLE OR A WHITE MOHAIR SWEATER, I SWEAR I'LL KILL YOU!!
You're like some weird life-form.
Light purple fur lining on a green coat.

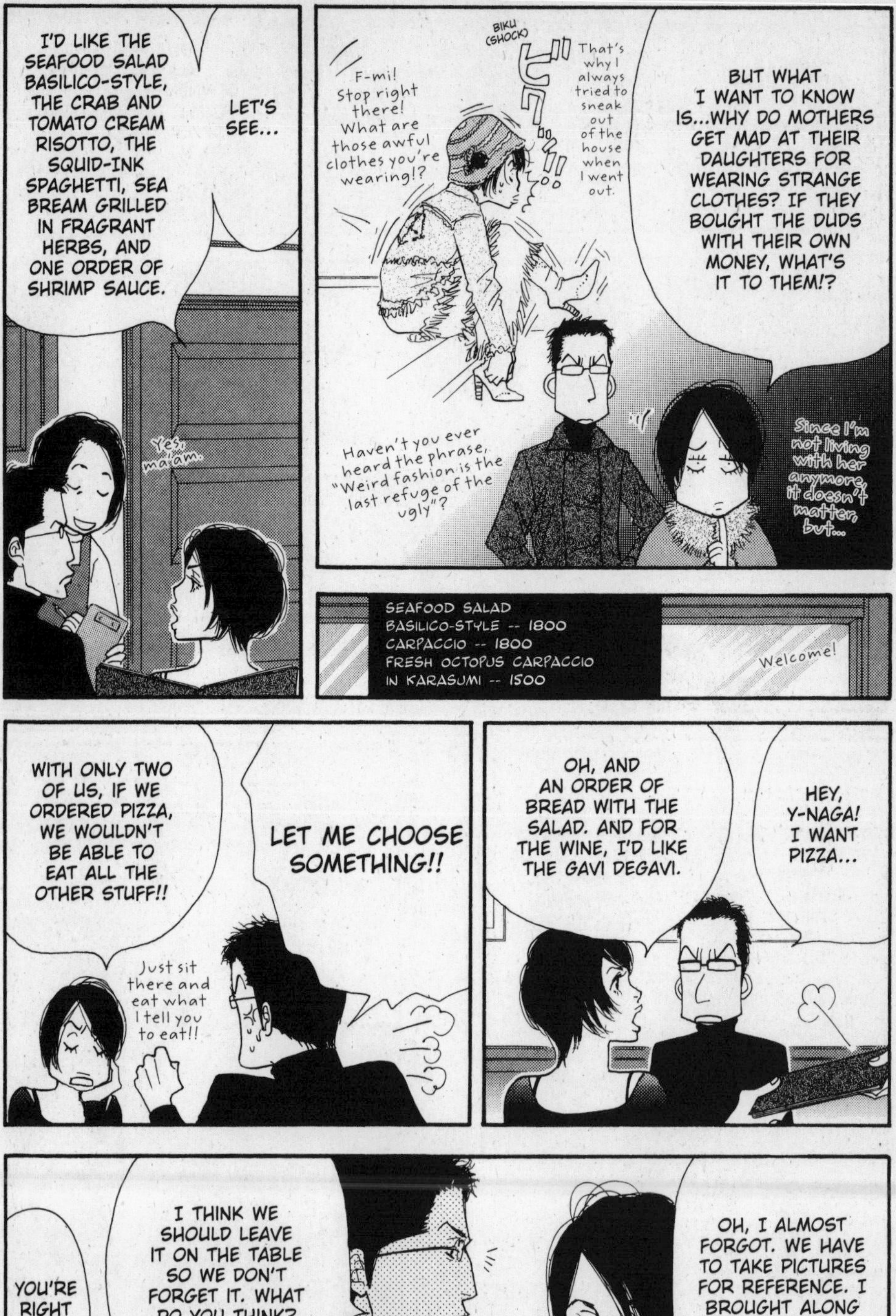
BUT WHAT I WANT TO KNOW IS...WHY DO MOTHERS GET MAD AT THEIR DAUGHTERS FOR WEARING STRANGE CLOTHES? IF THEY BOUGHT THE DUDS WITH THEIR OWN MONEY, WHAT'S IT TO THEM!?
Since I'm not living with her anymore, it doesn't matter, but...
That's why I always tried to sneak out of the house when I went out.
BIKU (SHOCK)
F-mi! Stop right there! What are those awful clothes you're wearing!?
Haven't you ever heard the phrase, "Weird fashion is the last refuge of the ugly"?
Welcome!
SEAFOOD SALAD
BASILICO-STYLE -- 1800
CARPACCIO -- 1800
FRESH OCTOPUS CARPACCIO
IN KARASUMI -- 1500
LET'S SEE...
I'D LIKE THE SEAFOOD SALAD BASILICO-STYLE, THE CRAB AND TOMATO CREAM RISOTTO, THE SQUID-INK SPAGHETTI, SEA BREAM GRILLED IN FRAGRANT HERBS, AND ONE ORDER OF SHRIMP SAUCE.
Yes, ma'am.
HEY, Y-NAGA! I WANT PIZZA...
OH, AND AN ORDER OF BREAD WITH THE SALAD. AND FOR THE WINE, I'D LIKE THE GAVI DEGAVI.
LET ME CHOOSE SOMETHING!!
WITH ONLY TWO OF US, IF WE ORDERED PIZZA, WE WOULDN'T BE ABLE TO EAT ALL THE OTHER STUFF!!
Just sit there and eat what I tell you to eat!!
OH, I ALMOST FORGOT. WE HAVE TO TAKE PICTURES FOR REFERENCE. I BROUGHT ALONG A CAMERA.
I THINK WE SHOULD LEAVE IT ON THE TABLE SO WE DON'T FORGET IT. WHAT DO YOU THINK?
YOU'RE RIGHT ...

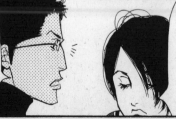

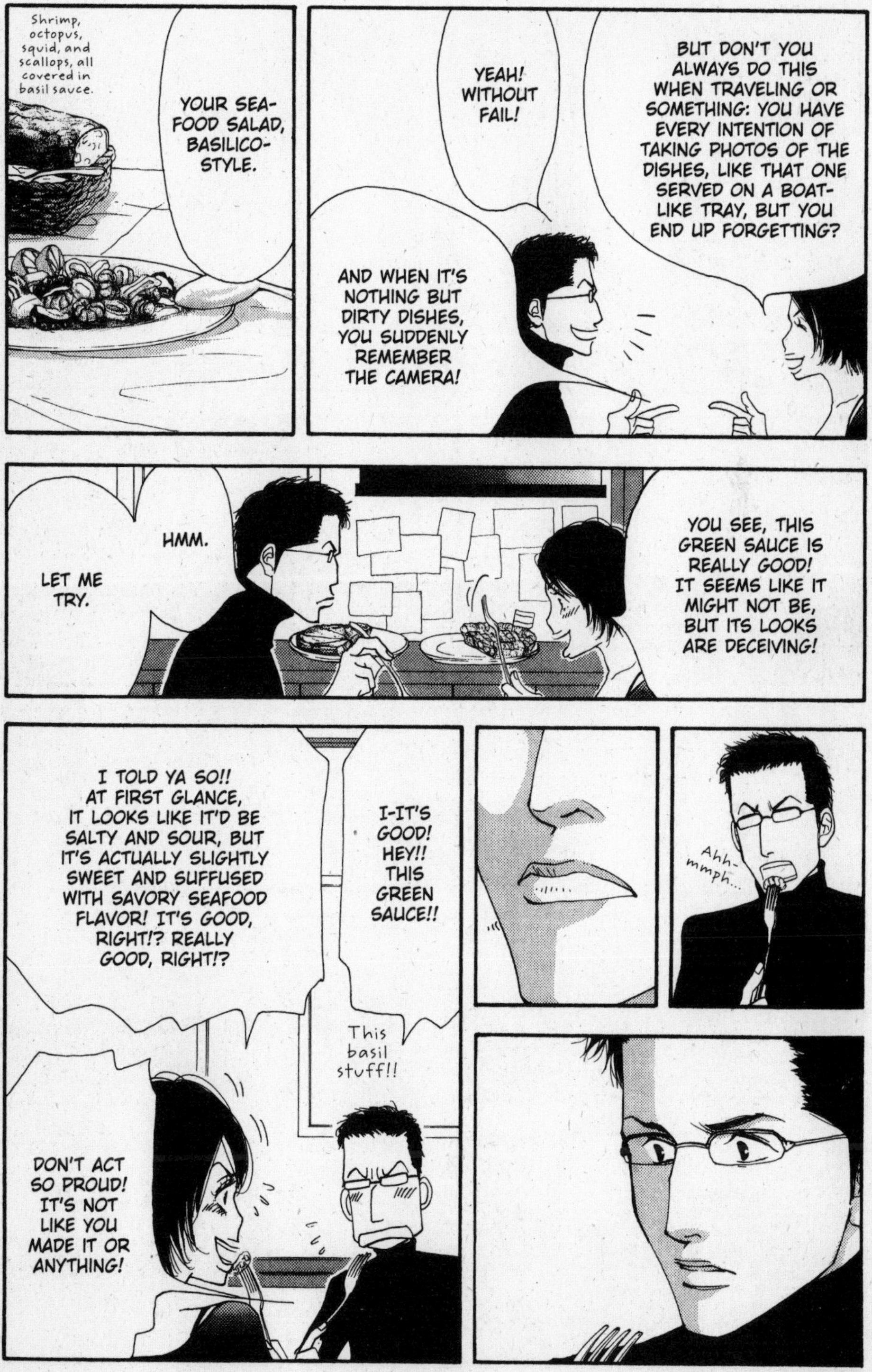
BUT DON'T YOU ALWAYS DO THIS WHEN TRAVELING OR SOMETHING: YOU HAVE EVERY INTENTION OF TAKING PHOTOS OF THE DISHES, LIKE THAT ONE SERVED ON A BOAT-LIKE TRAY, BUT YOU END UP FORGETTING?
YEAH! WITHOUT FAIL!
AND WHEN IT'S NOTHING BUT DIRTY DISHES, YOU SUDDENLY REMEMBER THE CAMERA!
YOUR SEA-FOOD SALAD, BASILICO-STYLE.
Shrimp, octopus, squid, and scallops, all covered in basil sauce.
YOU SEE, THIS GREEN SAUCE IS REALLY GOOD! IT SEEMS LIKE IT MIGHT NOT BE, BUT ITS LOOKS ARE DECEIVING!
HMM.
LET ME TRY.
Ahh-mmph...
I-IT'S GOOD! HEY!! THIS GREEN SAUCE!!
I TOLD YA SO!! AT FIRST GLANCE, IT LOOKS LIKE IT'D BE SALTY AND SOUR, BUT IT'S ACTUALLY SLIGHTLY SWEET AND SUFFUSED WITH SAVORY SEAFOOD FLAVOR! IT'S GOOD, RIGHT!? REALLY GOOD, RIGHT!?
This basil stuff!!
DON'T ACT SO PROUD! IT'S NOT LIKE YOU MADE IT OR ANYTHING!

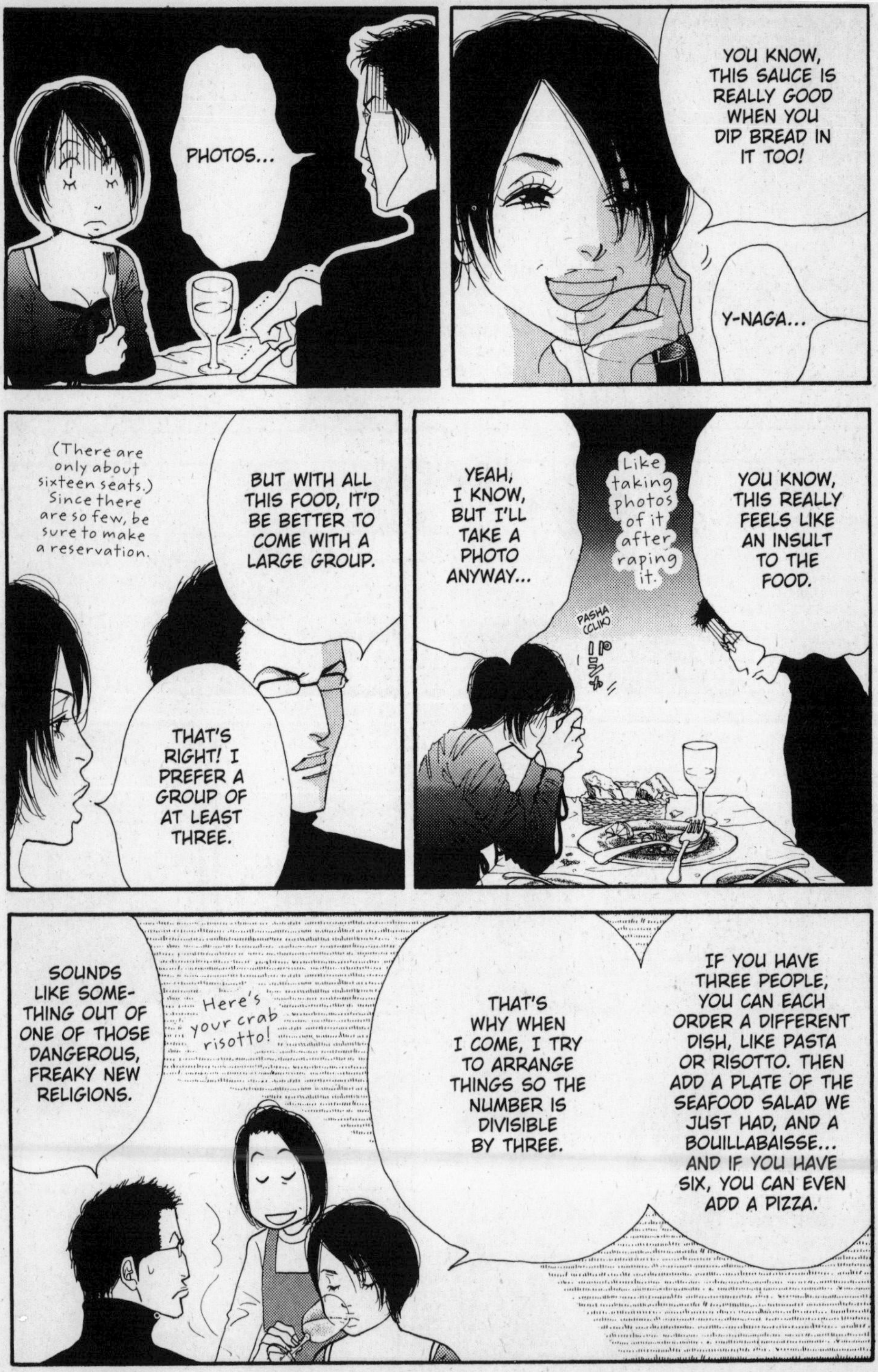
YOU KNOW, THIS SAUCE IS REALLY GOOD WHEN YOU DIP BREAD IN IT TOO!
Y-NAGA...
PHOTOS...
YOU KNOW, THIS REALLY FEELS LIKE AN INSULT TO THE FOOD.
Like taking photos of it after raping it.
YEAH, I KNOW, BUT I'LL TAKE A PHOTO ANYWAY...
PASHA (CLIK)
BUT WITH ALL THIS FOOD, IT'D BE BETTER TO COME WITH A LARGE GROUP.
(There are only about sixteen seats.) Since there are so few, be sure to make a reservation.
THAT'S RIGHT! I PREFER A GROUP OF AT LEAST THREE.
IF YOU HAVE THREE PEOPLE, YOU CAN EACH ORDER A DIFFERENT DISH, LIKE PASTA OR RISOTTO. THEN ADD A PLATE OF THE SEAFOOD SALAD WE JUST HAD, AND A BOUILLABAISSE... AND IF YOU HAVE SIX, YOU CAN EVEN ADD A PIZZA.
THAT'S WHY WHEN I COME, I TRY TO ARRANGE THINGS SO THE NUMBER IS DIVISIBLE BY THREE.
Here's your crab risotto!
SOUNDS LIKE SOME-THING OUT OF ONE OF THOSE DANGEROUS, FREAKY NEW RELIGIONS.

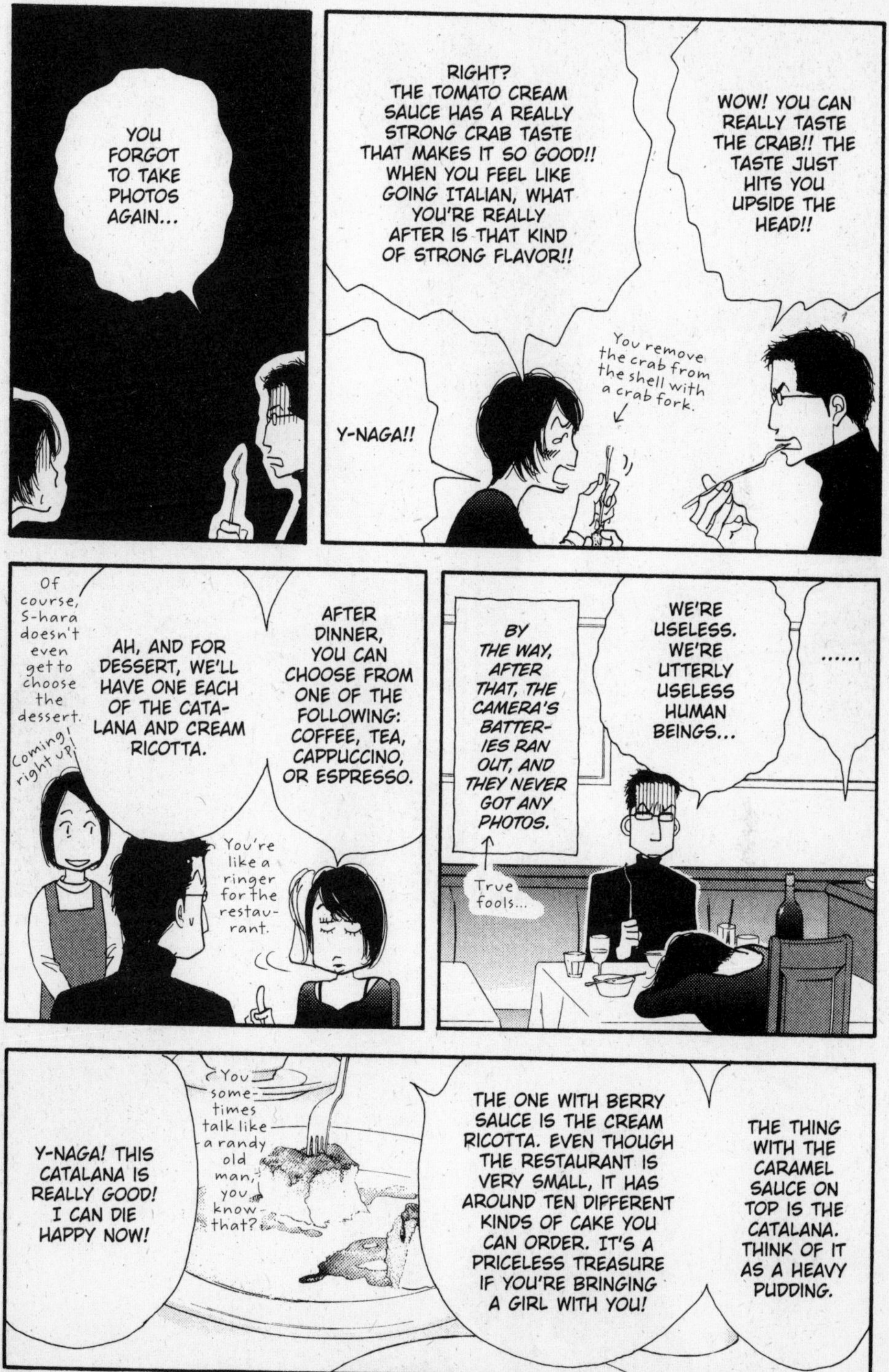
WOW! YOU CAN REALLY TASTE THE CRAB!! THE TASTE JUST HITS YOU UPSIDE THE HEAD!!
RIGHT? THE TOMATO CREAM SAUCE HAS A REALLY STRONG CRAB TASTE THAT MAKES IT SO GOOD!! WHEN YOU FEEL LIKE GOING ITALIAN, WHAT YOU'RE REALLY AFTER IS THAT KIND OF STRONG FLAVOR!!
You remove the crab from the shell with a crab fork.
Y-NAGA!!
YOU FORGOT TO TAKE PHOTOS AGAIN...
......
WE'RE USELESS. WE'RE UTTERLY USELESS HUMAN BEINGS...
BY THE WAY, AFTER THAT, THE CAMERA'S BATTERIES RAN OUT, AND THEY NEVER GOT ANY PHOTOS.
True fools...
AFTER DINNER, YOU CAN CHOOSE FROM ONE OF THE FOLLOWING: COFFEE, TEA, CAPPUCCINO, OR ESPRESSO.
AH, AND FOR DESSERT, WE'LL HAVE ONE EACH OF THE CATALANA AND CREAM RICOTTA.
Of course, S-hara doesn't even get to choose the dessert.
Coming right up!
You're like a ringer for the restaurant.
THE THING WITH THE CARAMEL SAUCE ON TOP IS THE CATALANA. THINK OF IT AS A HEAVY PUDDING.
THE ONE WITH BERRY SAUCE IS THE CREAM RICOTTA. EVEN THOUGH THE RESTAURANT IS VERY SMALL, IT HAS AROUND TEN DIFFERENT KINDS OF CAKE YOU CAN ORDER. IT'S A PRICELESS TREASURE IF YOU'RE BRINGING A GIRL WITH YOU!
You sometimes talk like a randy old man, you know that?
Y-NAGA! THIS CATALANA IS REALLY GOOD! I CAN DIE HAPPY NOW!

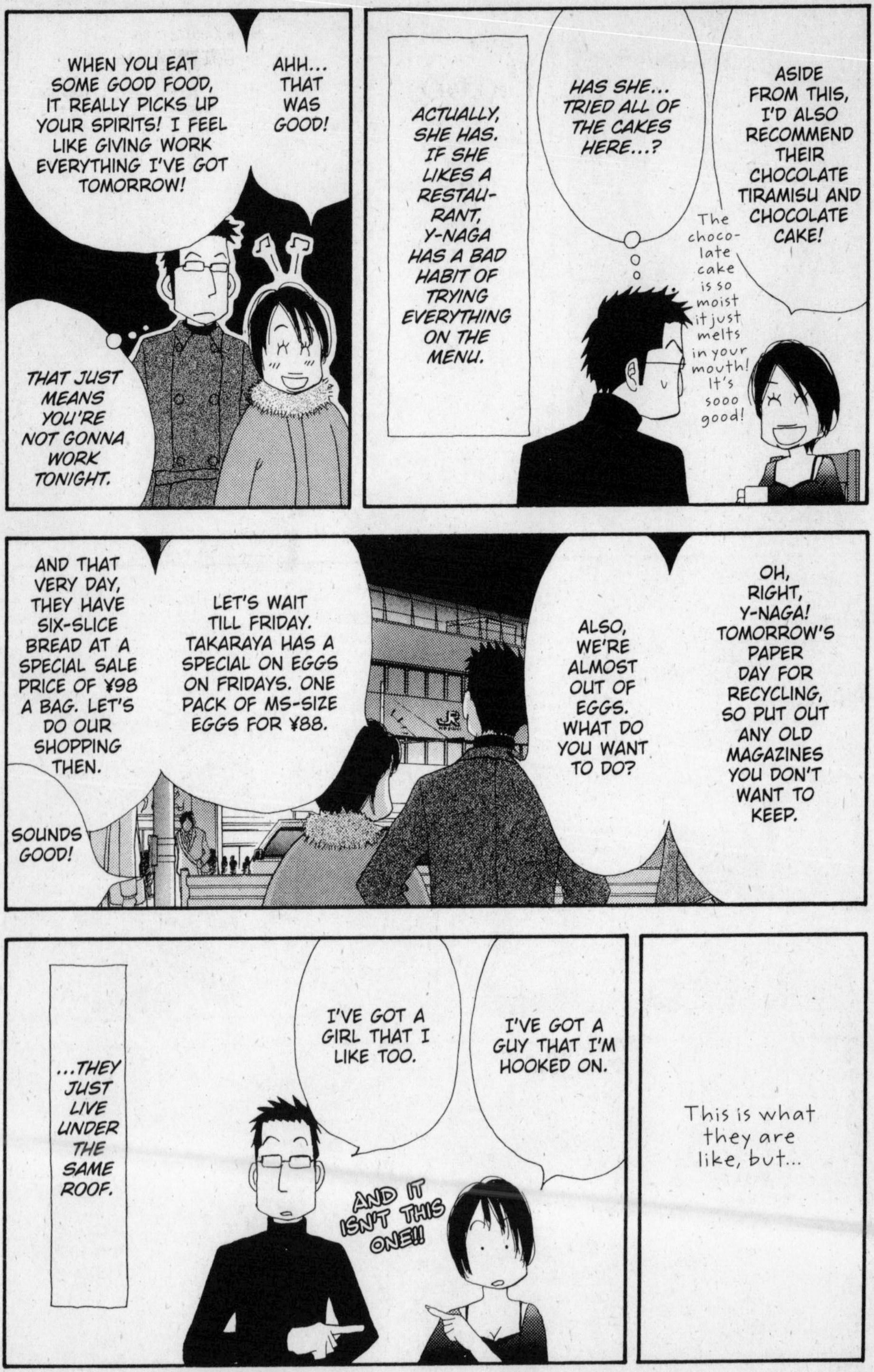
ASIDE FROM THIS, I'D ALSO RECOMMEND THEIR CHOCOLATE TIRAMISU AND CHOCOLATE CAKE!
The chocolate cake is so moist it just melts in your mouth! It's sooo good!
HAS SHE... TRIED ALL OF THE CAKES HERE...?
ACTUALLY, SHE HAS. IF SHE LIKES A RESTAU-RANT, Y-NAGA HAS A BAD HABIT OF TRYING EVERYTHING ON THE MENU.
AHH... THAT WAS GOOD!
WHEN YOU EAT SOME GOOD FOOD, IT REALLY PICKS UP YOUR SPIRITS! I FEEL LIKE GIVING WORK EVERYTHING I'VE GOT TOMORROW!
THAT JUST MEANS YOU'RE NOT GONNA WORK TONIGHT.
OH, RIGHT, Y-NAGA! TOMORROW'S PAPER DAY FOR RECYCLING, SO PUT OUT ANY OLD MAGAZINES YOU DON'T WANT TO KEEP.
ALSO, WE'RE ALMOST OUT OF EGGS. WHAT DO YOU WANT TO DO?
LET'S WAIT TILL FRIDAY. TAKARAYA HAS A SPECIAL ON EGGS ON FRIDAYS. ONE PACK OF MS-SIZE EGGS FOR ¥88.
AND THAT VERY DAY, THEY HAVE SIX-SLICE BREAD AT A SPECIAL SALE PRICE OF ¥98 A BAG. LET'S DO OUR SHOPPING THEN.
SOUNDS GOOD!
This is what they are like, but...
I'VE GOT A GUY THAT I'M HOOKED ON.
I'VE GOT A GIRL THAT I LIKE TOO.
AND IT ISN'T THIS ONE!!
...THEY JUST LIVE UNDER THE SAME ROOF.

Il Primo

[Address]
Ikeda Building, 1st Floor
5-46-5 Chuuou, Nakano-ku, Tokyo
[Telephone]
03-3384-3981
[Hours]
11:00 AM - 2:00 PM,
5:00 PM - 10:00 PM
[Closed On]
Wednesdays and every third Tuesday of the month
[Directions]
A ten-minute walk from the south entrance of Nakano Station on the JR Chuuou Line.
[Parking]
None. (There are paid parking lots nearby.)

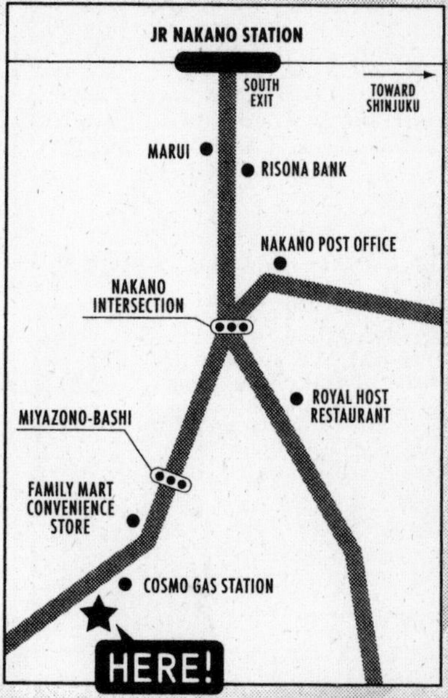

JR NAKANO STATION
SOUTH EXIT
TOWARD SHINJUKU
MARUI
RISONA BANK
NAKANO POST OFFICE
NAKANO INTERSECTION
ROYAL HOST RESTAURANT
MIYAZONO-BASHI
FAMILY MART CONVENIENCE STORE
COSMO GAS STATION
HERE!

FUMI YOSHINAGA'S COMMENTS

I WASN'T ABLE TO DRAW IT HERE, BUT I ALSO RECOMMEND THE SEA URCHIN SPAGHETTI SARDINIAN. THEY REALLY PUT A GENEROUS PORTION OF SEA URCHIN ON IT AND FLAVOR IT WITH A SIMPLE COMBINATION OF PEPPERONCINI AND OTHER PEPPERS. (NOT A CREAM BASE.) IT'S REALLY GOOD! I ALSO RECOMMEND THE SQUID-INK RISOTTO.
PRICE RANGE: EVENING, APPRX. ¥3500 - 6000.

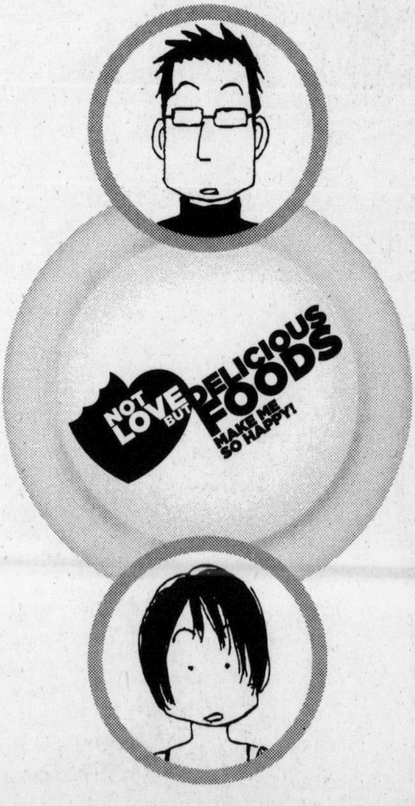
NOT LOVE BUT DELICIOUS FOODS
MAKE ME SO HAPPY!

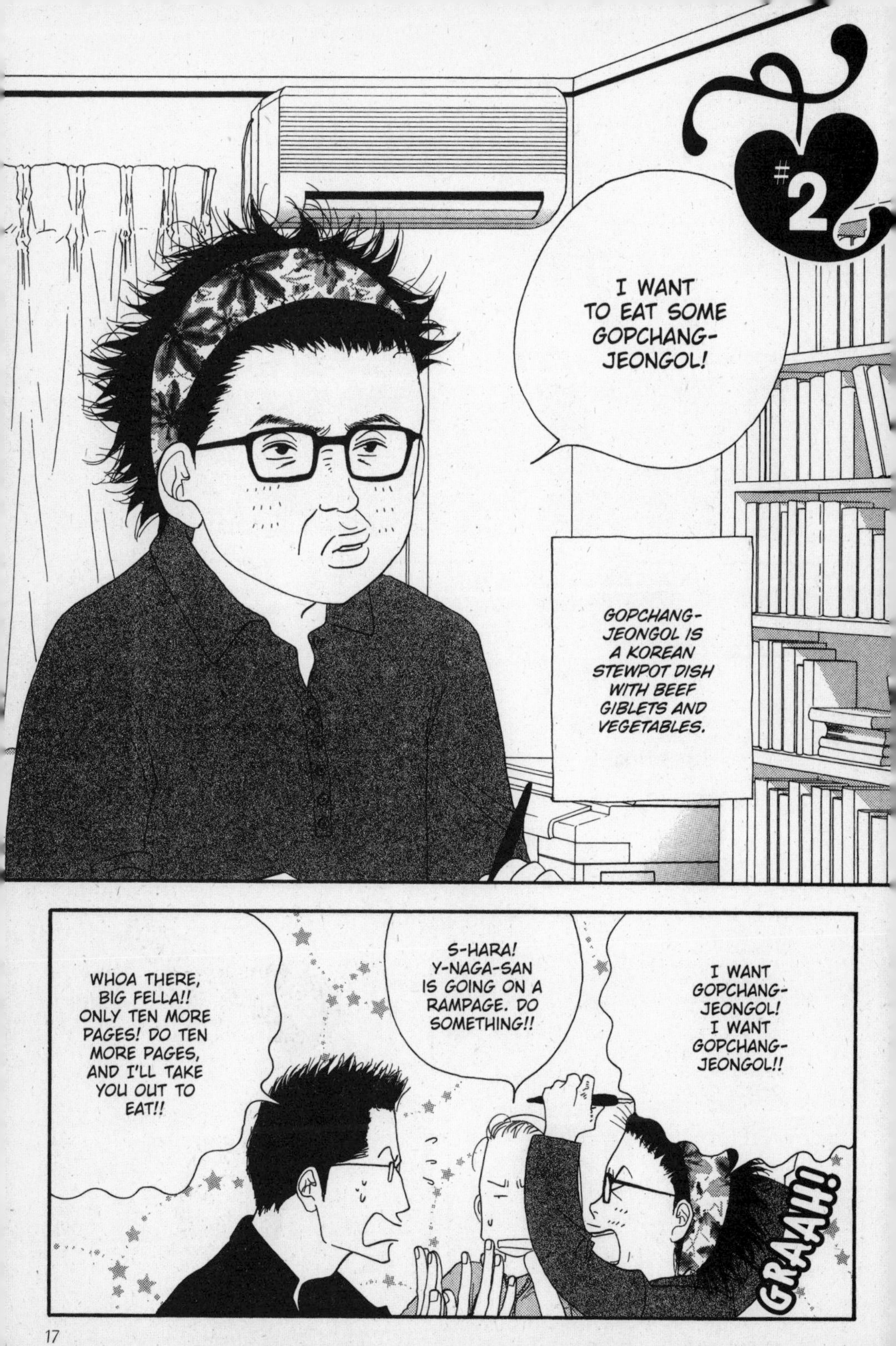
#2
I WANT TO EAT SOME GOPCHANG-JEONGOL!
GOPCHANG-JEONGOL IS A KOREAN STEWPOT DISH WITH BEEF GIBLETS AND VEGETABLES.
I WANT GOPCHANG-JEONGOL! I WANT GOPCHANG-JEONGOL!!
GRAAH!
S-HARA! Y-NAGA-SAN IS GOING ON A RAMPAGE. DO SOMETHING!!
WHOA THERE, BIG FELLA!! ONLY TEN MORE PAGES! DO TEN MORE PAGES, AND I'LL TAKE YOU OUT TO EAT!!

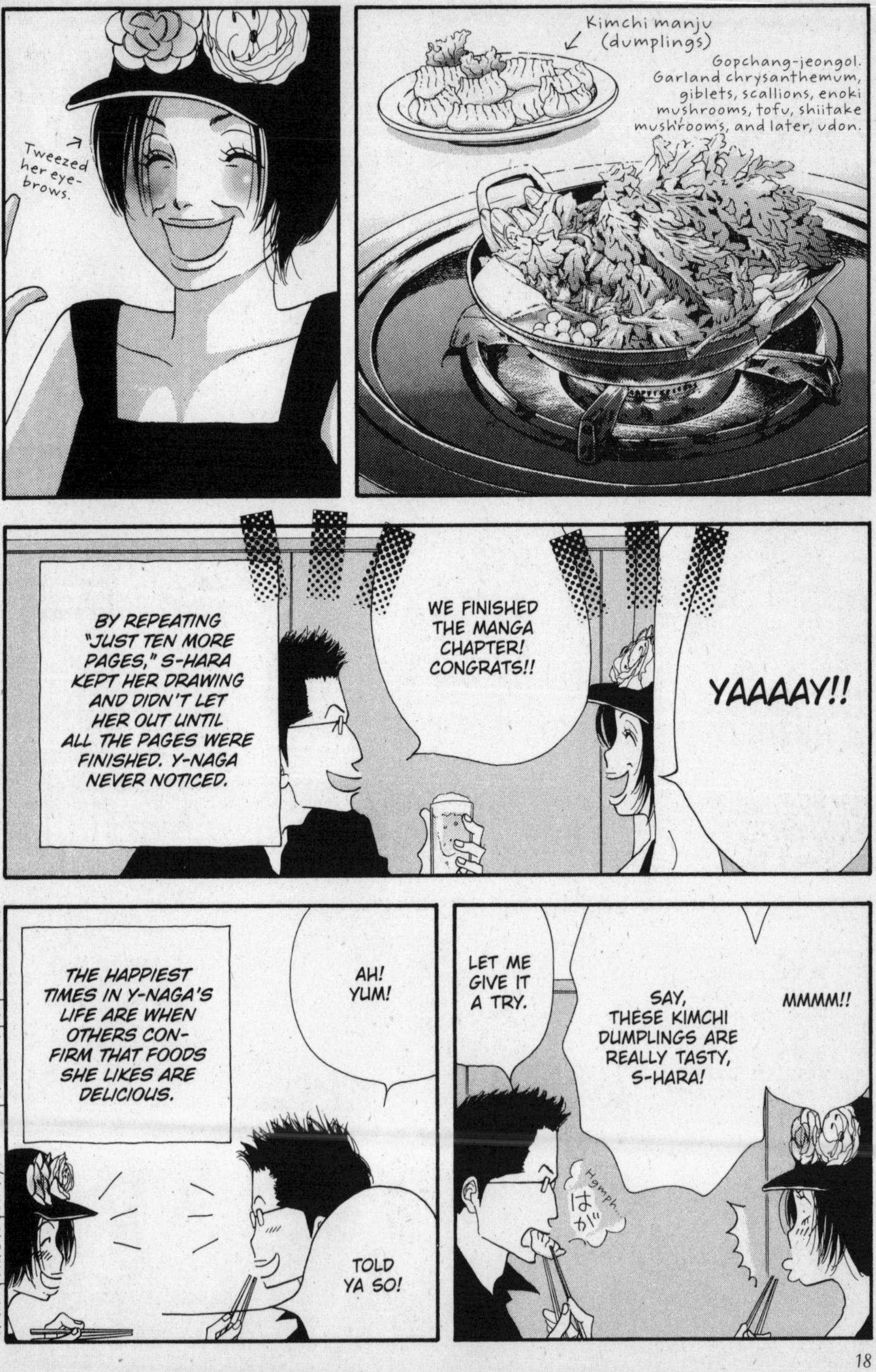
Kimchi manju (dumplings)
Gopchang-jeongol. Garland chrysanthemum, giblets, scallions, enoki mushrooms, tofu, shiitake mushrooms, and later, udon.
Tweezed her eye-brows.
YAAAAY!!
WE FINISHED THE MANGA CHAPTER! CONGRATS!!
BY REPEATING "JUST TEN MORE PAGES," S-HARA KEPT HER DRAWING AND DIDN'T LET HER OUT UNTIL ALL THE PAGES WERE FINISHED. Y-NAGA NEVER NOTICED.
MMMM!!
SAY, THESE KIMCHI DUMPLINGS ARE REALLY TASTY, S-HARA!
LET ME GIVE IT A TRY.
Hgmph...
はが
AH! YUM!
THE HAPPIEST TIMES IN Y-NAGA'S LIFE ARE WHEN OTHERS CON-FIRM THAT FOODS SHE LIKES ARE DELICIOUS.
TOLD YA SO!

*It's impolite to point your chopsticks at people like that.

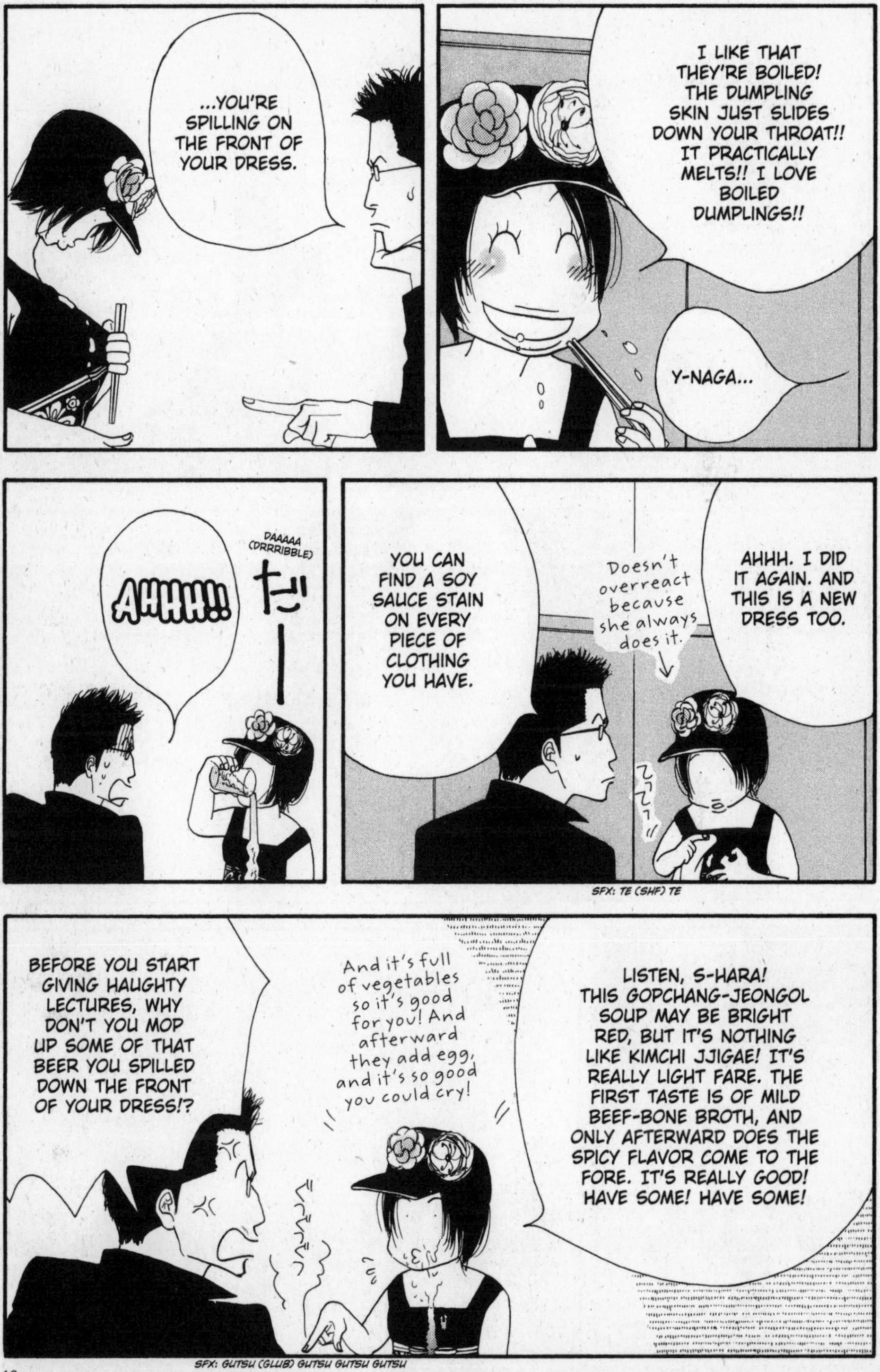
I LIKE THAT THEY'RE BOILED! THE DUMPLING SKIN JUST SLIDES DOWN YOUR THROAT!! IT PRACTICALLY MELTS!! I LOVE BOILED DUMPLINGS!!
Y-NAGA...
...YOU'RE SPILLING ON THE FRONT OF YOUR DRESS.
AHHH. I DID IT AGAIN. AND THIS IS A NEW DRESS TOO.
Doesn't overreact because she always does it.
YOU CAN FIND A SOY SAUCE STAIN ON EVERY PIECE OF CLOTHING YOU HAVE.
SFX: TE (SHF) TE
DAAAAA (DRRRIBBLE)
AHHH!!
LISTEN, S-HARA! THIS GOPCHANG-JEONGOL SOUP MAY BE BRIGHT RED, BUT IT'S NOTHING LIKE KIMCHI JJIGAE! IT'S REALLY LIGHT FARE. THE FIRST TASTE IS OF MILD BEEF-BONE BROTH, AND ONLY AFTERWARD DOES THE SPICY FLAVOR COME TO THE FORE. IT'S REALLY GOOD! HAVE SOME! HAVE SOME!
And it's full of vegetables so it's good for you! And afterward they add egg, and it's so good you could cry!
BEFORE YOU START GIVING HAUGHTY LECTURES, WHY DON'T YOU MOP UP SOME OF THAT BEER YOU SPILLED DOWN THE FRONT OF YOUR DRESS!?
SFX: GUTSU (GLUB) GUTSU GUTSU GUTSU

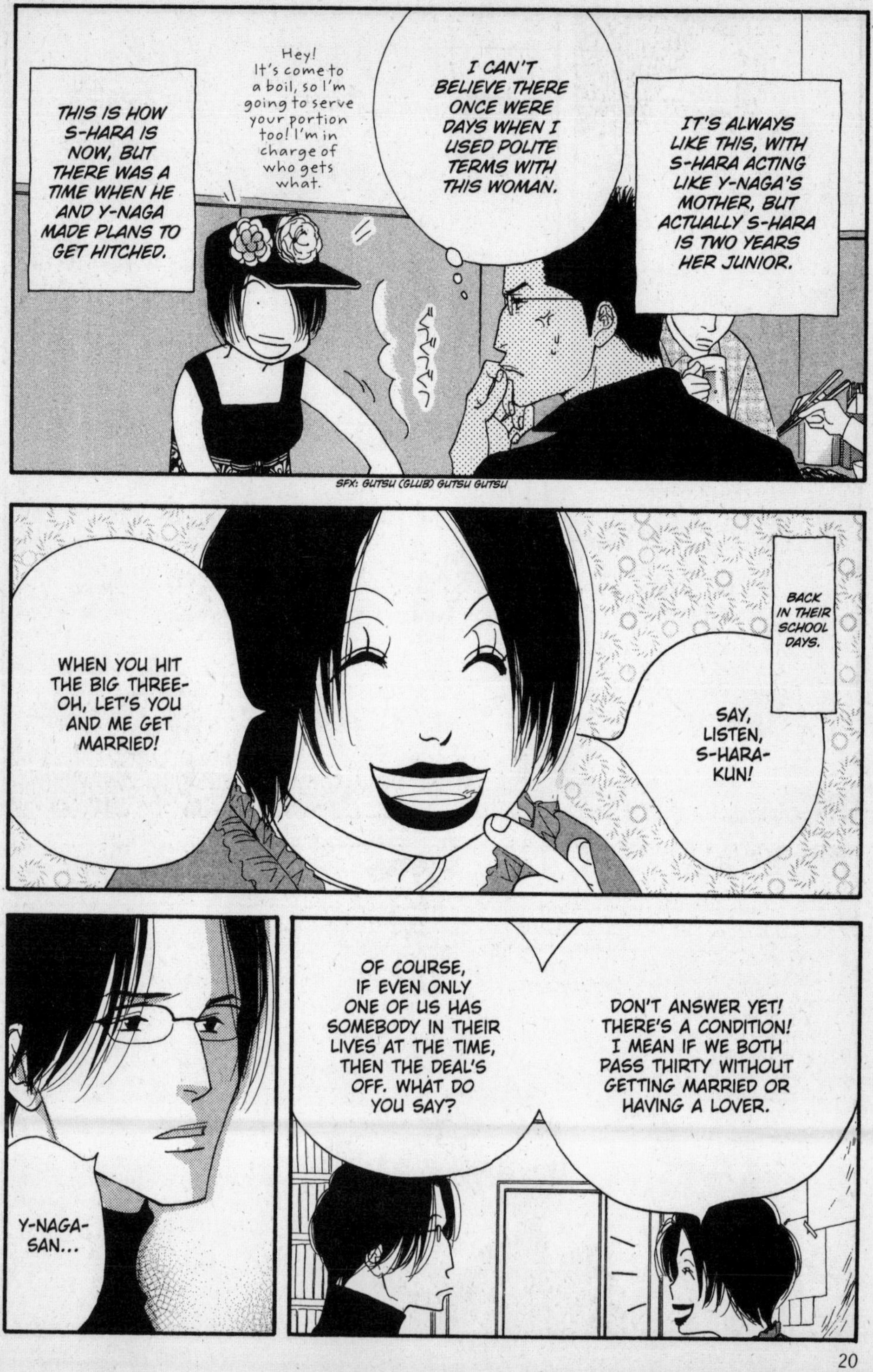
IT'S ALWAYS LIKE THIS, WITH S-HARA ACTING LIKE Y-NAGA'S MOTHER, BUT ACTUALLY S-HARA IS TWO YEARS HER JUNIOR.
I CAN'T BELIEVE THERE ONCE WERE DAYS WHEN I USED POLITE TERMS WITH THIS WOMAN.
Hey! It's come to a boil, so I'm going to serve your portion too! I'm in charge of who gets what.
THIS IS HOW S-HARA IS NOW, BUT THERE WAS A TIME WHEN HE AND Y-NAGA MADE PLANS TO GET HITCHED.
SFX: GUTSU (GLUB) GUTSU GUTSU
BACK IN THEIR SCHOOL DAYS.
SAY, LISTEN, S-HARA-KUN!
WHEN YOU HIT THE BIG THREE-OH, LET'S YOU AND ME GET MARRIED!
DON'T ANSWER YET! THERE'S A CONDITION! I MEAN IF WE BOTH PASS THIRTY WITHOUT GETTING MARRIED OR HAVING A LOVER.
OF COURSE, IF EVEN ONLY ONE OF US HAS SOMEBODY IN THEIR LIVES AT THE TIME, THEN THE DEAL'S OFF. WHAT DO YOU SAY?
Y-NAGA-SAN...

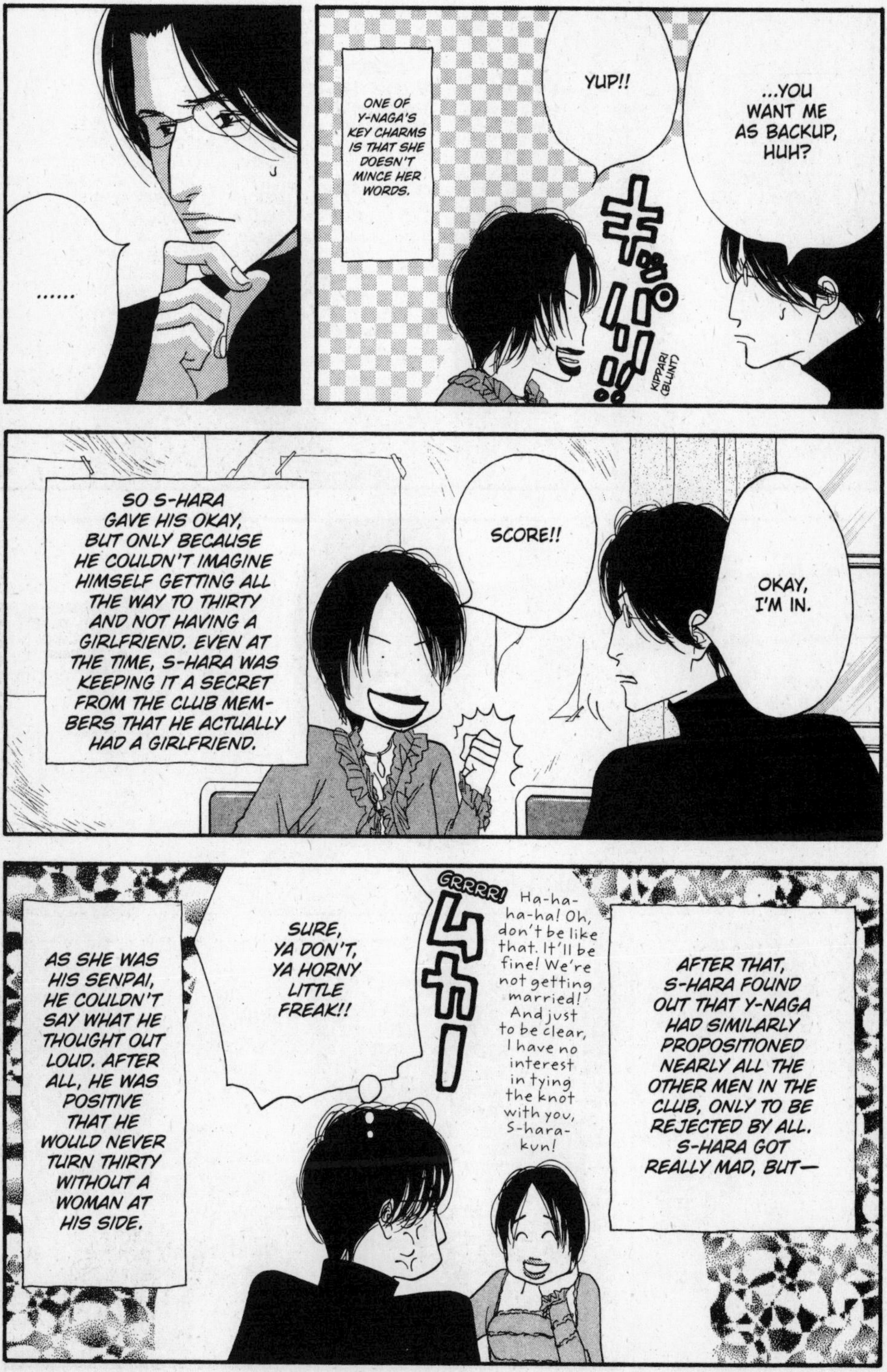
...YOU WANT ME AS BACKUP, HUH?
YUP!!
キッパリ!!
KIPPARI (BLUNT)
ONE OF Y-NAGA'S KEY CHARMS IS THAT SHE DOESN'T MINCE HER WORDS.
......
OKAY, I'M IN.
SCORE!!
SO S-HARA GAVE HIS OKAY, BUT ONLY BECAUSE HE COULDN'T IMAGINE HIMSELF GETTING ALL THE WAY TO THIRTY AND NOT HAVING A GIRLFRIEND. EVEN AT THE TIME, S-HARA WAS KEEPING IT A SECRET FROM THE CLUB MEMBERS THAT HE ACTUALLY HAD A GIRLFRIEND.
AFTER THAT, S-HARA FOUND OUT THAT Y-NAGA HAD SIMILARLY PROPOSITIONED NEARLY ALL THE OTHER MEN IN THE CLUB, ONLY TO BE REJECTED BY ALL. S-HARA GOT REALLY MAD, BUT—
Ha-ha-ha-ha! Oh, don't be like that. It'll be fine! We're not getting married! And just to be clear, I have no interest in tying the knot with you, S-hara-kun!
GRRRR!
ムカー
SURE, YA DON'T, YA HORNY LITTLE FREAK!!
AS SHE WAS HIS SENPAI, HE COULDN'T SAY WHAT HE THOUGHT OUT LOUD. AFTER ALL, HE WAS POSITIVE THAT HE WOULD NEVER TURN THIRTY WITHOUT A WOMAN AT HIS SIDE.

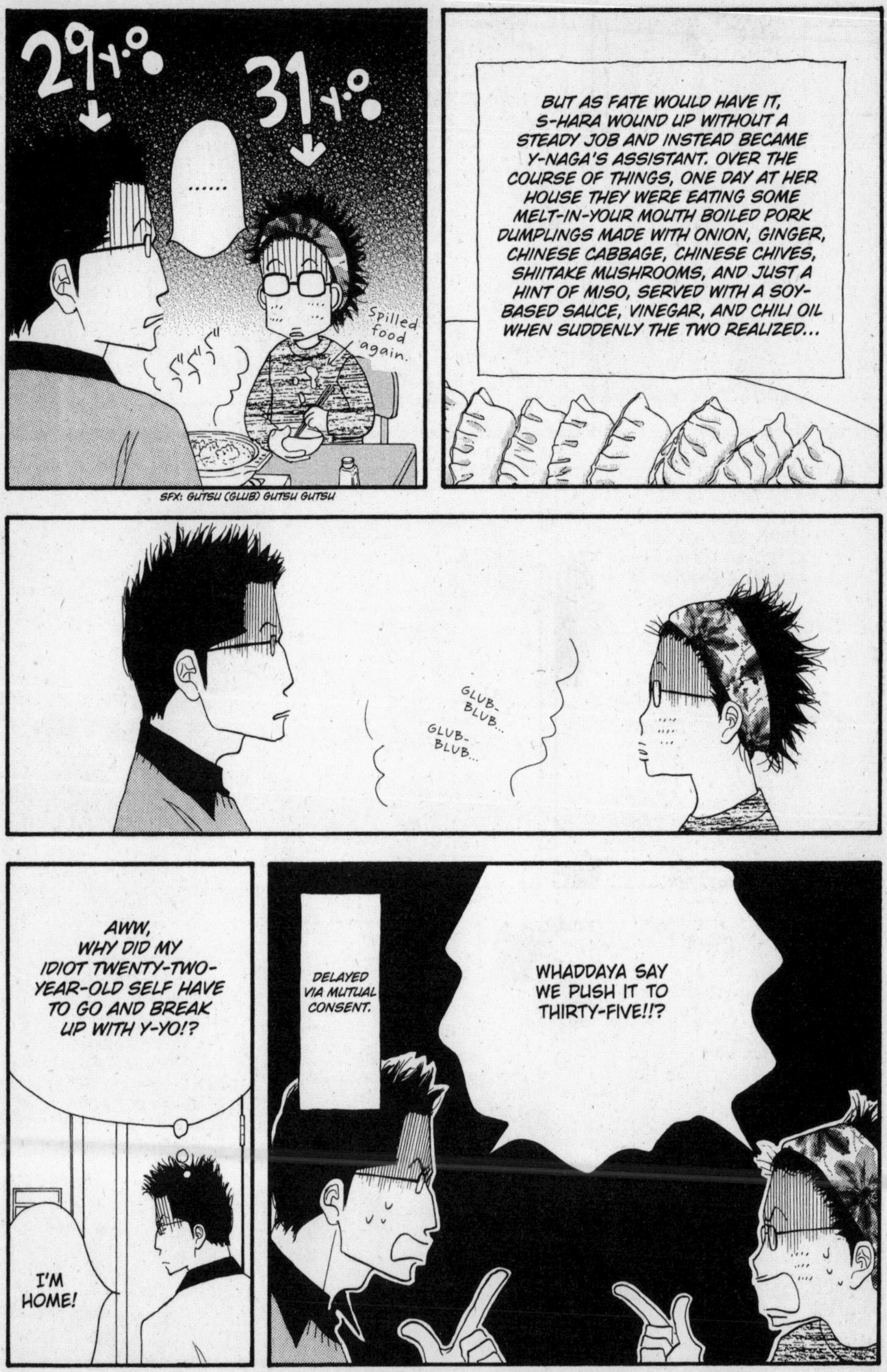

BUT AS FATE WOULD HAVE IT, S-HARA WOUND UP WITHOUT A STEADY JOB AND INSTEAD BECAME Y-NAGA'S ASSISTANT. OVER THE COURSE OF THINGS, ONE DAY AT HER HOUSE THEY WERE EATING SOME MELT-IN-YOUR MOUTH BOILED PORK DUMPLINGS MADE WITH ONION, GINGER, CHINESE CABBAGE, CHINESE CHIVES, SHIITAKE MUSHROOMS, AND JUST A HINT OF MISO, SERVED WITH A SOY-BASED SAUCE, VINEGAR, AND CHILI OIL WHEN SUDDENLY THE TWO REALIZED...
31 Y.O.
29 Y.O.
......
Spilled food again.
SFX: GUTSU (GLUB) GUTSU GUTSU
GLUB-BLUB...
GLUB-BLUB...
WHADDAYA SAY WE PUSH IT TO THIRTY-FIVE!!?
DELAYED VIA MUTUAL CONSENT.
AWW, WHY DID MY IDIOT TWENTY-TWO-YEAR-OLD SELF HAVE TO GO AND BREAK UP WITH Y-YO!?
I'M HOME!

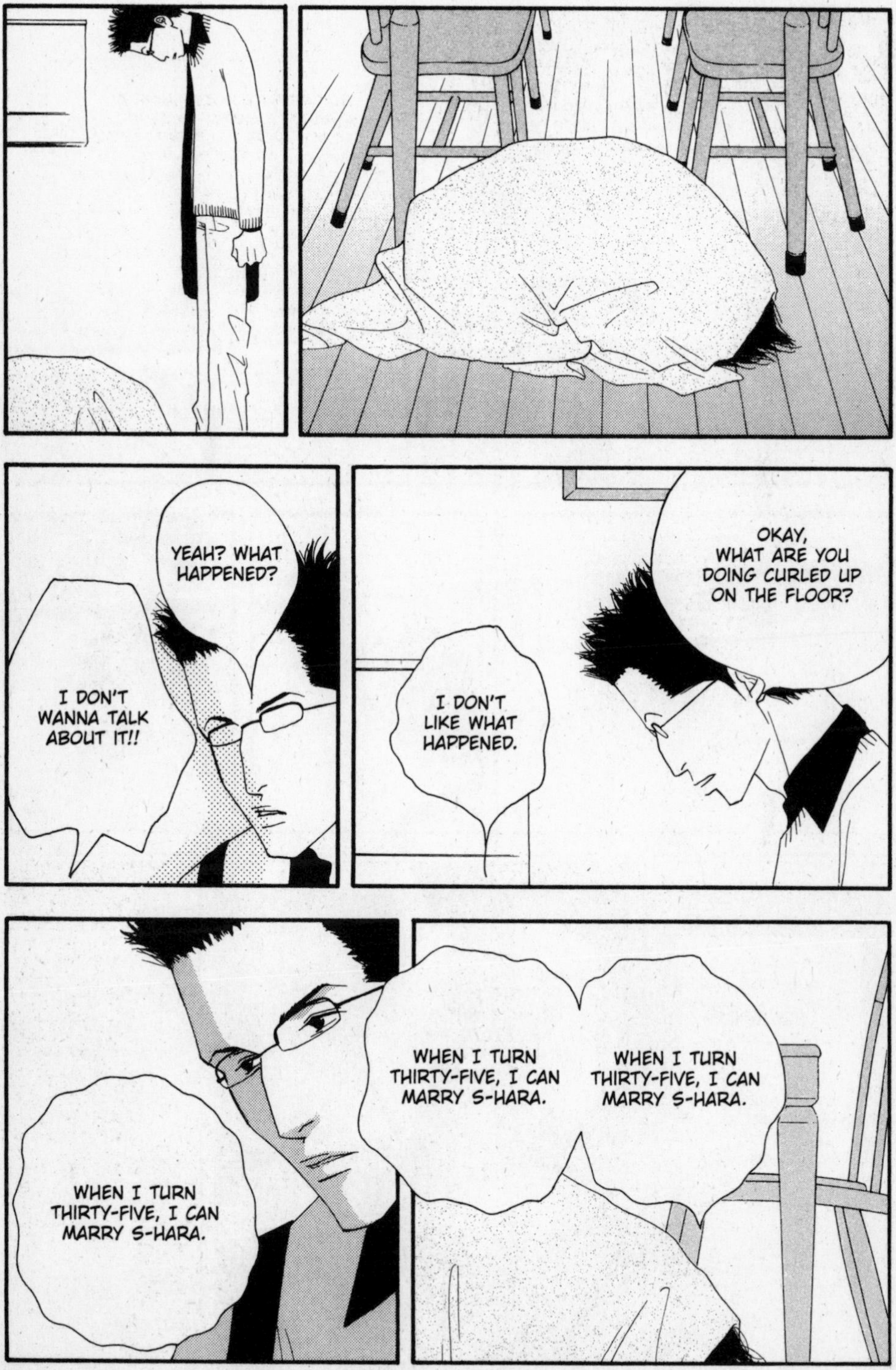
OKAY, WHAT ARE YOU DOING CURLED UP ON THE FLOOR?
I DON'T LIKE WHAT HAPPENED.
YEAH? WHAT HAPPENED?
I DON'T WANNA TALK ABOUT IT!!
WHEN I TURN THIRTY-FIVE, I CAN MARRY S-HARA.
WHEN I TURN THIRTY-FIVE, I CAN MARRY S-HARA.
WHEN I TURN THIRTY-FIVE, I CAN MARRY S-HARA.

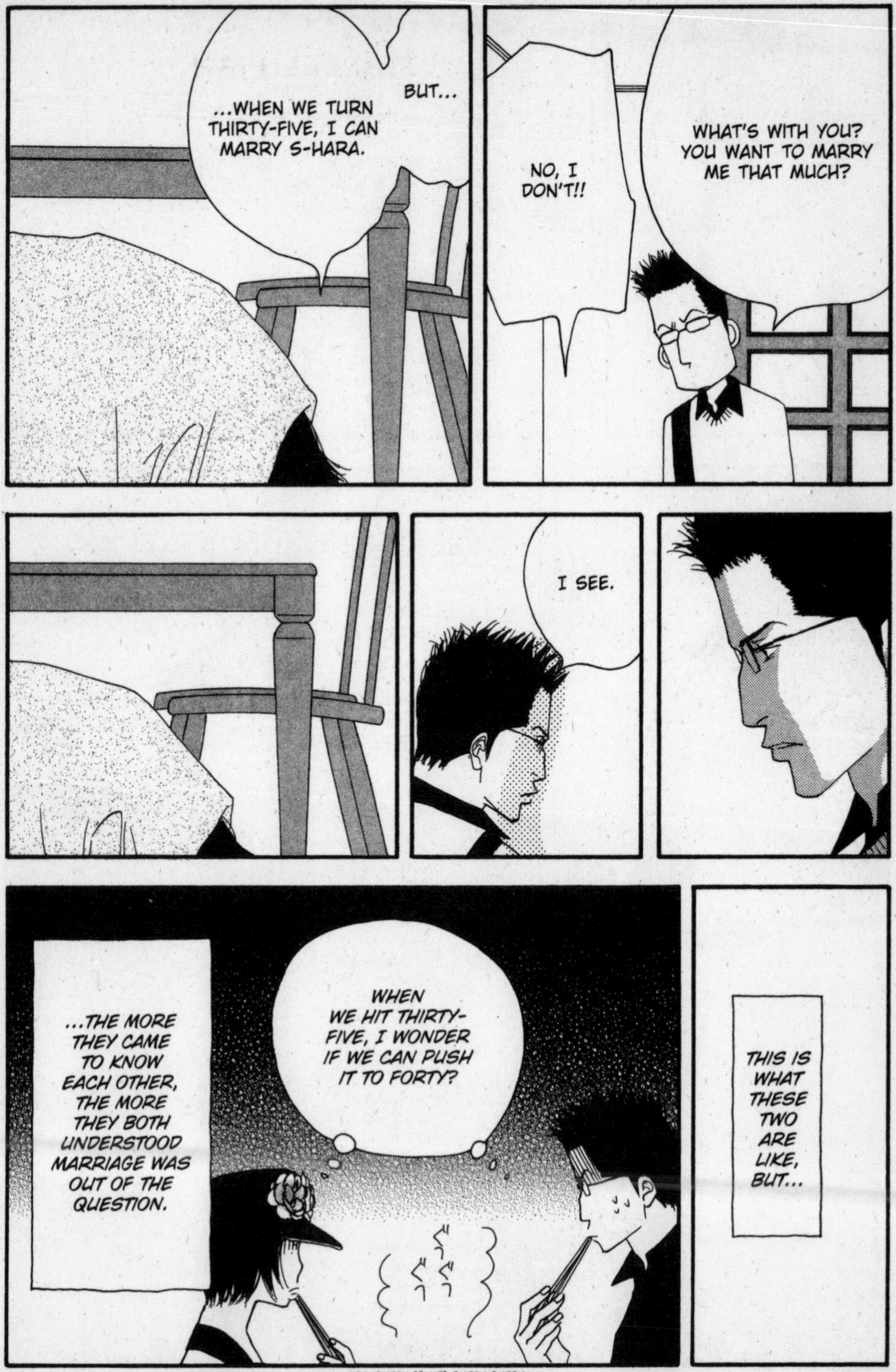
WHAT'S WITH YOU? YOU WANT TO MARRY ME THAT MUCH?
NO, I DON'T!!
BUT...
...WHEN WE TURN THIRTY-FIVE, I CAN MARRY S-HARA.
I SEE.
THIS IS WHAT THESE TWO ARE LIKE, BUT...
WHEN WE HIT THIRTY-FIVE, I WONDER IF WE CAN PUSH IT TO FORTY?
...THE MORE THEY CAME TO KNOW EACH OTHER, THE MORE THEY BOTH UNDERSTOOD MARRIAGE WAS OUT OF THE QUESTION.

SFX: GUTSU (GLUB) GUTSU GUTSU

KOREAN HOME COOKING RESTAURANT

Hallelujah

[Address] Shirahage Building, 1st Floor 1-5-6 Hyakunin-cho, Shinjuku-ku, Tokyo
[Telephone] 03-3200-0112
[Hours] Mon-Thurs 5:00 PM - 12:00 AM, Fri 5:00 PM - 1:00 AM
Sat, Sun, Holidays 12:00 PM - 12:00 AM (Special lunchtime hours
12:00 PM - 3:00 PM on Sat & Sun only.)
[Closed] Never.
[Directions] A five-minute walk from either JR Okubo Station or JR Shin-Okubu Station.
A two-minute walk from Seibu Shinjuku Station.
[Parking] None. (There are paid parking lots nearby.)

JR SHIN-OKUBO STATION
HERE!
JR OKUBO STATION
SHIRAHAGI FASHION TECHNICAL SCHOOL
JOMO GAS STATION
DON QUIXOTE
SHOKUAN DOORI ROAD
HELLO WORK SHINJUKU
SEIBU SHINJUKU LINE SHINJUKU STATION

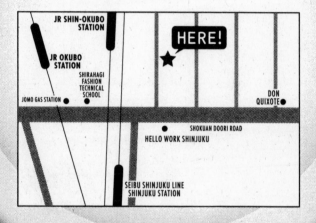

FUMI YOSHINAGA'S COMMENTS

HERE YOU CAN GET BULGOGI (A SORT OF KOREAN SUKIYAKI DISH) THAT IS REALLY DELICIOUS. IF YOU BRING FOUR OR MORE PEOPLE, YOU CAN TRY OUT A WHOLE LOT OF DISHES. PRICE RANGE: APPRX. ¥2000 - 4000. SUCH REASONABLE PRICES. THEY'RE SUPER BUSY WITH END-OF-THE-YEAR PARTIES, SO IT'S RECOMMENDED THAT YOU BOOK AHEAD DURING THAT SEASON.

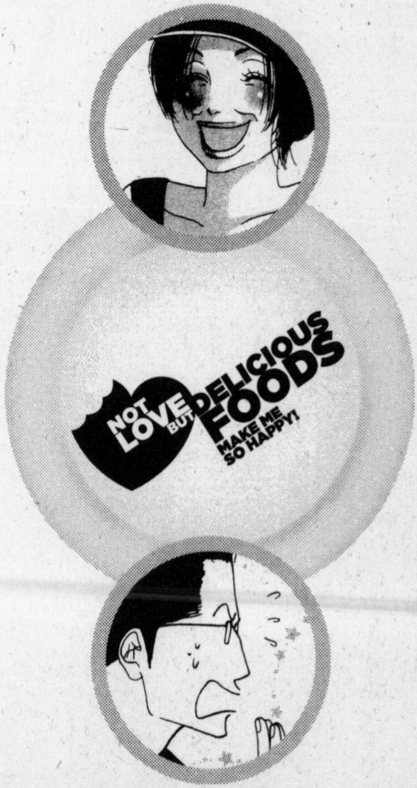
NOT LOVE BUT DELICIOUS FOODS MAKE ME SO HAPPY!

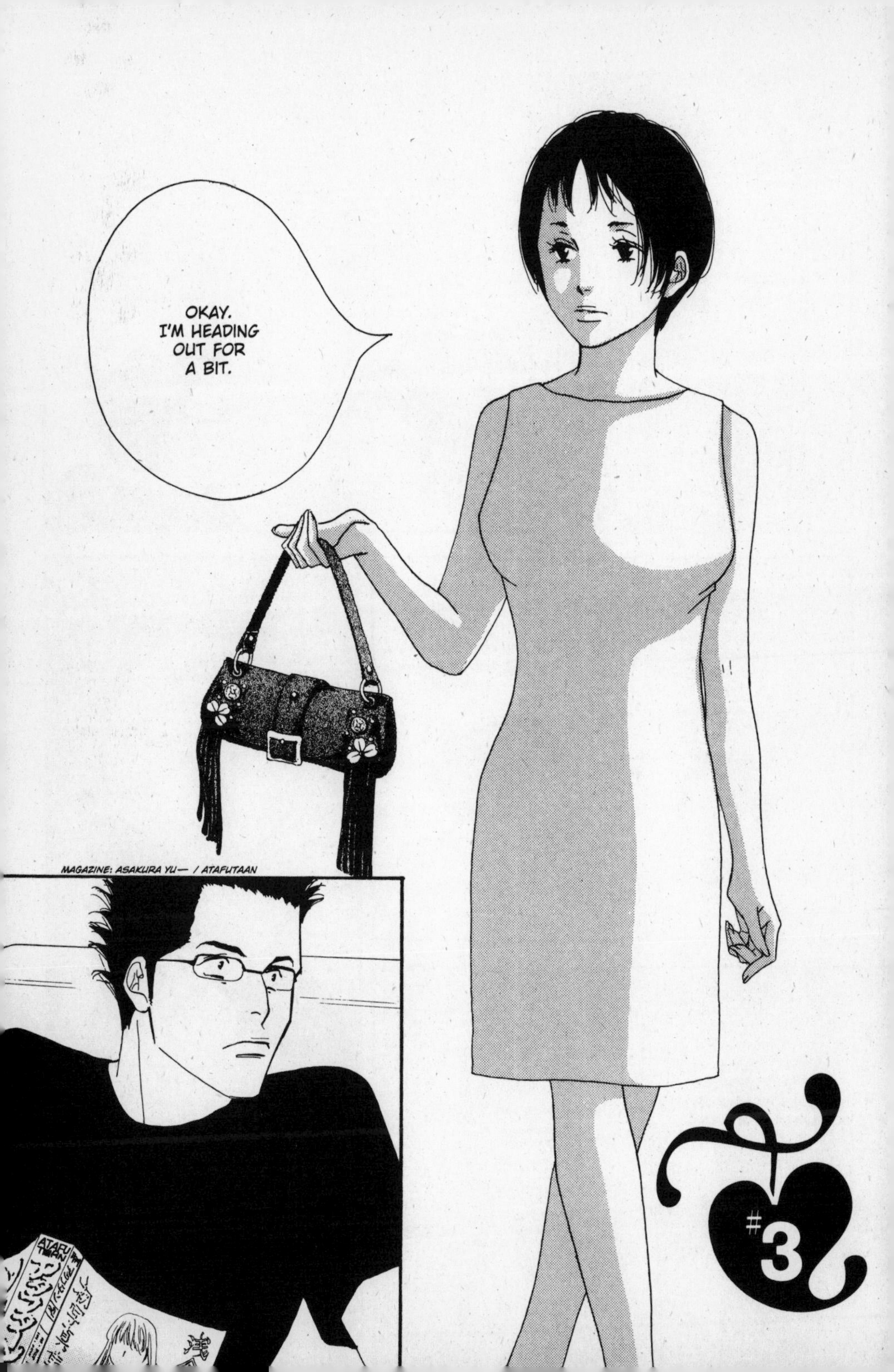
OKAY. I'M HEADING OUT FOR A BIT.
MAGAZINE: ASAKURA YU— / ATAFUTAAN
#3

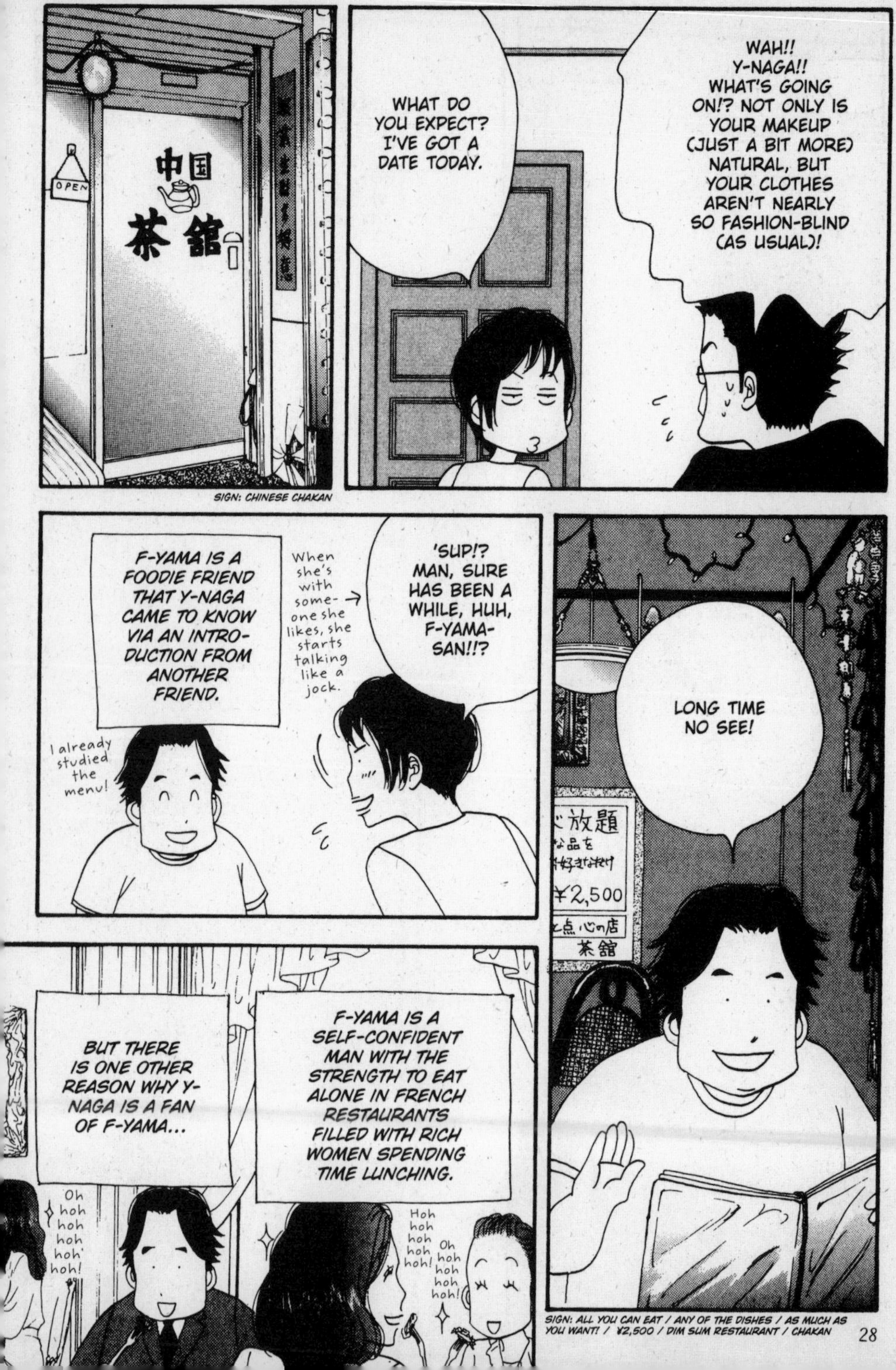
WAH!! Y-NAGA!! WHAT'S GOING ON!? NOT ONLY IS YOUR MAKEUP (JUST A BIT MORE) NATURAL, BUT YOUR CLOTHES AREN'T NEARLY SO FASHION-BLIND (AS USUAL)!
WHAT DO YOU EXPECT? I'VE GOT A DATE TODAY.
中国
茶館
OPEN
LONG TIME NO SEE!
放題
な品を
好きなだけ
¥2,500
点心の店
茶館
'SUP!? MAN, SURE HAS BEEN A WHILE, HUH, F-YAMA-SAN!!?
When she's with someone she likes, she starts talking like a jock.
F-YAMA IS A FOODIE FRIEND THAT Y-NAGA CAME TO KNOW VIA AN INTRODUCTION FROM ANOTHER FRIEND.
I already studied the menu!
F-YAMA IS A SELF-CONFIDENT MAN WITH THE STRENGTH TO EAT ALONE IN FRENCH RESTAURANTS FILLED WITH RICH WOMEN SPENDING TIME LUNCHING.
BUT THERE IS ONE OTHER REASON WHY Y-NAGA IS A FAN OF F-YAMA...
Hoh hoh hoh hoh hoh!
Oh hoh hoh hoh hoh!
Oh hoh hoh hoh hoh' hoh!

SIGN: CHINESE CHAKAN

SIGN: ALL YOU CAN EAT / ANY OF THE DISHES / AS MUCH AS YOU WANT! / ¥2,500 / DIM SUM RESTAURANT / CHAKAN

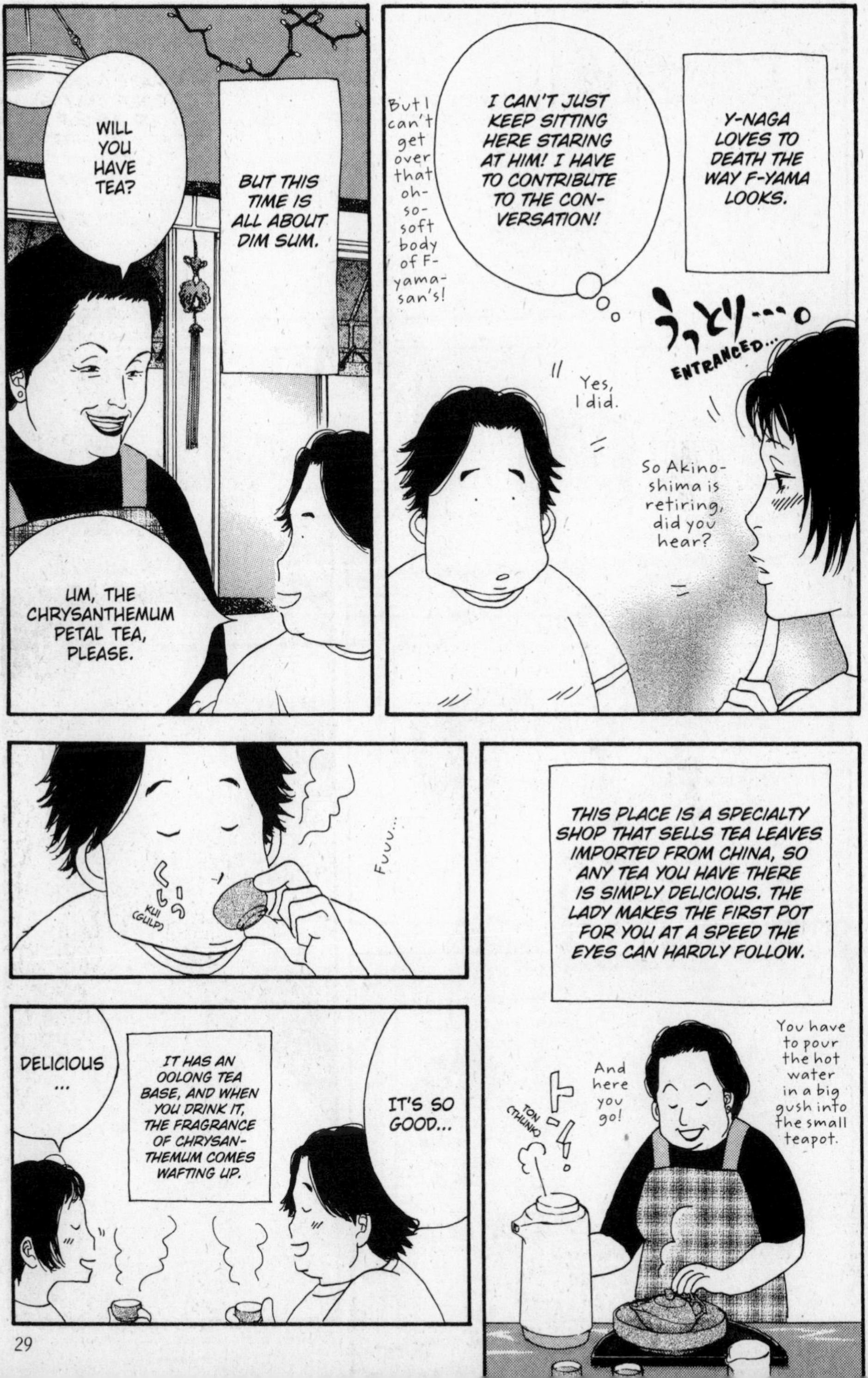

Y-NAGA LOVES TO DEATH THE WAY F-YAMA LOOKS.
I CAN'T JUST KEEP SITTING HERE STARING AT HIM! I HAVE TO CONTRIBUTE TO THE CONVERSATION!
But I can't get over that oh-so-soft body of F-yama-san's!
うっとり…。
ENTRANCED...
So Akinoshima is retiring, did you hear?
Yes, I did.
WILL YOU HAVE TEA?
BUT THIS TIME IS ALL ABOUT DIM SUM.
UM, THE CHRYSANTHEMUM PETAL TEA, PLEASE.
THIS PLACE IS A SPECIALTY SHOP THAT SELLS TEA LEAVES IMPORTED FROM CHINA, SO ANY TEA YOU HAVE THERE IS SIMPLY DELICIOUS. THE LADY MAKES THE FIRST POT FOR YOU AT A SPEED THE EYES CAN HARDLY FOLLOW.
You have to pour the hot water in a big gush into the small teapot.
And here you go!
TON (THUNK)
FUUU...
KUI (GULP)
IT'S SO GOOD...
IT HAS AN OOLONG TEA BASE, AND WHEN YOU DRINK IT, THE FRAGRANCE OF CHRYSANTHEMUM COMES WAFTING UP.
DELICIOUS ...

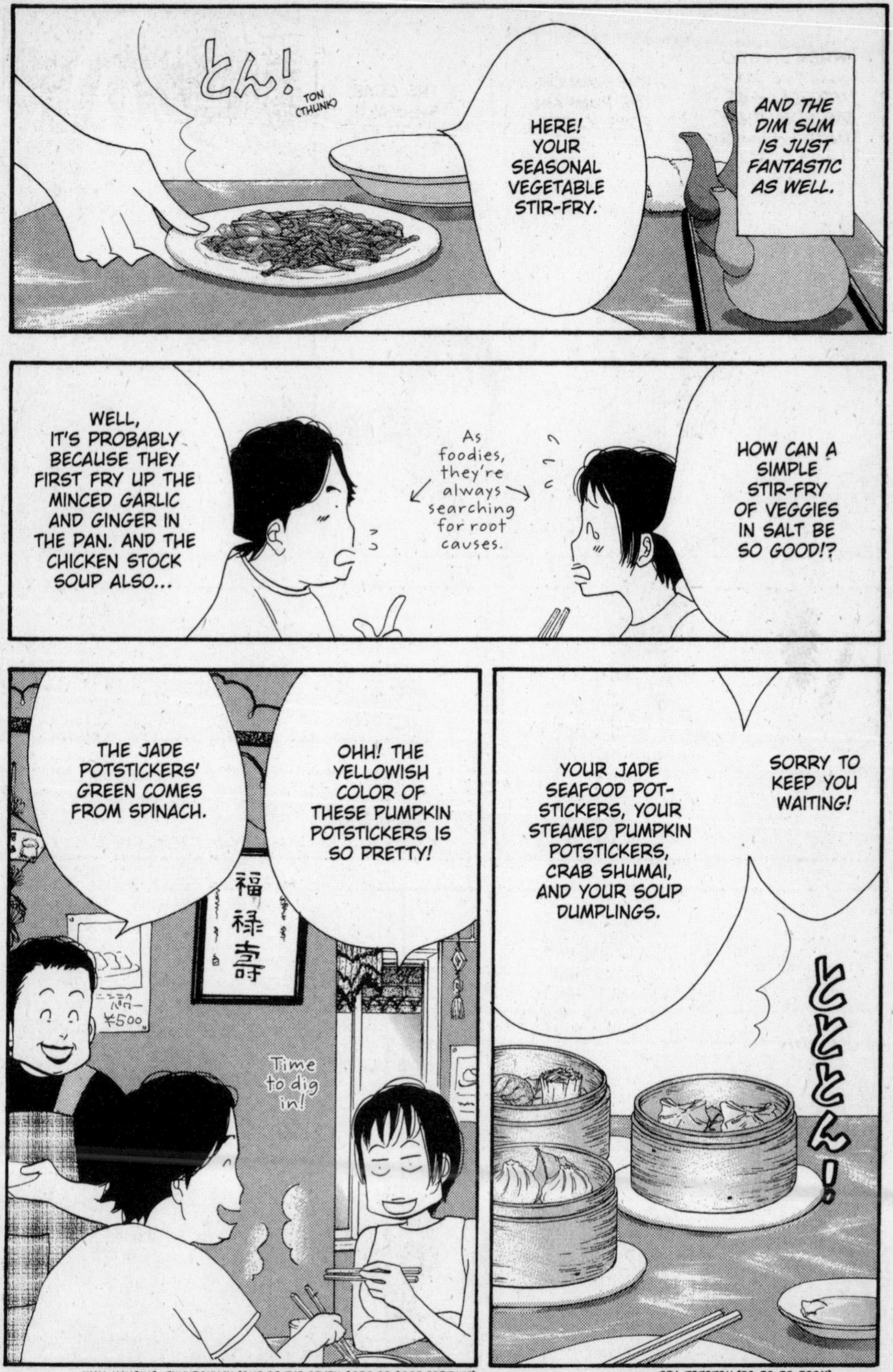
AND THE DIM SUM IS JUST FANTASTIC AS WELL.
HERE! YOUR SEASONAL VEGETABLE STIR-FRY.
とん!
TON (THUNK)
HOW CAN A SIMPLE STIR-FRY OF VEGGIES IN SALT BE SO GOOD!?
As foodies, they're always searching for root causes.
WELL, IT'S PROBABLY BECAUSE THEY FIRST FRY UP THE MINCED GARLIC AND GINGER IN THE PAN. AND THE CHICKEN STOCK SOUP ALSO...
SORRY TO KEEP YOU WAITING!
YOUR JADE SEAFOOD POT-STICKERS, YOUR STEAMED PUMPKIN POTSTICKERS, CRAB SHUMAI, AND YOUR SOUP DUMPLINGS.
とととん!
OHH! THE YELLOWISH COLOR OF THESE PUMPKIN POTSTICKERS IS SO PRETTY!
THE JADE POTSTICKERS' GREEN COMES FROM SPINACH.
福禄壽
¥500
Time to dig in!

SFX: TOTOTON (DO-DO-DO-DOOM)

WALL HANGING: FUKUROKUJU (ONE OF THE SEVEN GODS OF GOOD FORTUNE); SIGN: GARLIC POWER ¥500!

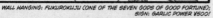

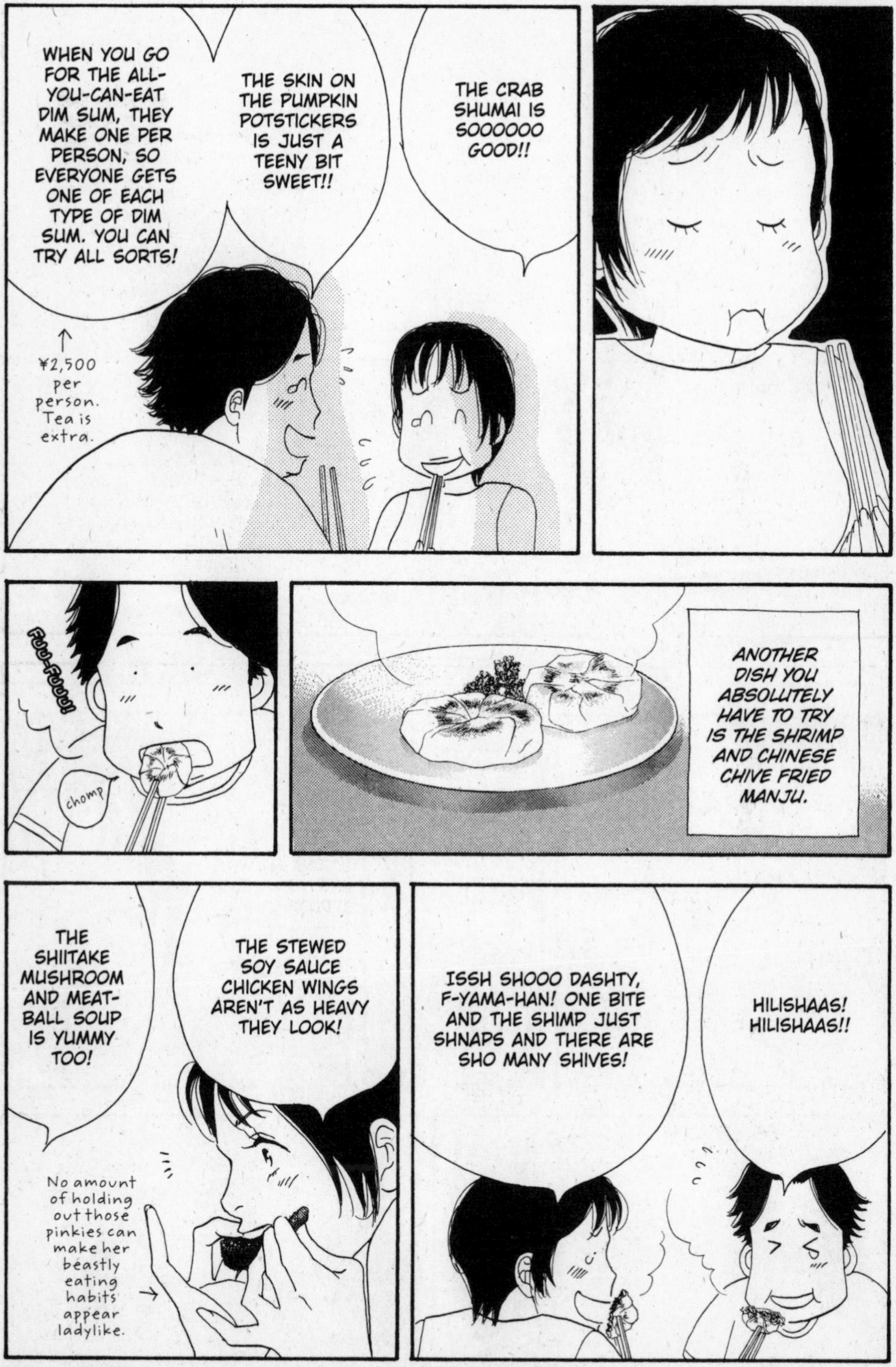

THE CRAB SHUMAI IS SOOOOOO GOOD!!
THE SKIN ON THE PUMPKIN POTSTICKERS IS JUST A TEENY BIT SWEET!!
WHEN YOU GO FOR THE ALL-YOU-CAN-EAT DIM SUM, THEY MAKE ONE PER PERSON, SO EVERYONE GETS ONE OF EACH TYPE OF DIM SUM. YOU CAN TRY ALL SORTS!
↑ ¥2,500 per person. Tea is extra.
ANOTHER DISH YOU ABSOLUTELY HAVE TO TRY IS THE SHRIMP AND CHINESE CHIVE FRIED MANJU.
Fuu-Fuuu!
chomp
HILISHAAS! HILISHAAS!!
ISSH SHOOO DASHTY, F-YAMA-HAN! ONE BITE AND THE SHIMP JUST SHNAPS AND THERE ARE SHO MANY SHIVES!
THE STEWED SOY SAUCE CHICKEN WINGS AREN'T AS HEAVY THEY LOOK!
THE SHIITAKE MUSHROOM AND MEAT-BALL SOUP IS YUMMY TOO!
No amount of holding out those pinkies can make her beastly eating habits appear ladylike. →

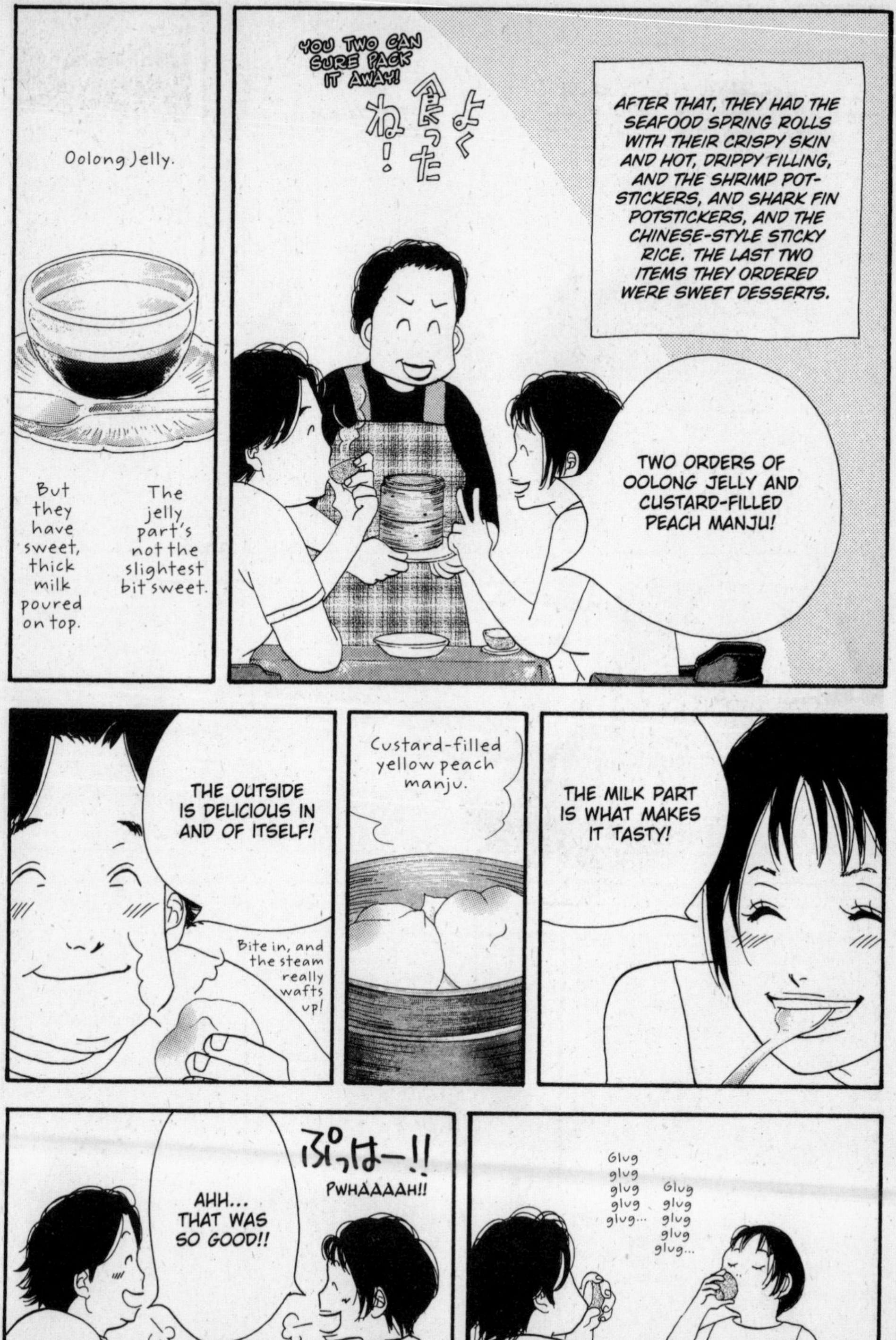
AFTER THAT, THEY HAD THE SEAFOOD SPRING ROLLS WITH THEIR CRISPY SKIN AND HOT, DRIPPY FILLING, AND THE SHRIMP POT-STICKERS, AND SHARK FIN POTSTICKERS, AND THE CHINESE-STYLE STICKY RICE. THE LAST TWO ITEMS THEY ORDERED WERE SWEET DESSERTS.
よく食ったね!
YOU TWO CAN SURE PACK IT AWAY!
TWO ORDERS OF OOLONG JELLY AND CUSTARD-FILLED PEACH MANJU!
Oolong Jelly.
The jelly part's not the slightest bit sweet.
But they have sweet, thick milk poured on top.
THE MILK PART IS WHAT MAKES IT TASTY!
Custard-filled yellow peach manju.
THE OUTSIDE IS DELICIOUS IN AND OF ITSELF!
Bite in, and the steam really wafts up!
Glug glug glug glug...
Glug glug glug glug glug...
ぷっはー!!
PWHAAAAH!!
AHH... THAT WAS SO GOOD!!

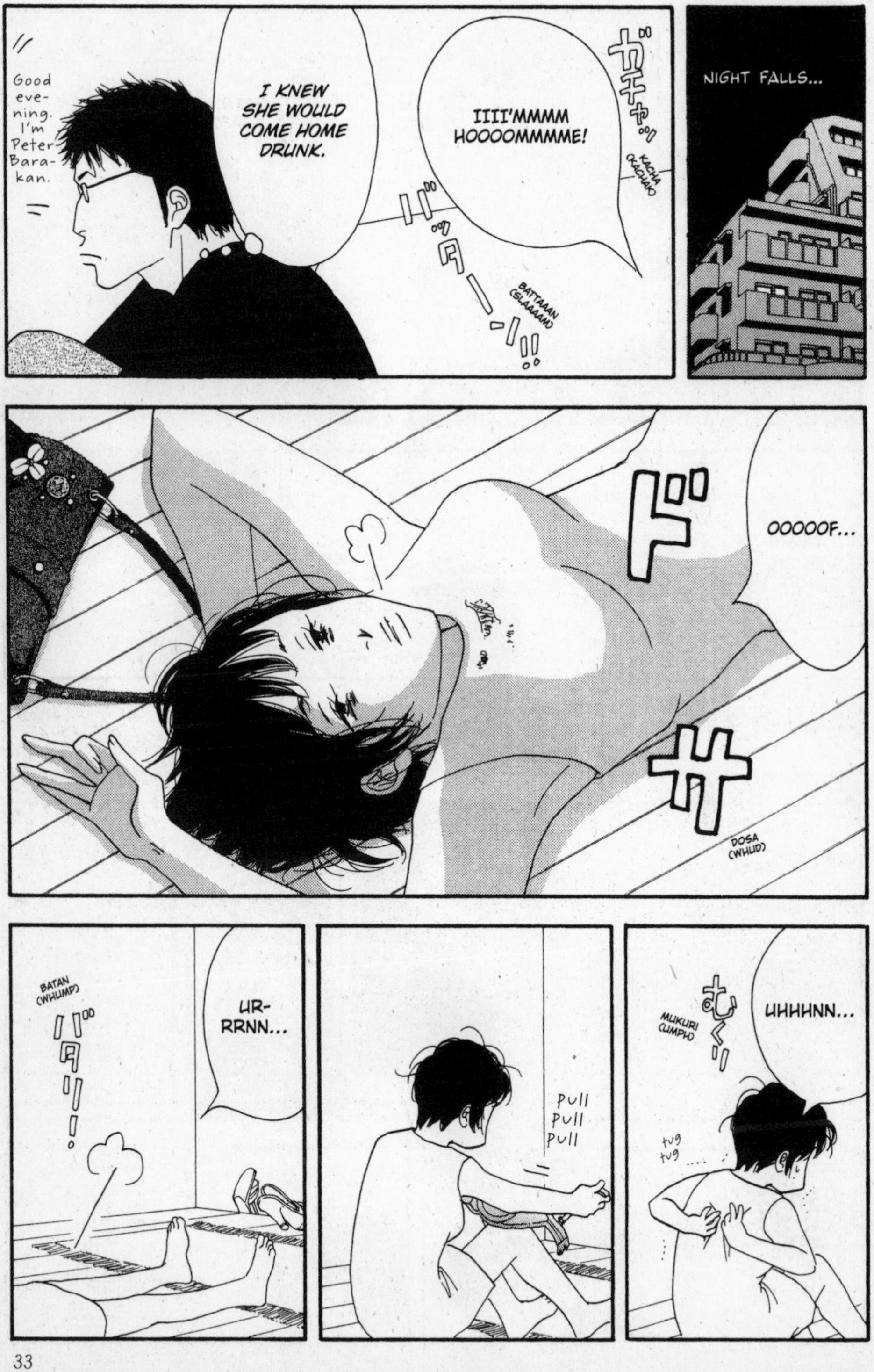
NIGHT FALLS...
ガチャッ
KACHA (KACHAK)
IIII'MMMM HOOOOMMMME!
バターン!!
BATTAAAN (SLAAAAM)
I KNEW SHE WOULD COME HOME DRUNK.
Good evening. I'm Peter Barakan.
OOOOOF...
ドサ
DOSA (WHUD)
UHHHNN...
MUKURI (UMPH)
tug tug
pull pull pull
UR-RRNN...
バタリ!
BATAN (WHUMP)

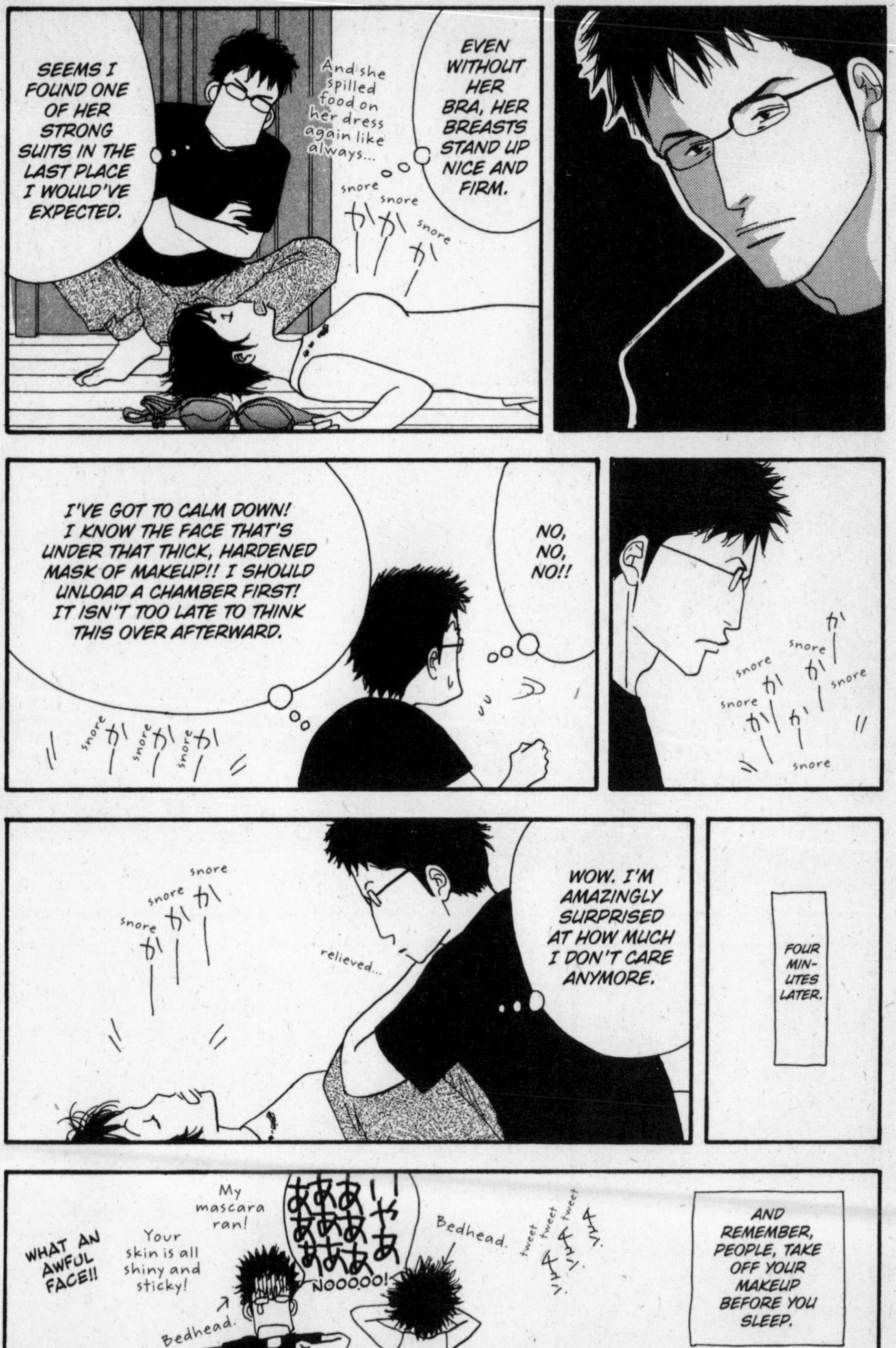
EVEN WITHOUT HER BRA, HER BREASTS STAND UP NICE AND FIRM.
And she spilled food on her dress again like always...
SEEMS I FOUND ONE OF HER STRONG SUITS IN THE LAST PLACE I WOULD'VE EXPECTED.
snore snore snore
snore snore snore snore snore
NO, NO, NO!!
I'VE GOT TO CALM DOWN! I KNOW THE FACE THAT'S UNDER THAT THICK, HARDENED MASK OF MAKEUP!! I SHOULD UNLOAD A CHAMBER FIRST! IT ISN'T TOO LATE TO THINK THIS OVER AFTERWARD.
snore snore snore
FOUR MIN-UTES LATER.
WOW. I'M AMAZINGLY SURPRISED AT HOW MUCH I DON'T CARE ANYMORE.
relieved...
snore snore snore
AND REMEMBER, PEOPLE, TAKE OFF YOUR MAKEUP BEFORE YOU SLEEP.
tweet tweet tweet
Bedhead.
NOOOOO!
My mascara ran!
Your skin is all shiny and sticky!
WHAT AN AWFUL FACE!!
Bedhead.

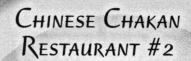

Chinese Chakan Restaurant #2

[Address] Mikasa Building, 2nd Floor, 1-22-8 Nishi-Ikebukuro, Toshima-ku, Tokyo
[Telephone] 03-3985-5183
[Hours] Mon-Fri 11:30 AM - 12:30 AM Sat, Sun, Holidays 11:30 AM - Midnight
[Closed] Never.
[Directions] A two-minute walk from the JR Ikebukuro West Exit.
[Parking] None.

GEKIJOU DOORI ROAD
CINEMA ROSA
ROMANCE DOORI ROAD
HERE!
BUNKA DOORI ROAD
MITSUI SUMITOMO GINKO BANK
TOKYO MITSUBISHI GINKO BANK
KENTUCKY FRIED CHICKEN
HOTEL SUNSHINE CITY IKEBUKURO
MIZUKI DOORI ROAD
KANAME-CHOU DOORI ROAD
WEST EXIT
TOBU DEPARTMENT STORE
JR IKEBUKURO STATION
TO SHINJUKU

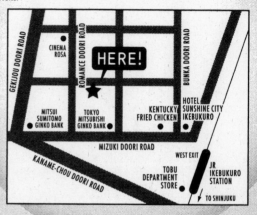

FUMI YOSHINAGA'S COMMENTS

IT DOESN'T MATTER IF IT'S AFTERNOON OR EVENING, YOU CAN ORDER THE ALL-YOU-CAN-EAT COURSE FOR ¥2500. THE ALL-YOU-CAN-EAT IS LIMITED TO NINETY MINUTES, BUT THAT'S JUST THE TIME LIMIT FOR PLACING YOUR ORDER, SO YOU CAN STAY AT THE TABLE AND TAKE YOUR TIME ENJOYING THE FOOD EVEN AFTER YOUR NINETY MINUTES ARE DONE.

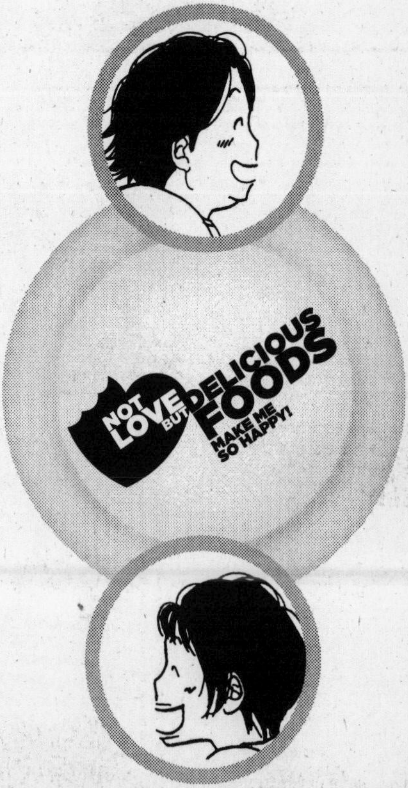
NOT LOVE BUT DELICIOUS FOODS
MAKE ME SO HAPPY!

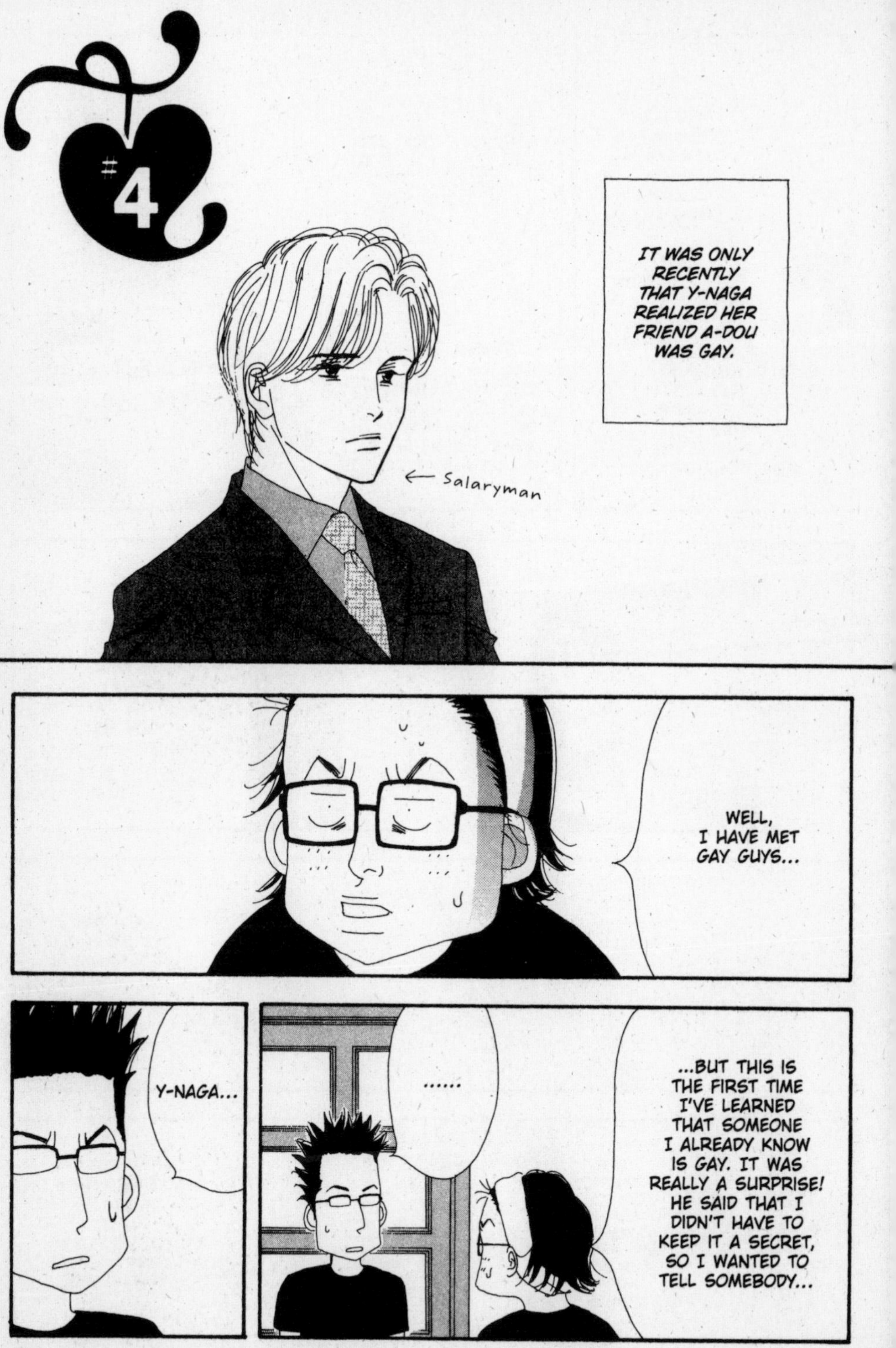
#4
IT WAS ONLY RECENTLY THAT Y-NAGA REALIZED HER FRIEND A-DOU WAS GAY.
← Salaryman
WELL, I HAVE MET GAY GUYS...
...BUT THIS IS THE FIRST TIME I'VE LEARNED THAT SOMEONE I ALREADY KNOW IS GAY. IT WAS REALLY A SURPRISE! HE SAID THAT I DIDN'T HAVE TO KEEP IT A SECRET, SO I WANTED TO TELL SOMEBODY...
......
Y-NAGA...

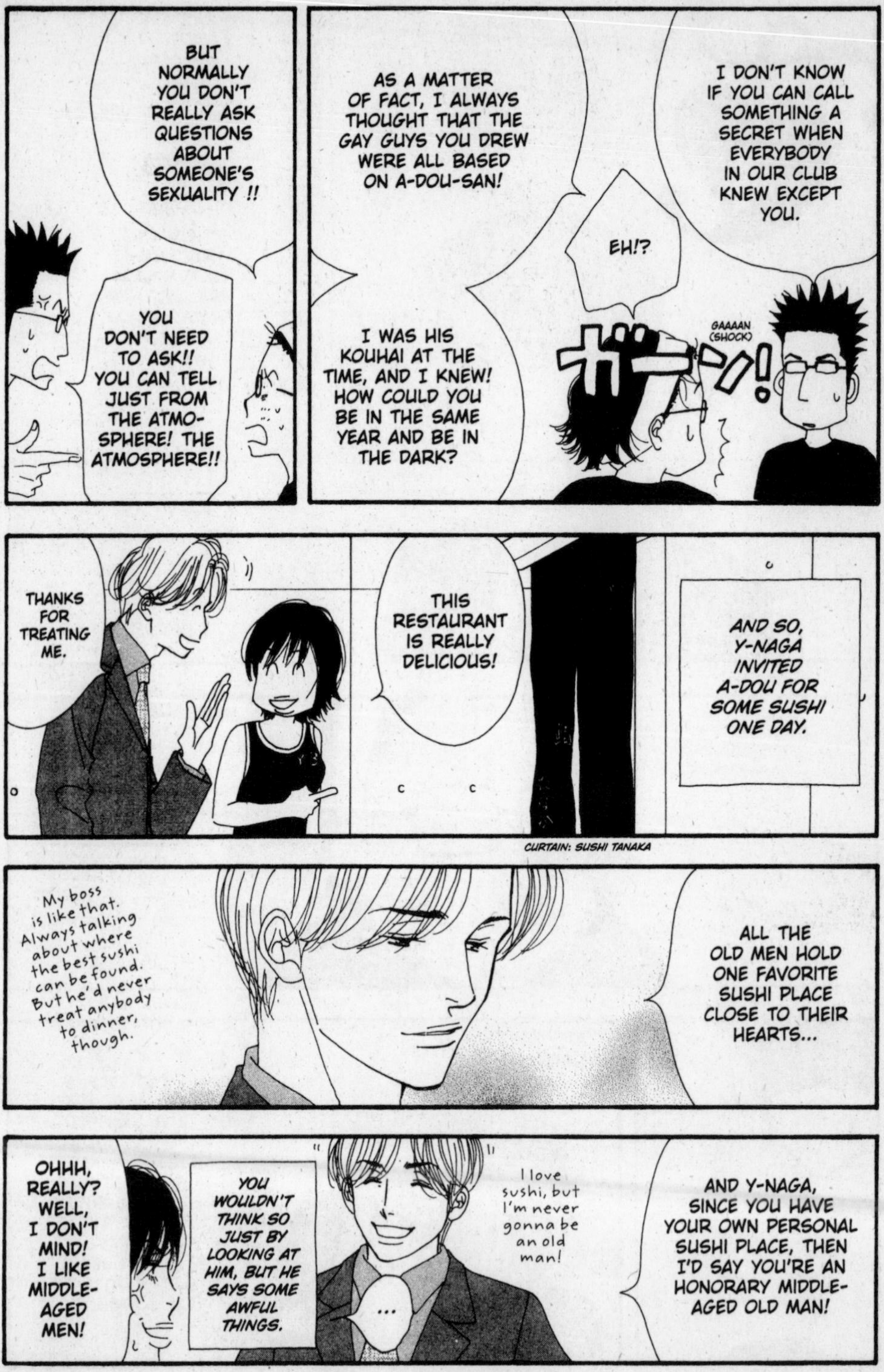
I DON'T KNOW IF YOU CAN CALL SOMETHING A SECRET WHEN EVERYBODY IN OUR CLUB KNEW EXCEPT YOU.
AS A MATTER OF FACT, I ALWAYS THOUGHT THAT THE GAY GUYS YOU DREW WERE ALL BASED ON A-DOU-SAN!
EH!?
GAAAAN (SHOCK)
I WAS HIS KOUHAI AT THE TIME, AND I KNEW! HOW COULD YOU BE IN THE SAME YEAR AND BE IN THE DARK?
BUT NORMALLY YOU DON'T REALLY ASK QUESTIONS ABOUT SOMEONE'S SEXUALITY !!
YOU DON'T NEED TO ASK!! YOU CAN TELL JUST FROM THE ATMOSPHERE! THE ATMOSPHERE!!
AND SO, Y-NAGA INVITED A-DOU FOR SOME SUSHI ONE DAY.
THIS RESTAURANT IS REALLY DELICIOUS!
THANKS FOR TREATING ME.
CURTAIN: SUSHI TANAKA
ALL THE OLD MEN HOLD ONE FAVORITE SUSHI PLACE CLOSE TO THEIR HEARTS...
My boss is like that. Always talking about where the best sushi can be found. But he'd never treat anybody to dinner, though.
AND Y-NAGA, SINCE YOU HAVE YOUR OWN PERSONAL SUSHI PLACE, THEN I'D SAY YOU'RE AN HONORARY MIDDLE-AGED OLD MAN!
I love sushi, but I'm never gonna be an old man!
...
YOU WOULDN'T THINK SO JUST BY LOOKING AT HIM, BUT HE SAYS SOME AWFUL THINGS.
OHHH, REALLY? WELL, I DON'T MIND! I LIKE MIDDLE-AGED MEN!

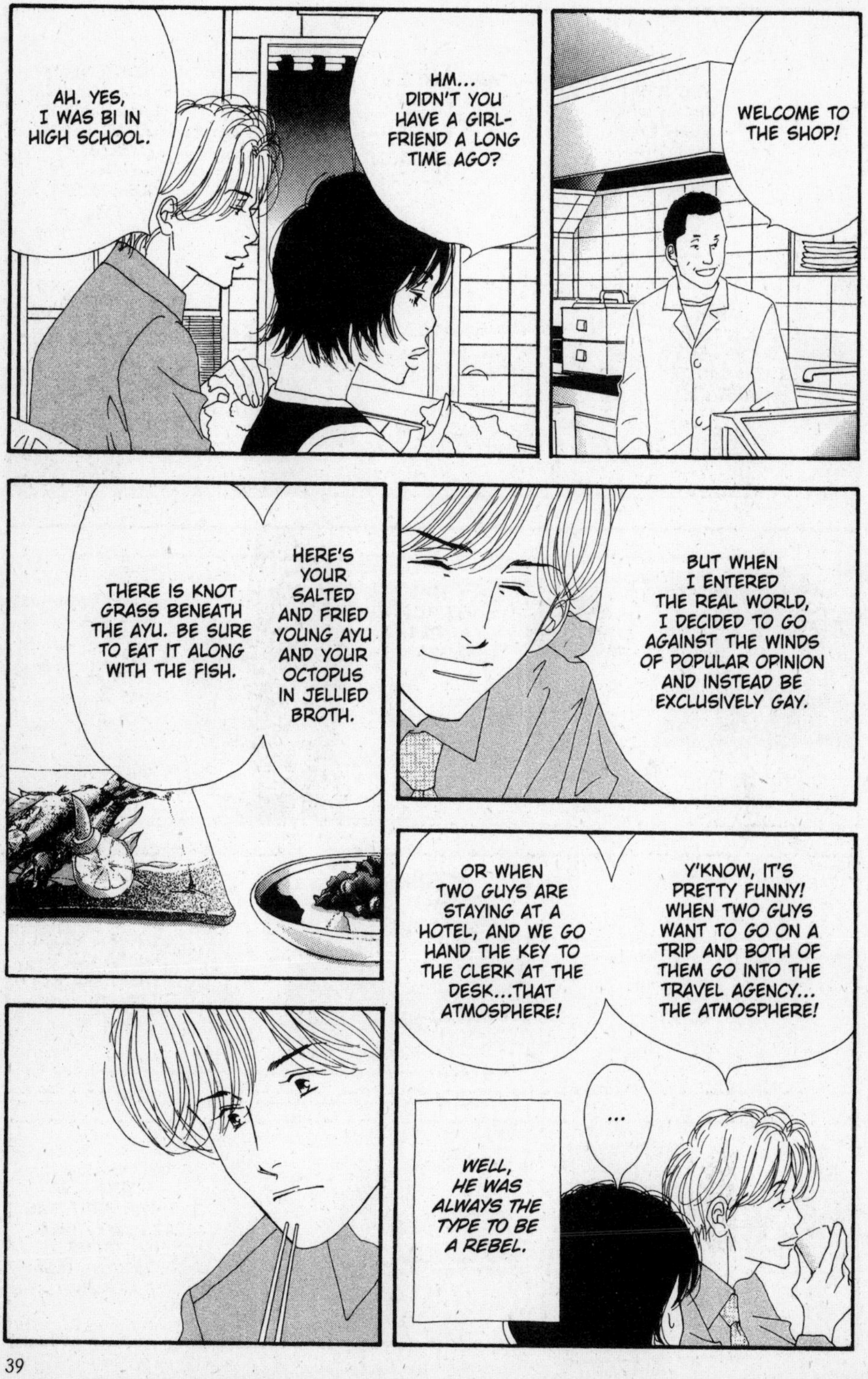
WELCOME TO THE SHOP!
HM... DIDN'T YOU HAVE A GIRL-FRIEND A LONG TIME AGO?
AH. YES, I WAS BI IN HIGH SCHOOL.
BUT WHEN I ENTERED THE REAL WORLD, I DECIDED TO GO AGAINST THE WINDS OF POPULAR OPINION AND INSTEAD BE EXCLUSIVELY GAY.
HERE'S YOUR SALTED AND FRIED YOUNG AYU AND YOUR OCTOPUS IN JELLIED BROTH.
THERE IS KNOT GRASS BENEATH THE AYU. BE SURE TO EAT IT ALONG WITH THE FISH.
Y'KNOW, IT'S PRETTY FUNNY! WHEN TWO GUYS WANT TO GO ON A TRIP AND BOTH OF THEM GO INTO THE TRAVEL AGENCY... THE ATMOSPHERE!
OR WHEN TWO GUYS ARE STAYING AT A HOTEL, AND WE GO HAND THE KEY TO THE CLERK AT THE DESK...THAT ATMOSPHERE!
...
WELL, HE WAS ALWAYS THE TYPE TO BE A REBEL.

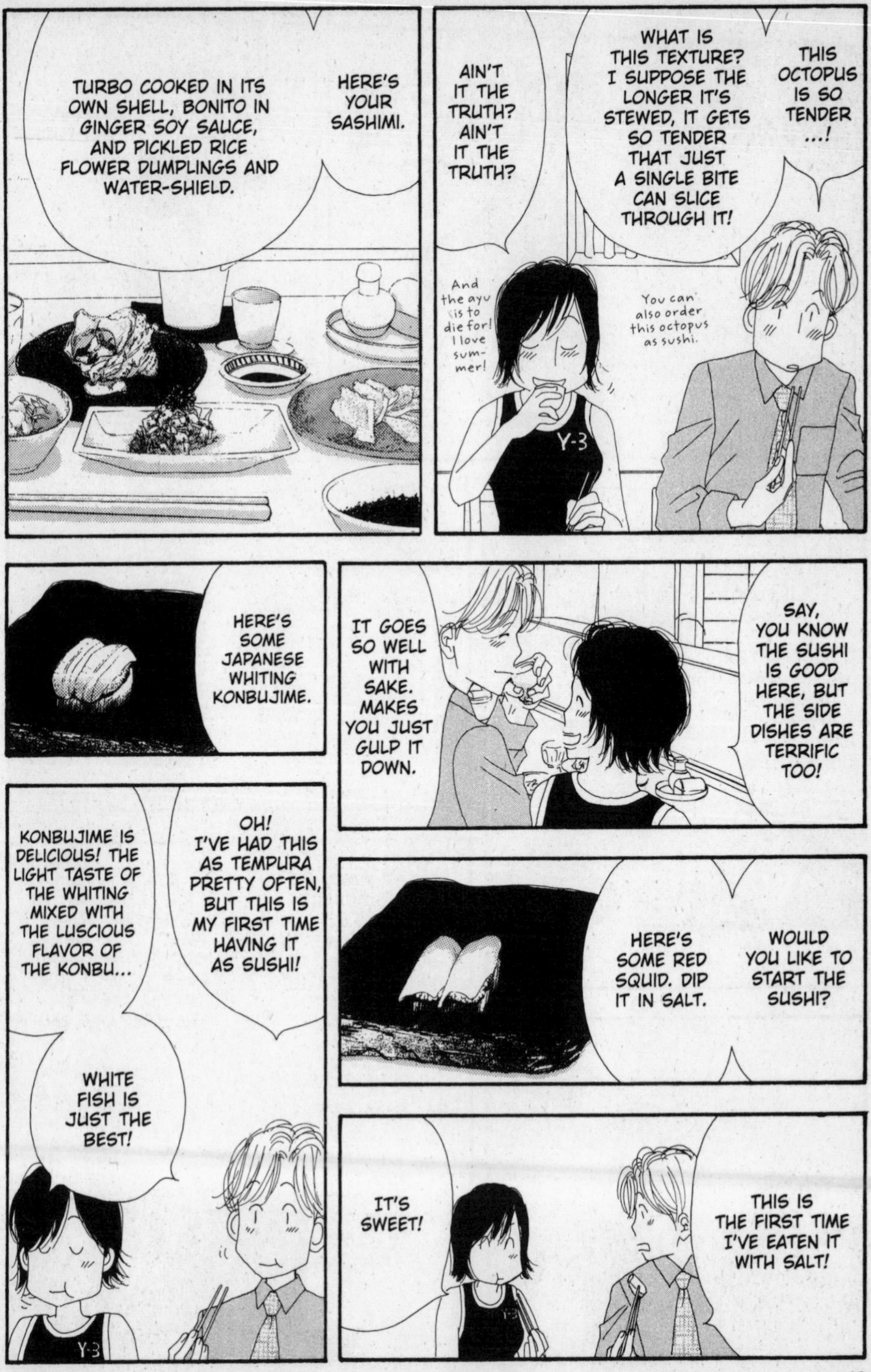
THIS OCTOPUS IS SO TENDER ...!
WHAT IS THIS TEXTURE? I SUPPOSE THE LONGER IT'S STEWED, IT GETS SO TENDER THAT JUST A SINGLE BITE CAN SLICE THROUGH IT!
AIN'T IT THE TRUTH? AIN'T IT THE TRUTH?
You can also order this octopus as sushi.
And the ayu is to die for! I love sum-mer!
HERE'S YOUR SASHIMI.
TURBO COOKED IN ITS OWN SHELL, BONITO IN GINGER SOY SAUCE, AND PICKLED RICE FLOWER DUMPLINGS AND WATER-SHIELD.
SAY, YOU KNOW THE SUSHI IS GOOD HERE, BUT THE SIDE DISHES ARE TERRIFIC TOO!
IT GOES SO WELL WITH SAKE. MAKES YOU JUST GULP IT DOWN.
WOULD YOU LIKE TO START THE SUSHI?
HERE'S SOME RED SQUID. DIP IT IN SALT.
THIS IS THE FIRST TIME I'VE EATEN IT WITH SALT!
IT'S SWEET!
HERE'S SOME JAPANESE WHITING KONBUJIME.
OH! I'VE HAD THIS AS TEMPURA PRETTY OFTEN, BUT THIS IS MY FIRST TIME HAVING IT AS SUSHI!
KONBUJIME IS DELICIOUS! THE LIGHT TASTE OF THE WHITING MIXED WITH THE LUSCIOUS FLAVOR OF THE KONBU...
WHITE FISH IS JUST THE BEST!

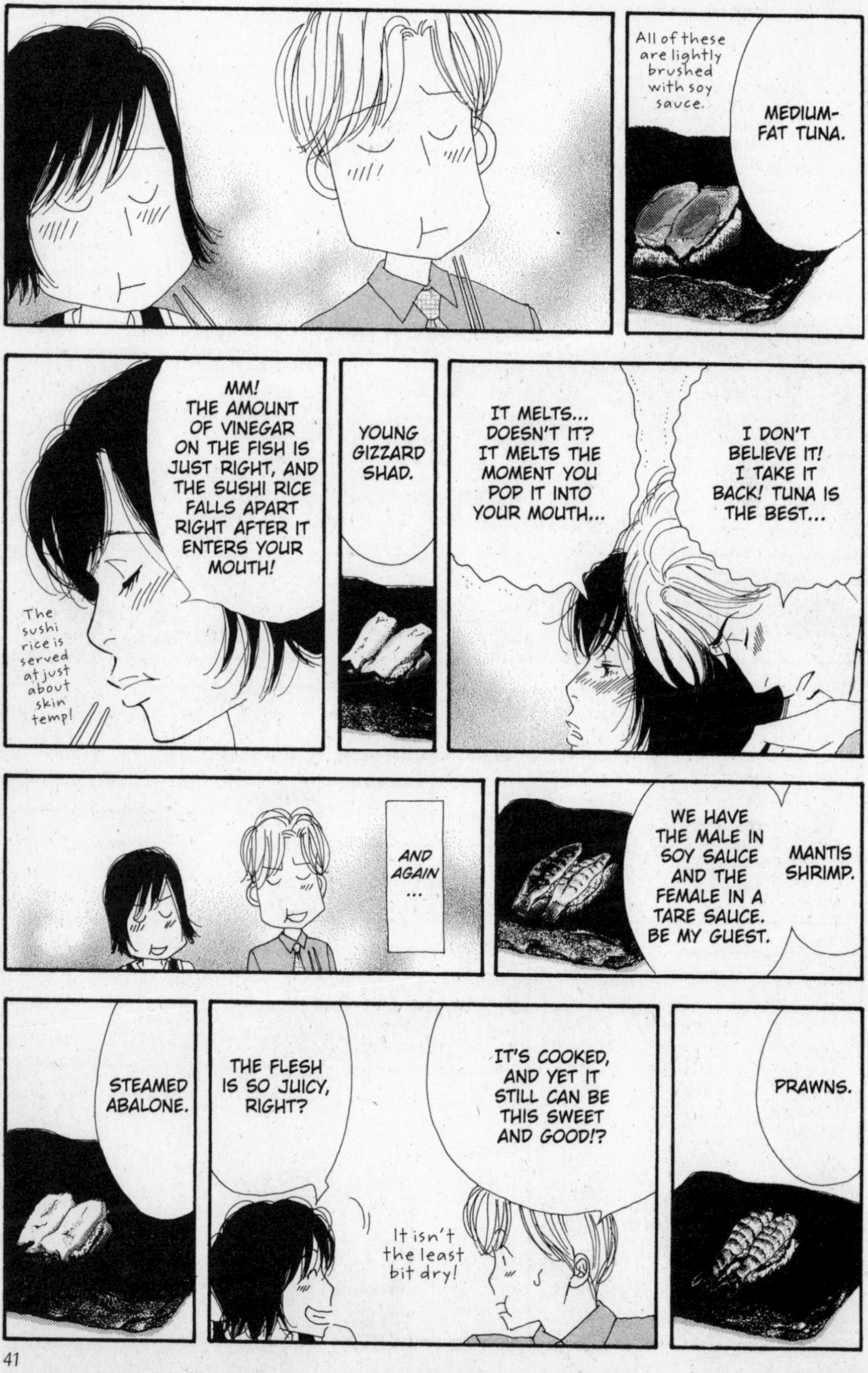
All of these are lightly brushed with soy sauce.
MEDIUM-FAT TUNA.
I DON'T BELIEVE IT! I TAKE IT BACK! TUNA IS THE BEST...
IT MELTS... DOESN'T IT? IT MELTS THE MOMENT YOU POP IT INTO YOUR MOUTH...
YOUNG GIZZARD SHAD.
MM! THE AMOUNT OF VINEGAR ON THE FISH IS JUST RIGHT, AND THE SUSHI RICE FALLS APART RIGHT AFTER IT ENTERS YOUR MOUTH!
The sushi rice is served at just about skin temp!
MANTIS SHRIMP.
WE HAVE THE MALE IN SOY SAUCE AND THE FEMALE IN A TARE SAUCE. BE MY GUEST.
AND AGAIN ...
PRAWNS.
IT'S COOKED, AND YET IT STILL CAN BE THIS SWEET AND GOOD!?
THE FLESH IS SO JUICY, RIGHT?
It isn't the least bit dry!
STEAMED ABALONE.

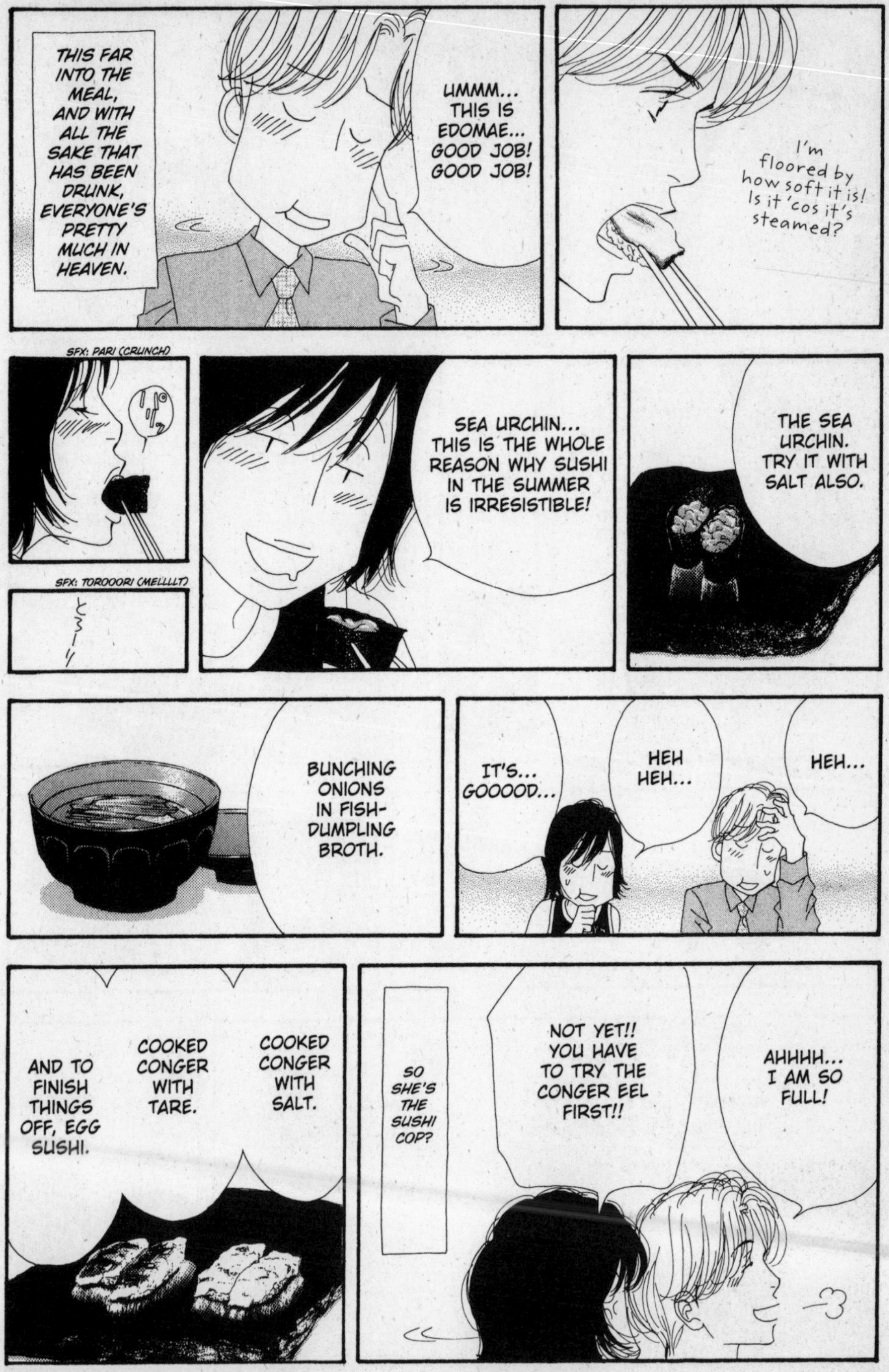
I'm floored by how soft it is! Is it 'cos it's steamed?
UMMM... THIS IS EDOMAE... GOOD JOB! GOOD JOB!
THIS FAR INTO THE MEAL, AND WITH ALL THE SAKE THAT HAS BEEN DRUNK, EVERYONE'S PRETTY MUCH IN HEAVEN.
THE SEA URCHIN. TRY IT WITH SALT ALSO.
SEA URCHIN... THIS IS THE WHOLE REASON WHY SUSHI IN THE SUMMER IS IRRESISTIBLE!
SFX: PARI (CRUNCH)
SFX: TOROOORI (MELLLLT)
HEH...
HEH HEH...
IT'S... GOOOOD...
BUNCHING ONIONS IN FISH-DUMPLING BROTH.
AHHHH... I AM SO FULL!
NOT YET!! YOU HAVE TO TRY THE CONGER EEL FIRST!!
SO SHE'S THE SUSHI COP?
COOKED CONGER WITH SALT.
COOKED CONGER WITH TARE.
AND TO FINISH THINGS OFF, EGG SUSHI.

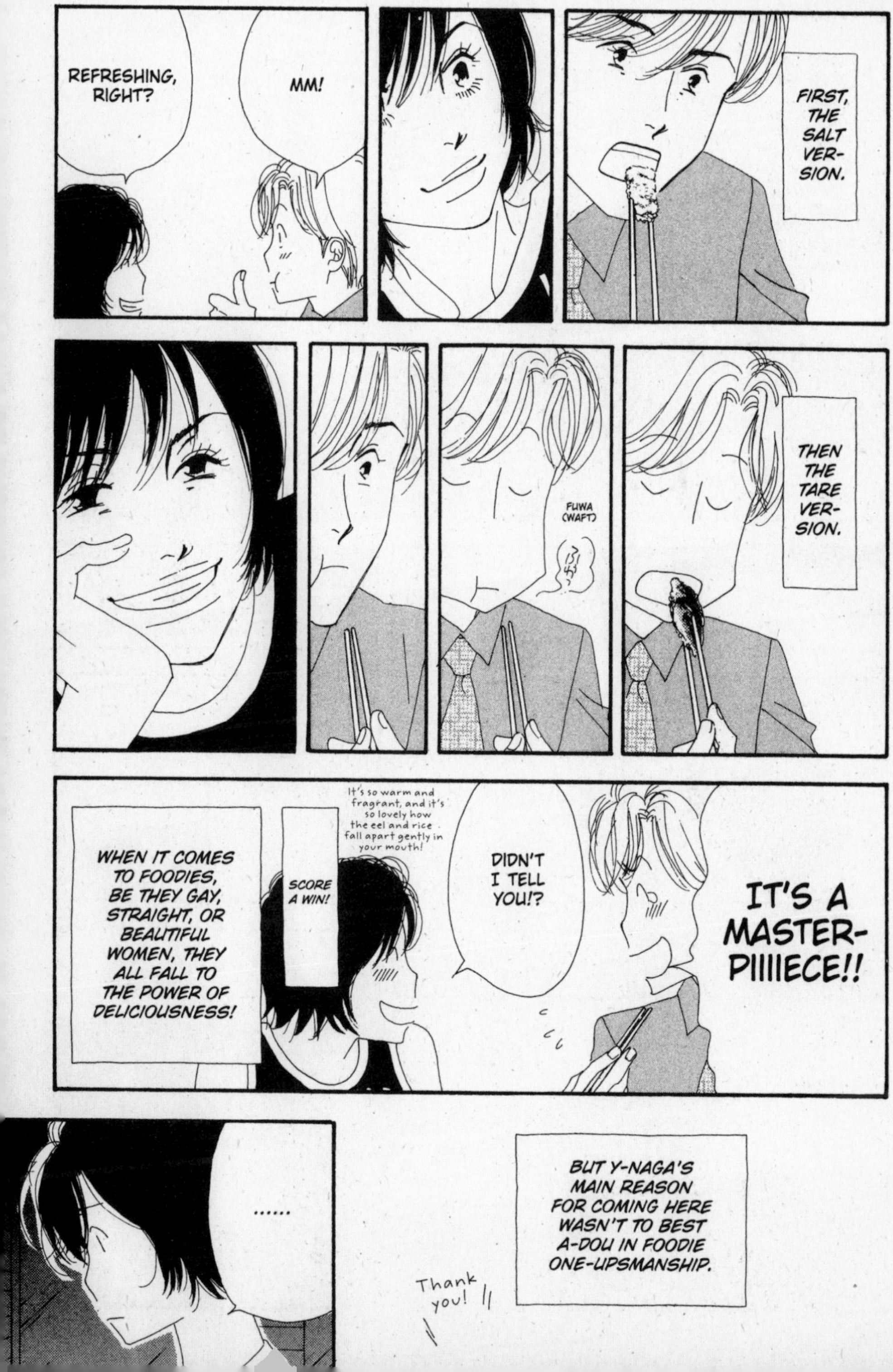
FIRST, THE SALT VERSION.
MM!
REFRESHING, RIGHT?
THEN THE TARE VERSION.
FUWA (WAFT)
IT'S A MASTER-PIIIIECE!!
DIDN'T I TELL YOU!?
It's so warm and fragrant, and it's so lovely how the eel and rice fall apart gently in your mouth!
SCORE A WIN!
WHEN IT COMES TO FOODIES, BE THEY GAY, STRAIGHT, OR BEAUTIFUL WOMEN, THEY ALL FALL TO THE POWER OF DELICIOUSNESS!
BUT Y-NAGA'S MAIN REASON FOR COMING HERE WASN'T TO BEST A-DOU IN FOODIE ONE-UPSMANSHIP.
Thank you!
......

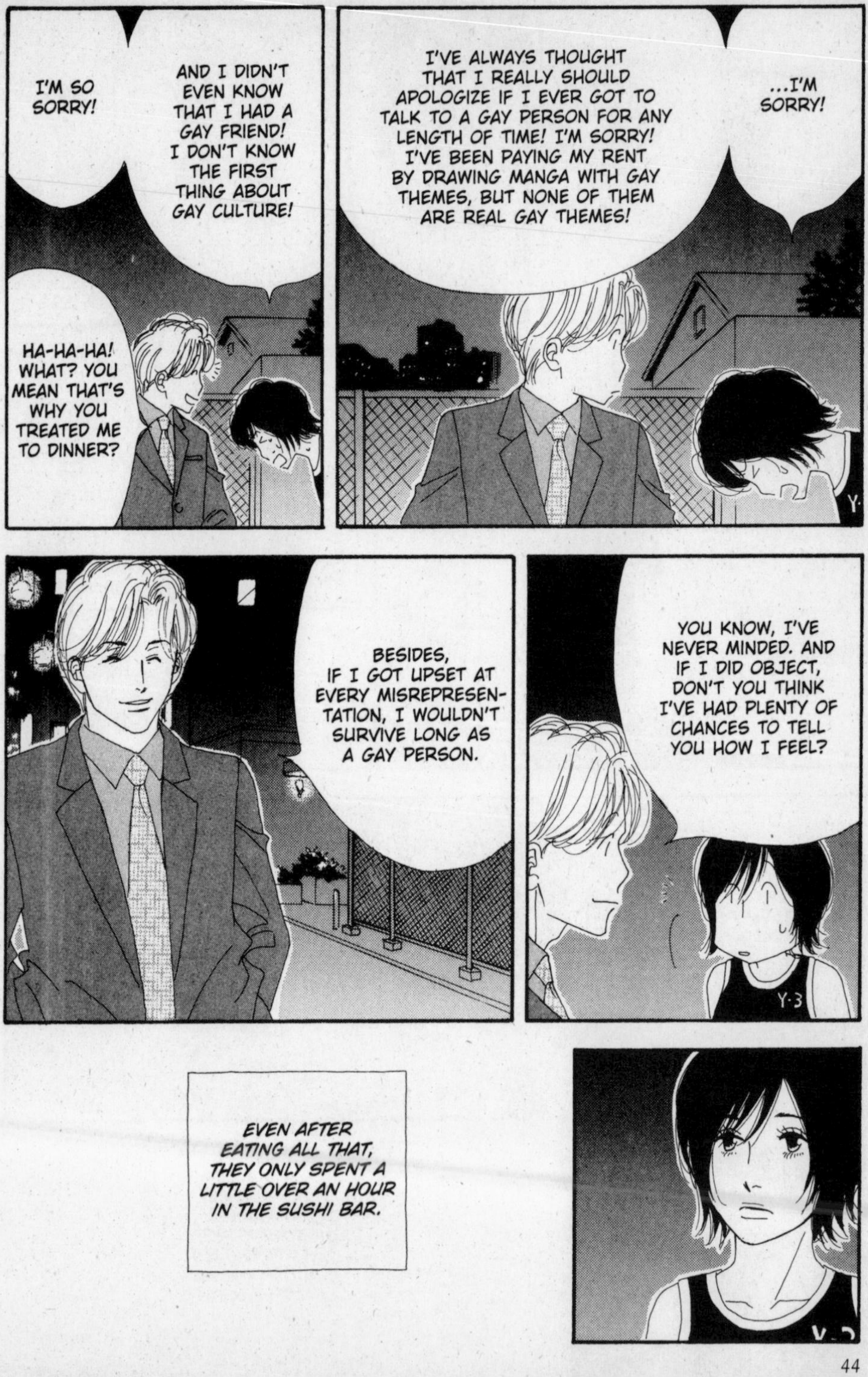
...I'M SORRY!
I'VE ALWAYS THOUGHT THAT I REALLY SHOULD APOLOGIZE IF I EVER GOT TO TALK TO A GAY PERSON FOR ANY LENGTH OF TIME! I'M SORRY! I'VE BEEN PAYING MY RENT BY DRAWING MANGA WITH GAY THEMES, BUT NONE OF THEM ARE REAL GAY THEMES!
AND I DIDN'T EVEN KNOW THAT I HAD A GAY FRIEND! I DON'T KNOW THE FIRST THING ABOUT GAY CULTURE!
I'M SO SORRY!
HA-HA-HA! WHAT? YOU MEAN THAT'S WHY YOU TREATED ME TO DINNER?
YOU KNOW, I'VE NEVER MINDED. AND IF I DID OBJECT, DON'T YOU THINK I'VE HAD PLENTY OF CHANCES TO TELL YOU HOW I FEEL?
BESIDES, IF I GOT UPSET AT EVERY MISREPRESEN-TATION, I WOULDN'T SURVIVE LONG AS A GAY PERSON.
EVEN AFTER EATING ALL THAT, THEY ONLY SPENT A LITTLE OVER AN HOUR IN THE SUSHI BAR.

SUSHI TANAKA

[Address]
2-6-3 Nishi-Ogi Minami,
Suginami-ku, Tokyo
[Telephone]
03-3335-3777
[Hours]
5:00 PM - 11:00 PM
[Closed]
Mondays.
[Directions]
A seven-minute walk
from the JR Nishi
Ogikubo Station.
[Parking]
There is parking (but
only a few spaces).

JR NISHI-OGIKUBO STATION
TO SHINJUKU
SOUTH EXIT
MIZUHO GINKO BANK
NISHI-OGI MINAMI 2
NISHI-OGI MINAMI POST OFFICE
NISHI-OGI MINAMI CHUUOU DOORI ROAD
HERE!
ITSUKAISHI KAIDOU ROAD
VIDEO RENTAL SHOP
NISHI-OGI MINAMI DAI-NI

FUMI YOSHINAGA'S COMMENTS

IF YOU WANT TO TRY ALL THE SUSHI, YOU SHOULD BUDGET IN THE NEIGHBORHOOD OF ¥8,000. IF YOU DO IT LIKE IN THE MANGA AND HAVE SAKE AND SNACKS BEFORE EATING THE SUSHI, YOU SHOULD BUDGET SOMEWHERE AROUND ¥13,000. EVERYONE WORKING IN THE RESTAURANT IS REALLY NICE, SO EVEN IF IT'S YOUR FIRST TIME, YOU'LL HAVE A FRIENDLY, GOOD TIME. RESERVATIONS NECESSARY.

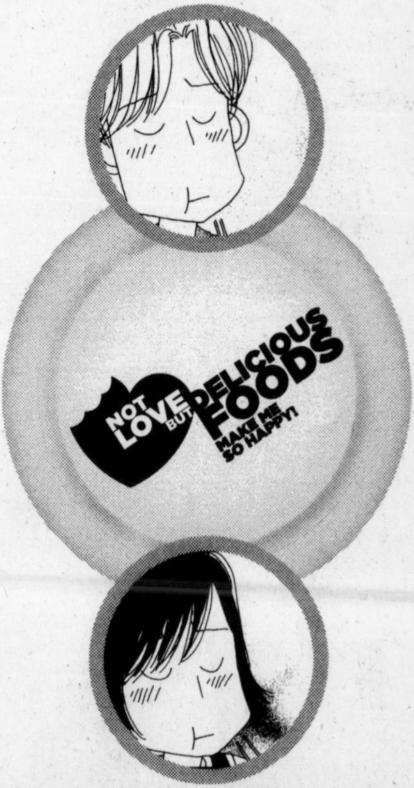
NOT LOVE BUT DELICIOUS FOODS MAKE ME SO HAPPY!

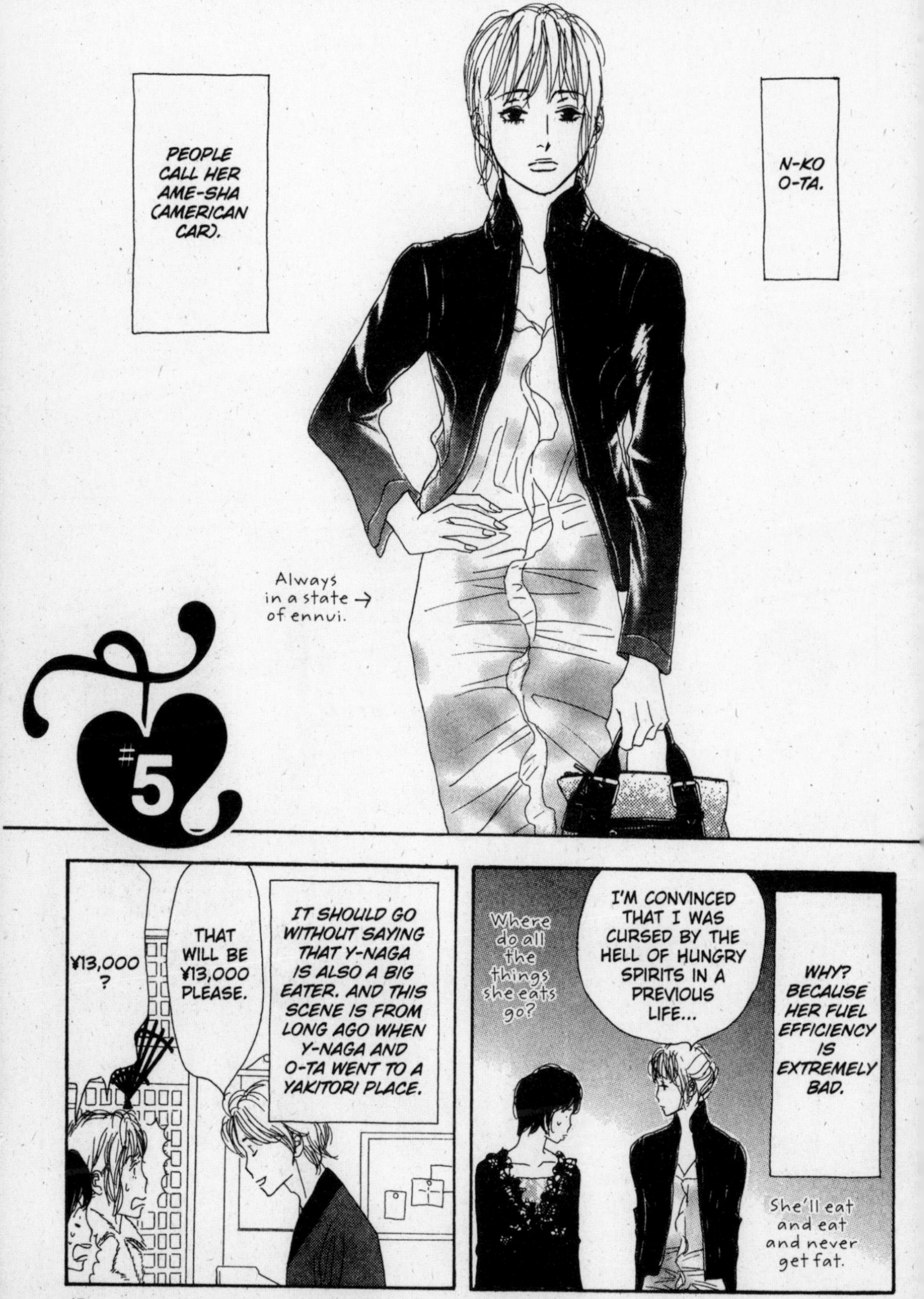
N-KO O-TA.
PEOPLE CALL HER AME-SHA (AMERICAN CAR).
Always in a state of ennui. →
#5
WHY? BECAUSE HER FUEL EFFICIENCY IS EXTREMELY BAD.
I'M CONVINCED THAT I WAS CURSED BY THE HELL OF HUNGRY SPIRITS IN A PREVIOUS LIFE...
Where do all the things she eats go?
She'll eat and eat and never get fat.
IT SHOULD GO WITHOUT SAYING THAT Y-NAGA IS ALSO A BIG EATER. AND THIS SCENE IS FROM LONG AGO WHEN Y-NAGA AND O-TA WENT TO A YAKITORI PLACE.
THAT WILL BE ¥13,000 PLEASE.
¥13,000?

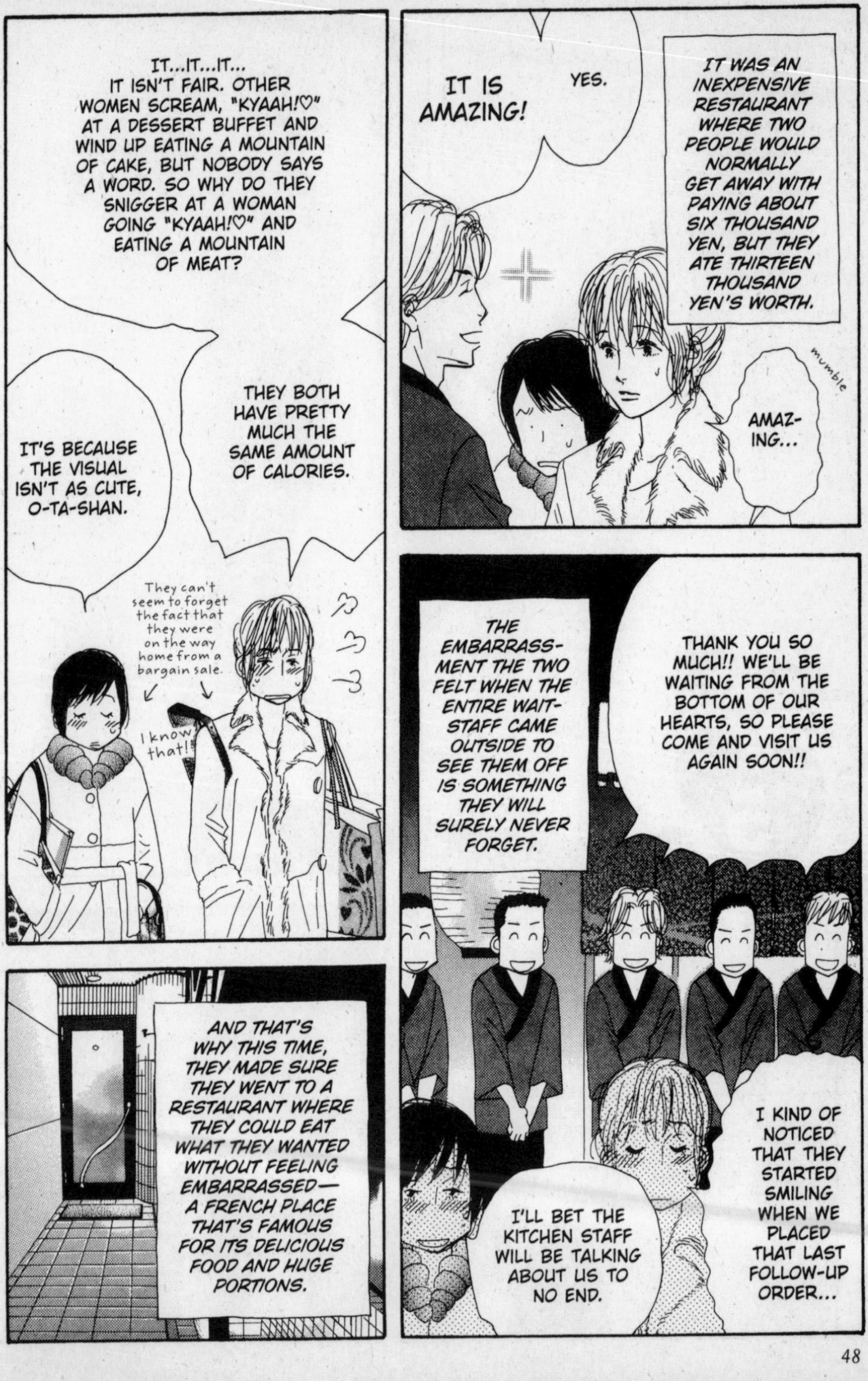
IT WAS AN INEXPENSIVE RESTAURANT WHERE TWO PEOPLE WOULD NORMALLY GET AWAY WITH PAYING ABOUT SIX THOUSAND YEN, BUT THEY ATE THIRTEEN THOUSAND YEN'S WORTH.
IT IS AMAZING!
YES.
mumble
AMAZ-ING...
THANK YOU SO MUCH!! WE'LL BE WAITING FROM THE BOTTOM OF OUR HEARTS, SO PLEASE COME AND VISIT US AGAIN SOON!!
THE EMBARRASS-MENT THE TWO FELT WHEN THE ENTIRE WAIT-STAFF CAME OUTSIDE TO SEE THEM OFF IS SOMETHING THEY WILL SURELY NEVER FORGET.
I KIND OF NOTICED THAT THEY STARTED SMILING WHEN WE PLACED THAT LAST FOLLOW-UP ORDER...
I'LL BET THE KITCHEN STAFF WILL BE TALKING ABOUT US TO NO END.
IT...IT...IT... IT ISN'T FAIR. OTHER WOMEN SCREAM, "KYAAH!♡" AT A DESSERT BUFFET AND WIND UP EATING A MOUNTAIN OF CAKE, BUT NOBODY SAYS A WORD. SO WHY DO THEY SNIGGER AT A WOMAN GOING "KYAAH!♡" AND EATING A MOUNTAIN OF MEAT?
THEY BOTH HAVE PRETTY MUCH THE SAME AMOUNT OF CALORIES.
IT'S BECAUSE THE VISUAL ISN'T AS CUTE, O-TA-SHAN.
They can't seem to forget the fact that they were on the way home from a bargain sale.
I know that!!
AND THAT'S WHY THIS TIME, THEY MADE SURE THEY WENT TO A RESTAURANT WHERE THEY COULD EAT WHAT THEY WANTED WITHOUT FEELING EMBARRASSED— A FRENCH PLACE THAT'S FAMOUS FOR ITS DELICIOUS FOOD AND HUGE PORTIONS.

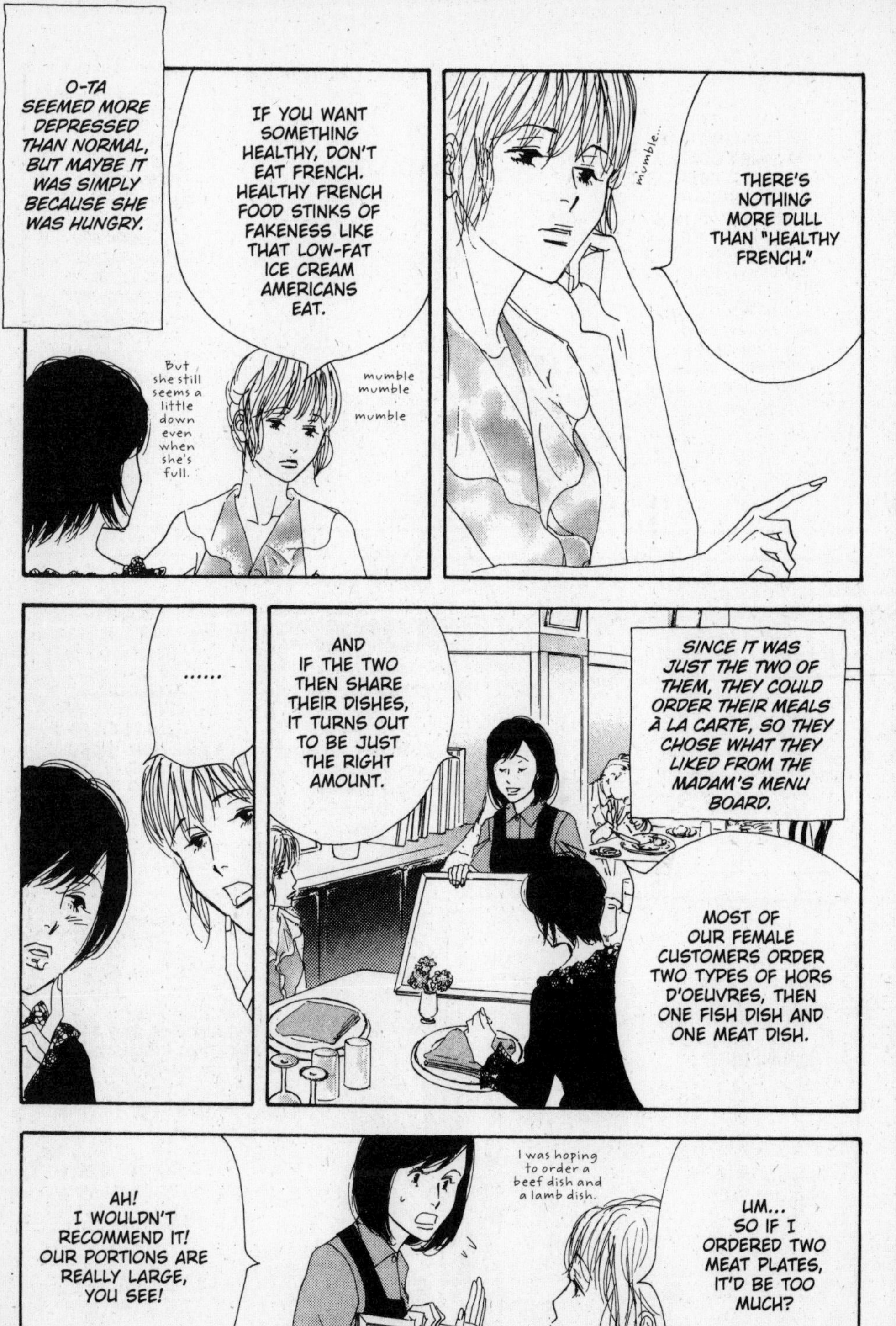
mumble...
THERE'S NOTHING MORE DULL THAN "HEALTHY FRENCH."
IF YOU WANT SOMETHING HEALTHY, DON'T EAT FRENCH. HEALTHY FRENCH FOOD STINKS OF FAKENESS LIKE THAT LOW-FAT ICE CREAM AMERICANS EAT.
O-TA SEEMED MORE DEPRESSED THAN NORMAL, BUT MAYBE IT WAS SIMPLY BECAUSE SHE WAS HUNGRY.
mumble mumble
mumble
But she still seems a little down even when she's full.
SINCE IT WAS JUST THE TWO OF THEM, THEY COULD ORDER THEIR MEALS À LA CARTE, SO THEY CHOSE WHAT THEY LIKED FROM THE MADAM'S MENU BOARD.
MOST OF OUR FEMALE CUSTOMERS ORDER TWO TYPES OF HORS D'OEUVRES, THEN ONE FISH DISH AND ONE MEAT DISH.
AND IF THE TWO THEN SHARE THEIR DISHES, IT TURNS OUT TO BE JUST THE RIGHT AMOUNT.
......
UM... SO IF I ORDERED TWO MEAT PLATES, IT'D BE TOO MUCH?
I was hoping to order a beef dish and a lamb dish.
AH! I WOULDN'T RECOMMEND IT! OUR PORTIONS ARE REALLY LARGE, YOU SEE!

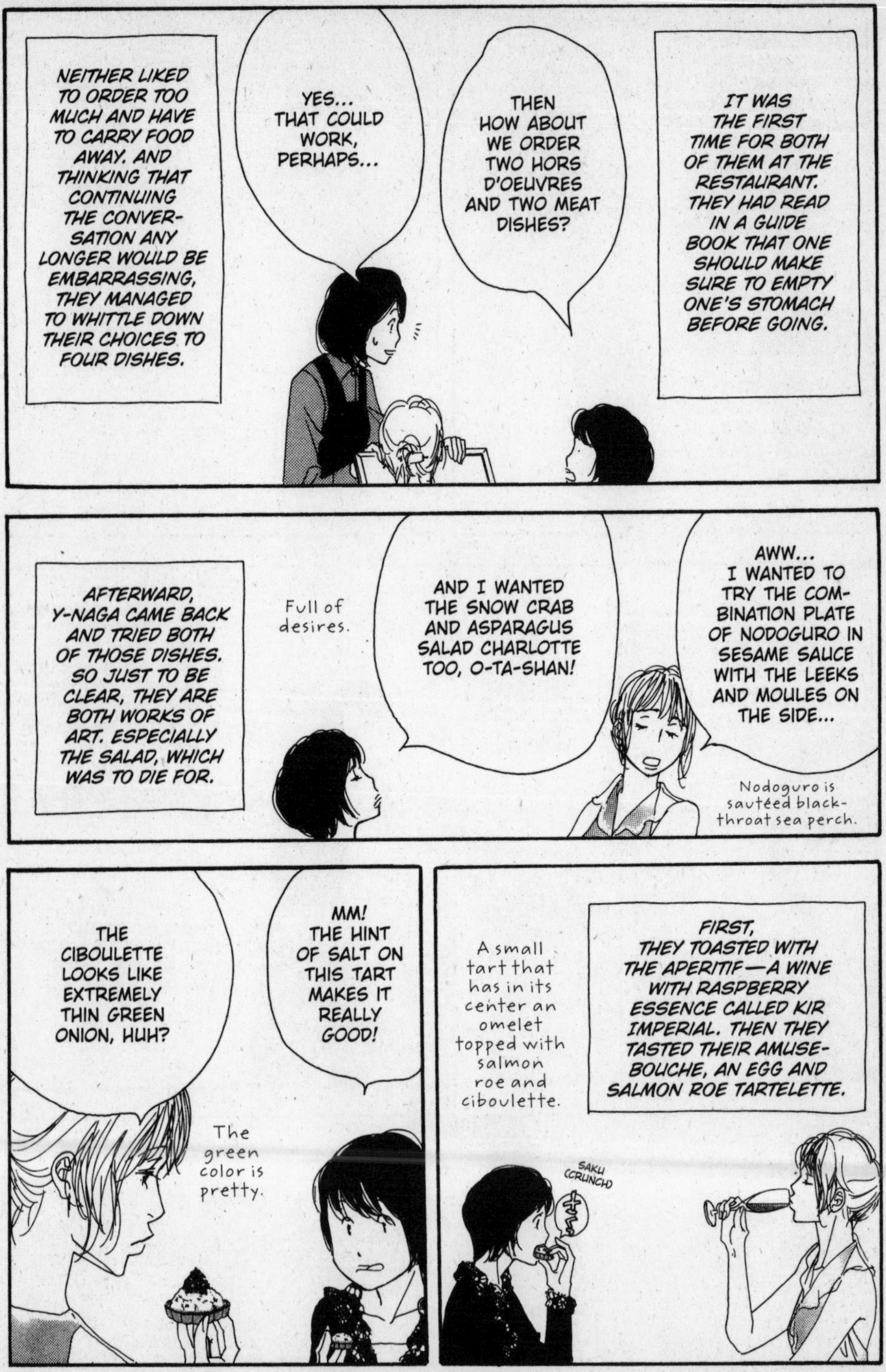
IT WAS THE FIRST TIME FOR BOTH OF THEM AT THE RESTAURANT. THEY HAD READ IN A GUIDE BOOK THAT ONE SHOULD MAKE SURE TO EMPTY ONE'S STOMACH BEFORE GOING.
THEN HOW ABOUT WE ORDER TWO HORS D'OEUVRES AND TWO MEAT DISHES?
YES... THAT COULD WORK, PERHAPS...
NEITHER LIKED TO ORDER TOO MUCH AND HAVE TO CARRY FOOD AWAY. AND THINKING THAT CONTINUING THE CONVERSATION ANY LONGER WOULD BE EMBARRASSING, THEY MANAGED TO WHITTLE DOWN THEIR CHOICES TO FOUR DISHES.
AWW... I WANTED TO TRY THE COMBINATION PLATE OF NODOGURO IN SESAME SAUCE WITH THE LEEKS AND MOULES ON THE SIDE...
Nodoguro is sautéed black-throat sea perch.
AND I WANTED THE SNOW CRAB AND ASPARAGUS SALAD CHARLOTTE TOO, O-TA-SHAN!
Full of desires.
AFTERWARD, Y-NAGA CAME BACK AND TRIED BOTH OF THOSE DISHES. SO JUST TO BE CLEAR, THEY ARE BOTH WORKS OF ART. ESPECIALLY THE SALAD, WHICH WAS TO DIE FOR.
FIRST, THEY TOASTED WITH THE APERITIF—A WINE WITH RASPBERRY ESSENCE CALLED KIR IMPERIAL. THEN THEY TASTED THEIR AMUSE-BOUCHE, AN EGG AND SALMON ROE TARTELETTE.
A small tart that has in its center an omelet topped with salmon roe and ciboulette.
SAKU (CRUNCH)
MM! THE HINT OF SALT ON THIS TART MAKES IT REALLY GOOD!
THE CIBOULETTE LOOKS LIKE EXTREMELY THIN GREEN ONION, HUH?
The green color is pretty.

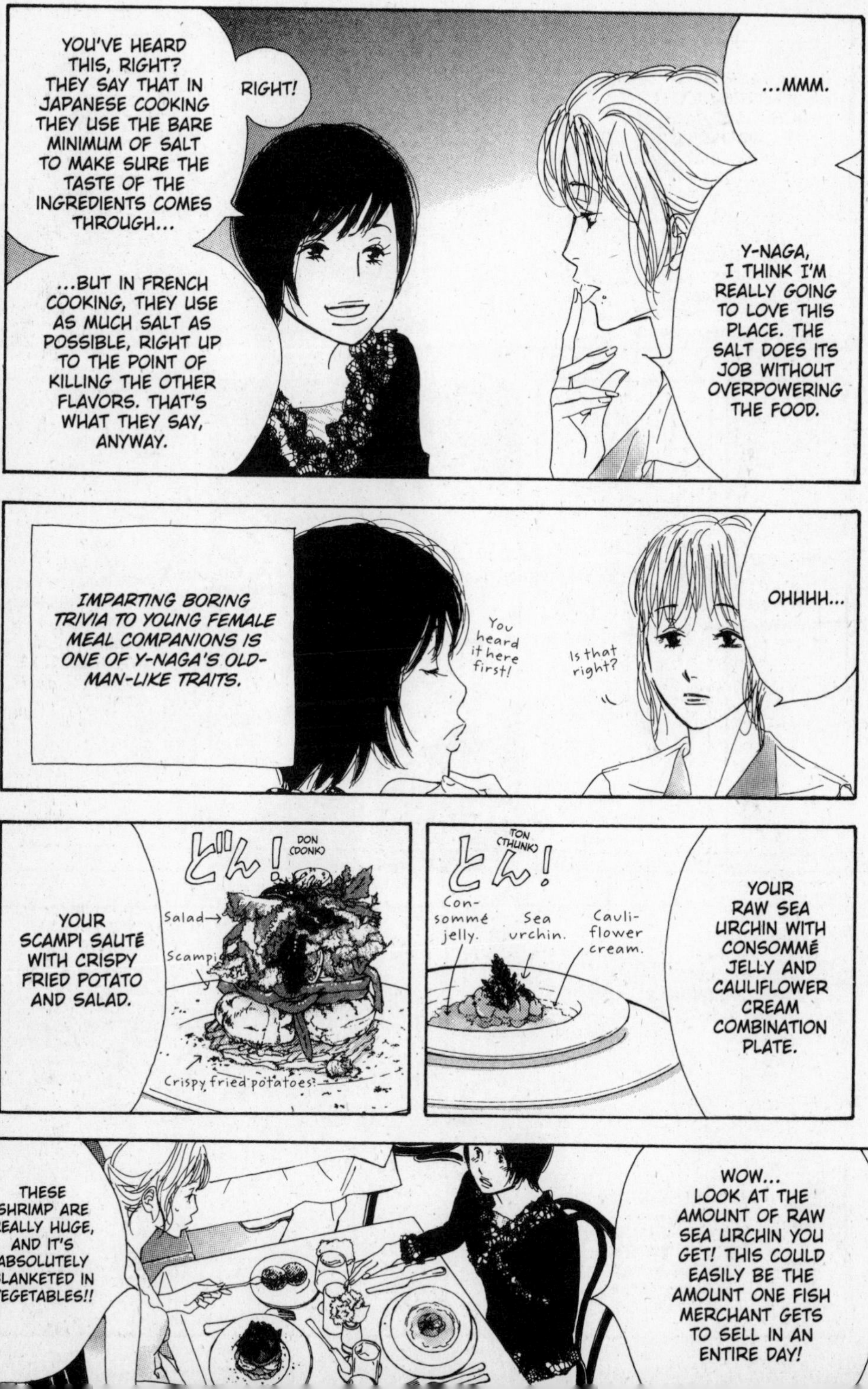
...MMM.
Y-NAGA, I THINK I'M REALLY GOING TO LOVE THIS PLACE. THE SALT DOES ITS JOB WITHOUT OVERPOWERING THE FOOD.
YOU'VE HEARD THIS, RIGHT? THEY SAY THAT IN JAPANESE COOKING THEY USE THE BARE MINIMUM OF SALT TO MAKE SURE THE TASTE OF THE INGREDIENTS COMES THROUGH...
RIGHT!
...BUT IN FRENCH COOKING, THEY USE AS MUCH SALT AS POSSIBLE, RIGHT UP TO THE POINT OF KILLING THE OTHER FLAVORS. THAT'S WHAT THEY SAY, ANYWAY.
OHHHH...
Is that right?
You heard it here first!
IMPARTING BORING TRIVIA TO YOUNG FEMALE MEAL COMPANIONS IS ONE OF Y-NAGA'S OLD-MAN-LIKE TRAITS.
TON (THUNK)
とん!
YOUR RAW SEA URCHIN WITH CONSOMMÉ JELLY AND CAULIFLOWER CREAM COMBINATION PLATE.
Consommé jelly.
Sea urchin.
Cauliflower cream.
DON (DONK)
どん!
YOUR SCAMPI SAUTÉ WITH CRISPY FRIED POTATO AND SALAD.
Salad
Scampi
Crispy fried potatoes
WOW... LOOK AT THE AMOUNT OF RAW SEA URCHIN YOU GET! THIS COULD EASILY BE THE AMOUNT ONE FISH MERCHANT GETS TO SELL IN AN ENTIRE DAY!
THESE SHRIMP ARE REALLY HUGE, AND IT'S ABSOLUTELY BLANKETED IN VEGETABLES!!

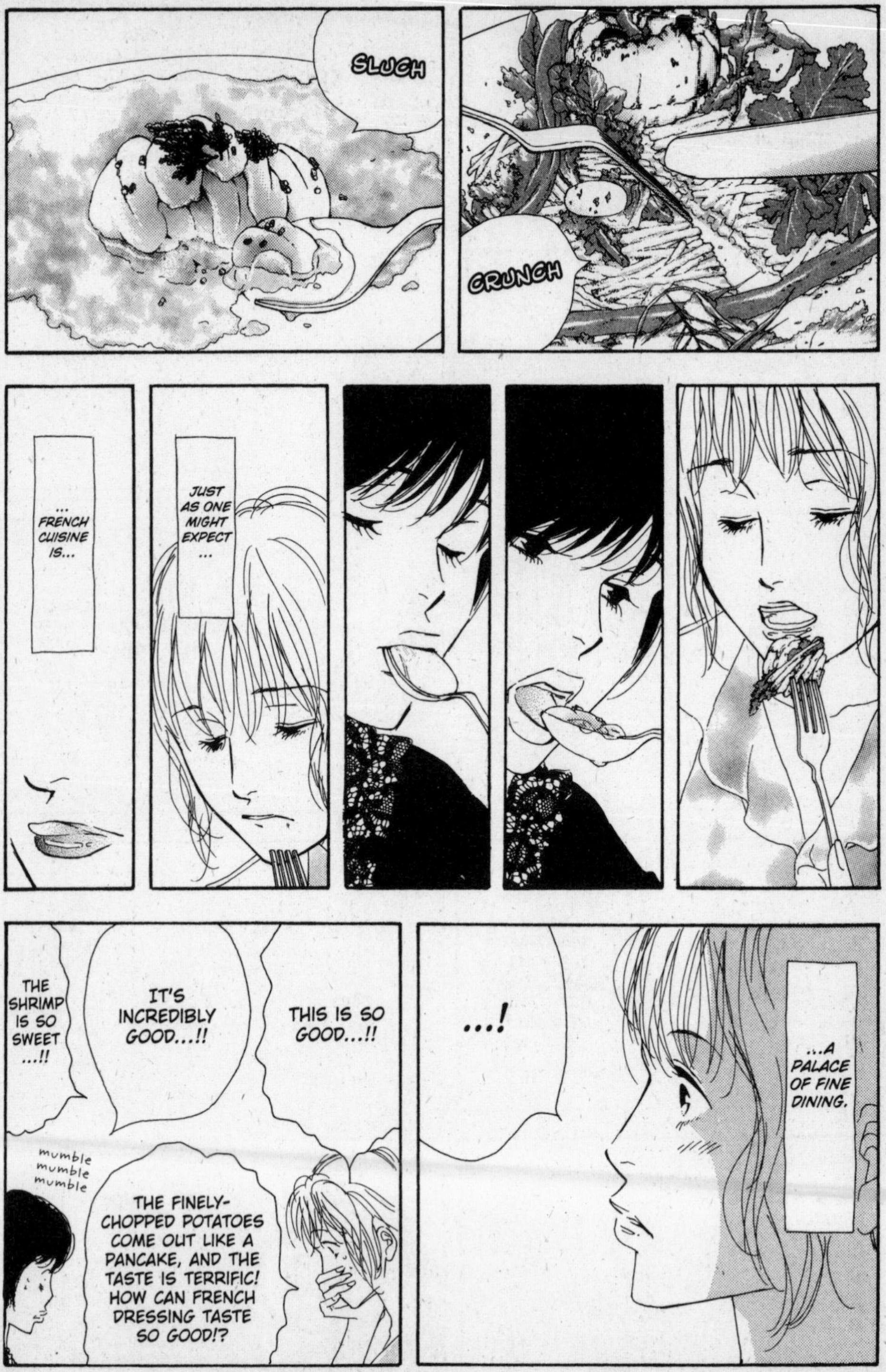
CRUNCH
SLUCH
JUST AS ONE MIGHT EXPECT ...
... FRENCH CUISINE IS...
...A PALACE OF FINE DINING.
...!
THIS IS SO GOOD...!!
IT'S INCREDIBLY GOOD...!!
THE SHRIMP IS SO SWEET ...!!
THE FINELY-CHOPPED POTATOES COME OUT LIKE A PANCAKE, AND THE TASTE IS TERRIFIC! HOW CAN FRENCH DRESSING TASTE SO GOOD!?
mumble mumble mumble

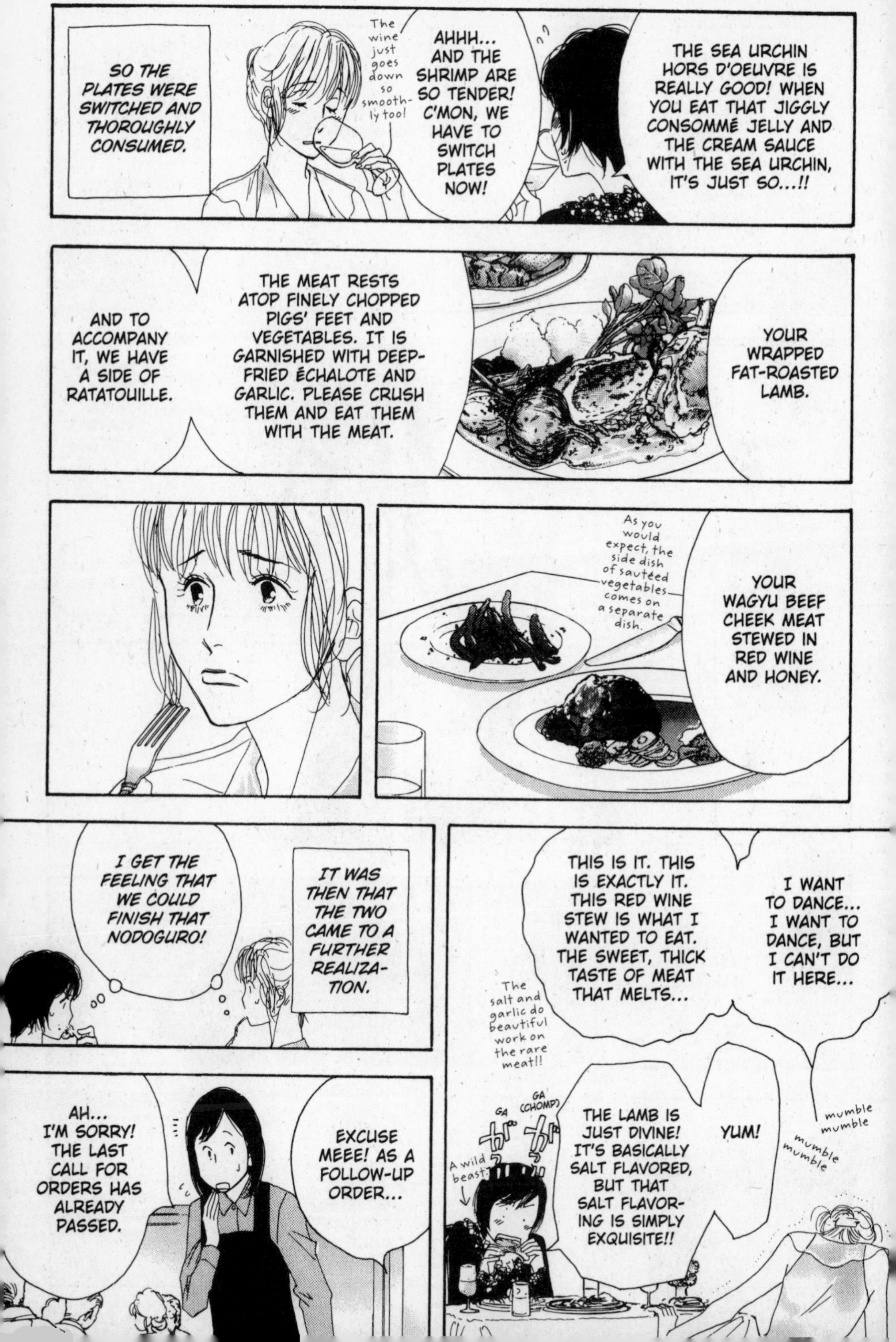
THE SEA URCHIN HORS D'OEUVRE IS REALLY GOOD! WHEN YOU EAT THAT JIGGLY CONSOMMÉ JELLY AND THE CREAM SAUCE WITH THE SEA URCHIN, IT'S JUST SO...!!
AHHH... AND THE SHRIMP ARE SO TENDER! C'MON, WE HAVE TO SWITCH PLATES NOW!
The wine just goes down so smoothly too!
SO THE PLATES WERE SWITCHED AND THOROUGHLY CONSUMED.
YOUR WRAPPED FAT-ROASTED LAMB.
THE MEAT RESTS ATOP FINELY CHOPPED PIGS' FEET AND VEGETABLES. IT IS GARNISHED WITH DEEP-FRIED ÉCHALOTE AND GARLIC. PLEASE CRUSH THEM AND EAT THEM WITH THE MEAT.
AND TO ACCOMPANY IT, WE HAVE A SIDE OF RATATOUILLE.
YOUR WAGYU BEEF CHEEK MEAT STEWED IN RED WINE AND HONEY.
As you would expect, the side dish of sautéed vegetables comes on a separate dish.
I WANT TO DANCE... I WANT TO DANCE, BUT I CAN'T DO IT HERE...
THIS IS IT. THIS IS EXACTLY IT. THIS RED WINE STEW IS WHAT I WANTED TO EAT. THE SWEET, THICK TASTE OF MEAT THAT MELTS...
mumble mumble
mumble mumble
YUM!
THE LAMB IS JUST DIVINE! IT'S BASICALLY SALT FLAVORED, BUT THAT SALT FLAVORING IS SIMPLY EXQUISITE!!
The salt and garlic do beautiful work on the rare meat!!
GA GA (CHOMP)
A wild beast.
IT WAS THEN THAT THE TWO CAME TO A FURTHER REALIZATION.
I GET THE FEELING THAT WE COULD FINISH THAT NODOGURO!
EXCUSE MEEE! AS A FOLLOW-UP ORDER...
AH... I'M SORRY! THE LAST CALL FOR ORDERS HAS ALREADY PASSED.

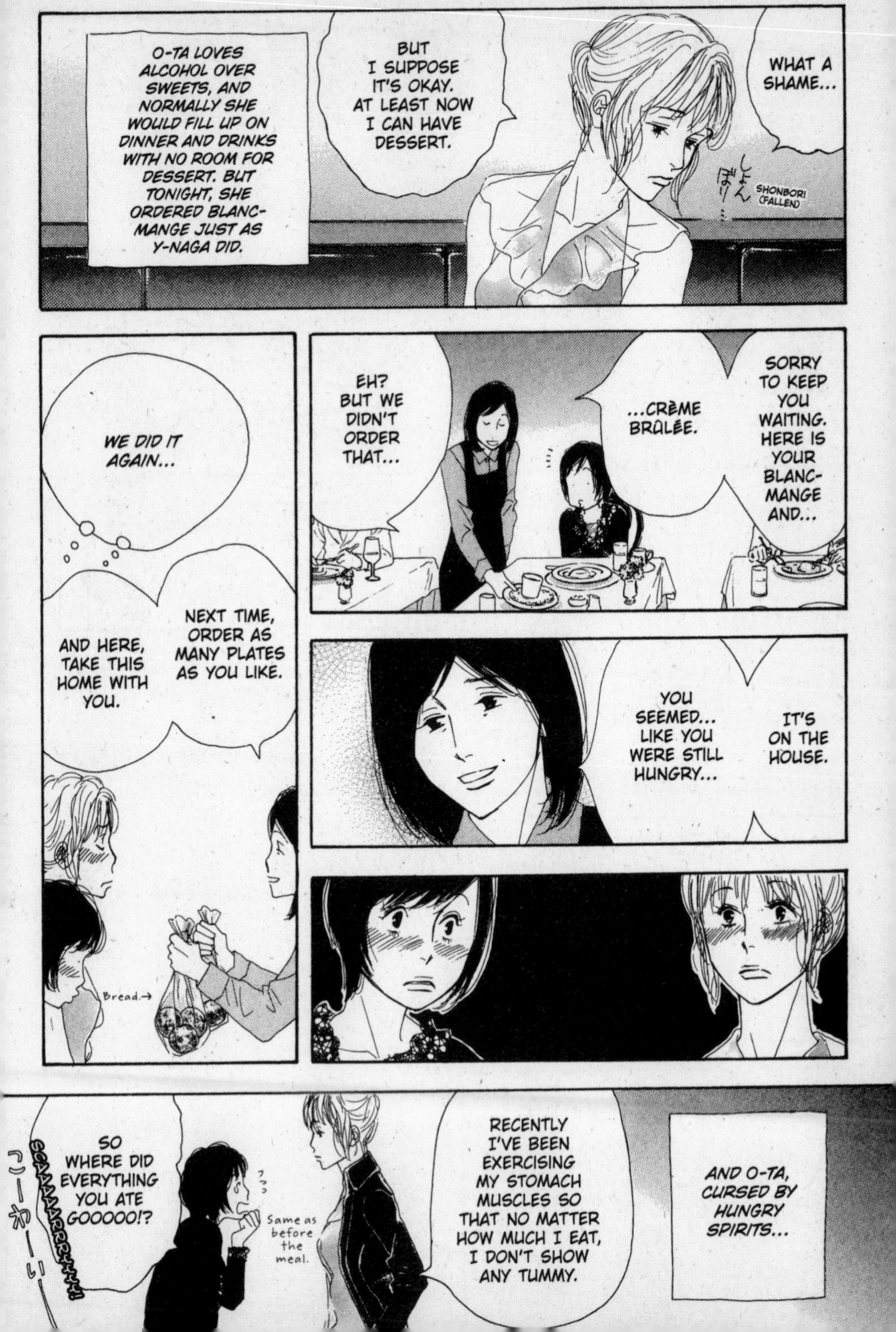
WHAT A SHAME...
SHONBORI (FALLEN)
BUT I SUPPOSE IT'S OKAY. AT LEAST NOW I CAN HAVE DESSERT.
O-TA LOVES ALCOHOL OVER SWEETS, AND NORMALLY SHE WOULD FILL UP ON DINNER AND DRINKS WITH NO ROOM FOR DESSERT. BUT TONIGHT, SHE ORDERED BLANC-MANGE JUST AS Y-NAGA DID.
SORRY TO KEEP YOU WAITING. HERE IS YOUR BLANC-MANGE AND...
...CRÈME BRÛLÉE.
EH? BUT WE DIDN'T ORDER THAT...
IT'S ON THE HOUSE.
YOU SEEMED... LIKE YOU WERE STILL HUNGRY...
WE DID IT AGAIN...
NEXT TIME, ORDER AS MANY PLATES AS YOU LIKE.
AND HERE, TAKE THIS HOME WITH YOU.
Bread.→
AND O-TA, CURSED BY HUNGRY SPIRITS...
RECENTLY I'VE BEEN EXERCISING MY STOMACH MUSCLES SO THAT NO MATTER HOW MUCH I EAT, I DON'T SHOW ANY TUMMY.
Same as before the meal.
SO WHERE DID EVERYTHING YOU ATE GOOOOO!?
SCAAAARRRHHH!

Kitajima Tei

[Address]
JHC Building 1F
7 San'ei-cho, Shinjuku-ku, Tokyo
[Telephone]
03-3355-6667
[Hours]
11:30 AM - 2:00 PM
6:00 PM - 9:00 PM
[Closed]
Sundays, and the 1st & 3rd Mondays of the month.
[Directions]
A five-minute walk from the Yotsuya Entrance of the Yotsuya Station for both the JR Chuuou Line and the Subway Maru-no-Uchi Nanboku Line.
[Parking]
None (there is metered parking in front of the restaurant).

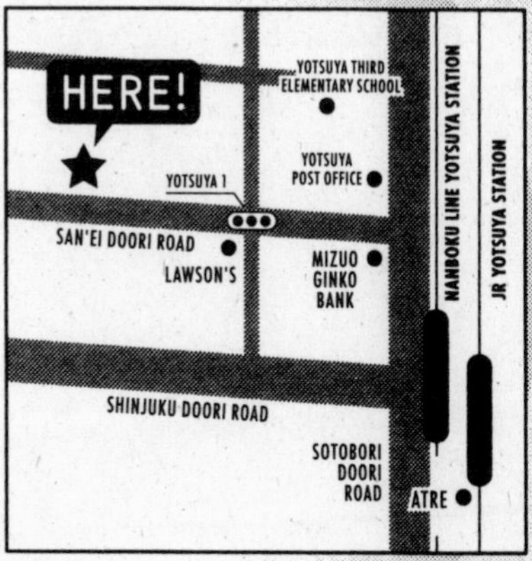

HERE!
YOTSUYA THIRD ELEMENTARY SCHOOL
YOTSUYA POST OFFICE
YOTSUYA 1
SAN'EI DOORI ROAD
LAWSON'S
MIZUO GINKO BANK
NANBOKU LINE YOTSUYA STATION
JR YOTSUYA STATION
SHINJUKU DOORI ROAD
SOTOBORI DOORI ROAD
ATRE

FUMI YOSHINAGA'S COMMENTS

THE NUMBER OF PEOPLE WHO CAN ORDER À LA CARTE IS LIMITED TO PARTIES OF THREE PEOPLE OR LESS. IF YOU HAVE FOUR OR MORE IN YOUR PARTY, YOU MUST MAKE A RESERVATION AND ORDER ONE OF THEIR COURSES. BUDGET FROM ¥10,000-20,000. IT'S A PERFECT MEAL FOR A SPECIAL DAY FOR YOUR FOODIE LOVED ONE. RESERVATIONS REQUIRED.

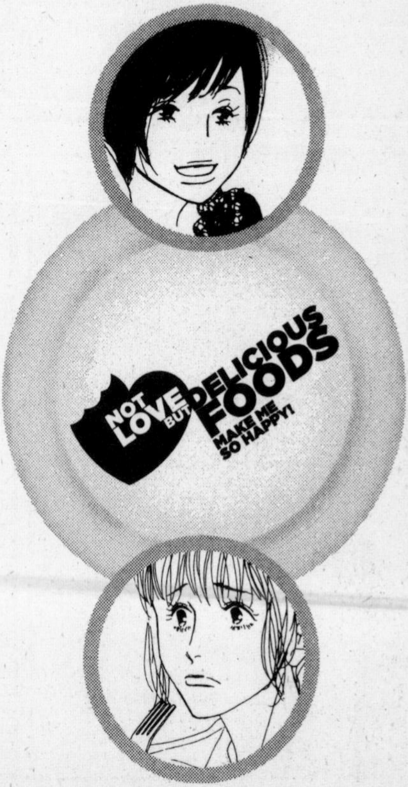
NOT LOVE BUT DELICIOUS FOODS
MAKE ME SO HAPPY!

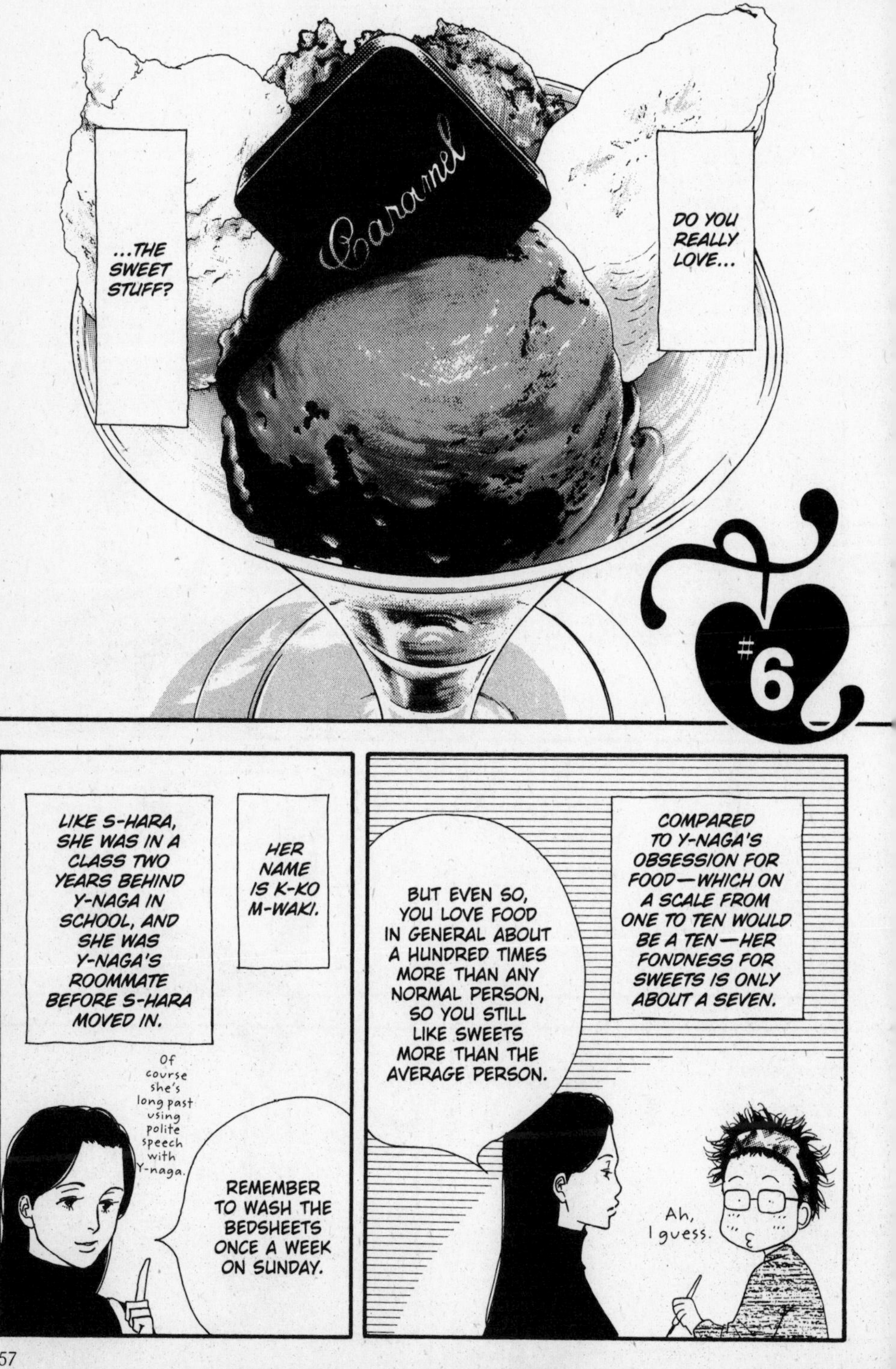
DO YOU REALLY LOVE...
...THE SWEET STUFF?
Caramel
#6
COMPARED TO Y-NAGA'S OBSESSION FOR FOOD—WHICH ON A SCALE FROM ONE TO TEN WOULD BE A TEN—HER FONDNESS FOR SWEETS IS ONLY ABOUT A SEVEN.
BUT EVEN SO, YOU LOVE FOOD IN GENERAL ABOUT A HUNDRED TIMES MORE THAN ANY NORMAL PERSON, SO YOU STILL LIKE SWEETS MORE THAN THE AVERAGE PERSON.
Ah, I guess.
HER NAME IS K-KO M-WAKI.
LIKE S-HARA, SHE WAS IN A CLASS TWO YEARS BEHIND Y-NAGA IN SCHOOL, AND SHE WAS Y-NAGA'S ROOMMATE BEFORE S-HARA MOVED IN.
Of course she's long past using polite speech with Y-naga.
REMEMBER TO WASH THE BEDSHEETS ONCE A WEEK ON SUNDAY.

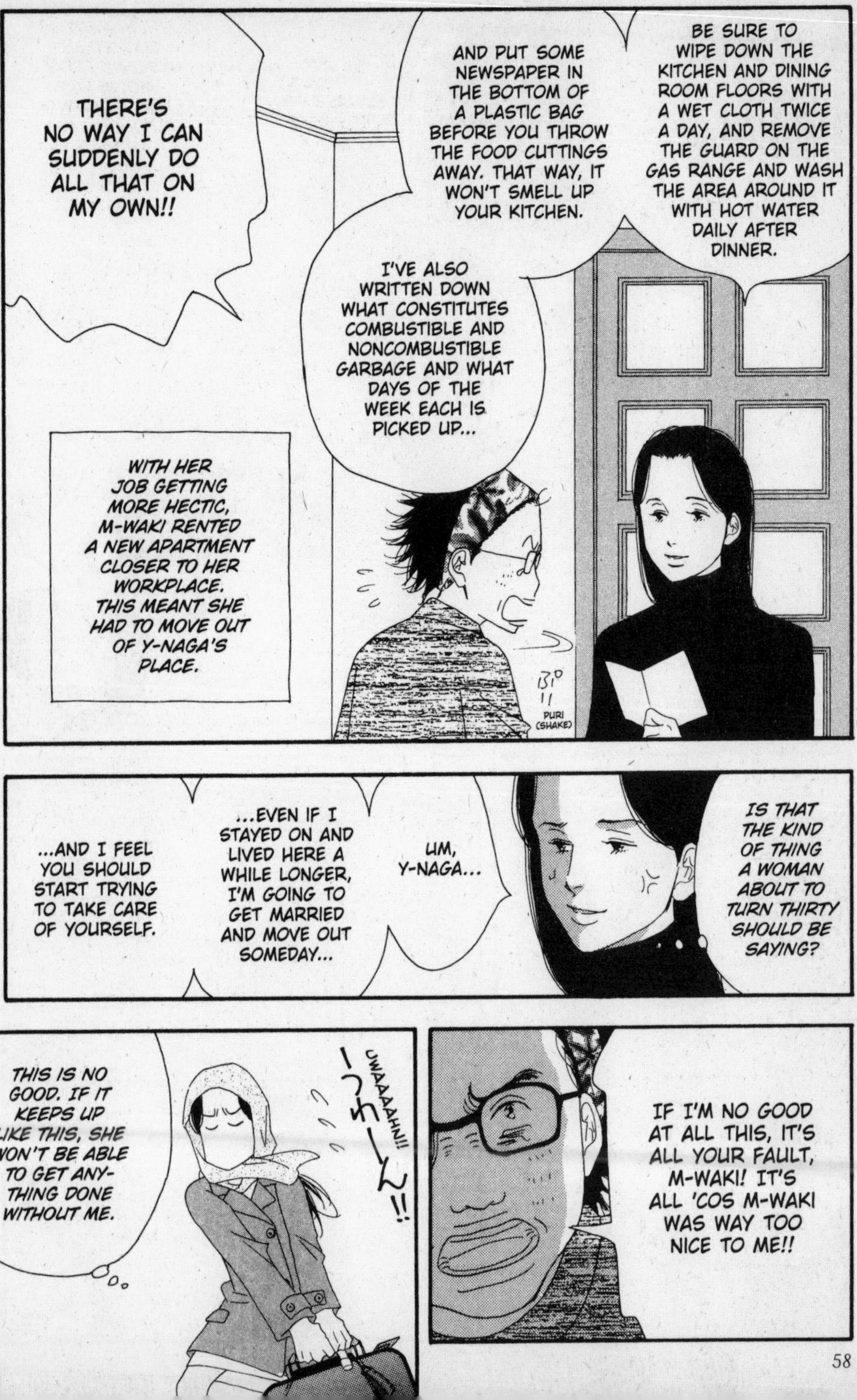
BE SURE TO WIPE DOWN THE KITCHEN AND DINING ROOM FLOORS WITH A WET CLOTH TWICE A DAY, AND REMOVE THE GUARD ON THE GAS RANGE AND WASH THE AREA AROUND IT WITH HOT WATER DAILY AFTER DINNER.
AND PUT SOME NEWSPAPER IN THE BOTTOM OF A PLASTIC BAG BEFORE YOU THROW THE FOOD CUTTINGS AWAY. THAT WAY, IT WON'T SMELL UP YOUR KITCHEN.
I'VE ALSO WRITTEN DOWN WHAT CONSTITUTES COMBUSTIBLE AND NONCOMBUSTIBLE GARBAGE AND WHAT DAYS OF THE WEEK EACH IS PICKED UP...
THERE'S NO WAY I CAN SUDDENLY DO ALL THAT ON MY OWN!!
WITH HER JOB GETTING MORE HECTIC, M-WAKI RENTED A NEW APARTMENT CLOSER TO HER WORKPLACE. THIS MEANT SHE HAD TO MOVE OUT OF Y-NAGA'S PLACE.
PURI (SHAKE)
IS THAT THE KIND OF THING A WOMAN ABOUT TO TURN THIRTY SHOULD BE SAYING?
UM, Y-NAGA...
...EVEN IF I STAYED ON AND LIVED HERE A WHILE LONGER, I'M GOING TO GET MARRIED AND MOVE OUT SOMEDAY...
...AND I FEEL YOU SHOULD START TRYING TO TAKE CARE OF YOURSELF.
IF I'M NO GOOD AT ALL THIS, IT'S ALL YOUR FAULT, M-WAKI! IT'S ALL 'COS M-WAKI WAS WAY TOO NICE TO ME!!
UWAAAAHN!!
THIS IS NO GOOD. IF IT KEEPS UP LIKE THIS, SHE WON'T BE ABLE TO GET ANYTHING DONE WITHOUT ME.

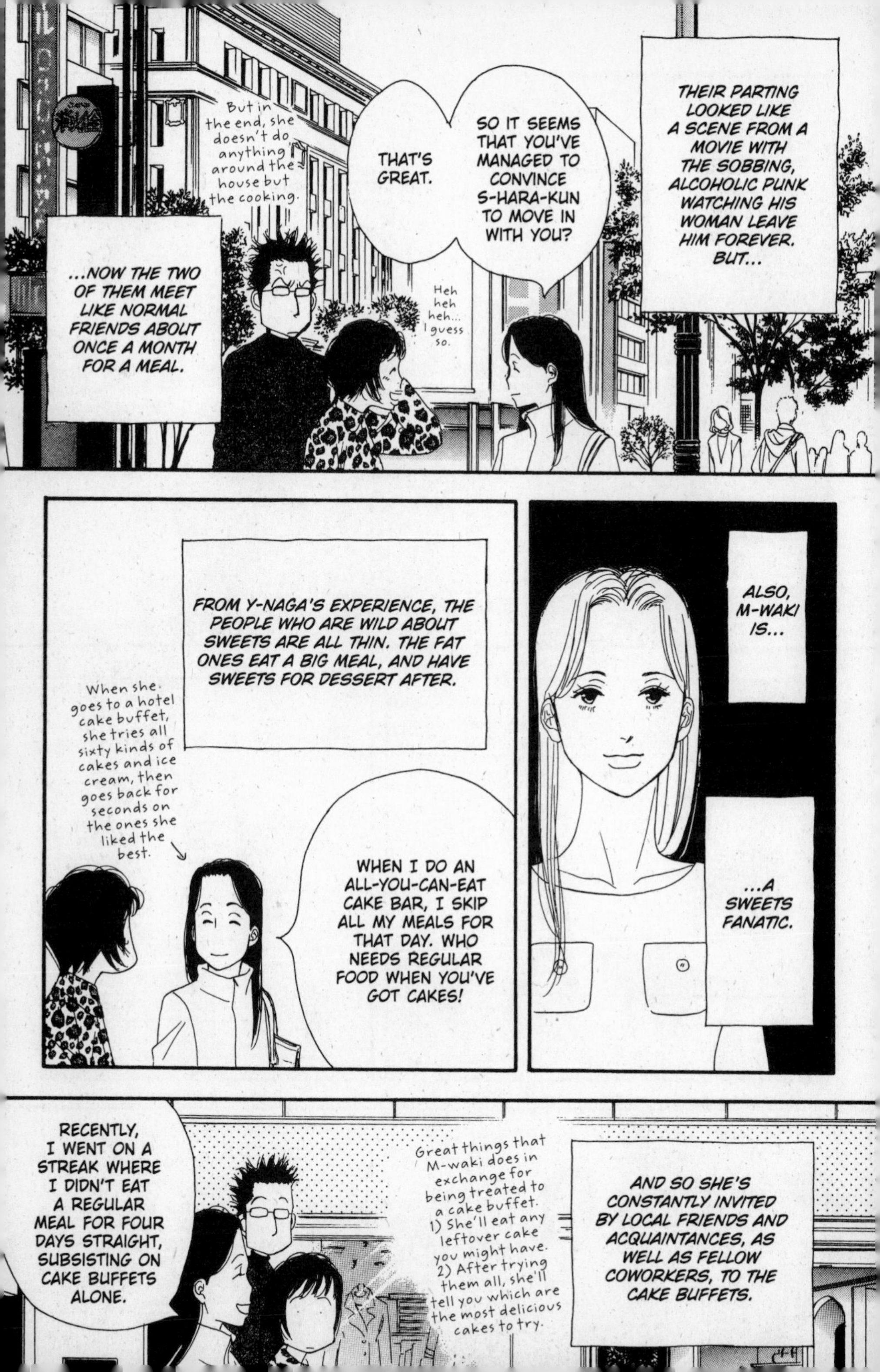
THEIR PARTING LOOKED LIKE A SCENE FROM A MOVIE WITH THE SOBBING, ALCOHOLIC PUNK WATCHING HIS WOMAN LEAVE HIM FOREVER. BUT...
SO IT SEEMS THAT YOU'VE MANAGED TO CONVINCE S-HARA-KUN TO MOVE IN WITH YOU?
THAT'S GREAT.
Heh heh heh... I guess so.
But in the end, she doesn't do anything around the house but the cooking.
...NOW THE TWO OF THEM MEET LIKE NORMAL FRIENDS ABOUT ONCE A MONTH FOR A MEAL.
ALSO, M-WAKI IS...
...A SWEETS FANATIC.
FROM Y-NAGA'S EXPERIENCE, THE PEOPLE WHO ARE WILD ABOUT SWEETS ARE ALL THIN. THE FAT ONES EAT A BIG MEAL, AND HAVE SWEETS FOR DESSERT AFTER.
WHEN I DO AN ALL-YOU-CAN-EAT CAKE BAR, I SKIP ALL MY MEALS FOR THAT DAY. WHO NEEDS REGULAR FOOD WHEN YOU'VE GOT CAKES!
When she goes to a hotel cake buffet, she tries all sixty kinds of cakes and ice cream, then goes back for seconds on the ones she liked the best.
AND SO SHE'S CONSTANTLY INVITED BY LOCAL FRIENDS AND ACQUAINTANCES, AS WELL AS FELLOW COWORKERS, TO THE CAKE BUFFETS.
Great things that M-waki does in exchange for being treated to a cake buffet. 1) She'll eat any leftover cake you might have. 2) After trying them all, she'll tell you which are the most delicious cakes to try.
RECENTLY, I WENT ON A STREAK WHERE I DIDN'T EAT A REGULAR MEAL FOR FOUR DAYS STRAIGHT, SUBSISTING ON CAKE BUFFETS ALONE.

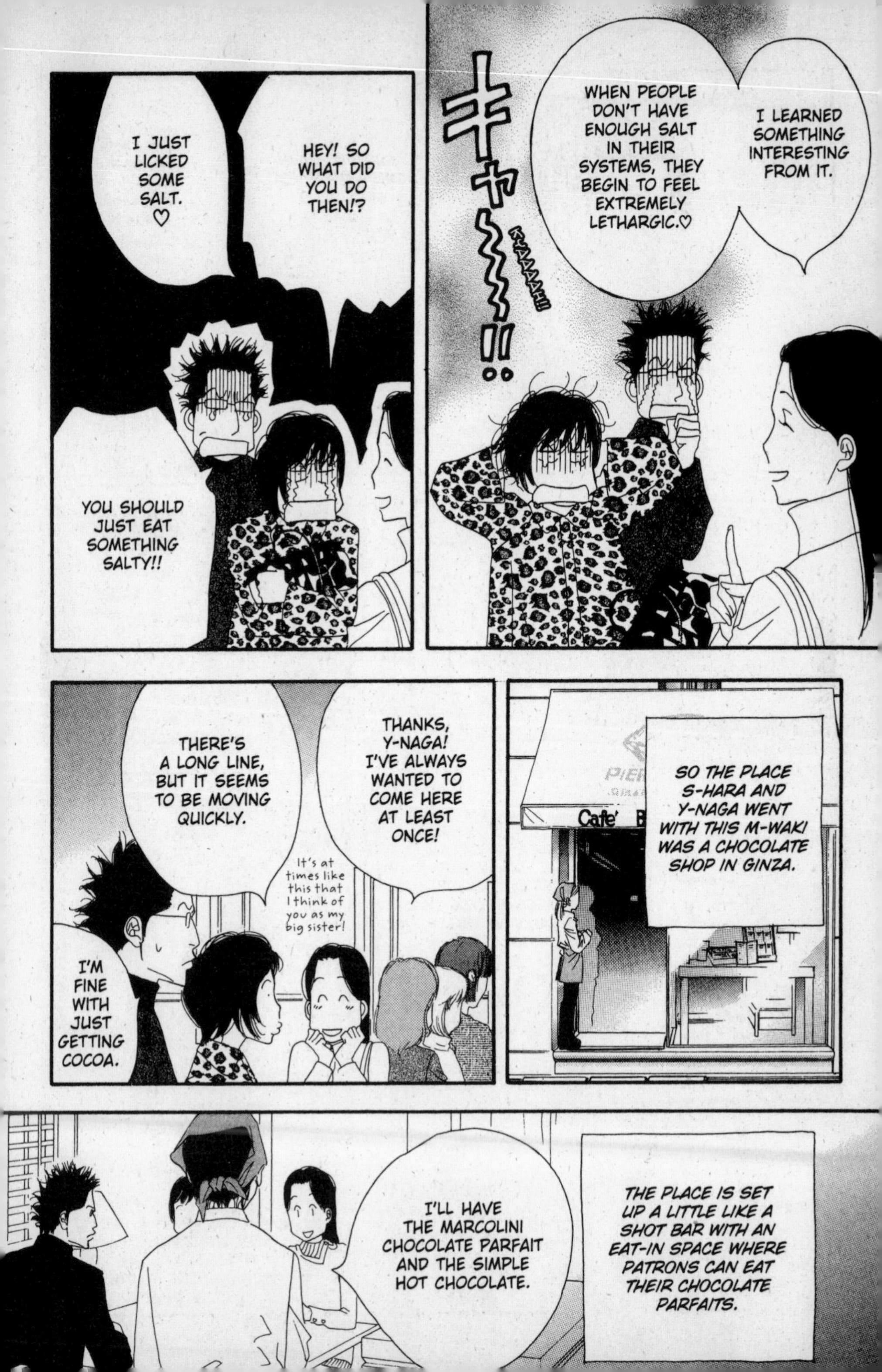
I LEARNED SOMETHING INTERESTING FROM IT.
WHEN PEOPLE DON'T HAVE ENOUGH SALT IN THEIR SYSTEMS, THEY BEGIN TO FEEL EXTREMELY LETHARGIC.♡
キャ〜〜!!
KYAAAAH!!
HEY! SO WHAT DID YOU DO THEN!?
I JUST LICKED SOME SALT. ♡
YOU SHOULD JUST EAT SOMETHING SALTY!!
SO THE PLACE S-HARA AND Y-NAGA WENT WITH THIS M-WAKI WAS A CHOCOLATE SHOP IN GINZA.
Cafe'
THANKS, Y-NAGA! I'VE ALWAYS WANTED TO COME HERE AT LEAST ONCE!
It's at times like this that I think of you as my big sister!
THERE'S A LONG LINE, BUT IT SEEMS TO BE MOVING QUICKLY.
I'M FINE WITH JUST GETTING COCOA.
THE PLACE IS SET UP A LITTLE LIKE A SHOT BAR WITH AN EAT-IN SPACE WHERE PATRONS CAN EAT THEIR CHOCOLATE PARFAITS.
I'LL HAVE THE MARCOLINI CHOCOLATE PARFAIT AND THE SIMPLE HOT CHOCOLATE.

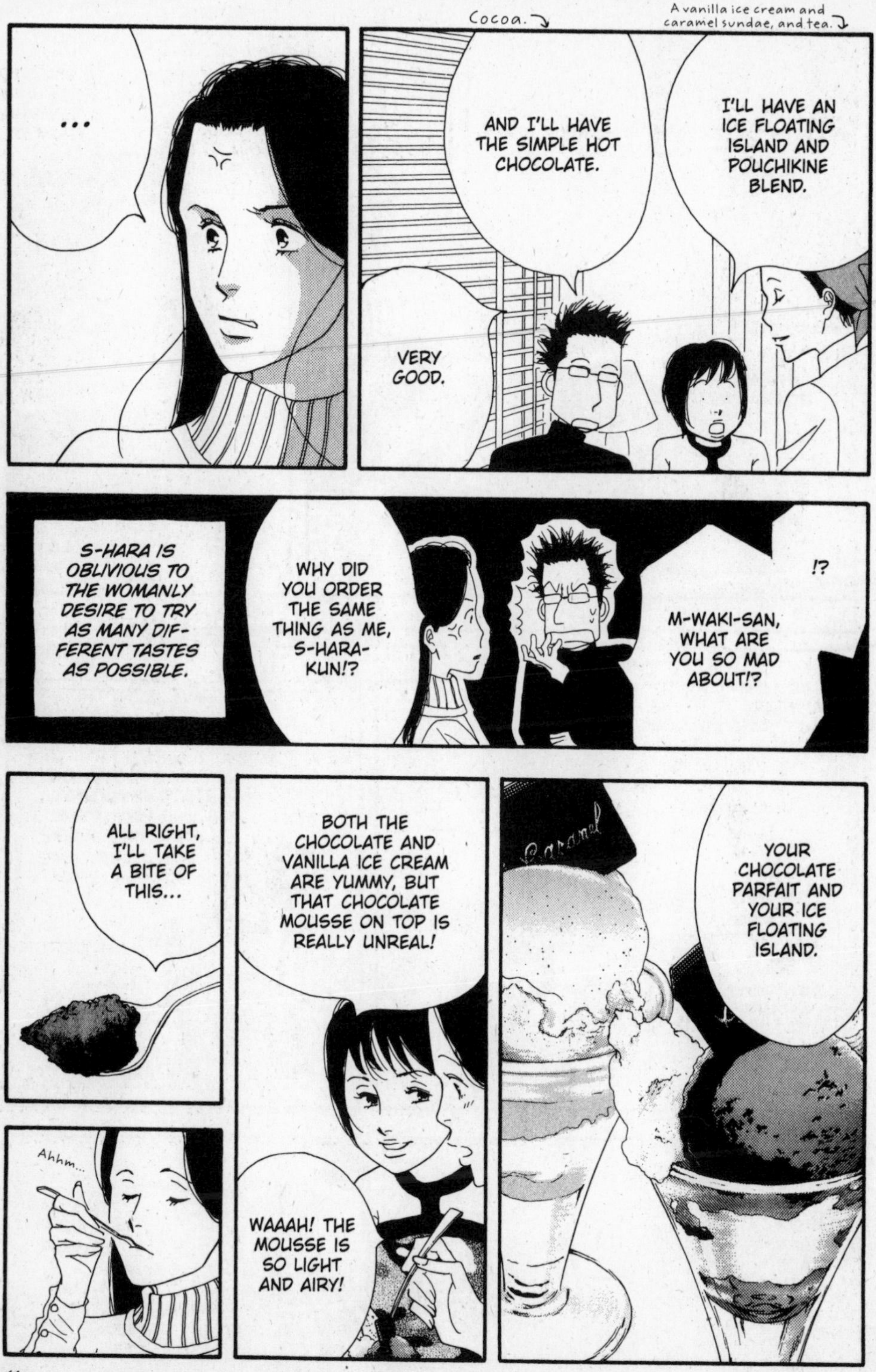
A vanilla ice cream and caramel sundae, and tea.
I'LL HAVE AN ICE FLOATING ISLAND AND POUCHIKINE BLEND.
Cocoa.
AND I'LL HAVE THE SIMPLE HOT CHOCOLATE.
VERY GOOD.
...
!?
M-WAKI-SAN, WHAT ARE YOU SO MAD ABOUT!?
WHY DID YOU ORDER THE SAME THING AS ME, S-HARA-KUN!?
S-HARA IS OBLIVIOUS TO THE WOMANLY DESIRE TO TRY AS MANY DIF-FERENT TASTES AS POSSIBLE.
YOUR CHOCOLATE PARFAIT AND YOUR ICE FLOATING ISLAND.
BOTH THE CHOCOLATE AND VANILLA ICE CREAM ARE YUMMY, BUT THAT CHOCOLATE MOUSSE ON TOP IS REALLY UNREAL!
WAAAH! THE MOUSSE IS SO LIGHT AND AIRY!
ALL RIGHT, I'LL TAKE A BITE OF THIS...
Ahhm...

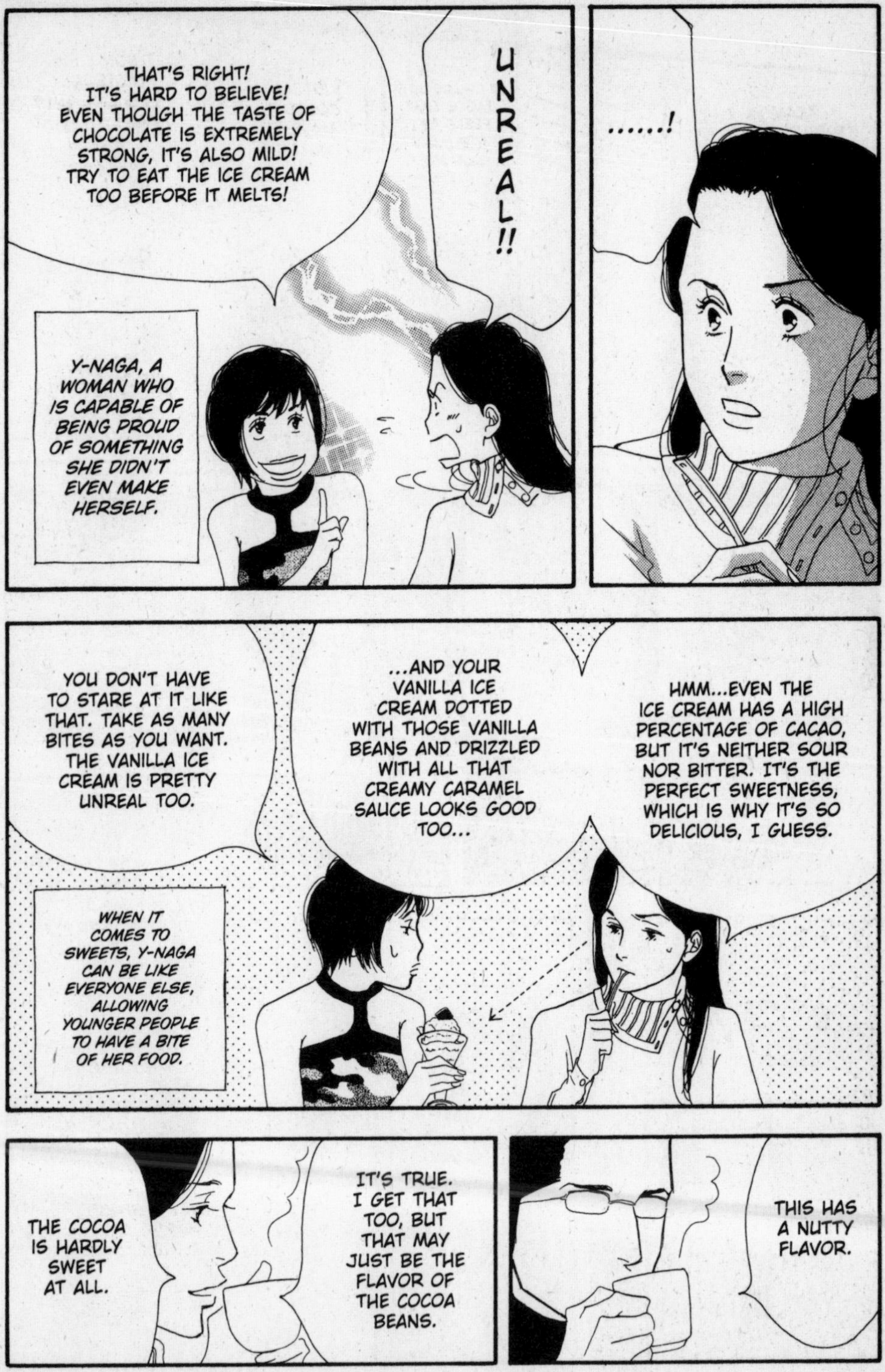
......!
UNREAL!!
THAT'S RIGHT! IT'S HARD TO BELIEVE! EVEN THOUGH THE TASTE OF CHOCOLATE IS EXTREMELY STRONG, IT'S ALSO MILD! TRY TO EAT THE ICE CREAM TOO BEFORE IT MELTS!
Y-NAGA, A WOMAN WHO IS CAPABLE OF BEING PROUD OF SOMETHING SHE DIDN'T EVEN MAKE HERSELF.
HMM...EVEN THE ICE CREAM HAS A HIGH PERCENTAGE OF CACAO, BUT IT'S NEITHER SOUR NOR BITTER. IT'S THE PERFECT SWEETNESS, WHICH IS WHY IT'S SO DELICIOUS, I GUESS.
...AND YOUR VANILLA ICE CREAM DOTTED WITH THOSE VANILLA BEANS AND DRIZZLED WITH ALL THAT CREAMY CARAMEL SAUCE LOOKS GOOD TOO...
YOU DON'T HAVE TO STARE AT IT LIKE THAT. TAKE AS MANY BITES AS YOU WANT. THE VANILLA ICE CREAM IS PRETTY UNREAL TOO.
WHEN IT COMES TO SWEETS, Y-NAGA CAN BE LIKE EVERYONE ELSE, ALLOWING YOUNGER PEOPLE TO HAVE A BITE OF HER FOOD.
THIS HAS A NUTTY FLAVOR.
IT'S TRUE. I GET THAT TOO, BUT THAT MAY JUST BE THE FLAVOR OF THE COCOA BEANS.
THE COCOA IS HARDLY SWEET AT ALL.

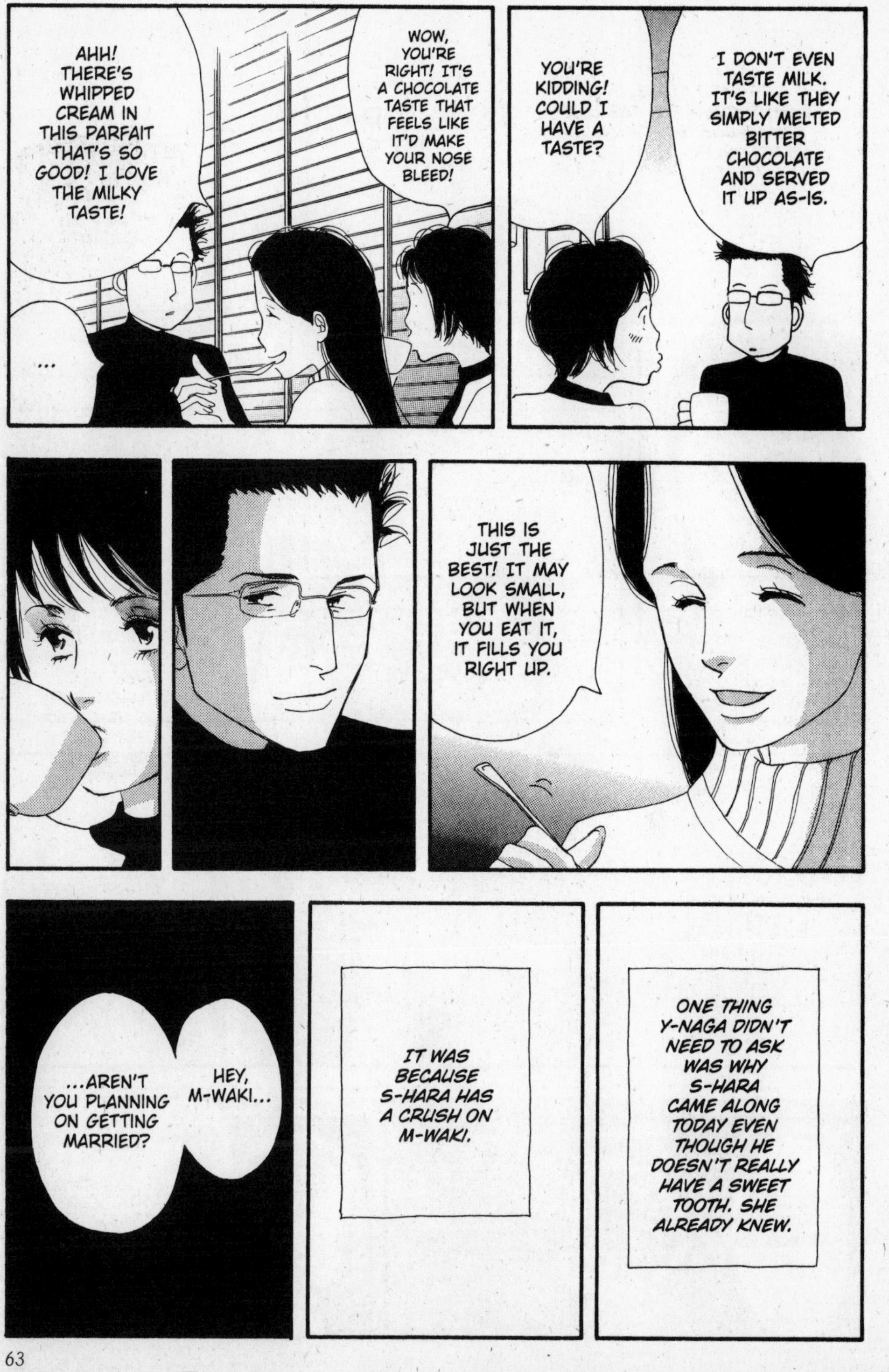
I DON'T EVEN TASTE MILK. IT'S LIKE THEY SIMPLY MELTED BITTER CHOCOLATE AND SERVED IT UP AS-IS.
YOU'RE KIDDING! COULD I HAVE A TASTE?
WOW, YOU'RE RIGHT! IT'S A CHOCOLATE TASTE THAT FEELS LIKE IT'D MAKE YOUR NOSE BLEED!
AHH! THERE'S WHIPPED CREAM IN THIS PARFAIT THAT'S SO GOOD! I LOVE THE MILKY TASTE!
...
THIS IS JUST THE BEST! IT MAY LOOK SMALL, BUT WHEN YOU EAT IT, IT FILLS YOU RIGHT UP.
ONE THING Y-NAGA DIDN'T NEED TO ASK WAS WHY S-HARA CAME ALONG TODAY EVEN THOUGH HE DOESN'T REALLY HAVE A SWEET TOOTH. SHE ALREADY KNEW.
IT WAS BECAUSE S-HARA HAS A CRUSH ON M-WAKI.
HEY, M-WAKI...
...AREN'T YOU PLANNING ON GETTING MARRIED?

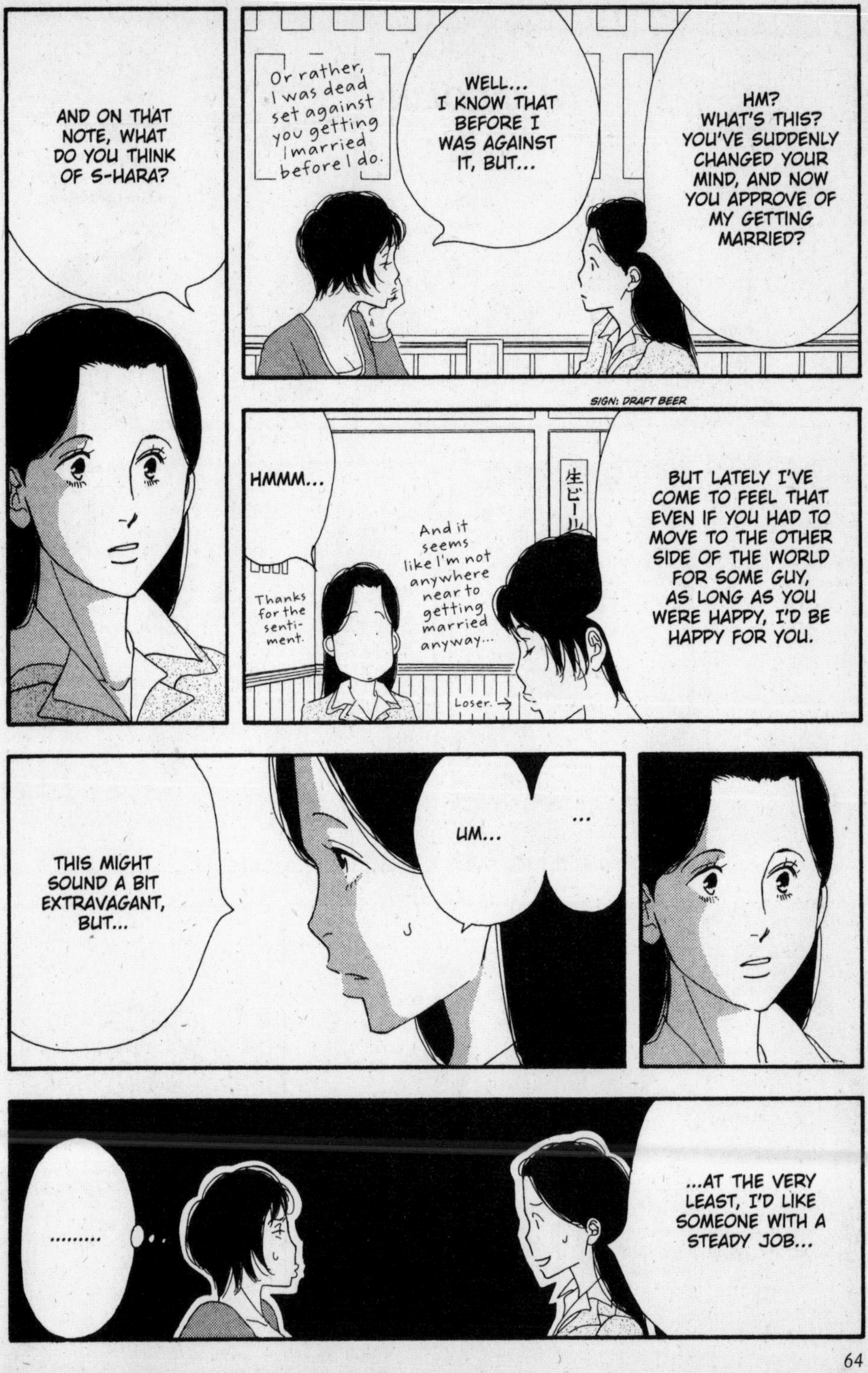
HM? WHAT'S THIS? YOU'VE SUDDENLY CHANGED YOUR MIND, AND NOW YOU APPROVE OF MY GETTING MARRIED?
WELL... I KNOW THAT BEFORE I WAS AGAINST IT, BUT...
Or rather, I was dead set against you getting married before I do.
SIGN: DRAFT BEER
BUT LATELY I'VE COME TO FEEL THAT EVEN IF YOU HAD TO MOVE TO THE OTHER SIDE OF THE WORLD FOR SOME GUY, AS LONG AS YOU WERE HAPPY, I'D BE HAPPY FOR YOU.
And it seems like I'm not anywhere near to getting married anyway...
Loser.
HMMM...
Thanks for the senti-ment.
AND ON THAT NOTE, WHAT DO YOU THINK OF S-HARA?
...
UM...
THIS MIGHT SOUND A BIT EXTRAVAGANT, BUT...
...AT THE VERY LEAST, I'D LIKE SOMEONE WITH A STEADY JOB...
....

PIERRE MARCOLINI GINZA

[Address]
5-5-8 Ginza, Chuuou-ku, Tokyo
[Telephone]
03-5537-0015
[Hours]
Mon-Sat 11:00 AM - 8:00 PM
Sun & Holidays 11:00 - 7:00 PM
[Closed]
Never.
[Directions]
A one-minute walk
from the Ginza Station
on both the Ginza Line
and the Hibiya Line.
[Parking]
None.

MIZUHO GINKO BANK

NAMIKI DOORI ROAD

MATSUMOTO KIYOSHI

HIBIYA LINE GINZA STATION

HARUMI DOORI ROAD

B5
B3

TOKYO MITSUBISHI GINKO BANK

WAKO

NISHI GOBAN-GAI DOORI ROAD

SUZURAN DOORI ROAD

A1
A2

MITSU-KOSHI

HERE!

GINZA LINE GINZA STATION

NEW MARUSA

FUMI YOSHINAGA'S COMMENTS

THE PARFAITS ARE ¥1,680. IT MIGHT LOOK SMALL, BUT WITH THIS AND ONE CUP OF HOT CHOCOLATE (COCOA), IT FEELS LIKE YOU ATE AN ENTIRE MEAL. THE HOT CHOCOLATE IS ¥1,050. THERE WAS A CHOCOLATE THAT I BOUGHT IN THE FIRST-FLOOR SHOP THAT WAS SHAPED LIKE A SHELL AND HAD CARAMEL INSIDE AND WAS ABSOLUTELY DELICIOUS. THEY DON'T TAKE RESERVATIONS.

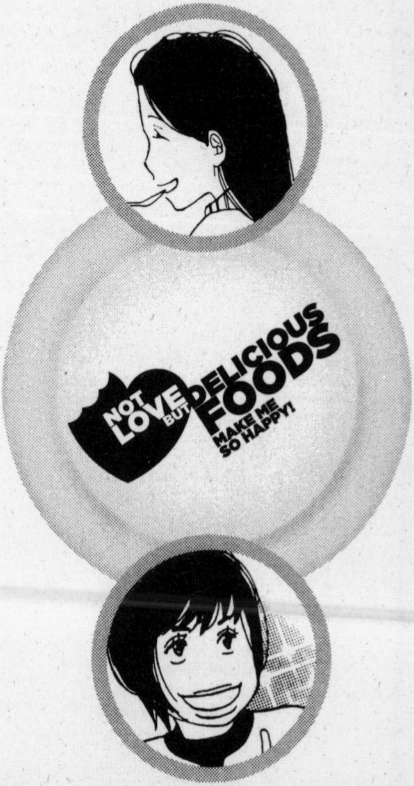
NOT LOVE BUT DELICIOUS FOODS
MAKE ME SO HAPPY!

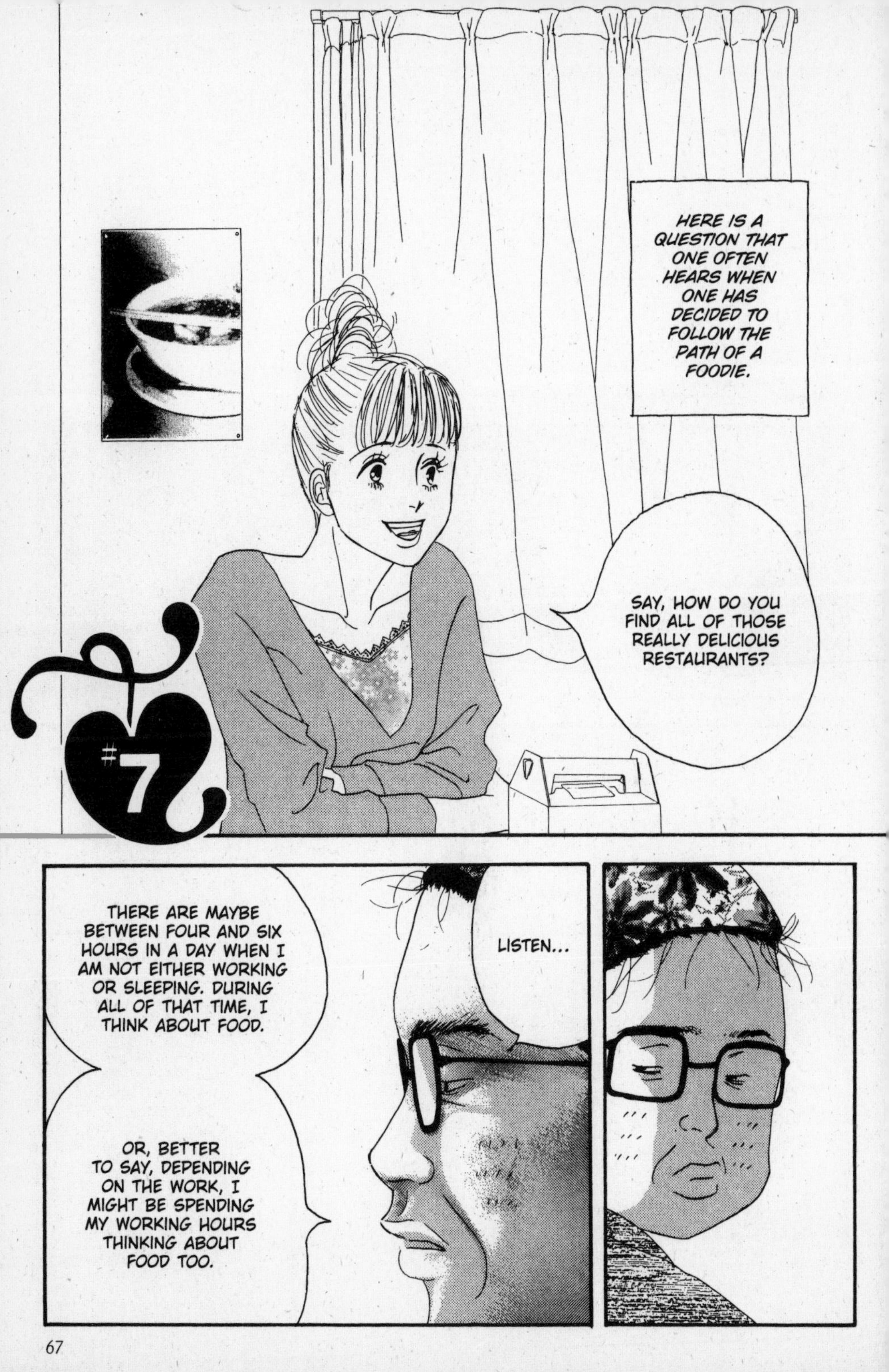
HERE IS A QUESTION THAT ONE OFTEN HEARS WHEN ONE HAS DECIDED TO FOLLOW THE PATH OF A FOODIE.
SAY, HOW DO YOU FIND ALL OF THOSE REALLY DELICIOUS RESTAURANTS?
#7
LISTEN...
THERE ARE MAYBE BETWEEN FOUR AND SIX HOURS IN A DAY WHEN I AM NOT EITHER WORKING OR SLEEPING. DURING ALL OF THAT TIME, I THINK ABOUT FOOD.
OR, BETTER TO SAY, DEPENDING ON THE WORK, I MIGHT BE SPENDING MY WORKING HOURS THINKING ABOUT FOOD TOO.

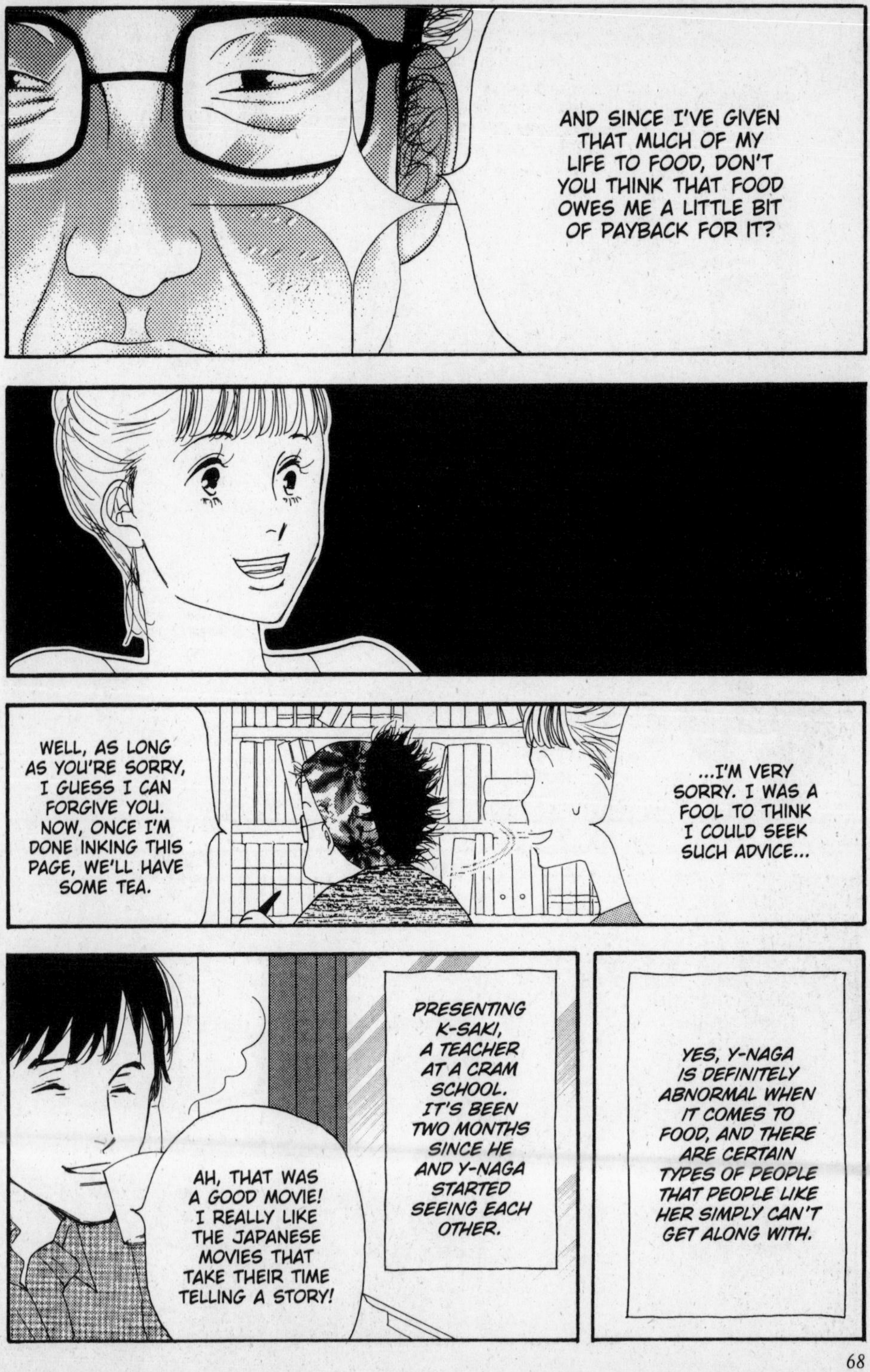
AND SINCE I'VE GIVEN THAT MUCH OF MY LIFE TO FOOD, DON'T YOU THINK THAT FOOD OWES ME A LITTLE BIT OF PAYBACK FOR IT?
...I'M VERY SORRY. I WAS A FOOL TO THINK I COULD SEEK SUCH ADVICE...
WELL, AS LONG AS YOU'RE SORRY, I GUESS I CAN FORGIVE YOU. NOW, ONCE I'M DONE INKING THIS PAGE, WE'LL HAVE SOME TEA.
YES, Y-NAGA IS DEFINITELY ABNORMAL WHEN IT COMES TO FOOD, AND THERE ARE CERTAIN TYPES OF PEOPLE THAT PEOPLE LIKE HER SIMPLY CAN'T GET ALONG WITH.
PRESENTING K-SAKI, A TEACHER AT A CRAM SCHOOL. IT'S BEEN TWO MONTHS SINCE HE AND Y-NAGA STARTED SEEING EACH OTHER.
AH, THAT WAS A GOOD MOVIE! I REALLY LIKE THE JAPANESE MOVIES THAT TAKE THEIR TIME TELLING A STORY!

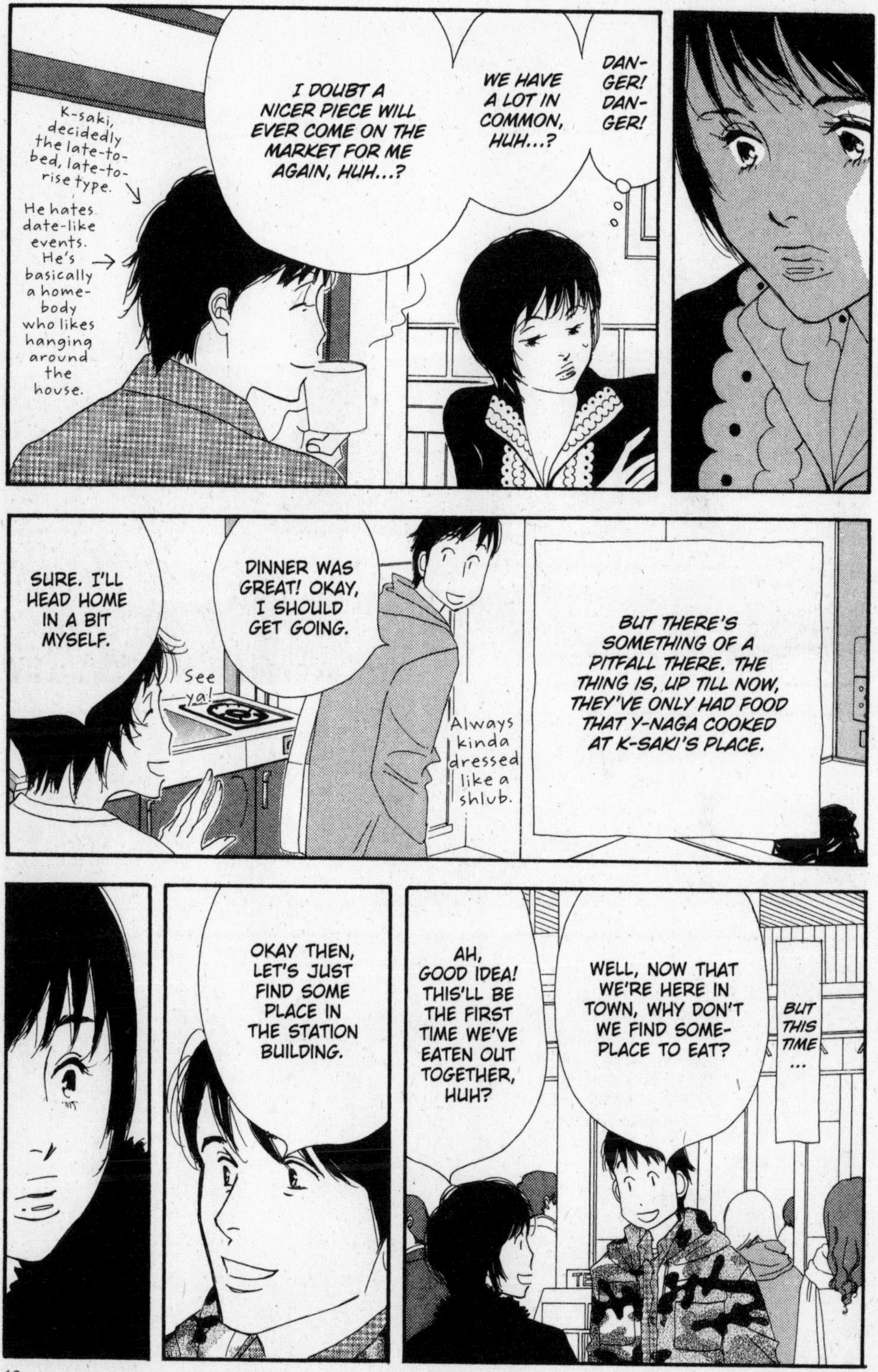
DAN-GER! DAN-GER!
WE HAVE A LOT IN COMMON, HUH...?
I DOUBT A NICER PIECE WILL EVER COME ON THE MARKET FOR ME AGAIN, HUH...?
K-saki, decidedly the late-to-bed, late-to-rise type.
He hates date-like events. He's basically a home-body who likes hanging around the house.
BUT THERE'S SOMETHING OF A PITFALL THERE. THE THING IS, UP TILL NOW, THEY'VE ONLY HAD FOOD THAT Y-NAGA COOKED AT K-SAKI'S PLACE.
DINNER WAS GREAT! OKAY, I SHOULD GET GOING.
Always kinda dressed like a shlub.
SURE. I'LL HEAD HOME IN A BIT MYSELF.
See ya!
BUT THIS TIME ...
WELL, NOW THAT WE'RE HERE IN TOWN, WHY DON'T WE FIND SOME-PLACE TO EAT?
AH, GOOD IDEA! THIS'LL BE THE FIRST TIME WE'VE EATEN OUT TOGETHER, HUH?
OKAY THEN, LET'S JUST FIND SOME PLACE IN THE STATION BUILDING.

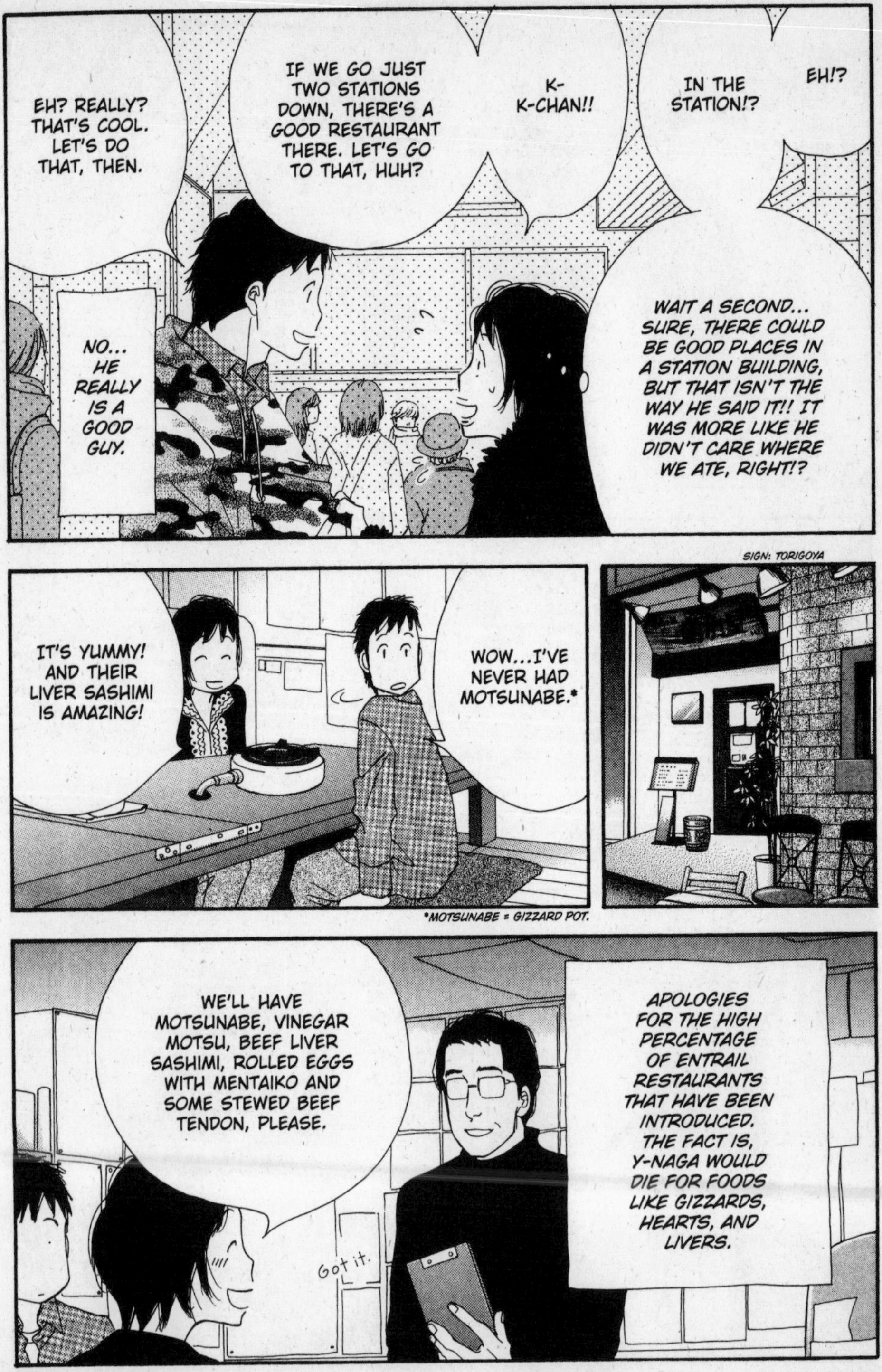
EH!?
IN THE STATION!?
K- K-CHAN!!
IF WE GO JUST TWO STATIONS DOWN, THERE'S A GOOD RESTAURANT THERE. LET'S GO TO THAT, HUH?
EH? REALLY? THAT'S COOL. LET'S DO THAT, THEN.
WAIT A SECOND... SURE, THERE COULD BE GOOD PLACES IN A STATION BUILDING, BUT THAT ISN'T THE WAY HE SAID IT!! IT WAS MORE LIKE HE DIDN'T CARE WHERE WE ATE, RIGHT!?
NO... HE REALLY IS A GOOD GUY.
SIGN: TORIGOYA
WOW...I'VE NEVER HAD MOTSUNABE.*
IT'S YUMMY! AND THEIR LIVER SASHIMI IS AMAZING!
*MOTSUNABE = GIZZARD POT.
APOLOGIES FOR THE HIGH PERCENTAGE OF ENTRAIL RESTAURANTS THAT HAVE BEEN INTRODUCED. THE FACT IS, Y-NAGA WOULD DIE FOR FOODS LIKE GIZZARDS, HEARTS, AND LIVERS.
WE'LL HAVE MOTSUNABE, VINEGAR MOTSU, BEEF LIVER SASHIMI, ROLLED EGGS WITH MENTAIKO AND SOME STEWED BEEF TENDON, PLEASE.
Got it.

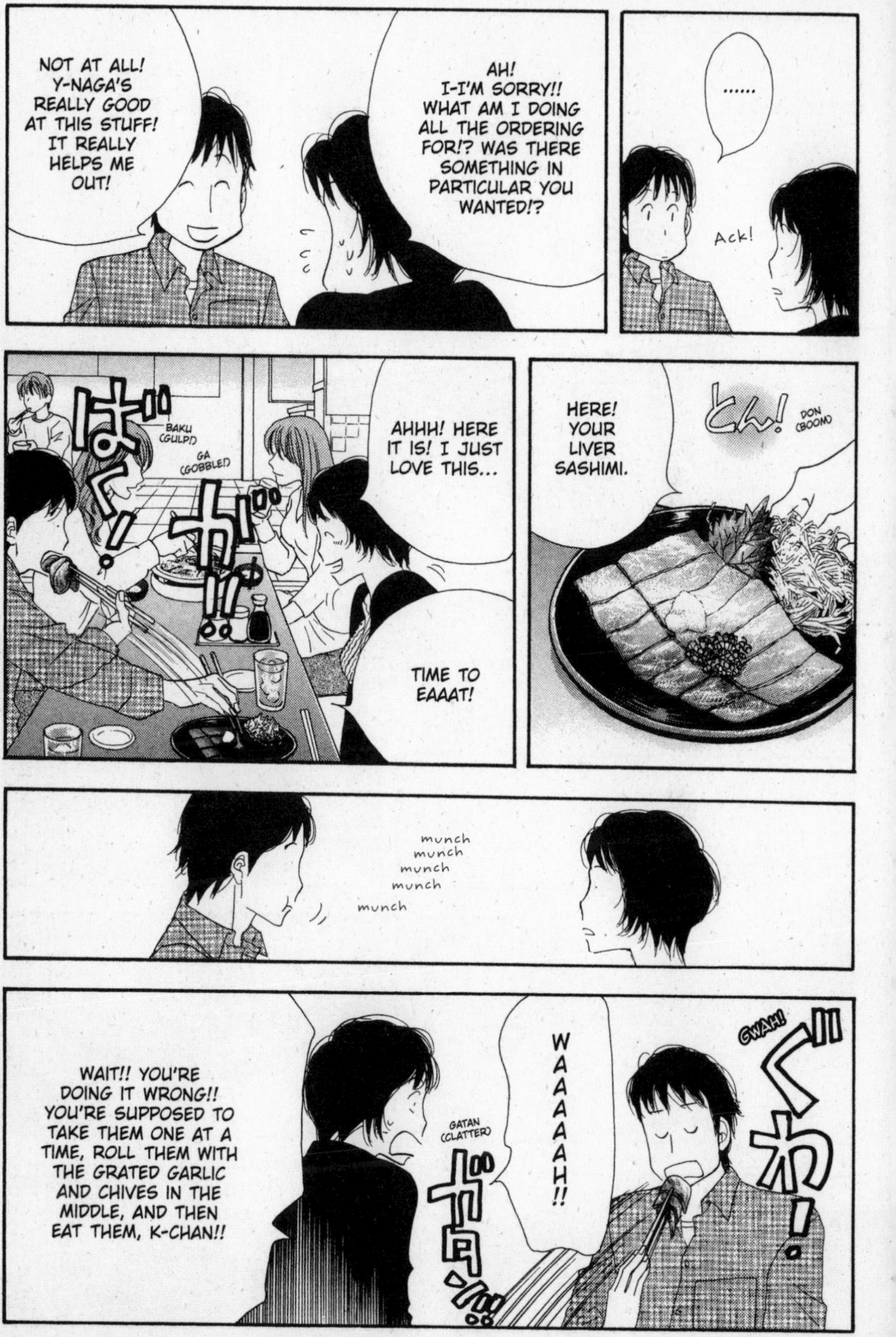

......
Ack!
AH! I-I'M SORRY!! WHAT AM I DOING ALL THE ORDERING FOR!? WAS THERE SOMETHING IN PARTICULAR YOU WANTED!?
NOT AT ALL! Y-NAGA'S REALLY GOOD AT THIS STUFF! IT REALLY HELPS ME OUT!
とん!
DON (BOOM)
HERE! YOUR LIVER SASHIMI.
AHHH! HERE IT IS! I JUST LOVE THIS...
TIME TO EAAAT!
GA (GOBBLE!)
BAKU (GULP!)
munch
munch
munch
munch
munch
GWAH!
ぐわ!
WAAAAAAAH!!
GATAN (CLATTER)
WAIT!! YOU'RE DOING IT WRONG!! YOU'RE SUPPOSED TO TAKE THEM ONE AT A TIME, ROLL THEM WITH THE GRATED GARLIC AND CHIVES IN THE MIDDLE, AND THEN EAT THEM, K-CHAN!!

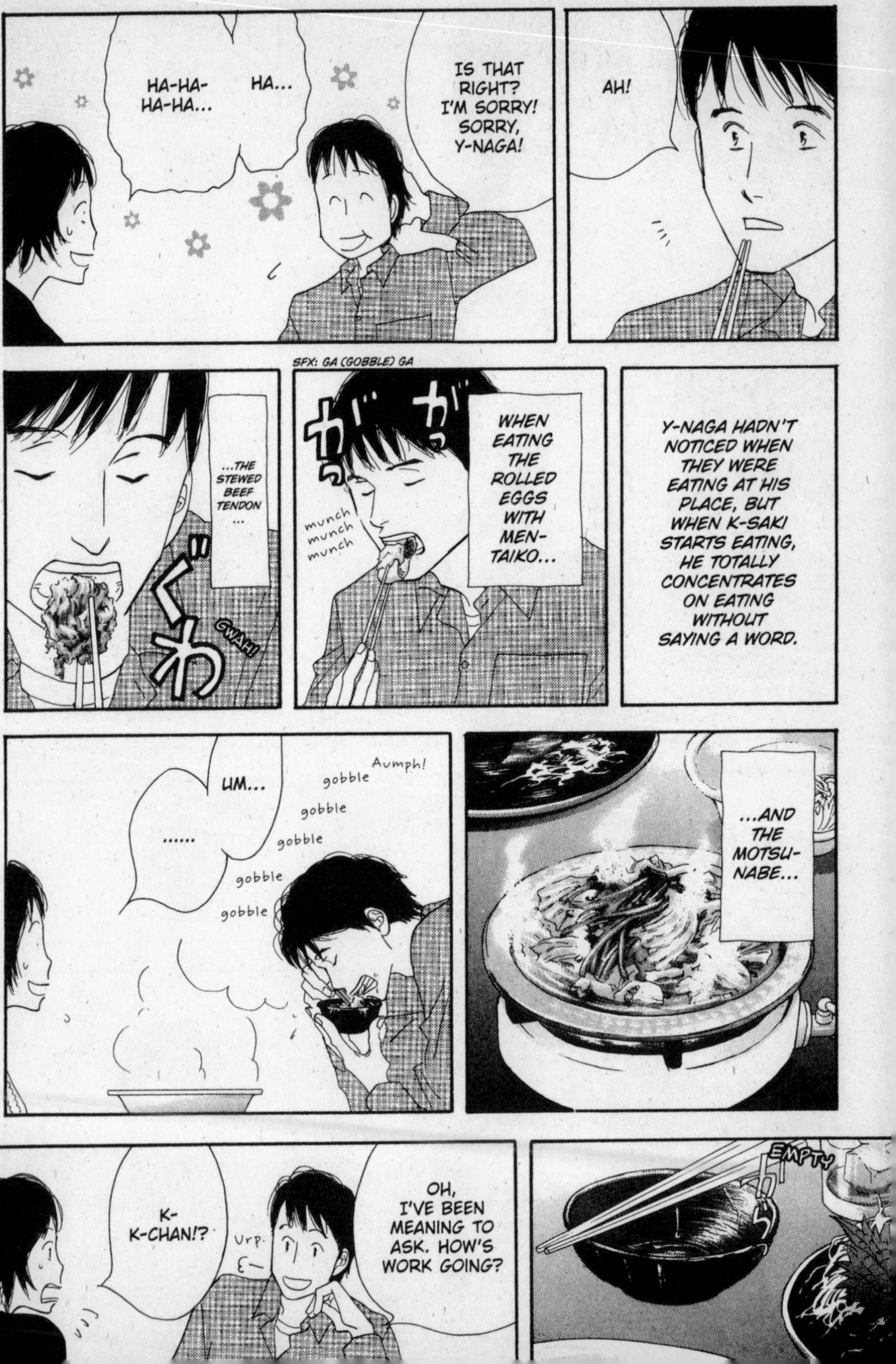
AH!
IS THAT RIGHT? I'M SORRY! SORRY, Y-NAGA!
HA-HA-HA-HA... HA...
Y-NAGA HADN'T NOTICED WHEN THEY WERE EATING AT HIS PLACE, BUT WHEN K-SAKI STARTS EATING, HE TOTALLY CONCENTRATES ON EATING WITHOUT SAYING A WORD.
SFX: GA (GOBBLE) GA
WHEN EATING THE ROLLED EGGS WITH MEN-TAIKO...
munch munch munch
...THE STEWED BEEF TENDON ...
GWAH!
...AND THE MOTSU-NABE...
Aumph!
gobble gobble gobble gobble gobble
UM... ......
EMPTY
OH, I'VE BEEN MEANING TO ASK. HOW'S WORK GOING?
Urp.
K-K-CHAN!?

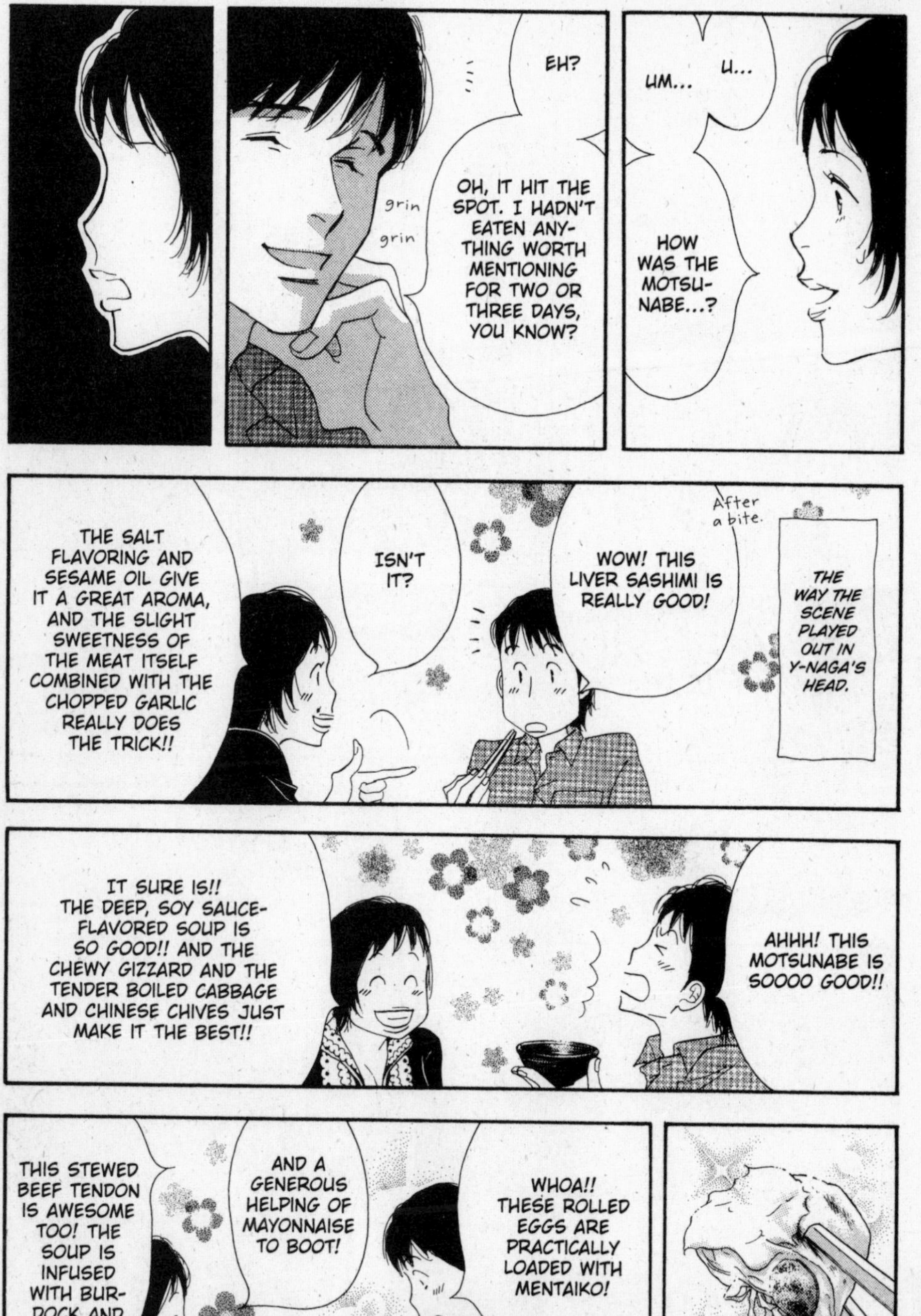
U...
UM...
HOW WAS THE MOTSUNABE...?
EH?
OH, IT HIT THE SPOT. I HADN'T EATEN ANYTHING WORTH MENTIONING FOR TWO OR THREE DAYS, YOU KNOW?
grin
grin
THE WAY THE SCENE PLAYED OUT IN Y-NAGA'S HEAD.
After a bite.
WOW! THIS LIVER SASHIMI IS REALLY GOOD!
ISN'T IT?
THE SALT FLAVORING AND SESAME OIL GIVE IT A GREAT AROMA, AND THE SLIGHT SWEETNESS OF THE MEAT ITSELF COMBINED WITH THE CHOPPED GARLIC REALLY DOES THE TRICK!!
AHHH! THIS MOTSUNABE IS SOOOO GOOD!!
IT SURE IS!! THE DEEP, SOY SAUCE-FLAVORED SOUP IS SO GOOD!! AND THE CHEWY GIZZARD AND THE TENDER BOILED CABBAGE AND CHINESE CHIVES JUST MAKE IT THE BEST!!
WHOA!! THESE ROLLED EGGS ARE PRACTICALLY LOADED WITH MENTAIKO!
AND A GENEROUS HELPING OF MAYONNAISE TO BOOT!
THIS STEWED BEEF TENDON IS AWESOME TOO! THE SOUP IS INFUSED WITH BURDOCK AND KONJAK!

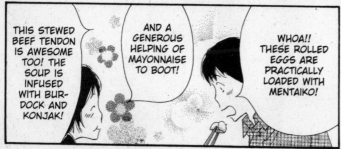

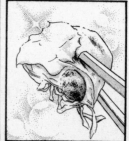

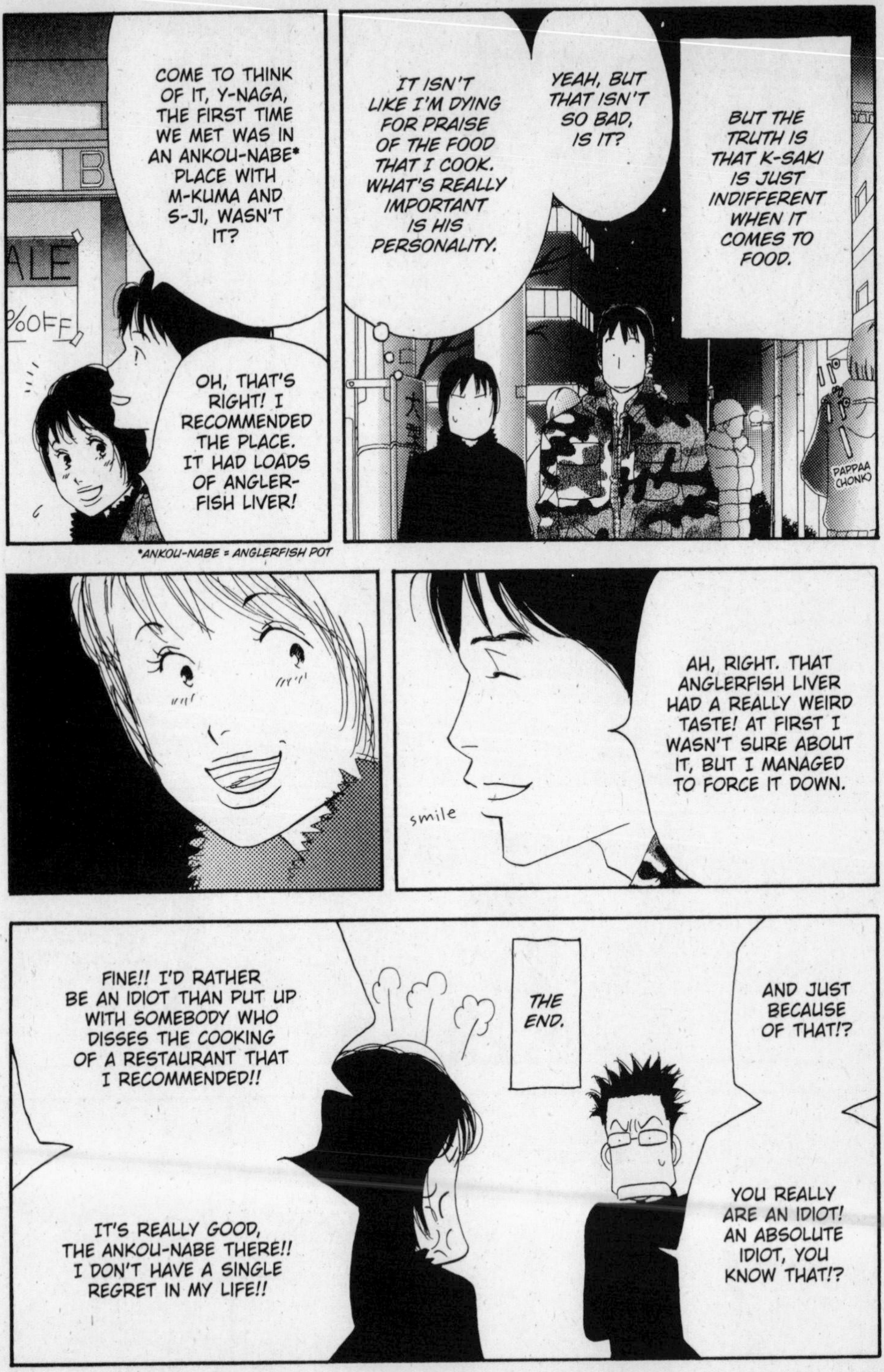
BUT THE TRUTH IS THAT K-SAKI IS JUST INDIFFERENT WHEN IT COMES TO FOOD.
YEAH, BUT THAT ISN'T SO BAD, IS IT?
IT ISN'T LIKE I'M DYING FOR PRAISE OF THE FOOD THAT I COOK. WHAT'S REALLY IMPORTANT IS HIS PERSONALITY.
PAPPAA (HONK)
COME TO THINK OF IT, Y-NAGA, THE FIRST TIME WE MET WAS IN AN ANKOU-NABE* PLACE WITH M-KUMA AND S-JI, WASN'T IT?
OH, THAT'S RIGHT! I RECOMMENDED THE PLACE. IT HAD LOADS OF ANGLER-FISH LIVER!
*ANKOU-NABE = ANGLERFISH POT
AH, RIGHT. THAT ANGLERFISH LIVER HAD A REALLY WEIRD TASTE! AT FIRST I WASN'T SURE ABOUT IT, BUT I MANAGED TO FORCE IT DOWN.
smile
AND JUST BECAUSE OF THAT!?
YOU REALLY ARE AN IDIOT! AN ABSOLUTE IDIOT, YOU KNOW THAT!?
THE END.
FINE!! I'D RATHER BE AN IDIOT THAN PUT UP WITH SOMEBODY WHO DISSES THE COOKING OF A RESTAURANT THAT I RECOMMENDED!!
IT'S REALLY GOOD, THE ANKOU-NABE THERE!! I DON'T HAVE A SINGLE REGRET IN MY LIFE!!

Torigoya Higashiyama

[Address]
1-5-11 Higashiyama,
Meguro-ku, Tokyo
[Telephone]
03-5074-1707
[Hours]
Mon-Sat
5:00 PM - 3:00 AM
Sun & Holidays
5:00 PM - 1:00 AM
[Closed]
Never.
[Directions]
A ten-minute walk from the Nakameguro Station on the Toukyuu-Touyoko Line and Hibiya Line.
[Parking]
None.

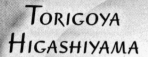

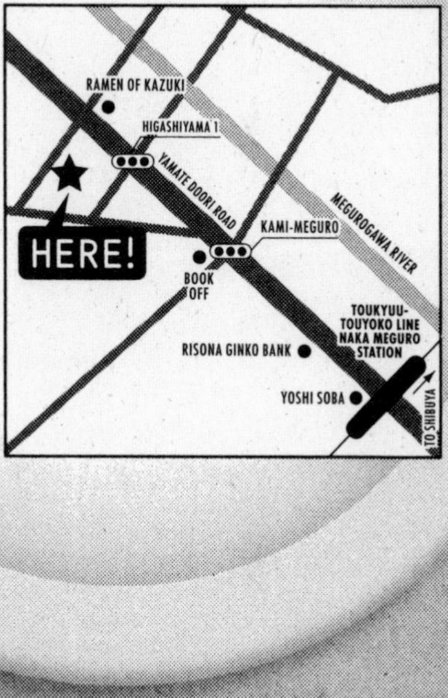

RAMEN OF KAZUKI
HIGASHIYAMA 1
YAMATE DOORI ROAD
MEGUROGAWA RIVER
KAMI-MEGURO
HERE!
BOOK OFF
TOUKYUU-TOUYOKO LINE NAKA MEGURO STATION
RISONA GINKO BANK
YOSHI SOBA
TO SHIBUYA

FUMI YOSHINAGA'S COMMENTS

THIS IS ANOTHER RESTAURANT WITH REASONABLE PRICES IN THE ¥3,000 RANGE. IT'S A GOOD PLACE FOR LARGE CROWDS. AND IT'S REALLY CONVENIENT SINCE IT'S OPEN SO LATE.

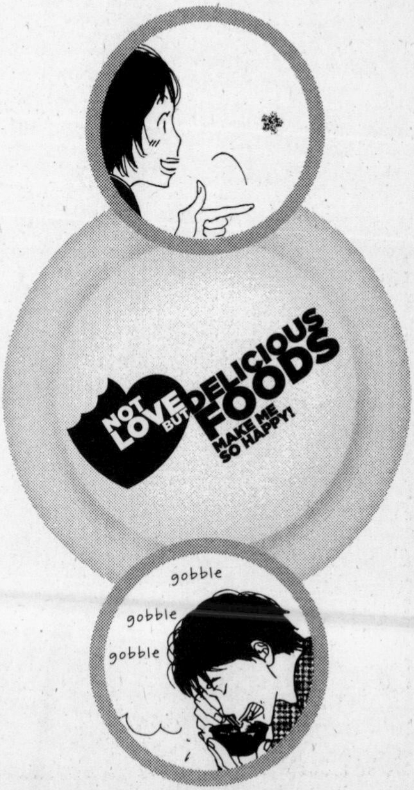
NOT LOVE BUT DELICIOUS FOODS MAKE ME SO HAPPY!
gobble
gobble
gobble

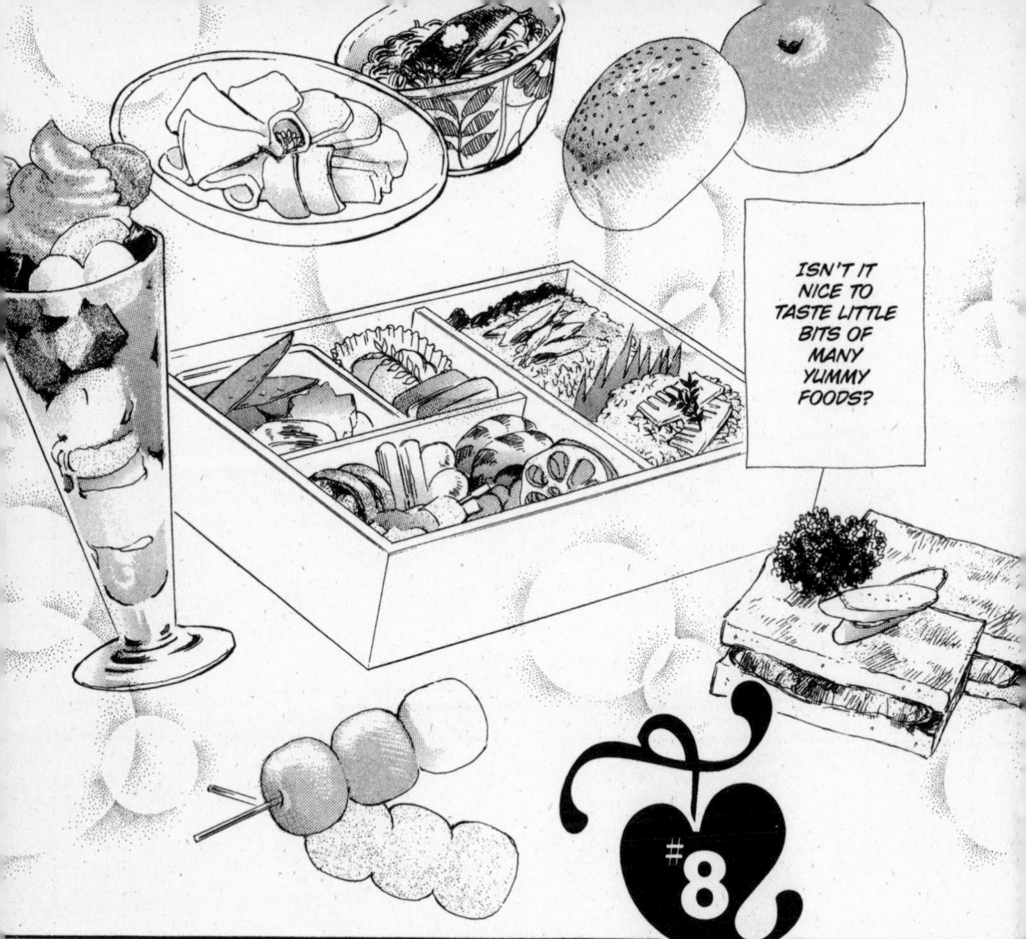
ISN'T IT NICE TO TASTE LITTLE BITS OF MANY YUMMY FOODS?
#8

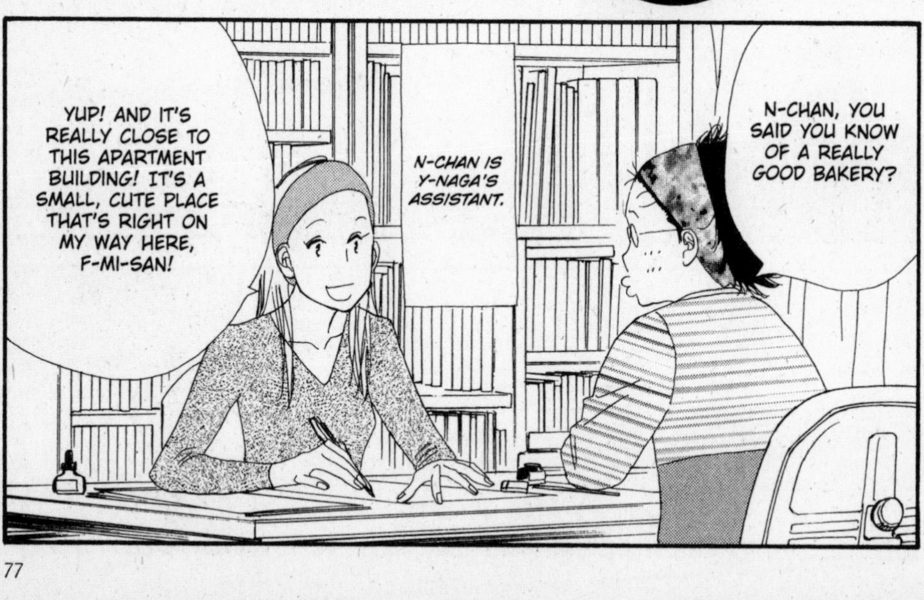
N-CHAN, YOU SAID YOU KNOW OF A REALLY GOOD BAKERY?
N-CHAN IS Y-NAGA'S ASSISTANT.
YUP! AND IT'S REALLY CLOSE TO THIS APARTMENT BUILDING! IT'S A SMALL, CUTE PLACE THAT'S RIGHT ON MY WAY HERE, F-MI-SAN!

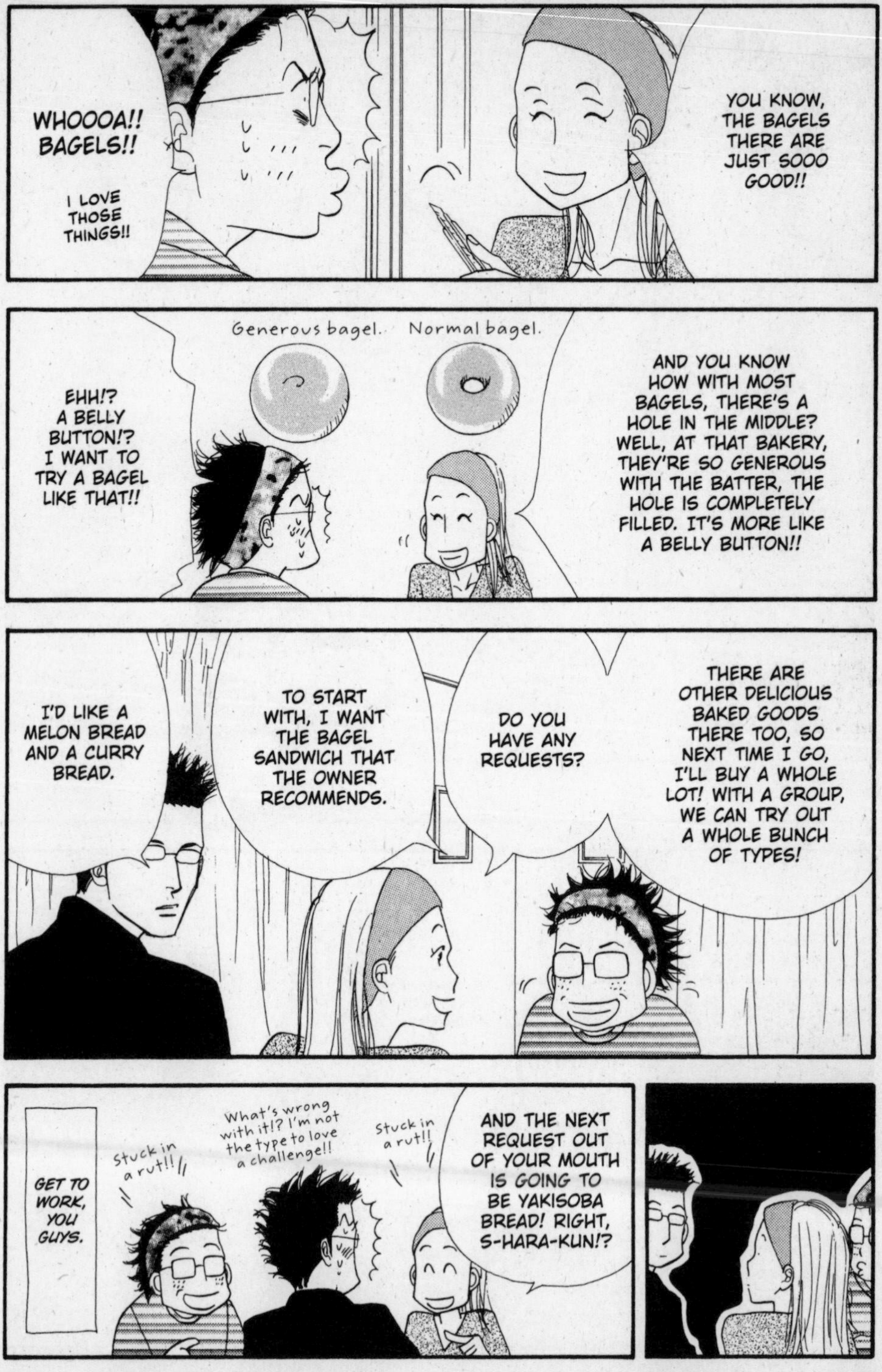
YOU KNOW, THE BAGELS THERE ARE JUST SOOO GOOD!!
WHOOOA!! BAGELS!!
I LOVE THOSE THINGS!!
AND YOU KNOW HOW WITH MOST BAGELS, THERE'S A HOLE IN THE MIDDLE? WELL, AT THAT BAKERY, THEY'RE SO GENEROUS WITH THE BATTER, THE HOLE IS COMPLETELY FILLED. IT'S MORE LIKE A BELLY BUTTON!!
Normal bagel.
Generous bagel.
EHH!? A BELLY BUTTON!? I WANT TO TRY A BAGEL LIKE THAT!!
THERE ARE OTHER DELICIOUS BAKED GOODS THERE TOO, SO NEXT TIME I GO, I'LL BUY A WHOLE LOT! WITH A GROUP, WE CAN TRY OUT A WHOLE BUNCH OF TYPES!
DO YOU HAVE ANY REQUESTS?
TO START WITH, I WANT THE BAGEL SANDWICH THAT THE OWNER RECOMMENDS.
I'D LIKE A MELON BREAD AND A CURRY BREAD.
AND THE NEXT REQUEST OUT OF YOUR MOUTH IS GOING TO BE YAKISOBA BREAD! RIGHT, S-HARA-KUN!?
Stuck in a rut!!
What's wrong with it!? I'm not the type to love a challenge!!
Stuck in a rut!!
GET TO WORK, YOU GUYS.

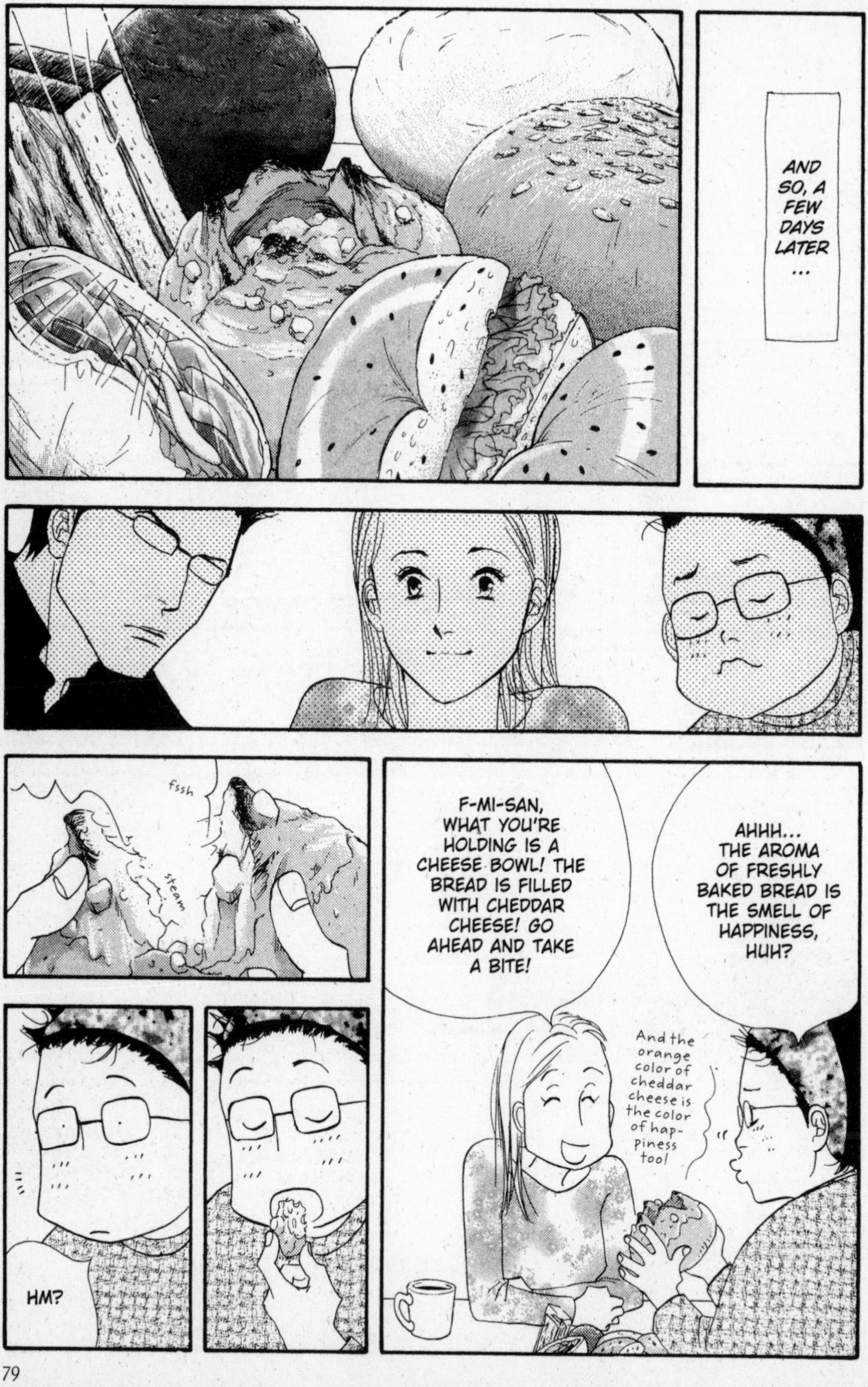
AND SO, A FEW DAYS LATER ...
fssh
steam
AHHH... THE AROMA OF FRESHLY BAKED BREAD IS THE SMELL OF HAPPINESS, HUH?
F-MI-SAN, WHAT YOU'RE HOLDING IS A CHEESE BOWL! THE BREAD IS FILLED WITH CHEDDAR CHEESE! GO AHEAD AND TAKE A BITE!
And the orange color of cheddar cheese is the color of happiness too!
HM?

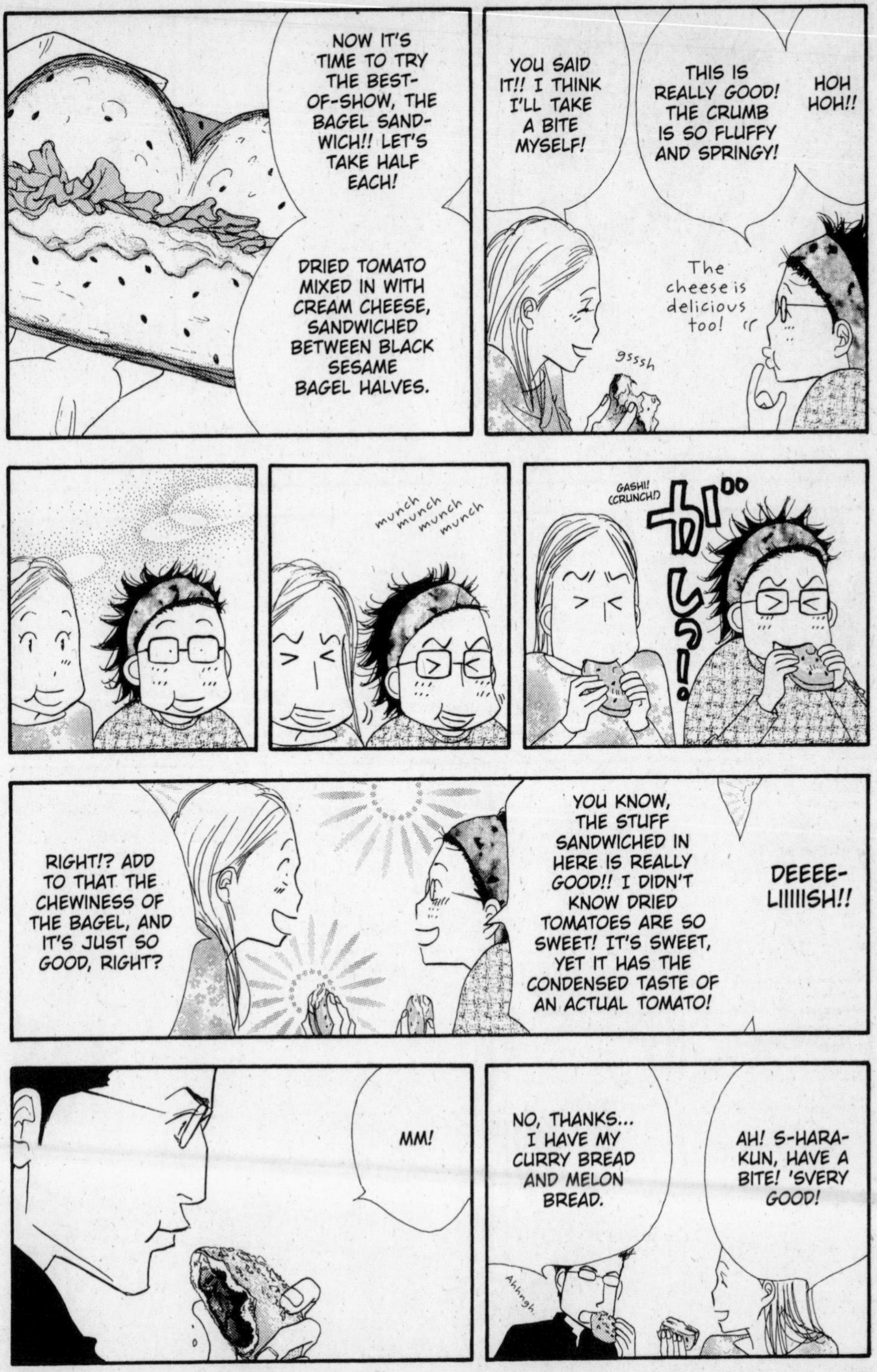
HOH HOH!!
THIS IS REALLY GOOD! THE CRUMB IS SO FLUFFY AND SPRINGY!
YOU SAID IT!! I THINK I'LL TAKE A BITE MYSELF!
The cheese is delicious too!
gsssh
NOW IT'S TIME TO TRY THE BEST-OF-SHOW, THE BAGEL SANDWICH!! LET'S TAKE HALF EACH!
DRIED TOMATO MIXED IN WITH CREAM CHEESE, SANDWICHED BETWEEN BLACK SESAME BAGEL HALVES.
GASHI! (CRUNCH!)
munch munch munch munch
DEEEE-LIIIIISH!!
YOU KNOW, THE STUFF SANDWICHED IN HERE IS REALLY GOOD!! I DIDN'T KNOW DRIED TOMATOES ARE SO SWEET! IT'S SWEET, YET IT HAS THE CONDENSED TASTE OF AN ACTUAL TOMATO!
RIGHT!? ADD TO THAT THE CHEWINESS OF THE BAGEL, AND IT'S JUST SO GOOD, RIGHT?
AH! S-HARA-KUN, HAVE A BITE! 'SVERY GOOD!
NO, THANKS... I HAVE MY CURRY BREAD AND MELON BREAD.
Ahhngh
MM!

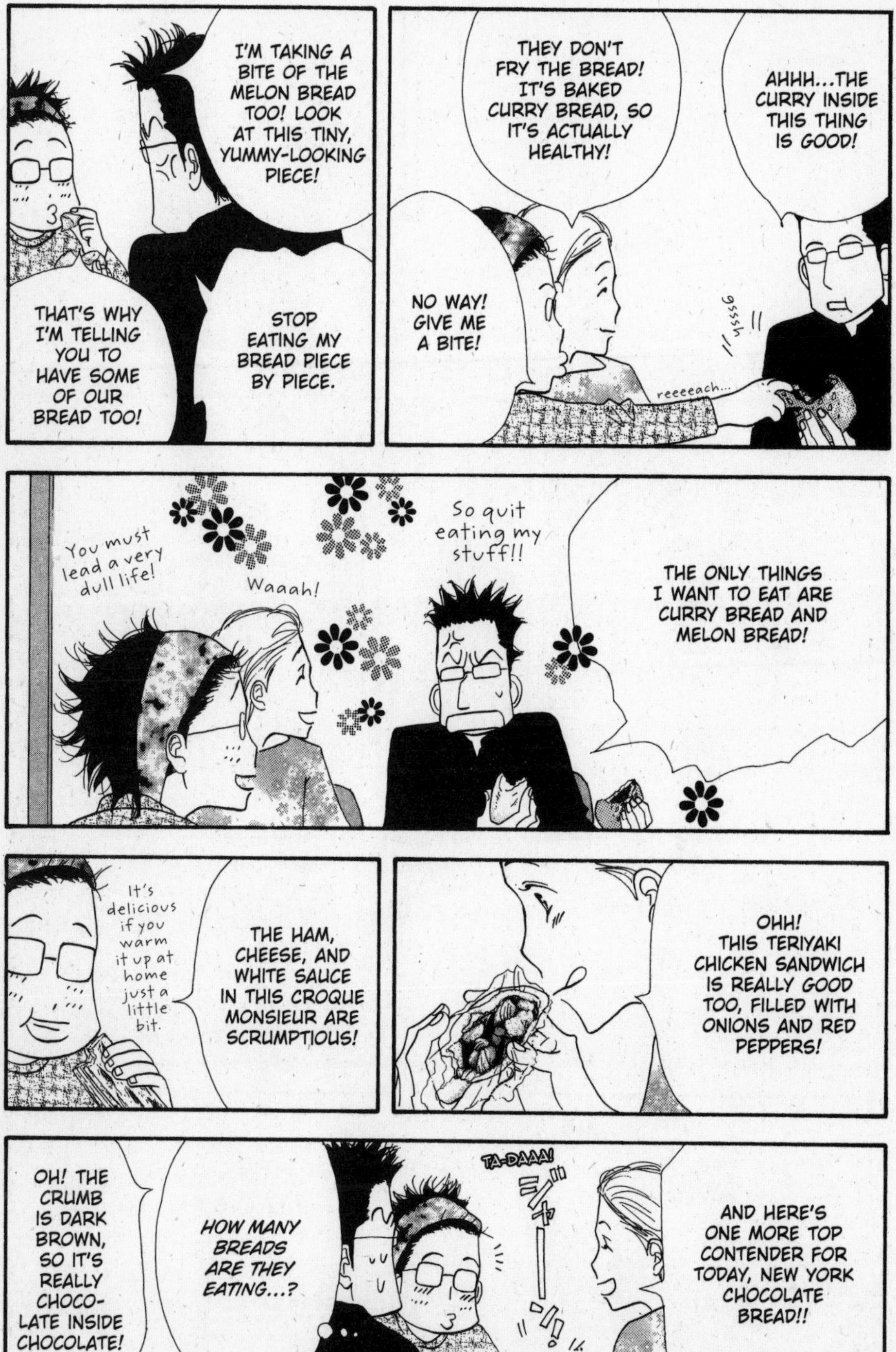
AHHH...THE CURRY INSIDE THIS THING IS GOOD!
THEY DON'T FRY THE BREAD! IT'S BAKED CURRY BREAD, SO IT'S ACTUALLY HEALTHY!
reeeeach...
NO WAY! GIVE ME A BITE!
I'M TAKING A BITE OF THE MELON BREAD TOO! LOOK AT THIS TINY, YUMMY-LOOKING PIECE!
STOP EATING MY BREAD PIECE BY PIECE.
THAT'S WHY I'M TELLING YOU TO HAVE SOME OF OUR BREAD TOO!
THE ONLY THINGS I WANT TO EAT ARE CURRY BREAD AND MELON BREAD!
So quit eating my stuff!!
Waaah!
You must lead a very dull life!
OHH! THIS TERIYAKI CHICKEN SANDWICH IS REALLY GOOD TOO, FILLED WITH ONIONS AND RED PEPPERS!
THE HAM, CHEESE, AND WHITE SAUCE IN THIS CROQUE MONSIEUR ARE SCRUMPTIOUS!
It's delicious if you warm it up at home just a little bit.
AND HERE'S ONE MORE TOP CONTENDER FOR TODAY, NEW YORK CHOCOLATE BREAD!!
TA-DAAA!
HOW MANY BREADS ARE THEY EATING...?
OH! THE CRUMB IS DARK BROWN, SO IT'S REALLY CHOCOLATE INSIDE CHOCOLATE!

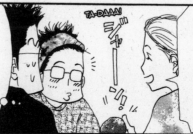

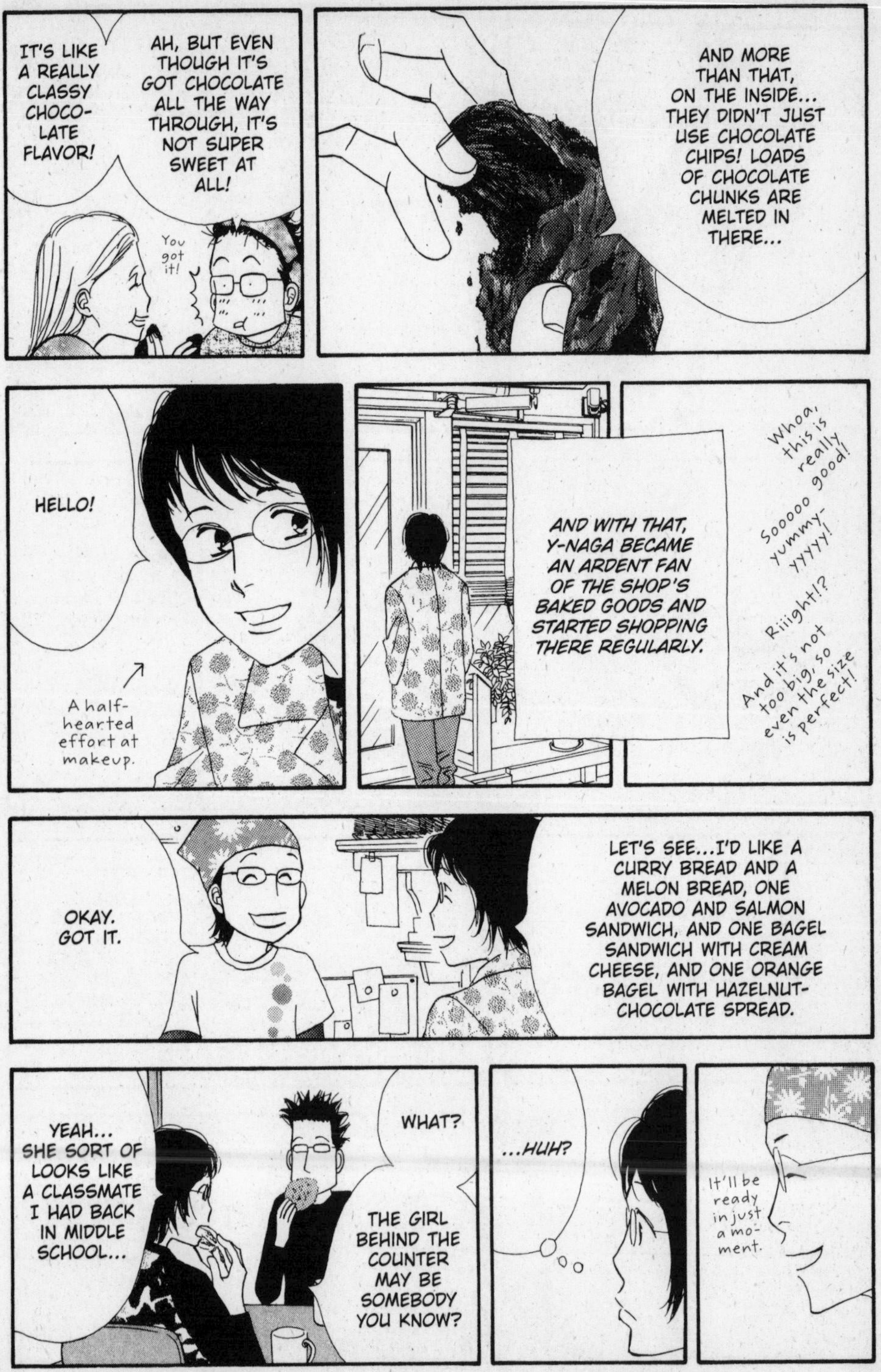
AND MORE THAN THAT, ON THE INSIDE... THEY DIDN'T JUST USE CHOCOLATE CHIPS! LOADS OF CHOCOLATE CHUNKS ARE MELTED IN THERE...
AH, BUT EVEN THOUGH IT'S GOT CHOCOLATE ALL THE WAY THROUGH, IT'S NOT SUPER SWEET AT ALL!
IT'S LIKE A REALLY CLASSY CHOCO-LATE FLAVOR!
You got it!
Whoa, this is really good!
Sooooo yummy-yyyyy!
Riiiight!?
And it's not too big, so even the size is perfect!
AND WITH THAT, Y-NAGA BECAME AN ARDENT FAN OF THE SHOP'S BAKED GOODS AND STARTED SHOPPING THERE REGULARLY.
HELLO!
A half-hearted effort at makeup.
LET'S SEE...I'D LIKE A CURRY BREAD AND A MELON BREAD, ONE AVOCADO AND SALMON SANDWICH, AND ONE BAGEL SANDWICH WITH CREAM CHEESE, AND ONE ORANGE BAGEL WITH HAZELNUT-CHOCOLATE SPREAD.
OKAY. GOT IT.
It'll be ready in just a moment.
...HUH?
WHAT?
THE GIRL BEHIND THE COUNTER MAY BE SOMEBODY YOU KNOW?
YEAH... SHE SORT OF LOOKS LIKE A CLASSMATE I HAD BACK IN MIDDLE SCHOOL...

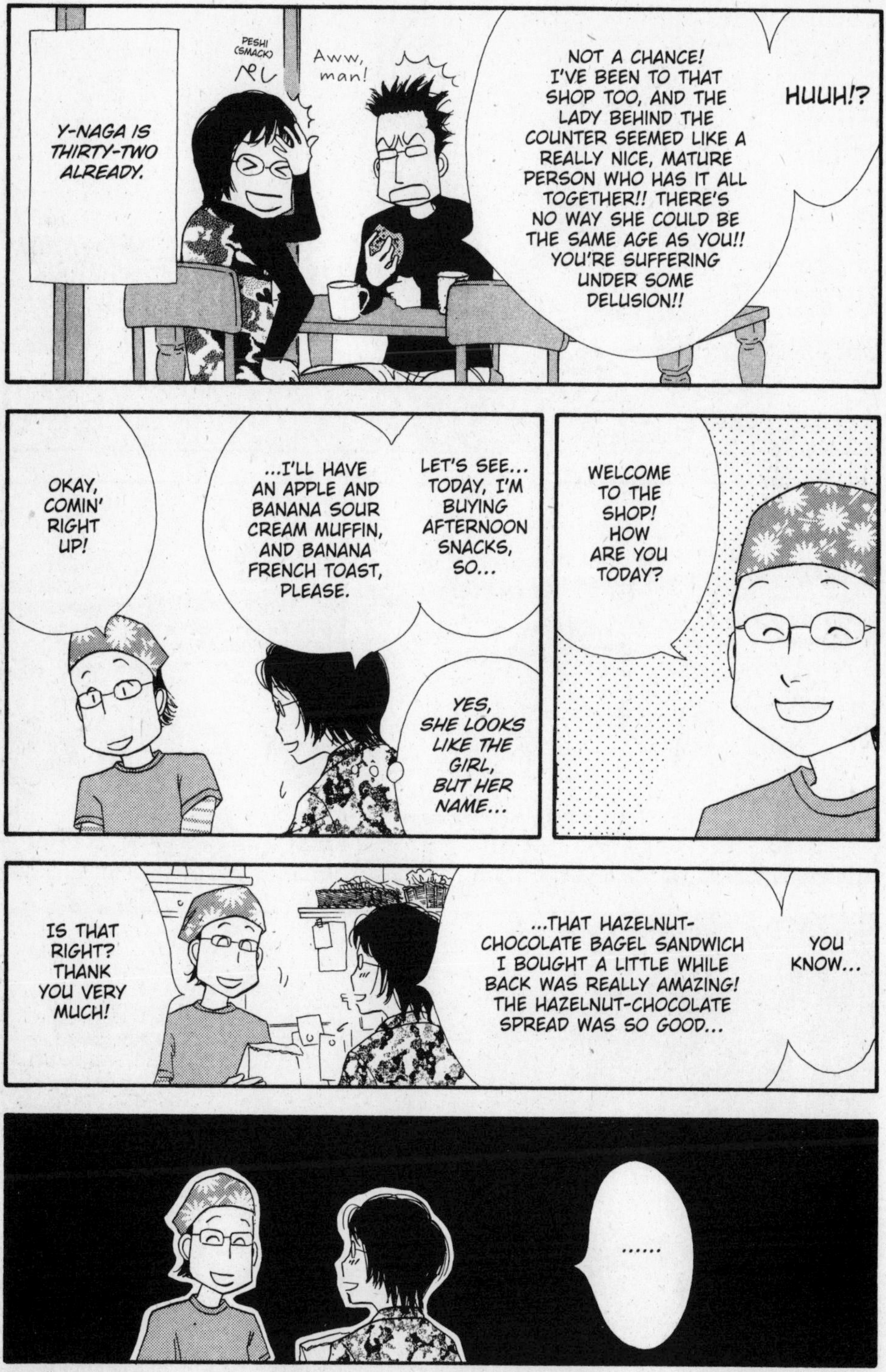
HUUH!?
NOT A CHANCE! I'VE BEEN TO THAT SHOP TOO, AND THE LADY BEHIND THE COUNTER SEEMED LIKE A REALLY NICE, MATURE PERSON WHO HAS IT ALL TOGETHER!! THERE'S NO WAY SHE COULD BE THE SAME AGE AS YOU!! YOU'RE SUFFERING UNDER SOME DELUSION!!
Aww, man!
PESHI (SMACK)
ぺし
Y-NAGA IS THIRTY-TWO ALREADY.
WELCOME TO THE SHOP! HOW ARE YOU TODAY?
LET'S SEE... TODAY, I'M BUYING AFTERNOON SNACKS, SO...
...I'LL HAVE AN APPLE AND BANANA SOUR CREAM MUFFIN, AND BANANA FRENCH TOAST, PLEASE.
YES, SHE LOOKS LIKE THE GIRL, BUT HER NAME...
OKAY, COMIN' RIGHT UP!
YOU KNOW...
...THAT HAZELNUT-CHOCOLATE BAGEL SANDWICH I BOUGHT A LITTLE WHILE BACK WAS REALLY AMAZING! THE HAZELNUT-CHOCOLATE SPREAD WAS SO GOOD...
IS THAT RIGHT? THANK YOU VERY MUCH!
......

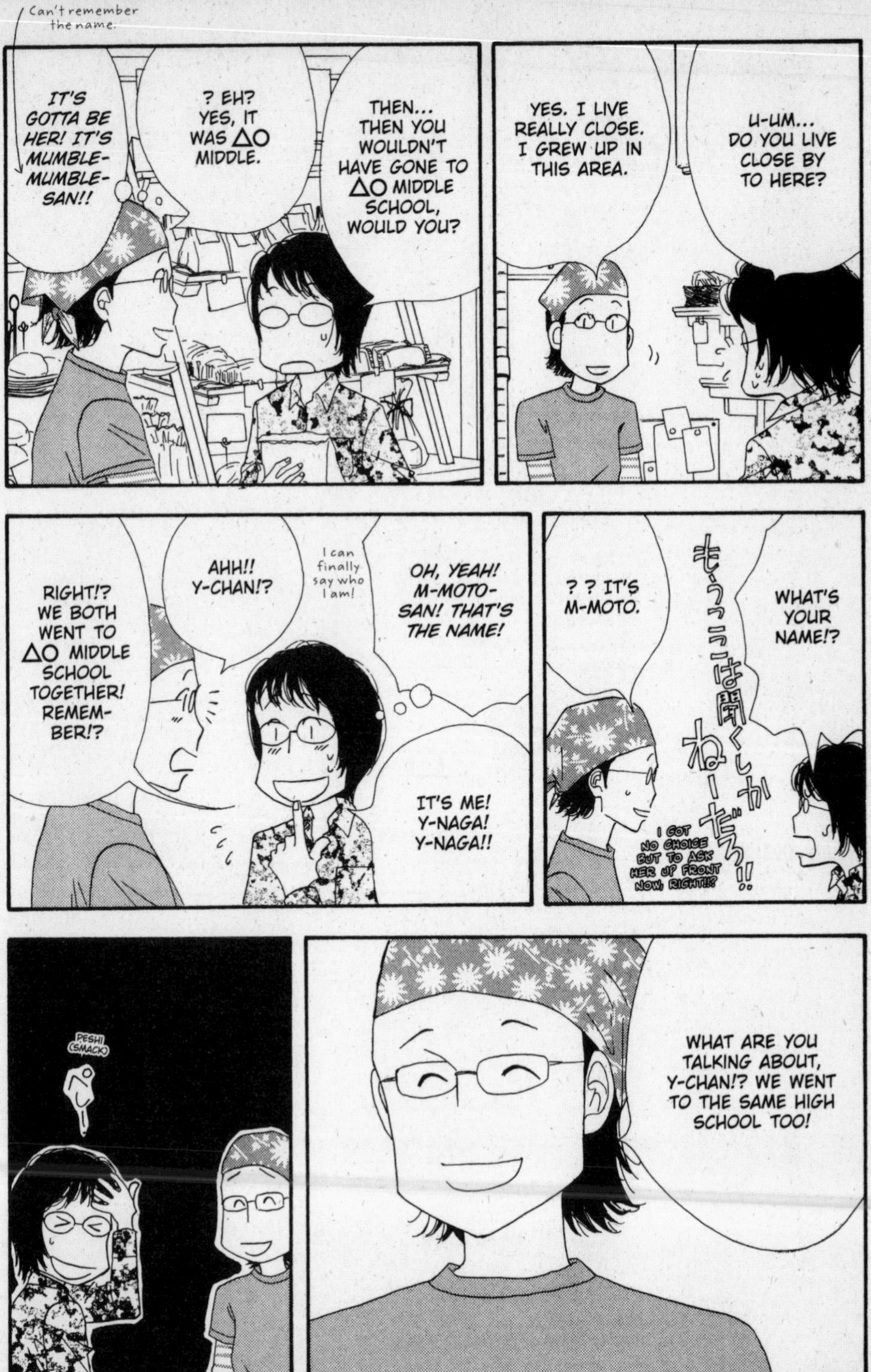
U-UM... DO YOU LIVE CLOSE BY TO HERE?
YES. I LIVE REALLY CLOSE. I GREW UP IN THIS AREA.
THEN... THEN YOU WOULDN'T HAVE GONE TO △O MIDDLE SCHOOL, WOULD YOU?
? EH? YES, IT WAS △O MIDDLE.
IT'S GOTTA BE HER! IT'S MUMBLE-MUMBLE-SAN!!
Can't remember the name.
WHAT'S YOUR NAME!?
もうここは聞くしかねーだろ!!
I GOT NO CHOICE BUT TO ASK HER UP FRONT NOW, RIGHT!!?
? ? IT'S M-MOTO.
OH, YEAH! M-MOTO-SAN! THAT'S THE NAME!
I can finally say who I am!
IT'S ME! Y-NAGA! Y-NAGA!!
AHH!! Y-CHAN!?
RIGHT!? WE BOTH WENT TO △O MIDDLE SCHOOL TOGETHER! REMEMBER!?
WHAT ARE YOU TALKING ABOUT, Y-CHAN!? WE WENT TO THE SAME HIGH SCHOOL TOO!
PESHI (SMACK)

BAGEL

[Address]
5-35-7 Narita
Higashi, Suginami-ku,
Tokyo
[Telephone]
03-5397-2339
[Hours]
7:00 AM - 3:00 PM
[Closed]
Tuesdays and
every third Monday
of the month.
[Directions]
A five-minute
walk from the Minami
Asagaya Station on the
Maru-no-Uchi Line.
[Parking]
None.

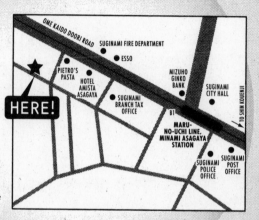

OME KAIDO DOORI ROAD
SUGINAMI FIRE DEPARTMENT
ESSO
PIETRO'S PASTA
HOTEL AMISTA ASAGAYA
MIZUHO GINKO BANK
SUGINAMI CITY HALL
TO SHIN KOUENJI
HERE!
SUGINAMI BRANCH TAX OFFICE
B1
MARU-NO-UCHI LINE, MINAMI ASAGAYA STATION
SUGINAMI POLICE OFFICE
SUGINAMI POST OFFICE

FUMI YOSHINAGA'S COMMENTS

IT'S A REALLY POPULAR BAKERY, SO EVERYTHING IS PRETTY MUCH SOLD OUT NEAR CLOSING TIME. AROUND NOON IS WHEN THEY HAVE THE MOST VARIETIES OF BREAD, SO THAT TIME IS BEST. THE CHEESE BOWL WHEN IT'S JUST OUT OF THE OVEN IS SO FLUFF, FLUFF AND SPRING, SPRING IT'S REALLY THE BEST!

gsssh

NOT LOVE BUT DELICIOUS FOODS MAKE ME SO HAPPY!

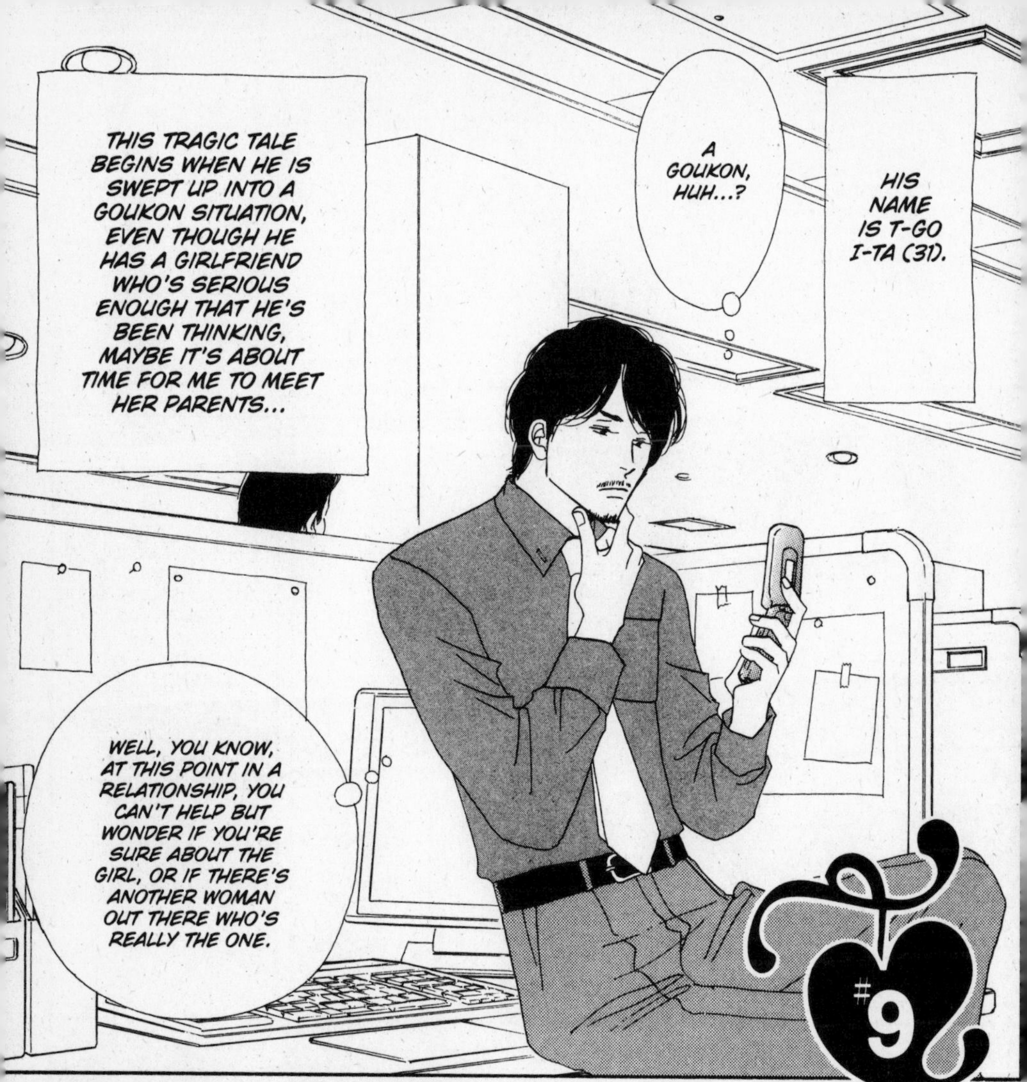
HIS NAME IS T-GO I-TA (31).
A GOUKON, HUH...?
THIS TRAGIC TALE BEGINS WHEN HE IS SWEPT UP INTO A GOUKON SITUATION, EVEN THOUGH HE HAS A GIRLFRIEND WHO'S SERIOUS ENOUGH THAT HE'S BEEN THINKING, MAYBE IT'S ABOUT TIME FOR ME TO MEET HER PARENTS...
WELL, YOU KNOW, AT THIS POINT IN A RELATIONSHIP, YOU CAN'T HELP BUT WONDER IF YOU'RE SURE ABOUT THE GIRL, OR IF THERE'S ANOTHER WOMAN OUT THERE WHO'S REALLY THE ONE.
#9
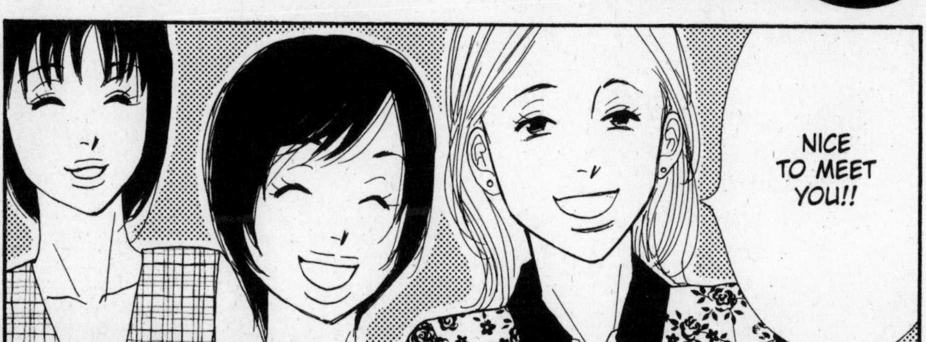
NICE TO MEET YOU!!

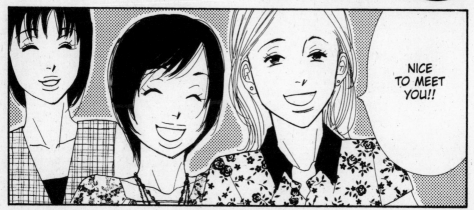

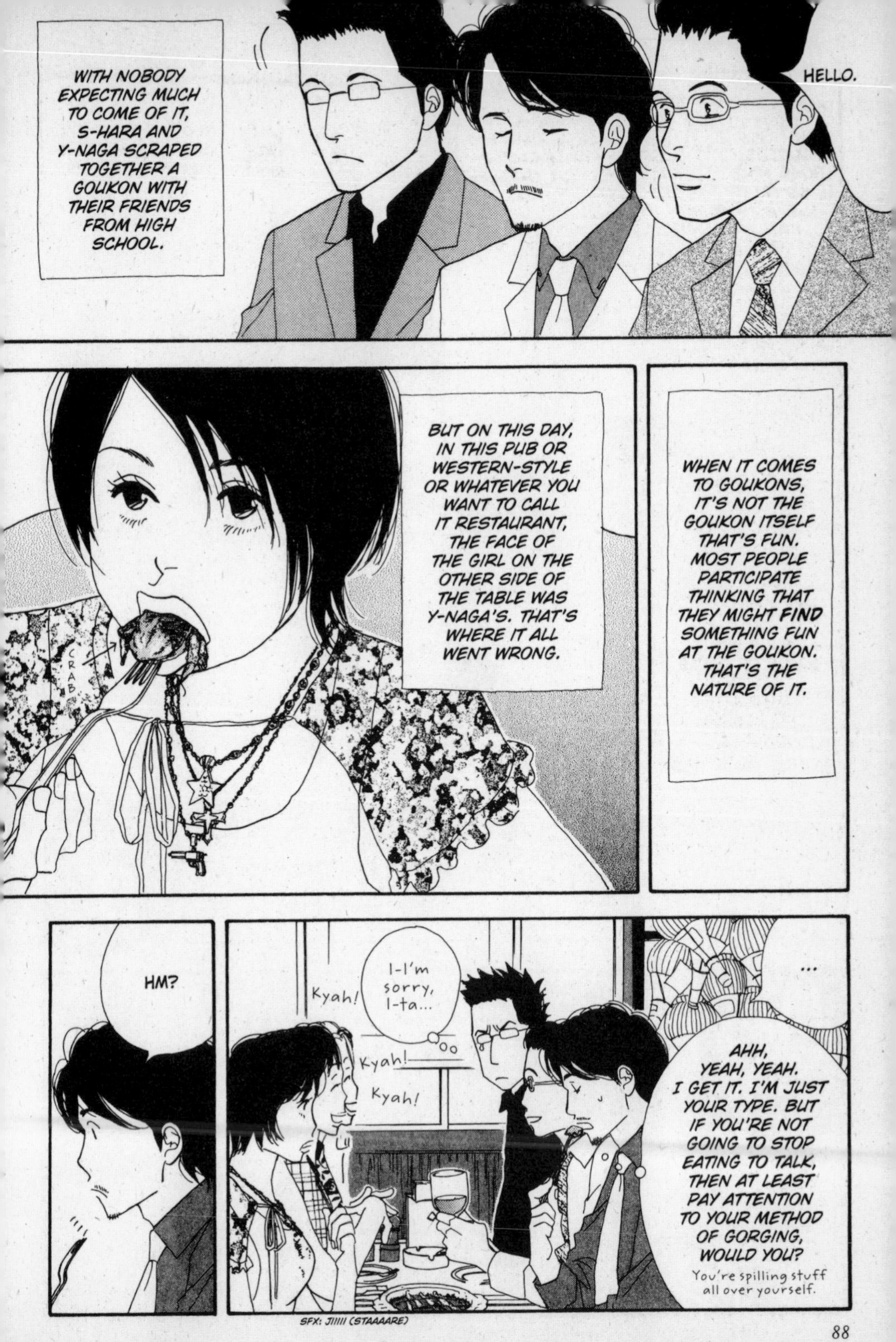
HELLO.
WITH NOBODY EXPECTING MUCH TO COME OF IT, S-HARA AND Y-NAGA SCRAPED TOGETHER A GOUKON WITH THEIR FRIENDS FROM HIGH SCHOOL.
WHEN IT COMES TO GOUKONS, IT'S NOT THE GOUKON ITSELF THAT'S FUN. MOST PEOPLE PARTICIPATE THINKING THAT THEY MIGHT **FIND** SOMETHING FUN AT THE GOUKON. THAT'S THE NATURE OF IT.
BUT ON THIS DAY, IN THIS PUB OR WESTERN-STYLE OR WHATEVER YOU WANT TO CALL IT RESTAURANT, THE FACE OF THE GIRL ON THE OTHER SIDE OF THE TABLE WAS Y-NAGA'S. THAT'S WHERE IT ALL WENT WRONG.
CRAB
...
AHH, YEAH, YEAH. I GET IT. I'M JUST YOUR TYPE. BUT IF YOU'RE NOT GOING TO STOP EATING TO TALK, THEN AT LEAST PAY ATTENTION TO YOUR METHOD OF GORGING, WOULD YOU?
You're spilling stuff all over yourself.
I-I'm sorry, I-ta...
Kyah!
Kyah!
Kyah!
HM?

SFX: JIIIII (STAAAARE)

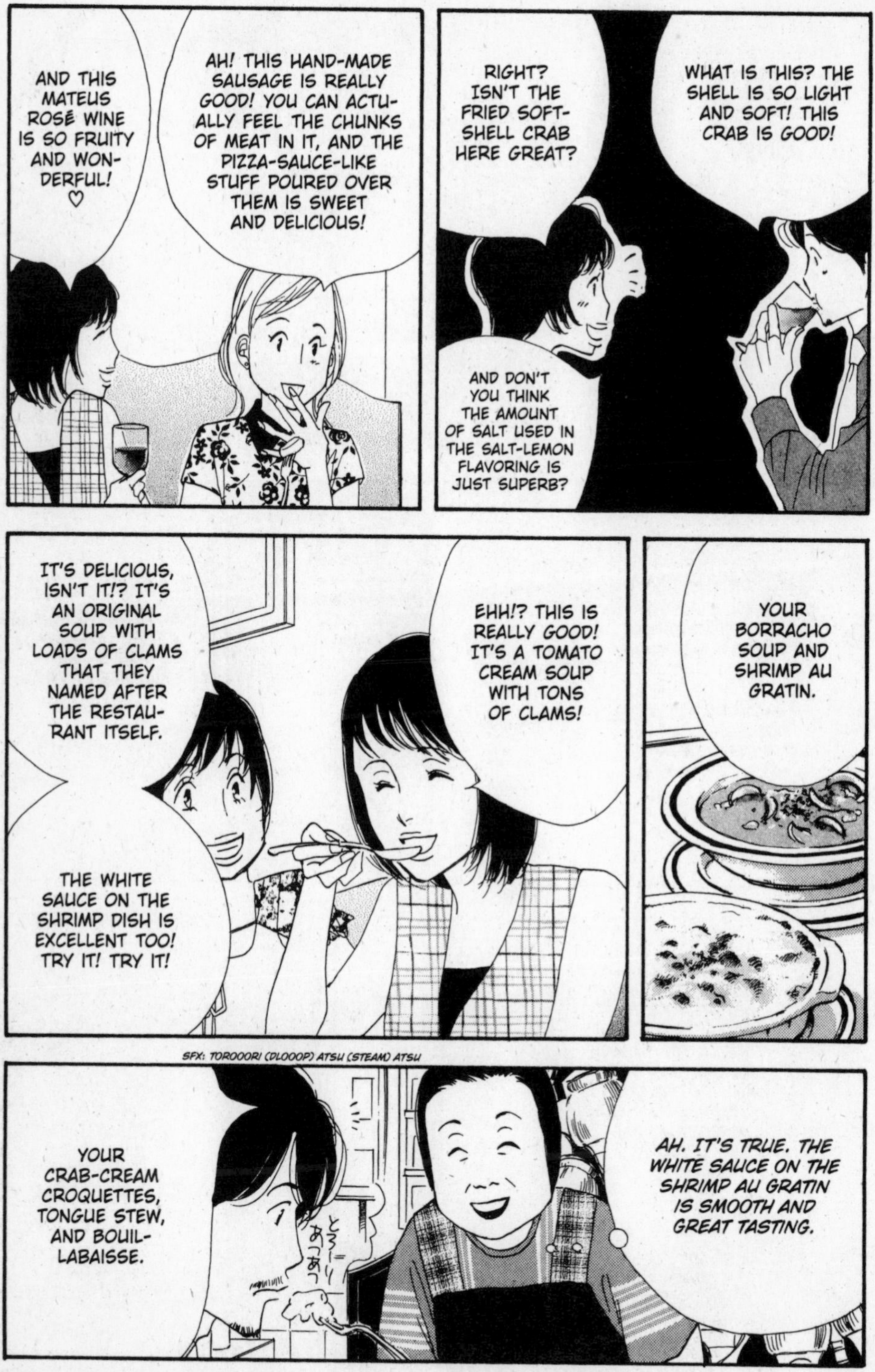
WHAT IS THIS? THE SHELL IS SO LIGHT AND SOFT! THIS CRAB IS GOOD!
RIGHT? ISN'T THE FRIED SOFT-SHELL CRAB HERE GREAT?
AND DON'T YOU THINK THE AMOUNT OF SALT USED IN THE SALT-LEMON FLAVORING IS JUST SUPERB?
AH! THIS HAND-MADE SAUSAGE IS REALLY GOOD! YOU CAN ACTU-ALLY FEEL THE CHUNKS OF MEAT IN IT, AND THE PIZZA-SAUCE-LIKE STUFF POURED OVER THEM IS SWEET AND DELICIOUS!
AND THIS MATEUS ROSÉ WINE IS SO FRUITY AND WON-DERFUL! ♡
YOUR BORRACHO SOUP AND SHRIMP AU GRATIN.
EHH!? THIS IS REALLY GOOD! IT'S A TOMATO CREAM SOUP WITH TONS OF CLAMS!
IT'S DELICIOUS, ISN'T IT!? IT'S AN ORIGINAL SOUP WITH LOADS OF CLAMS THAT THEY NAMED AFTER THE RESTAU-RANT ITSELF.
THE WHITE SAUCE ON THE SHRIMP DISH IS EXCELLENT TOO! TRY IT! TRY IT!
SFX: TOROOORI (DLOOOP) ATSU (STEAM) ATSU
AH. IT'S TRUE. THE WHITE SAUCE ON THE SHRIMP AU GRATIN IS SMOOTH AND GREAT TASTING.
YOUR CRAB-CREAM CROQUETTES, TONGUE STEW, AND BOUIL-LABAISSE.

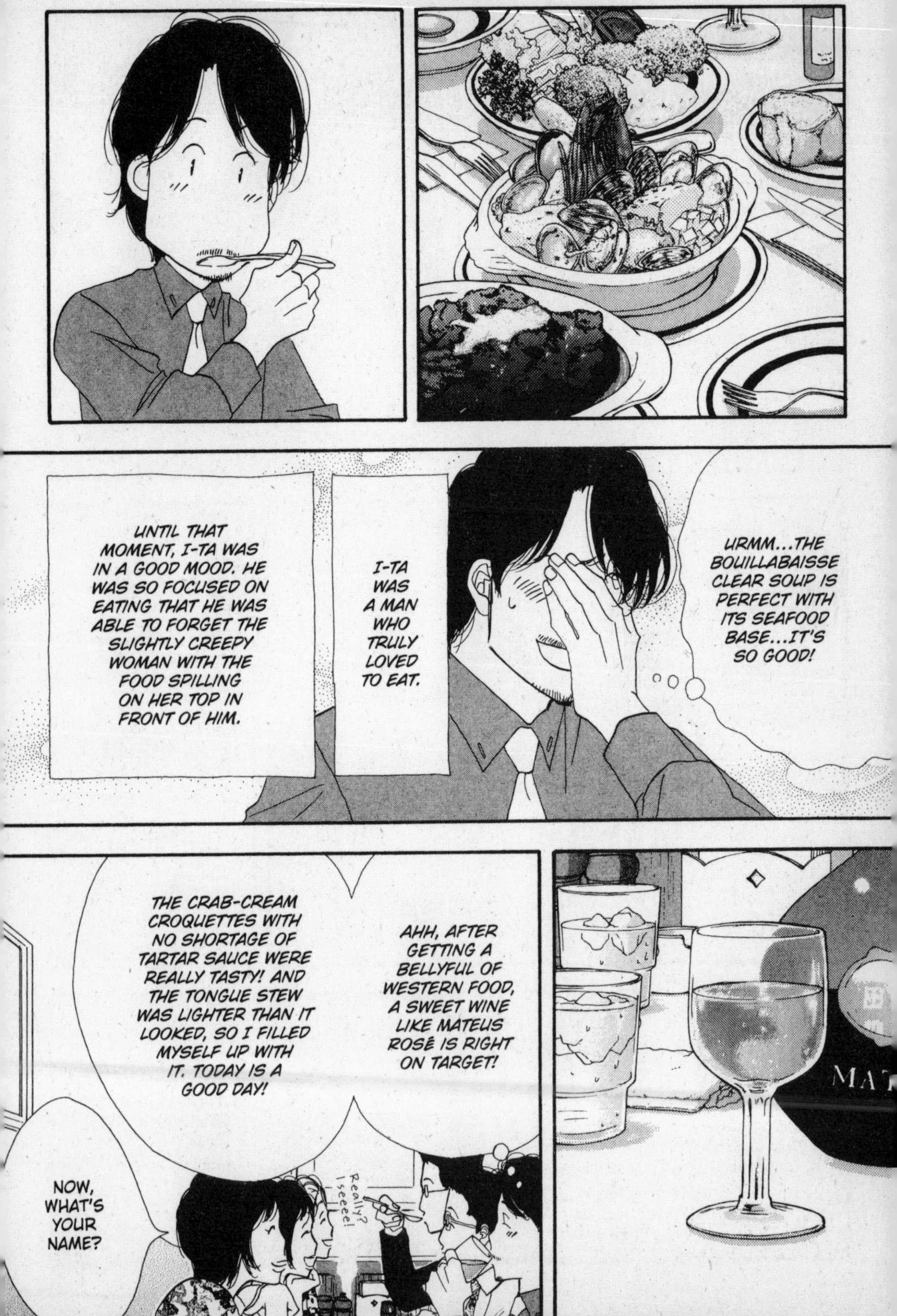
URMM...THE BOUILLABAISSE CLEAR SOUP IS PERFECT WITH ITS SEAFOOD BASE...IT'S SO GOOD!
I-TA WAS A MAN WHO TRULY LOVED TO EAT.
UNTIL THAT MOMENT, I-TA WAS IN A GOOD MOOD. HE WAS SO FOCUSED ON EATING THAT HE WAS ABLE TO FORGET THE SLIGHTLY CREEPY WOMAN WITH THE FOOD SPILLING ON HER TOP IN FRONT OF HIM.
AHH, AFTER GETTING A BELLYFUL OF WESTERN FOOD, A SWEET WINE LIKE MATEUS ROSÊ IS RIGHT ON TARGET!
THE CRAB-CREAM CROQUETTES WITH NO SHORTAGE OF TARTAR SAUCE WERE REALLY TASTY! AND THE TONGUE STEW WAS LIGHTER THAN IT LOOKED, SO I FILLED MYSELF UP WITH IT. TODAY IS A GOOD DAY!
Really? I seeee!
NOW, WHAT'S YOUR NAME?

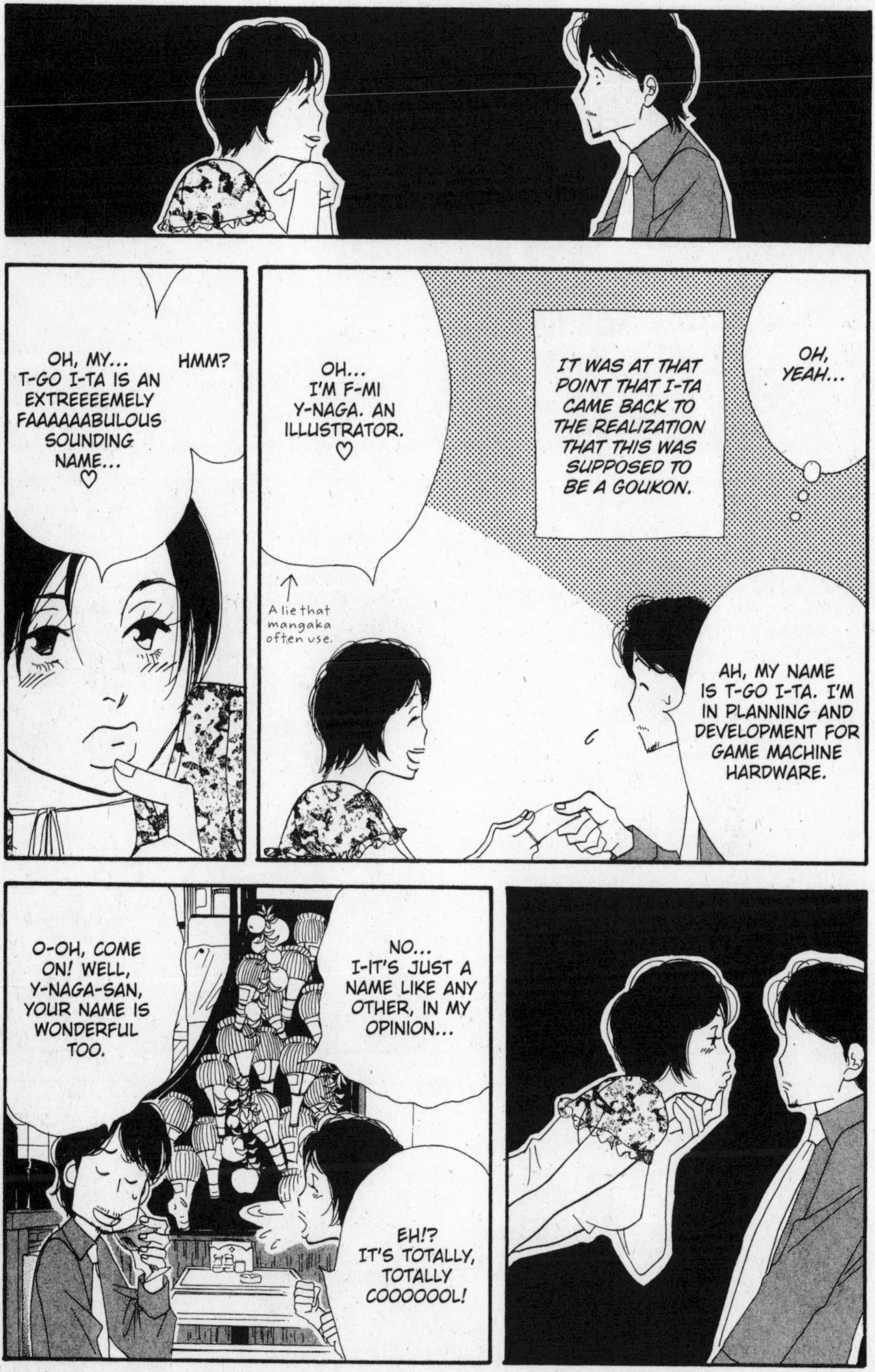
OH, YEAH...
IT WAS AT THAT POINT THAT I-TA CAME BACK TO THE REALIZATION THAT THIS WAS SUPPOSED TO BE A GOUKON.
AH, MY NAME IS T-GO I-TA. I'M IN PLANNING AND DEVELOPMENT FOR GAME MACHINE HARDWARE.
OH... I'M F-MI Y-NAGA. AN ILLUSTRATOR. ♡
A lie that mangaka often use.
HMM?
OH, MY... T-GO I-TA IS AN EXTREEEEMELY FAAAAAABULOUS SOUNDING NAME... ♡
NO... I-IT'S JUST A NAME LIKE ANY OTHER, IN MY OPINION...
O-OH, COME ON! WELL, Y-NAGA-SAN, YOUR NAME IS WONDERFUL TOO.
EH!? IT'S TOTALLY, TOTALLY COOOOOOL!

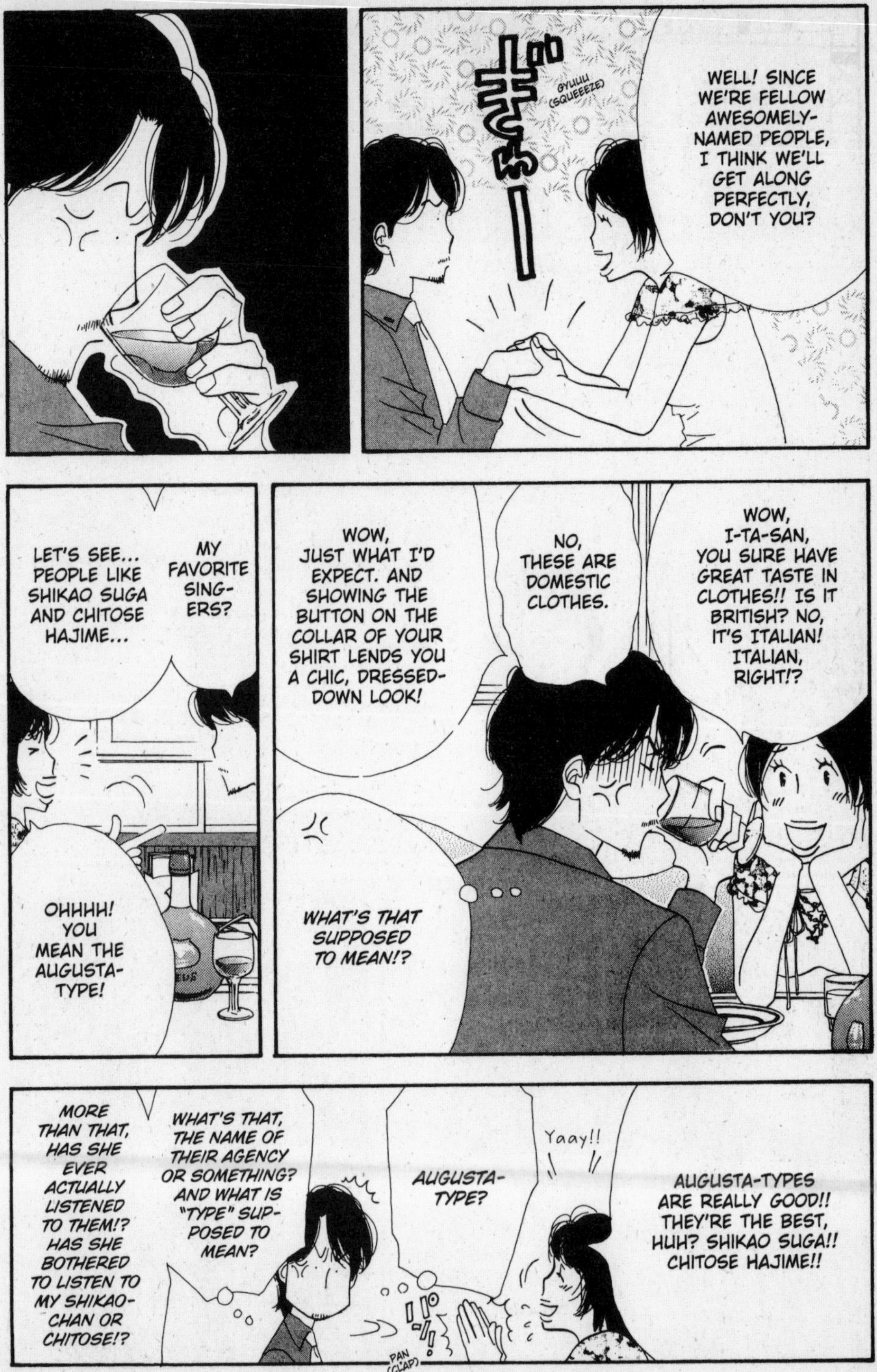
WELL! SINCE WE'RE FELLOW AWESOMELY-NAMED PEOPLE, I THINK WE'LL GET ALONG PERFECTLY, DON'T YOU?
GYUUUU (SQUEEEZE)
WOW, I-TA-SAN, YOU SURE HAVE GREAT TASTE IN CLOTHES!! IS IT BRITISH? NO, IT'S ITALIAN! ITALIAN, RIGHT!?
NO, THESE ARE DOMESTIC CLOTHES.
WOW, JUST WHAT I'D EXPECT. AND SHOWING THE BUTTON ON THE COLLAR OF YOUR SHIRT LENDS YOU A CHIC, DRESSED-DOWN LOOK!
WHAT'S THAT SUPPOSED TO MEAN!?
MY FAVORITE SINGERS?
LET'S SEE... PEOPLE LIKE SHIKAO SUGA AND CHITOSE HAJIME...
OHHHH! YOU MEAN THE AUGUSTA-TYPE!
AUGUSTA-TYPES ARE REALLY GOOD!! THEY'RE THE BEST, HUH? SHIKAO SUGA!! CHITOSE HAJIME!!
Yaay!!
AUGUSTA-TYPE?
PAN (CLAP)
WHAT'S THAT, THE NAME OF THEIR AGENCY OR SOMETHING? AND WHAT IS "TYPE" SUPPOSED TO MEAN?
MORE THAN THAT, HAS SHE EVER ACTUALLY LISTENED TO THEM!? HAS SHE BOTHERED TO LISTEN TO MY SHIKAO-CHAN OR CHITOSE!?

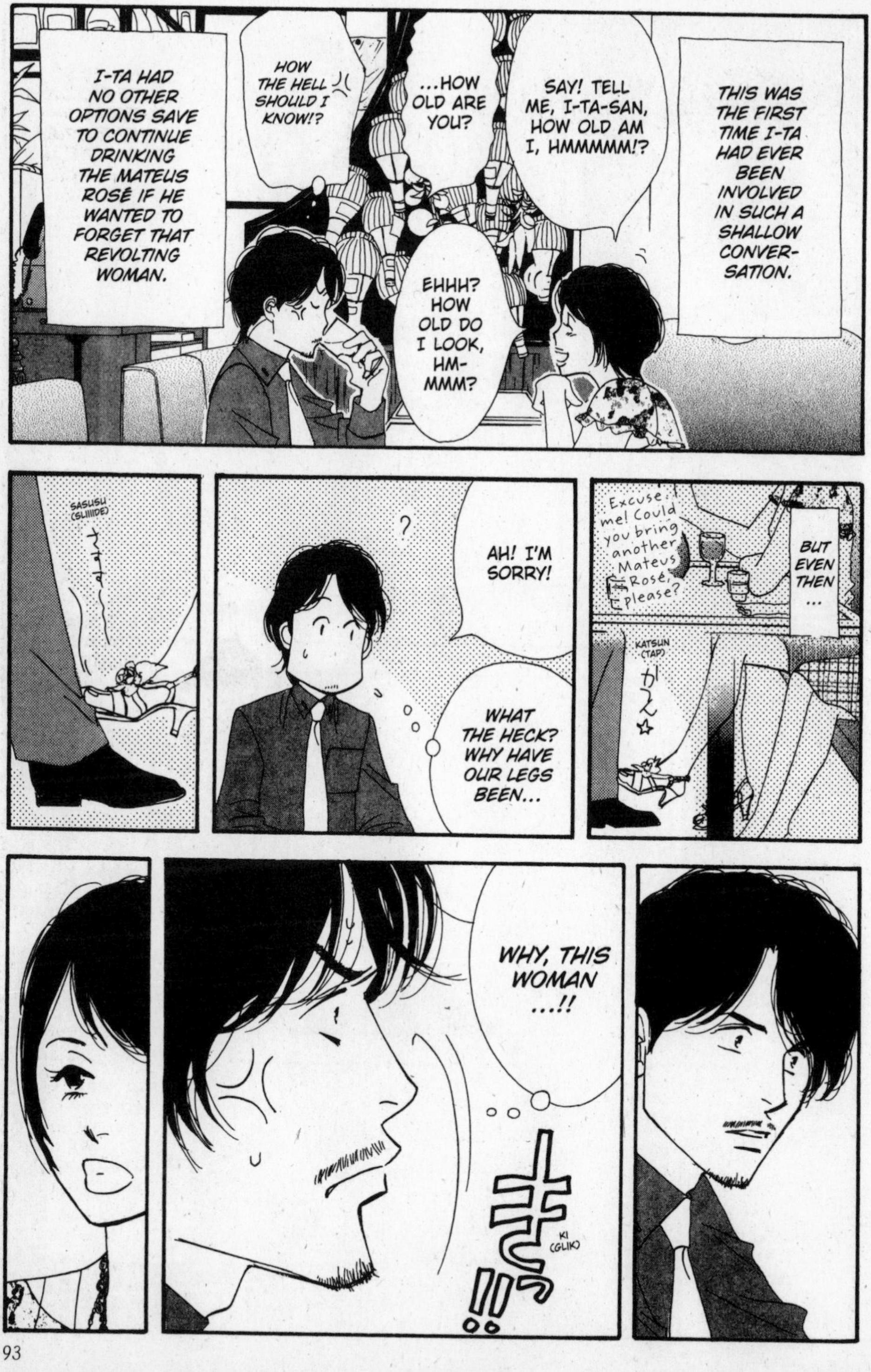
THIS WAS THE FIRST TIME I-TA HAD EVER BEEN INVOLVED IN SUCH A SHALLOW CONVER-SATION.
SAY! TELL ME, I-TA-SAN, HOW OLD AM I, HMMMMM!?
...HOW OLD ARE YOU?
HOW THE HELL SHOULD I KNOW!?
EHHH? HOW OLD DO I LOOK, HM-MMM?
I-TA HAD NO OTHER OPTIONS SAVE TO CONTINUE DRINKING THE MATEUS ROSÉ IF HE WANTED TO FORGET THAT REVOLTING WOMAN.
BUT EVEN THEN...
Excuse me! Could you bring another Mateus Rosé, please?
かつん
KATSUN (TAP)
AH! I'M SORRY!
?
WHAT THE HECK? WHY HAVE OUR LEGS BEEN...
すすー
SASUSU (SLIIIIDE)
WHY, THIS WOMAN ...!!
きっ!!
KI (GLIK)

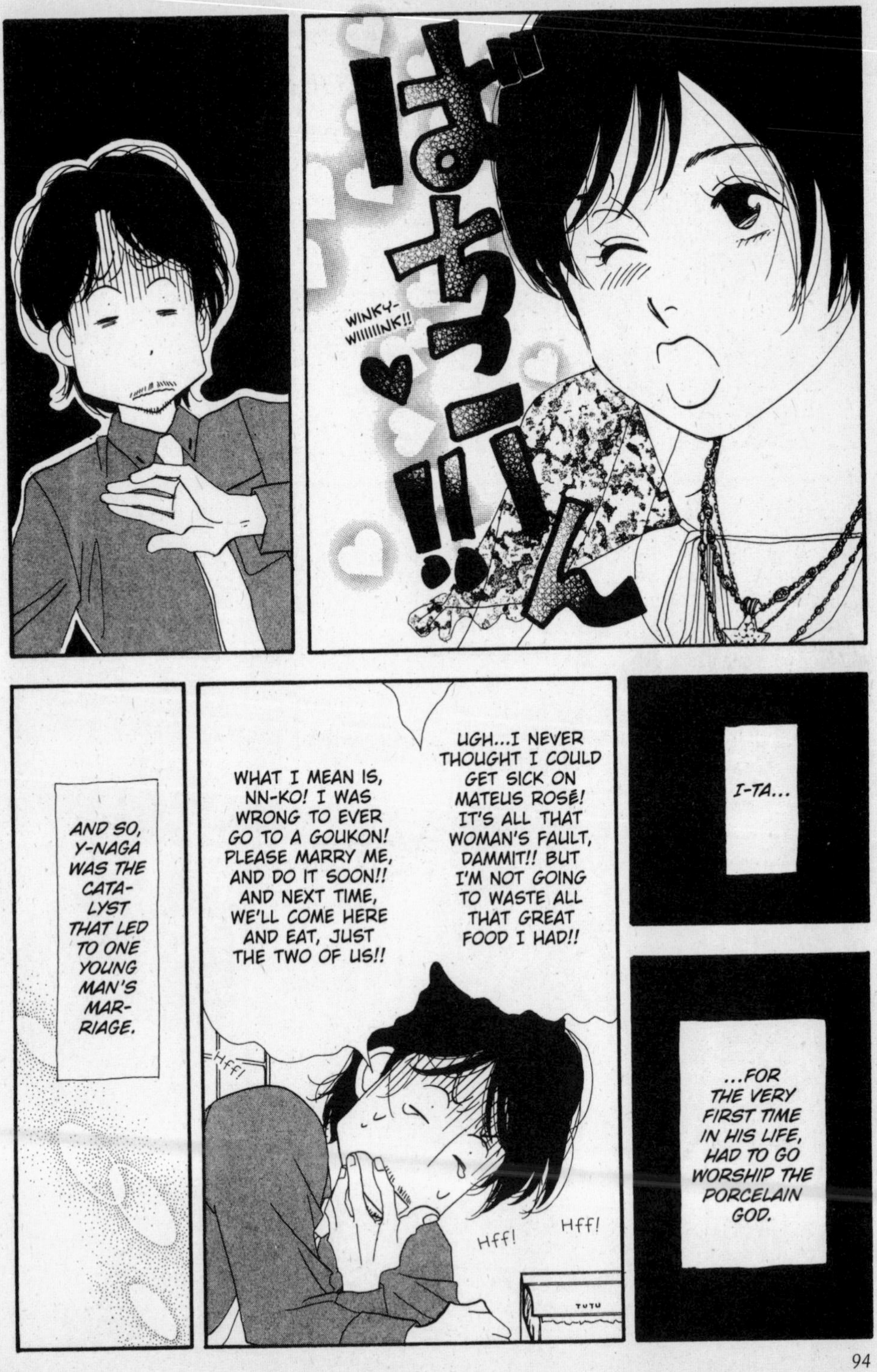
ばちこーん!!
WINKY-WIIIIIINK!!
I-TA...
...FOR THE VERY FIRST TIME IN HIS LIFE, HAD TO GO WORSHIP THE PORCELAIN GOD.
UGH...I NEVER THOUGHT I COULD GET SICK ON MATEUS ROSÉ! IT'S ALL THAT WOMAN'S FAULT, DAMMIT!! BUT I'M NOT GOING TO WASTE ALL THAT GREAT FOOD I HAD!!
WHAT I MEAN IS, NN-KO! I WAS WRONG TO EVER GO TO A GOUKON! PLEASE MARRY ME, AND DO IT SOON!! AND NEXT TIME, WE'LL COME HERE AND EAT, JUST THE TWO OF US!!
Hff!
Hff!
Hff!
AND SO, Y-NAGA WAS THE CATA-LYST THAT LED TO ONE YOUNG MAN'S MAR-RIAGE.

Borracho

[Address] 2-6-18 Ouhashi, Meguro-ku, Tokyo
[Telephone] 03-3465-4452
[Hours] 6:00 PM - 3:00 AM
[Closed] Mondays.
[Directions] A twelve-minute walk from the Komaba Toudai-mae Station on the Touou I-no-Kashira Line.
[Parking] None.

I-NO-KASHIRA LINE
KOMABA-TOUDAI-MAE STATION
McDONALD'S
WEST EXIT
LAWSON'S
KOMABA POST OFFICE
SUNKUS CONVENIENCE STORE
TOKYO ENGINEERING HIGH SCHOOL
MATSUBASHI 2
TO SHIBUYA
MATSUMISAKA KAMI
MATSUMISAKA
KOMABA
NATIONAL SOCIAL INSURANCE CHUUOU HALL
KOMABA CITY HIGH SCHOOL
7-11
BAKERY
HERE!

FUMI YOSHINAGA'S COMMENTS

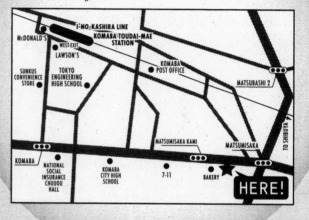

THE ATMOSPHERE IS SO WELCOMING THAT ONCE YOU SIT DOWN, YOU STAY THERE FOR HOURS WITHOUT REALIZING IT... IN WINTER, THEY ADD RAW OYSTERS TO THE MENU, WHICH I RECOMMEND TOO. IT'S PROBABLY EASIER FOR PEOPLE TO GET THERE BY CAR THAN TRAIN. BUDGET FOR ¥3,000, OR IF YOU WANT TO BE FILLED TO THE GILLS, ABOUT ¥5,000.

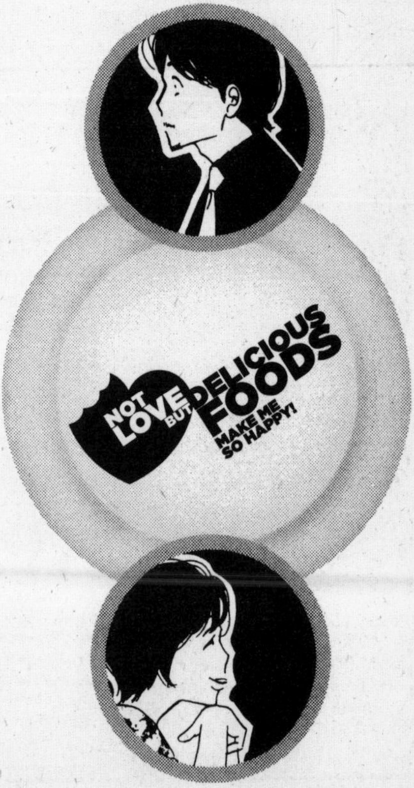
NOT LOVE BUT DELICIOUS FOODS
MAKE ME SO HAPPY!

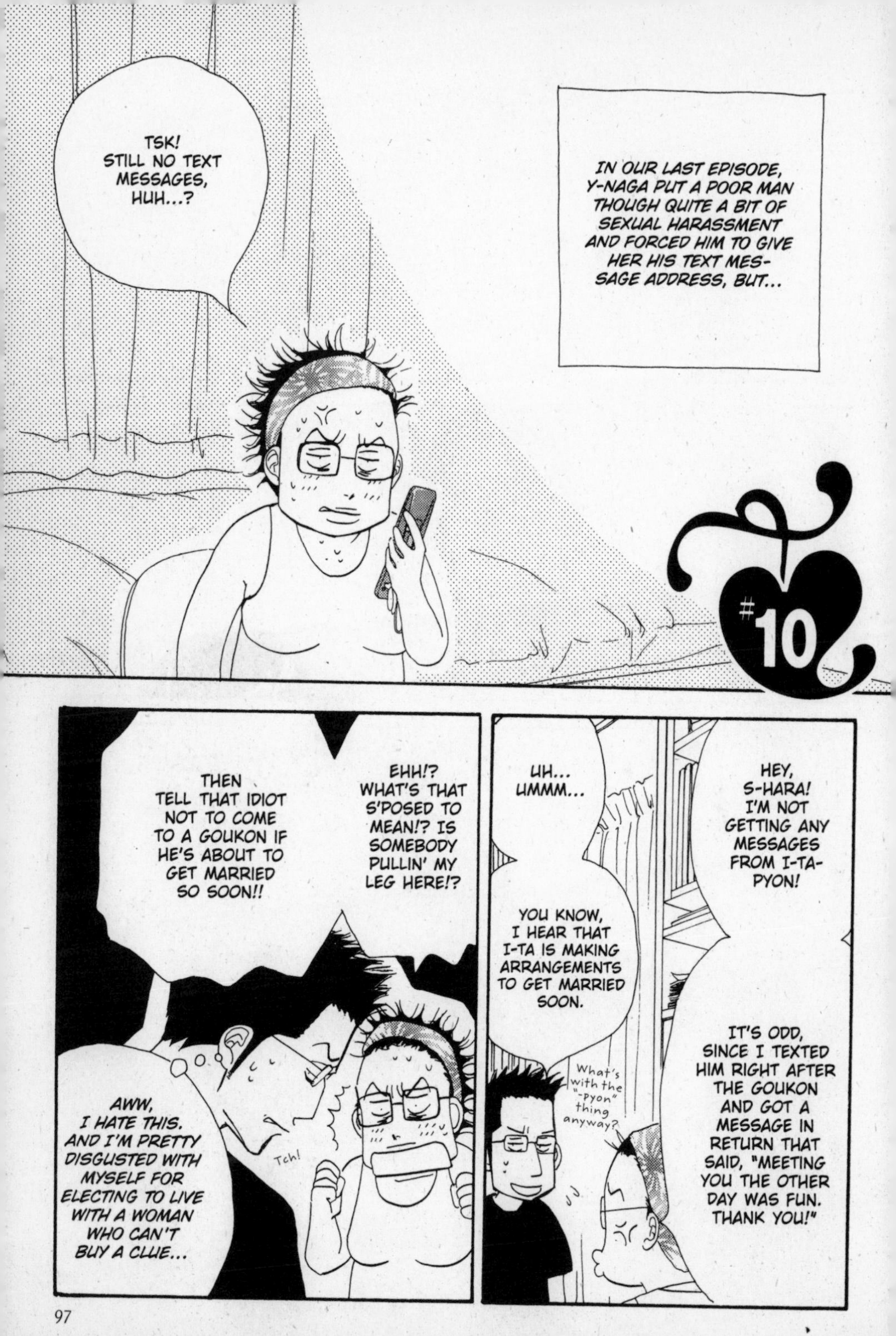
IN OUR LAST EPISODE, Y-NAGA PUT A POOR MAN THOUGH QUITE A BIT OF SEXUAL HARASSMENT AND FORCED HIM TO GIVE HER HIS TEXT MES-SAGE ADDRESS, BUT...
TSK! STILL NO TEXT MESSAGES, HUH...?
#10
HEY, S-HARA! I'M NOT GETTING ANY MESSAGES FROM I-TA-PYON!
IT'S ODD, SINCE I TEXTED HIM RIGHT AFTER THE GOUKON AND GOT A MESSAGE IN RETURN THAT SAID, "MEETING YOU THE OTHER DAY WAS FUN. THANK YOU!"
UH... UMMM...
YOU KNOW, I HEAR THAT I-TA IS MAKING ARRANGEMENTS TO GET MARRIED SOON.
What's with the "-pyon" thing anyway?
EHH!? WHAT'S THAT S'POSED TO MEAN!? IS SOMEBODY PULLIN' MY LEG HERE!?
THEN TELL THAT IDIOT NOT TO COME TO A GOUKON IF HE'S ABOUT TO GET MARRIED SO SOON!!
Tch!
AWW, I HATE THIS. AND I'M PRETTY DISGUSTED WITH MYSELF FOR ELECTING TO LIVE WITH A WOMAN WHO CAN'T BUY A CLUE...

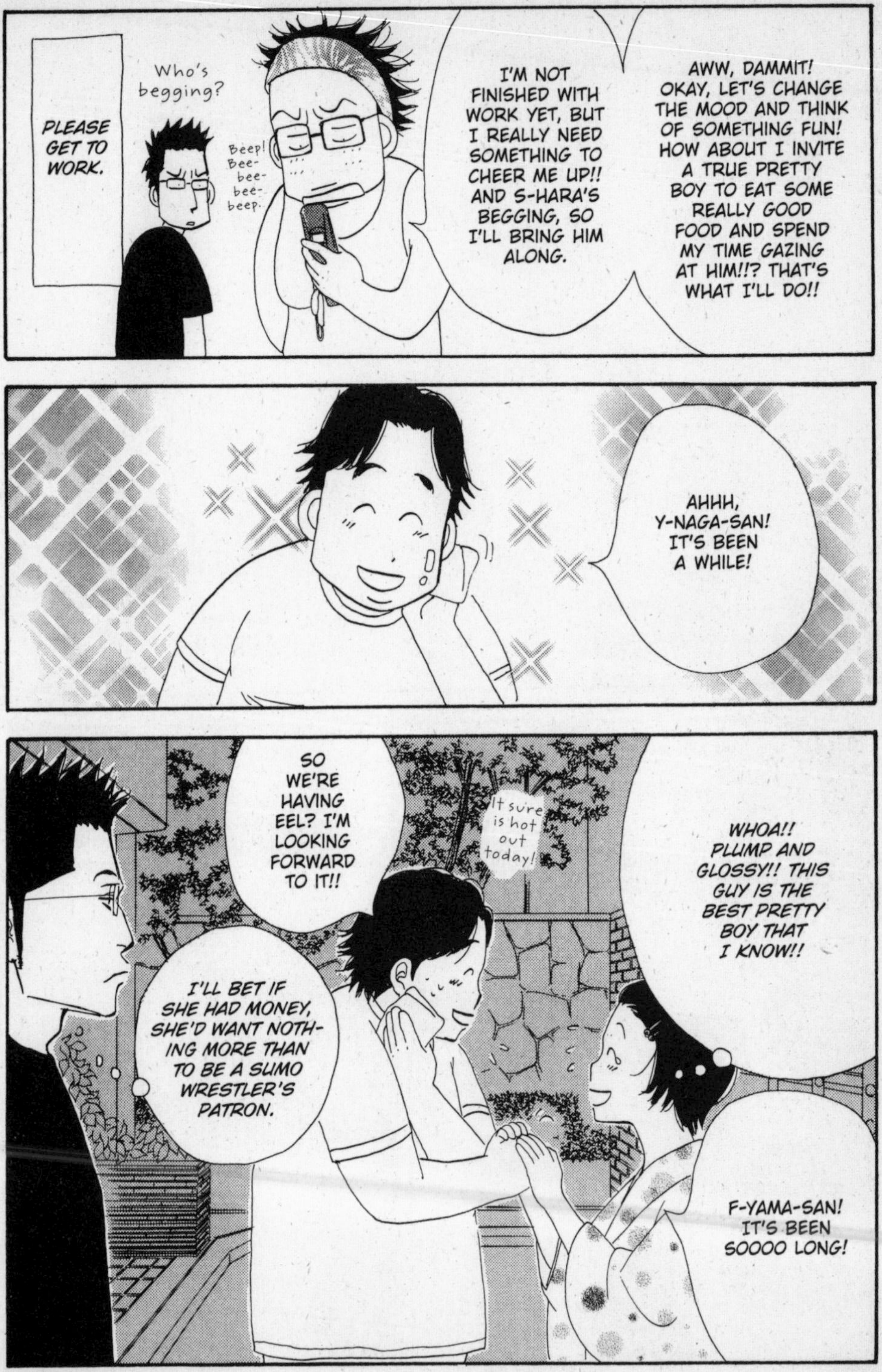
AWW, DAMMIT! OKAY, LET'S CHANGE THE MOOD AND THINK OF SOMETHING FUN! HOW ABOUT I INVITE A TRUE PRETTY BOY TO EAT SOME REALLY GOOD FOOD AND SPEND MY TIME GAZING AT HIM!!? THAT'S WHAT I'LL DO!!
I'M NOT FINISHED WITH WORK YET, BUT I REALLY NEED SOMETHING TO CHEER ME UP!! AND S-HARA'S BEGGING, SO I'LL BRING HIM ALONG.
Beep! Bee-bee-bee-beep.
Who's begging?
PLEASE GET TO WORK.
AHHH, Y-NAGA-SAN! IT'S BEEN A WHILE!
WHOA!! PLUMP AND GLOSSY!! THIS GUY IS THE BEST PRETTY BOY THAT I KNOW!!
It sure is hot out today!
SO WE'RE HAVING EEL? I'M LOOKING FORWARD TO IT!!
F-YAMA-SAN! IT'S BEEN SOOOO LONG!
I'LL BET IF SHE HAD MONEY, SHE'D WANT NOTHING MORE THAN TO BE A SUMO WRESTLER'S PATRON.

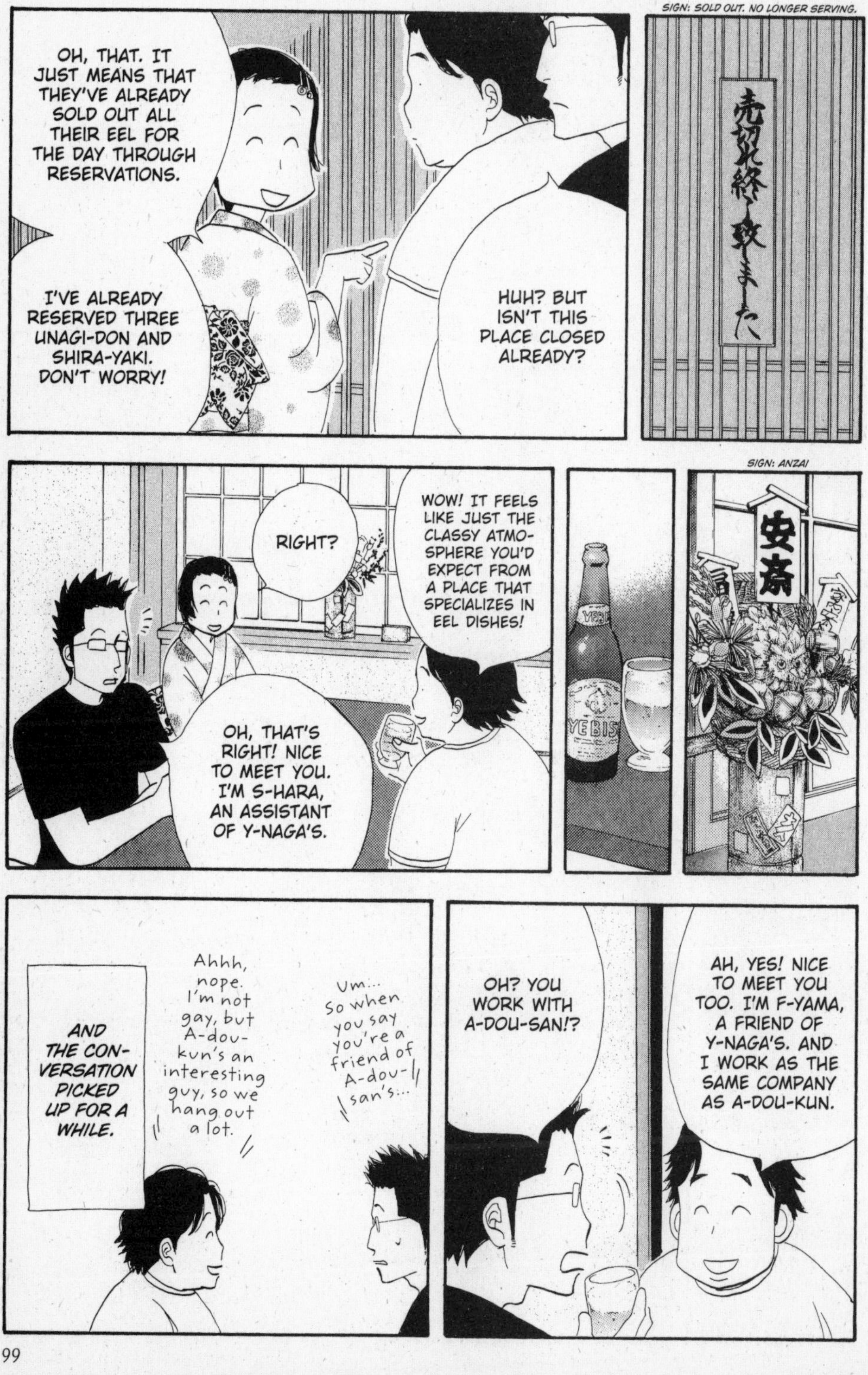
SIGN: SOLD OUT. NO LONGER SERVING.
売切れ終了致しました
HUH? BUT ISN'T THIS PLACE CLOSED ALREADY?
OH, THAT. IT JUST MEANS THAT THEY'VE ALREADY SOLD OUT ALL THEIR EEL FOR THE DAY THROUGH RESERVATIONS.
I'VE ALREADY RESERVED THREE UNAGI-DON AND SHIRA-YAKI. DON'T WORRY!
SIGN: ANZAI
安斎
YEBISU
WOW! IT FEELS LIKE JUST THE CLASSY ATMOSPHERE YOU'D EXPECT FROM A PLACE THAT SPECIALIZES IN EEL DISHES!
RIGHT?
OH, THAT'S RIGHT! NICE TO MEET YOU. I'M S-HARA, AN ASSISTANT OF Y-NAGA'S.
AH, YES! NICE TO MEET YOU TOO. I'M F-YAMA, A FRIEND OF Y-NAGA'S. AND I WORK AS THE SAME COMPANY AS A-DOU-KUN.
OH? YOU WORK WITH A-DOU-SAN!?
Um... So when you say you're a friend of A-dou-san's...
Ahhh, nope. I'm not gay, but A-dou-kun's an interesting guy, so we hang out a lot.
AND THE CONVERSATION PICKED UP FOR A WHILE.

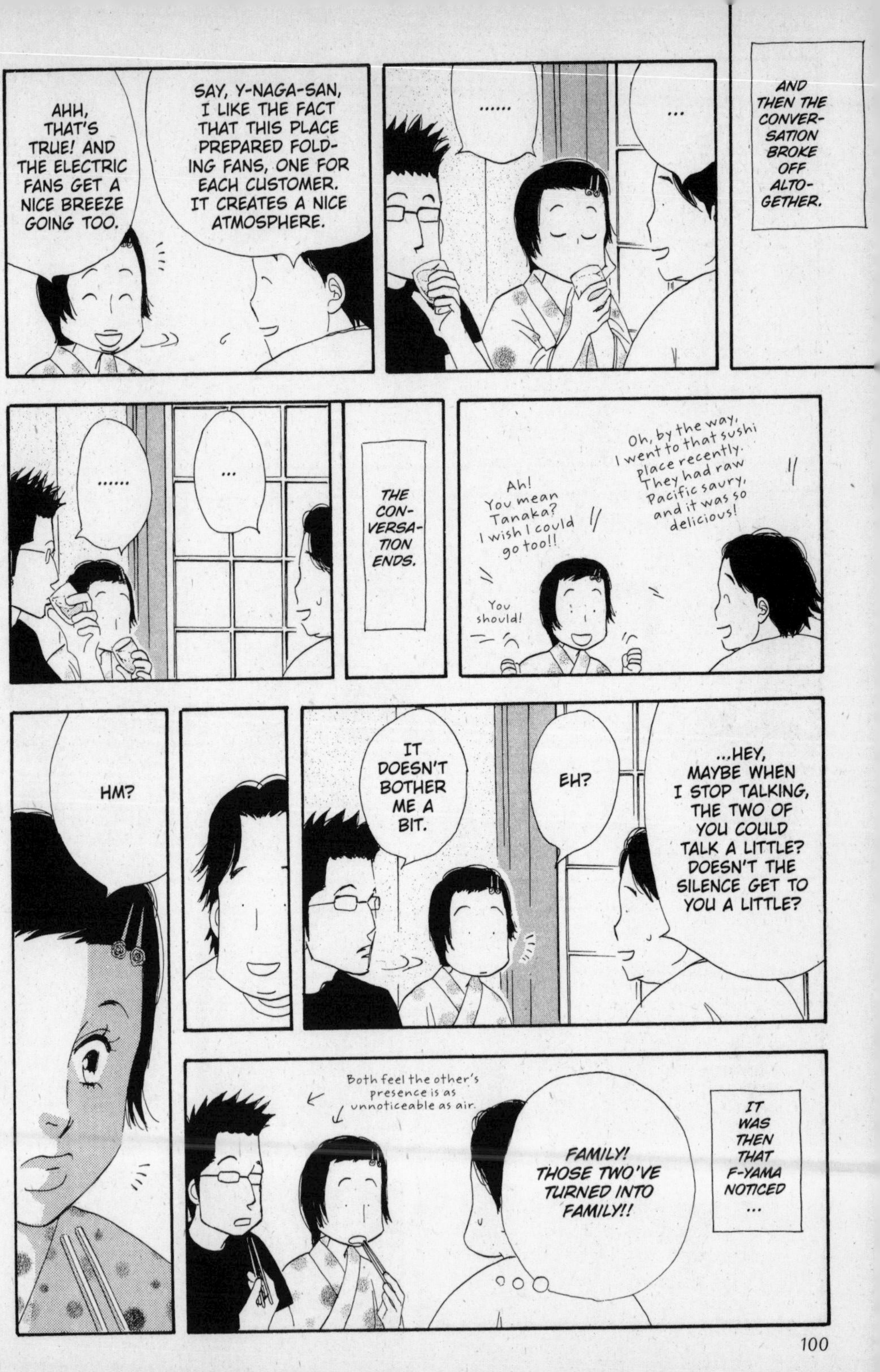
AND THEN THE CONVERSATION BROKE OFF ALTOGETHER.
...
......
SAY, Y-NAGA-SAN, I LIKE THE FACT THAT THIS PLACE PREPARED FOLDING FANS, ONE FOR EACH CUSTOMER. IT CREATES A NICE ATMOSPHERE.
AHH, THAT'S TRUE! AND THE ELECTRIC FANS GET A NICE BREEZE GOING TOO.
Oh, by the way, I went to that sushi place recently. They had raw Pacific saury, and it was so delicious!
Ah! You mean Tanaka? I wish I could go too!!
You should!
THE CONVERSATION ENDS.
...
......
...HEY, MAYBE WHEN I STOP TALKING, THE TWO OF YOU COULD TALK A LITTLE? DOESN'T THE SILENCE GET TO YOU A LITTLE?
EH?
IT DOESN'T BOTHER ME A BIT.
IT WAS THEN THAT F-YAMA NOTICED ...
FAMILY! THOSE TWO'VE TURNED INTO FAMILY!!
Both feel the other's presence is as unnoticeable as air.
HM?

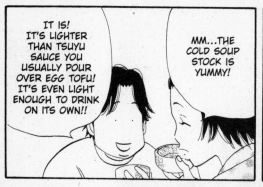

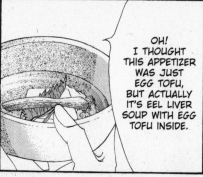

OH! I THOUGHT THIS APPETIZER WAS JUST EGG TOFU, BUT ACTUALLY IT'S EEL LIVER SOUP WITH EGG TOFU INSIDE.
MM...THE COLD SOUP STOCK IS YUMMY!
IT IS! IT'S LIGHTER THAN TSUYU SAUCE YOU USUALLY POUR OVER EGG TOFU! IT'S EVEN LIGHT ENOUGH TO DRINK ON ITS OWN!!
TON! (THUNK!)
とん!
HERE YOU GO! YOUR SHIRA-YAKI.
WOW!! AND IT HAS THE LIVER ON TOP! IT LOOKS DELICIOUS!
DISSOLVE SOME WASABI IN THE SWEET SOY SAUCE DIP. THEN PLOP IT IN AND TRY OUT THE TASTE!
USUALLY SHIRA-YAKI MEANS THAT THE EEL IS STEAMED, THEN GRILLED WITHOUT SAUCE, BUT...
WHOA! I LOVE IT WHEN IT LEAVES OILS FLOATING IN THE SOY SAUCE!!
chlip
Mwahh!

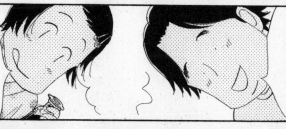

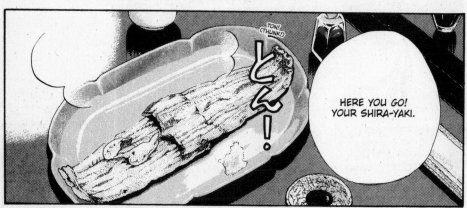

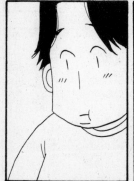

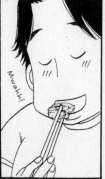

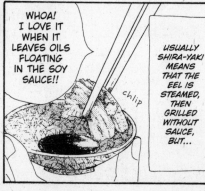

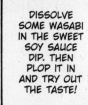

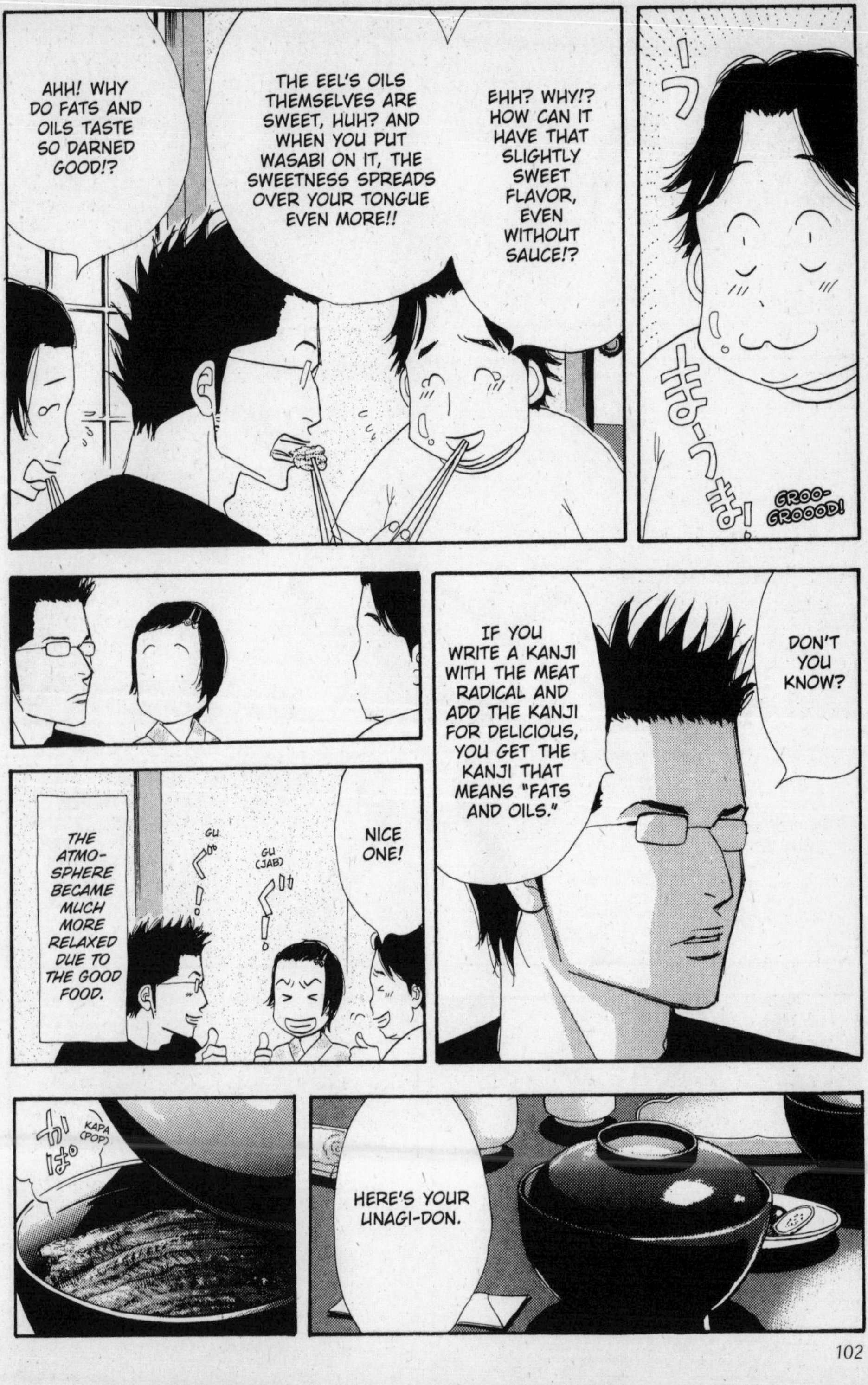
GROO-GROOOD!
EHH? WHY!? HOW CAN IT HAVE THAT SLIGHTLY SWEET FLAVOR, EVEN WITHOUT SAUCE!?
THE EEL'S OILS THEMSELVES ARE SWEET, HUH? AND WHEN YOU PUT WASABI ON IT, THE SWEETNESS SPREADS OVER YOUR TONGUE EVEN MORE!!
AHH! WHY DO FATS AND OILS TASTE SO DARNED GOOD!?
DON'T YOU KNOW?
IF YOU WRITE A KANJI WITH THE MEAT RADICAL AND ADD THE KANJI FOR DELICIOUS, YOU GET THE KANJI THAT MEANS "FATS AND OILS."
NICE ONE!
GU
GU (JAB)
THE ATMOSPHERE BECAME MUCH MORE RELAXED DUE TO THE GOOD FOOD.
HERE'S YOUR UNAGI-DON.
KAPA (POP)

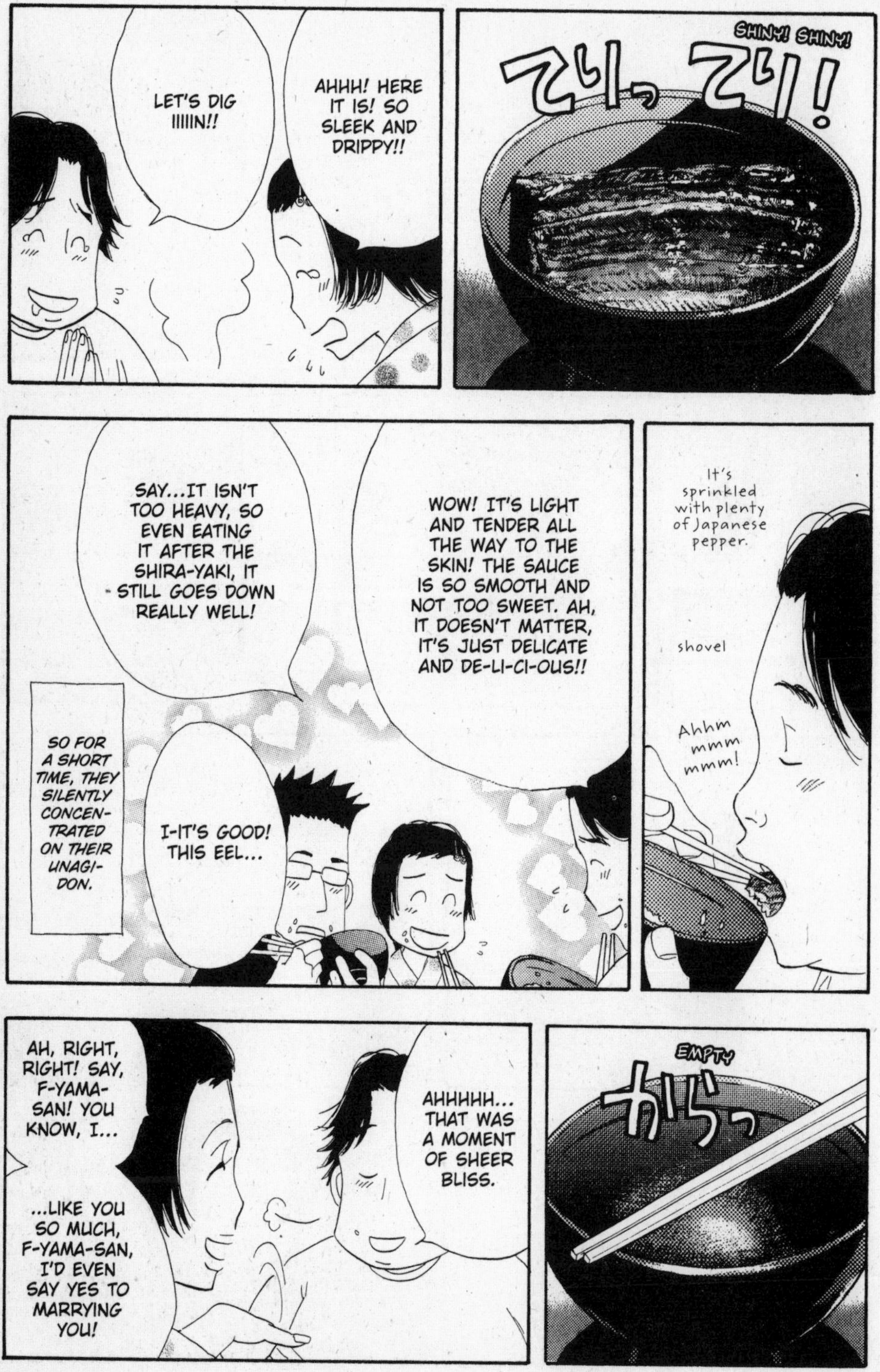
SHINY! SHINY!
てりっ てりっ!
AHHH! HERE IT IS! SO SLEEK AND DRIPPY!!
LET'S DIG IIIIIN!!
It's sprinkled with plenty of Japanese pepper.
shovel
Ahhm mmm mmm!
WOW! IT'S LIGHT AND TENDER ALL THE WAY TO THE SKIN! THE SAUCE IS SO SMOOTH AND NOT TOO SWEET. AH, IT DOESN'T MATTER, IT'S JUST DELICATE AND DE-LI-CI-OUS!!
SAY...IT ISN'T TOO HEAVY, SO EVEN EATING IT AFTER THE SHIRA-YAKI, IT STILL GOES DOWN REALLY WELL!
I-IT'S GOOD! THIS EEL...
SO FOR A SHORT TIME, THEY SILENTLY CONCENTRATED ON THEIR UNAGI-DON.
EMPTY
からっ
AHHHHH... THAT WAS A MOMENT OF SHEER BLISS.
AH, RIGHT, RIGHT! SAY, F-YAMA-SAN! YOU KNOW, I...
...LIKE YOU SO MUCH, F-YAMA-SAN, I'D EVEN SAY YES TO MARRYING YOU!

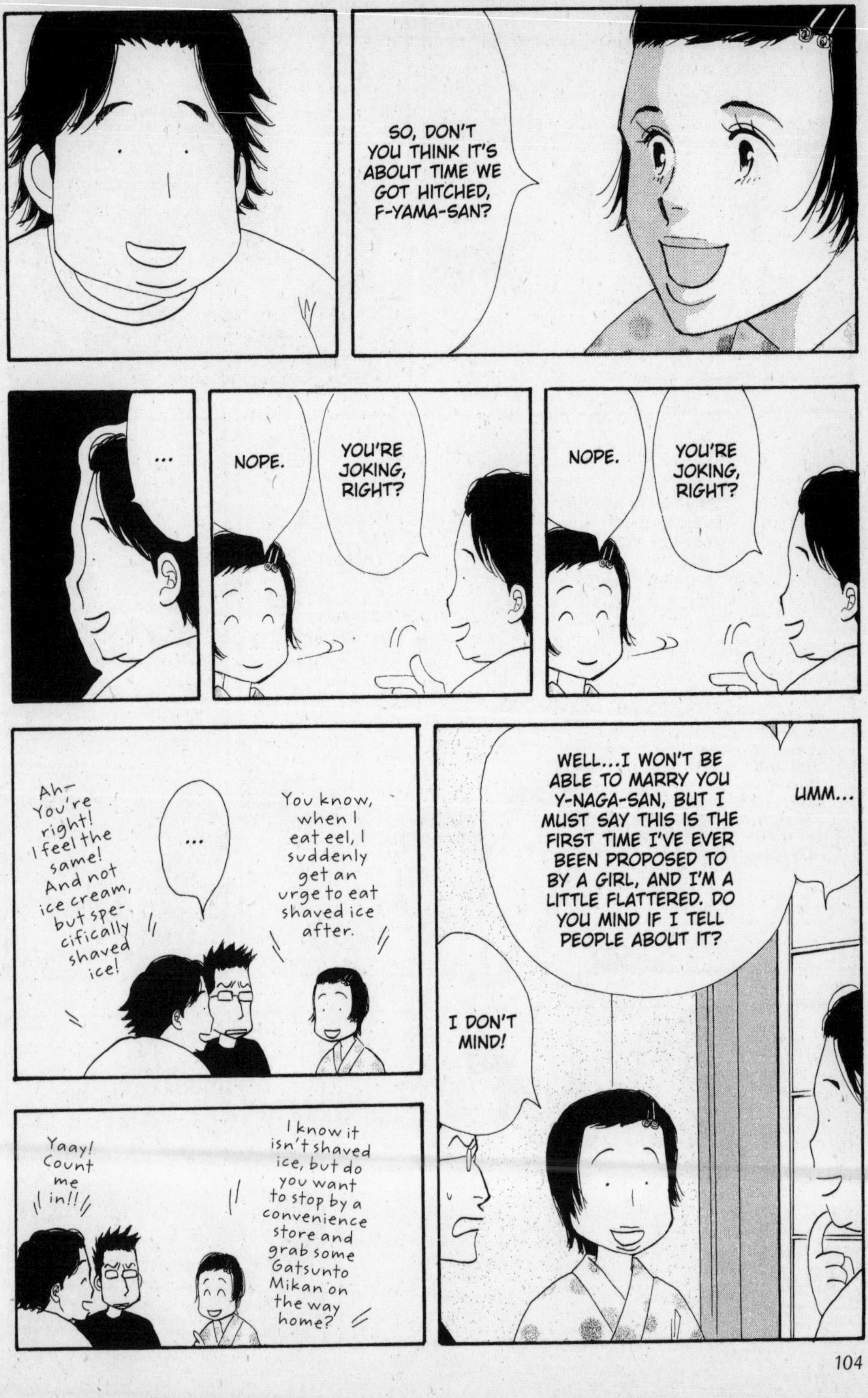

SO, DON'T YOU THINK IT'S ABOUT TIME WE GOT HITCHED, F-YAMA-SAN?
YOU'RE JOKING, RIGHT?
NOPE.
YOU'RE JOKING, RIGHT?
NOPE.
...
UMM...
WELL...I WON'T BE ABLE TO MARRY YOU Y-NAGA-SAN, BUT I MUST SAY THIS IS THE FIRST TIME I'VE EVER BEEN PROPOSED TO BY A GIRL, AND I'M A LITTLE FLATTERED. DO YOU MIND IF I TELL PEOPLE ABOUT IT?
I DON'T MIND!
You know, when I eat eel, I suddenly get an urge to eat shaved ice after.
...
Ah— You're right! I feel the same! And not ice cream, but specifically shaved ice!
I know it isn't shaved ice, but do you want to stop by a convenience store and grab some Gatsunto Mikan on the way home?
Yaay! Count me in!!

ANZAI

[Address]
4-12-16 Ogikubo,
Suginami-ku, Tokyo
[Telephone]
03-3392-2059
[Hours]
11:30 AM - O.S 1:40 PM
5:00 PM - Until Sold Out.
[Closed]
Tuesdays.
[Directions]
A five-minute walk from
the Ogikubo Station on the
JR Chuuou line.
[Parking]
None. (There is paid
parking nearby.)

JR OGIKUBO STATION | TO SHINJUKU

SOUTH EXIT | I-NO-KASHIRA LINE
OGIKUBO STATION

TOKYO MITSUBISHI GINKO BANK
TOYOSAKA PLAZA
SEIBU SHINYOU GINKO BANK
NTT
FLORIST
P
OGIKUBO DENWAKYOKU MAE
SUGINAMI INSURANCE OFFICE
MINAMIGUCHI SHOPPING STREET
OGIKUBO HIGH SCHOOL

HERE!

FUMI YOSHINAGA'S COMMENTS

UNAGI-DON, ¥2,600...SHIRA-YAKI, ¥3,000.
THE SHIRA-YAKI WAS JUST DELICIOUS!
WHEN YOU DECIDE TO GO, YOU TELEPHONE
AHEAD WITH BOTH YOUR RESERVATIONS AND
YOUR FOOD ORDER. THE ATMOSPHERE IS JUST
WHAT YOU EXPECT FROM A JAPANESE EEL
RESTAURANT. A SNUG AND COZY PLACE.

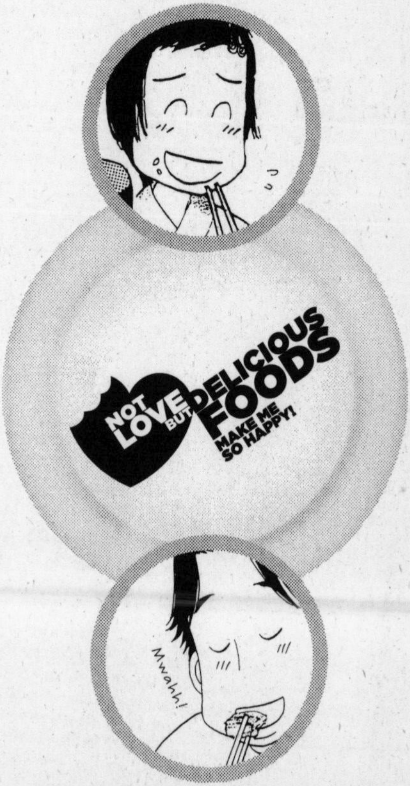
NOT LOVE BUT DELICIOUS FOODS MAKE ME SO HAPPY!
Mwahh!

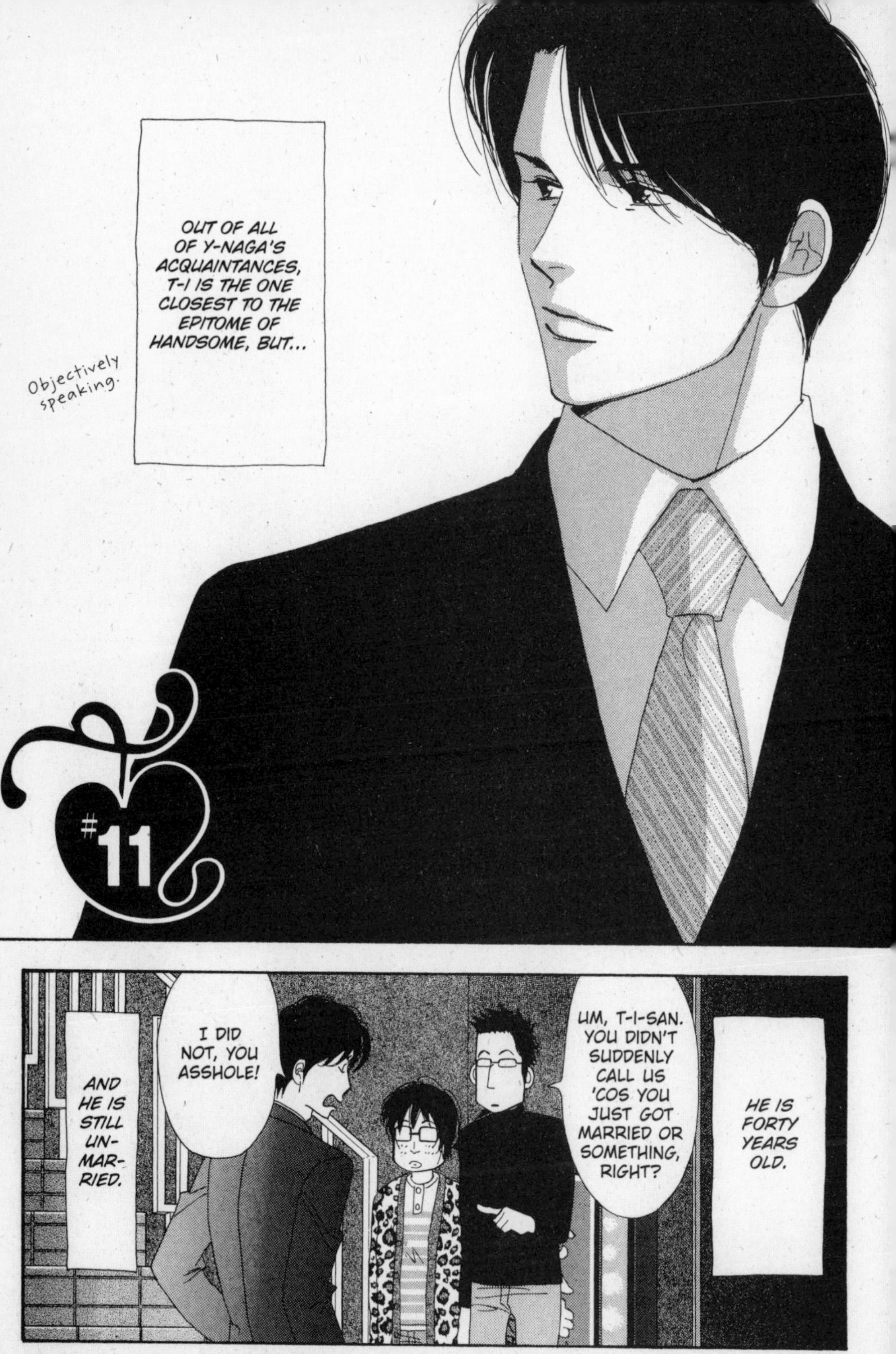
OUT OF ALL OF Y-NAGA'S ACQUAINTANCES, T-I IS THE ONE CLOSEST TO THE EPITOME OF HANDSOME, BUT...
Objectively speaking.
#11
HE IS FORTY YEARS OLD.
UM, T-I-SAN. YOU DIDN'T SUDDENLY CALL US 'COS YOU JUST GOT MARRIED OR SOMETHING, RIGHT?
I DID NOT, YOU ASSHOLE!
AND HE IS STILL UN-MAR-RIED.

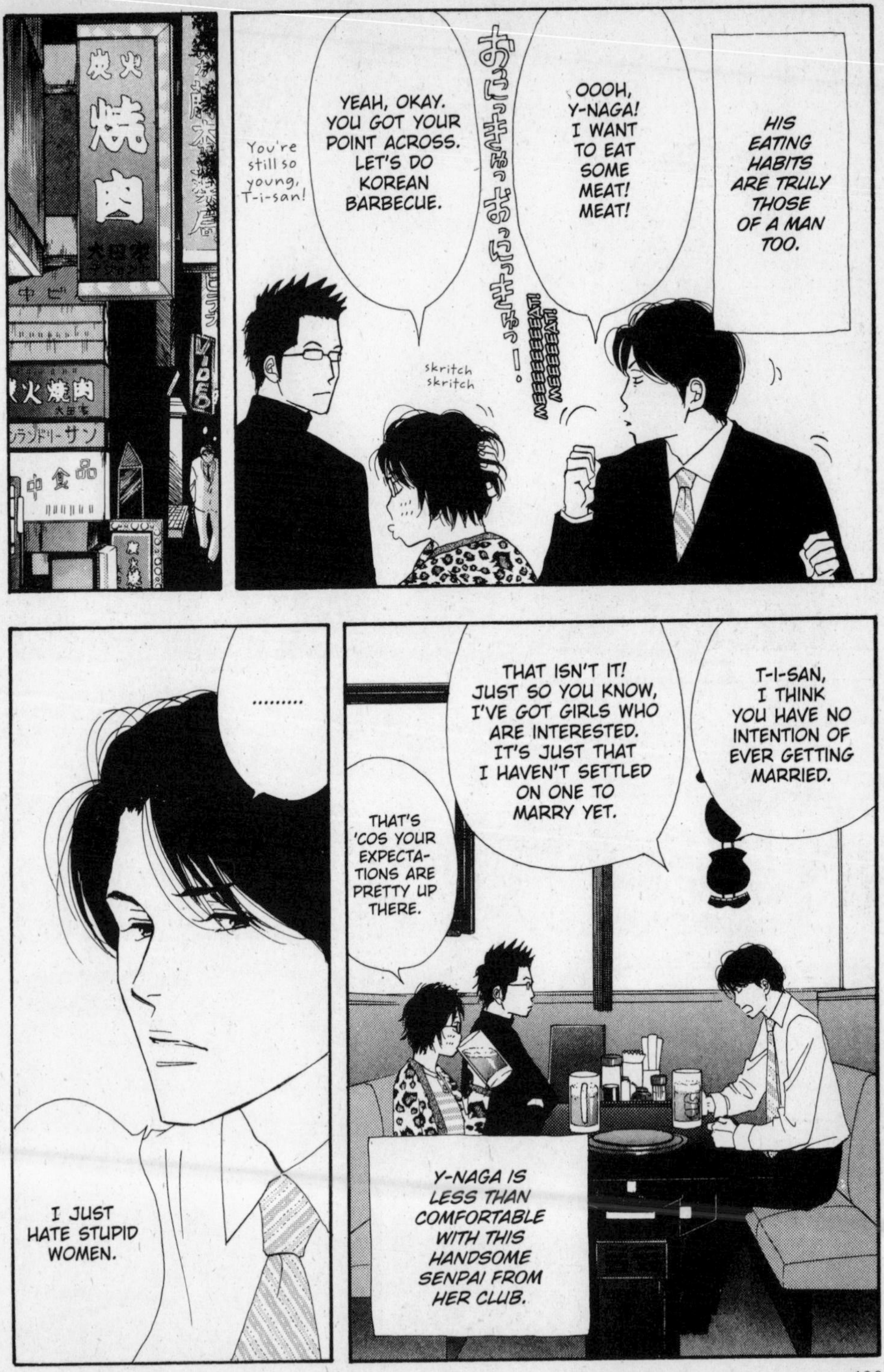
HIS EATING HABITS ARE TRULY THOSE OF A MAN TOO.
OOOH, Y-NAGA! I WANT TO EAT SOME MEAT! MEAT!
おにっきゅっおにっきゅっー。
MEEEEEEEEAT! MEEEEEEEAT!
skritch skritch
YEAH, OKAY. YOU GOT YOUR POINT ACROSS. LET'S DO KOREAN BARBECUE.
You're still so young, T-i-san!
炭火焼肉
VIDEO
中食品
T-I-SAN, I THINK YOU HAVE NO INTENTION OF EVER GETTING MARRIED.
THAT ISN'T IT! JUST SO YOU KNOW, I'VE GOT GIRLS WHO ARE INTERESTED. IT'S JUST THAT I HAVEN'T SETTLED ON ONE TO MARRY YET.
THAT'S 'COS YOUR EXPECTATIONS ARE PRETTY UP THERE.
Y-NAGA IS LESS THAN COMFORTABLE WITH THIS HANDSOME SENPAI FROM HER CLUB.
....
I JUST HATE STUPID WOMEN.

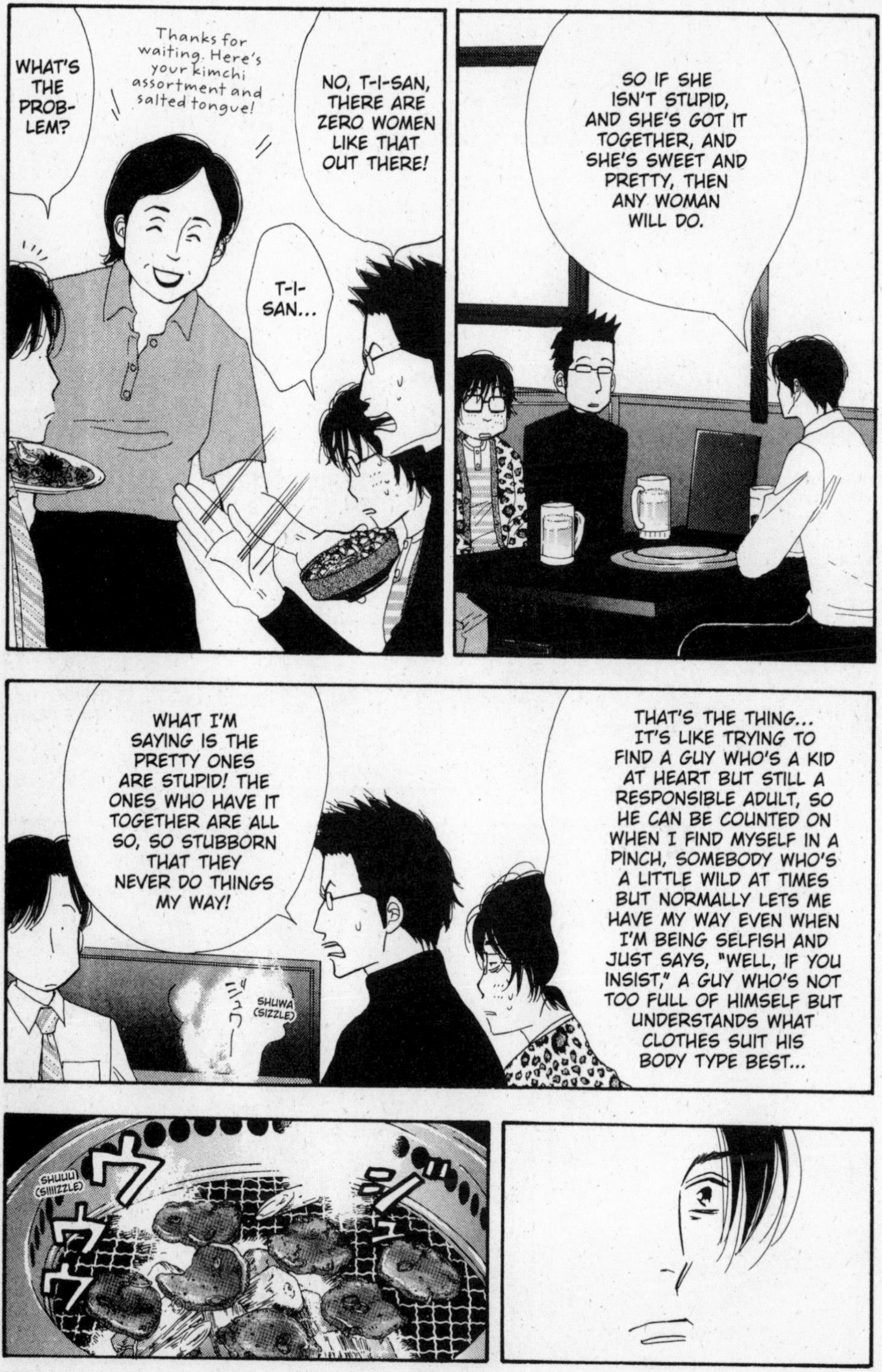
SO IF SHE ISN'T STUPID, AND SHE'S GOT IT TOGETHER, AND SHE'S SWEET AND PRETTY, THEN ANY WOMAN WILL DO.
NO, T-I-SAN, THERE ARE ZERO WOMEN LIKE THAT OUT THERE!
Thanks for waiting. Here's your kimchi assortment and salted tongue!
WHAT'S THE PROB-LEM?
T-I-SAN...
THAT'S THE THING... IT'S LIKE TRYING TO FIND A GUY WHO'S A KID AT HEART BUT STILL A RESPONSIBLE ADULT, SO HE CAN BE COUNTED ON WHEN I FIND MYSELF IN A PINCH, SOMEBODY WHO'S A LITTLE WILD AT TIMES BUT NORMALLY LETS ME HAVE MY WAY EVEN WHEN I'M BEING SELFISH AND JUST SAYS, "WELL, IF YOU INSIST," A GUY WHO'S NOT TOO FULL OF HIMSELF BUT UNDERSTANDS WHAT CLOTHES SUIT HIS BODY TYPE BEST...
WHAT I'M SAYING IS THE PRETTY ONES ARE STUPID! THE ONES WHO HAVE IT TOGETHER ARE ALL SO, SO STUBBORN THAT THEY NEVER DO THINGS MY WAY!
SHUWA (SIZZLE)
SHUUU (SIIIIZZLE)

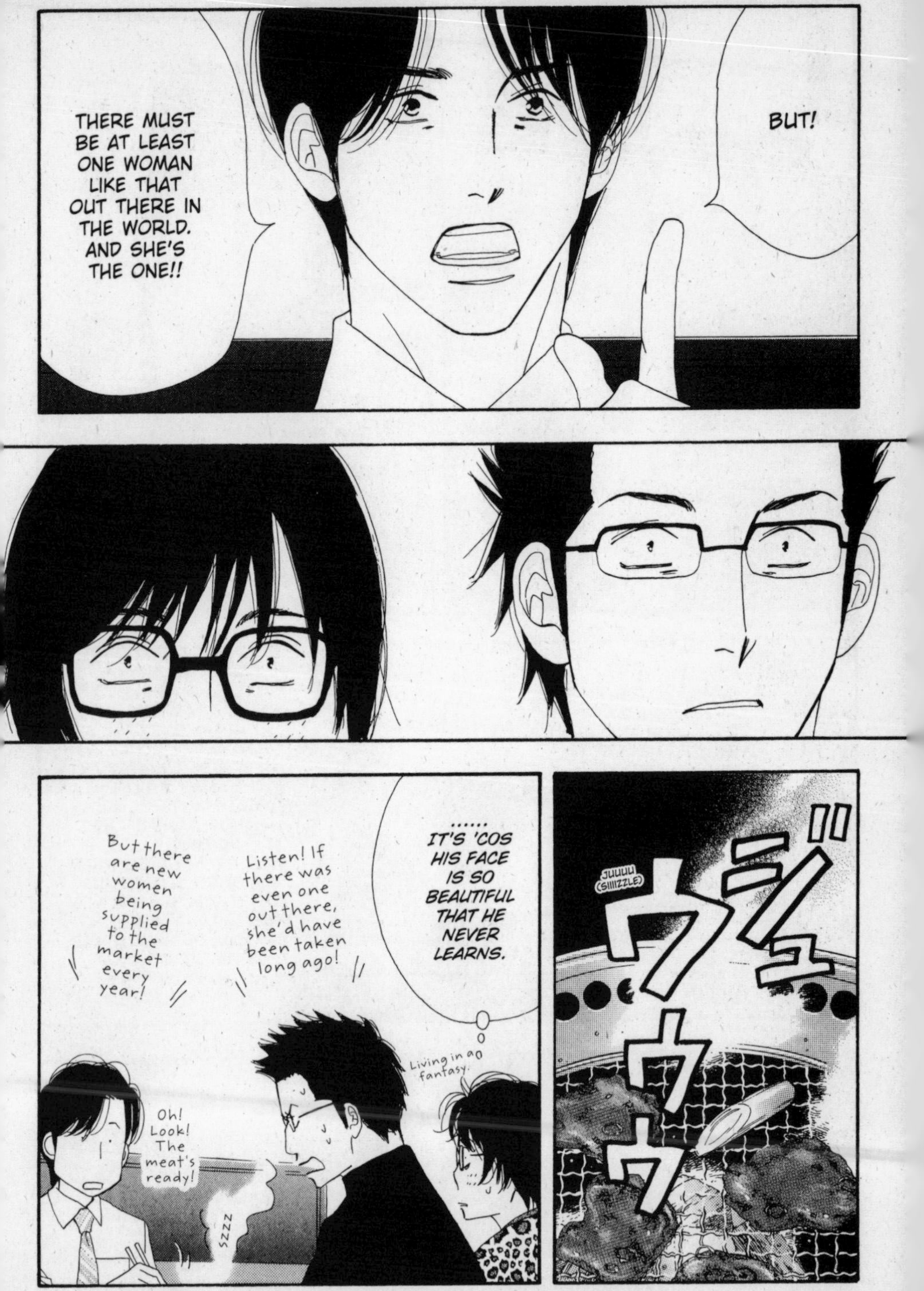
BUT!
THERE MUST BE AT LEAST ONE WOMAN LIKE THAT OUT THERE IN THE WORLD. AND SHE'S THE ONE!!
JUUUU (SIIIIZZLE)
ジュウウウウ
...... IT'S 'COS HIS FACE IS SO BEAUTIFUL THAT HE NEVER LEARNS.
Listen! If there was even one out there, she'd have been taken long ago!
But there are new women being supplied to the market every year!
Living in a fantasy.
Oh! Look! The meat's ready!
SZZZ

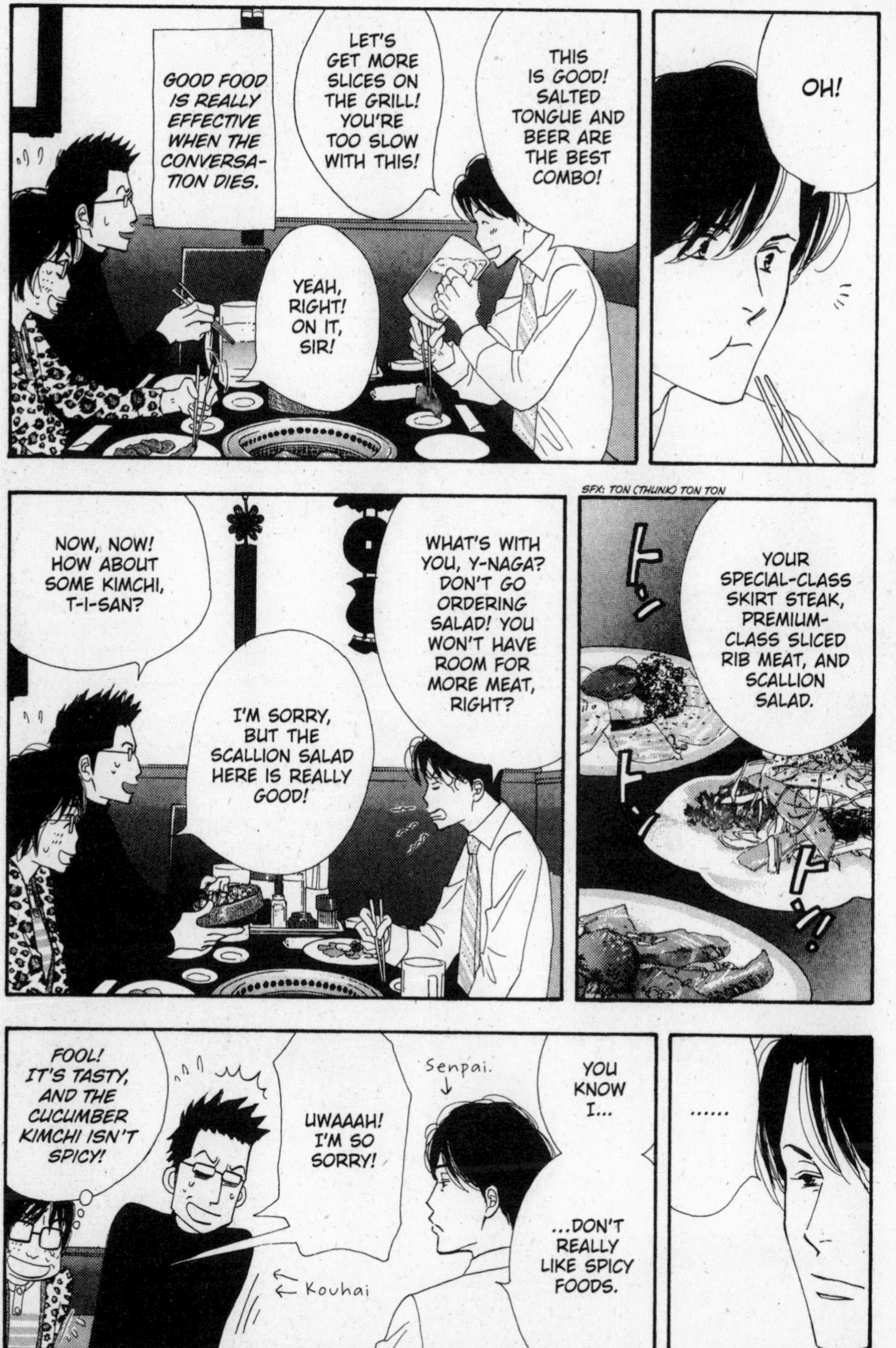
OH!
THIS IS GOOD! SALTED TONGUE AND BEER ARE THE BEST COMBO!
LET'S GET MORE SLICES ON THE GRILL! YOU'RE TOO SLOW WITH THIS!
GOOD FOOD IS REALLY EFFECTIVE WHEN THE CONVERSATION DIES.
YEAH, RIGHT! ON IT, SIR!
SFX: TON (THUNK) TON TON
YOUR SPECIAL-CLASS SKIRT STEAK, PREMIUM-CLASS SLICED RIB MEAT, AND SCALLION SALAD.
WHAT'S WITH YOU, Y-NAGA? DON'T GO ORDERING SALAD! YOU WON'T HAVE ROOM FOR MORE MEAT, RIGHT?
NOW, NOW! HOW ABOUT SOME KIMCHI, T-I-SAN?
I'M SORRY, BUT THE SCALLION SALAD HERE IS REALLY GOOD!
......
YOU KNOW I...
...DON'T REALLY LIKE SPICY FOODS.
Senpai.
UWAAAH! I'M SO SORRY!
FOOL! IT'S TASTY, AND THE CUCUMBER KIMCHI ISN'T SPICY!
Kouhai

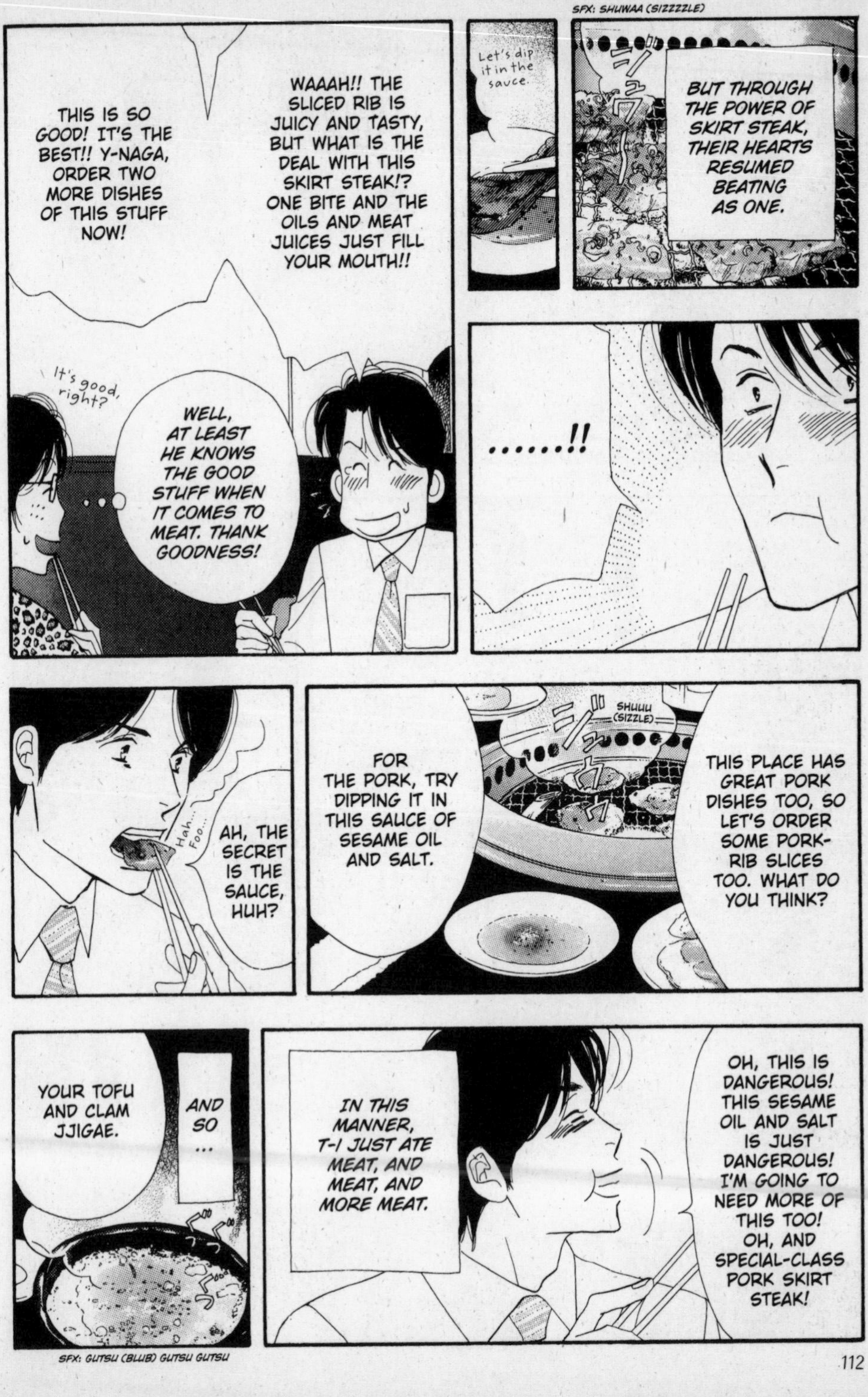
SFX: SHUWAA (SIZZZZLE)
BUT THROUGH THE POWER OF SKIRT STEAK, THEIR HEARTS RESUMED BEATING AS ONE.
Let's dip it in the sauce.
......!!
WAAAH!! THE SLICED RIB IS JUICY AND TASTY, BUT WHAT IS THE DEAL WITH THIS SKIRT STEAK!? ONE BITE AND THE OILS AND MEAT JUICES JUST FILL YOUR MOUTH!!
THIS IS SO GOOD! IT'S THE BEST!! Y-NAGA, ORDER TWO MORE DISHES OF THIS STUFF NOW!
WELL, AT LEAST HE KNOWS THE GOOD STUFF WHEN IT COMES TO MEAT. THANK GOODNESS!
It's good, right?
THIS PLACE HAS GREAT PORK DISHES TOO, SO LET'S ORDER SOME PORK-RIB SLICES TOO. WHAT DO YOU THINK?
SHUUU (SIZZLE)
FOR THE PORK, TRY DIPPING IT IN THIS SAUCE OF SESAME OIL AND SALT.
AH, THE SECRET IS THE SAUCE, HUH?
Hah... Foo...
OH, THIS IS DANGEROUS! THIS SESAME OIL AND SALT IS JUST DANGEROUS! I'M GOING TO NEED MORE OF THIS TOO! OH, AND SPECIAL-CLASS PORK SKIRT STEAK!
IN THIS MANNER, T-I JUST ATE MEAT, AND MEAT, AND MORE MEAT.
AND SO ...
YOUR TOFU AND CLAM JJIGAE.
SFX: GUTSU (BLUB) GUTSU GUTSU

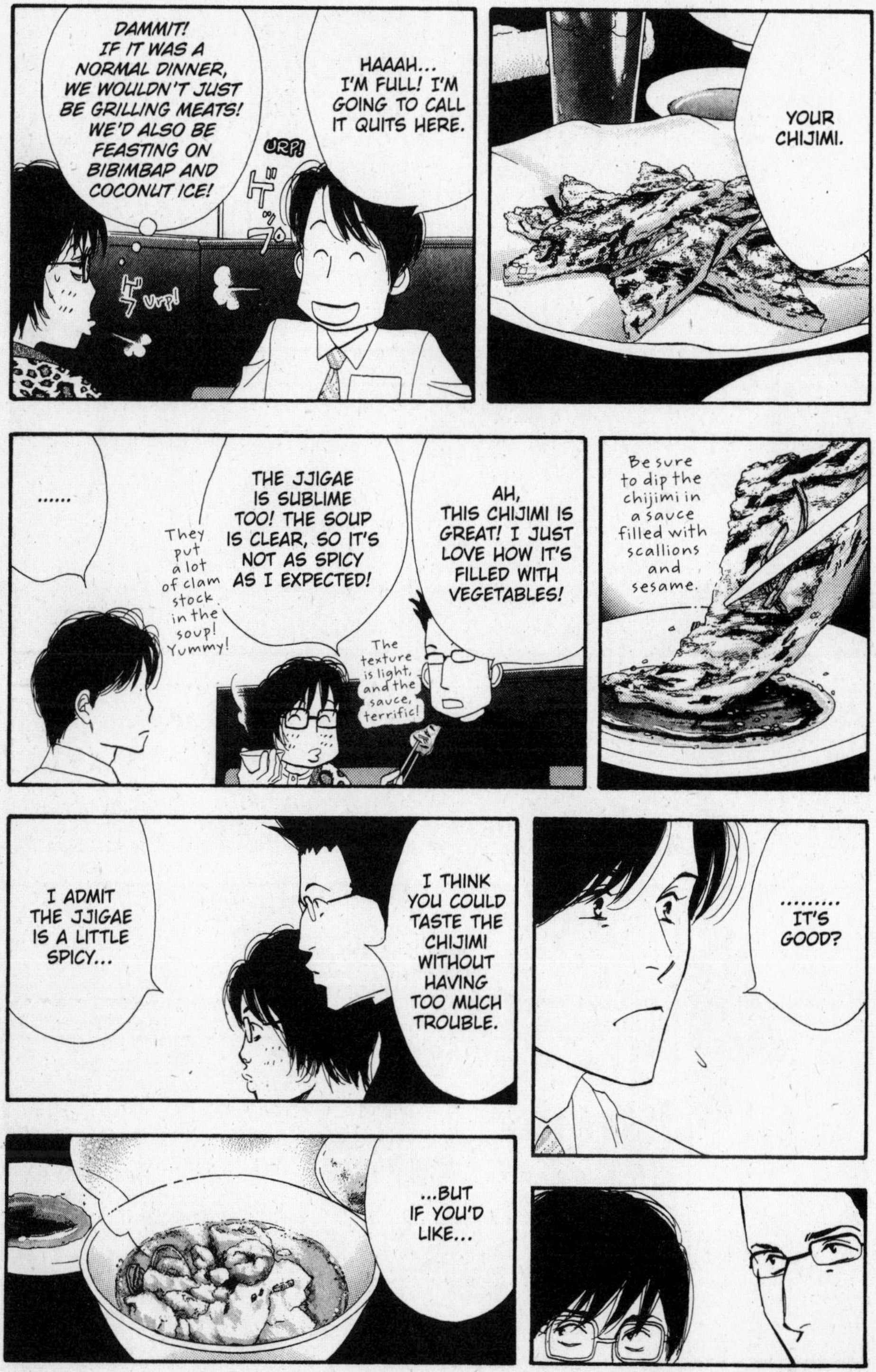
YOUR CHIJIMI.
HAAAH... I'M FULL! I'M GOING TO CALL IT QUITS HERE.
URP!
DAMMIT! IF IT WAS A NORMAL DINNER, WE WOULDN'T JUST BE GRILLING MEATS! WE'D ALSO BE FEASTING ON BIBIMBAP AND COCONUT ICE!
Urp!
Be sure to dip the chijimi in a sauce filled with scallions and sesame.
AH, THIS CHIJIMI IS GREAT! I JUST LOVE HOW IT'S FILLED WITH VEGETABLES!
The texture is light, and the sauce, terrific!
THE JJIGAE IS SUBLIME TOO! THE SOUP IS CLEAR, SO IT'S NOT AS SPICY AS I EXPECTED!
They put a lot of clam stock in the soup! Yummy!
......
.... IT'S GOOD?
I THINK YOU COULD TASTE THE CHIJIMI WITHOUT HAVING TOO MUCH TROUBLE.
I ADMIT THE JJIGAE IS A LITTLE SPICY...
...BUT IF YOU'D LIKE...

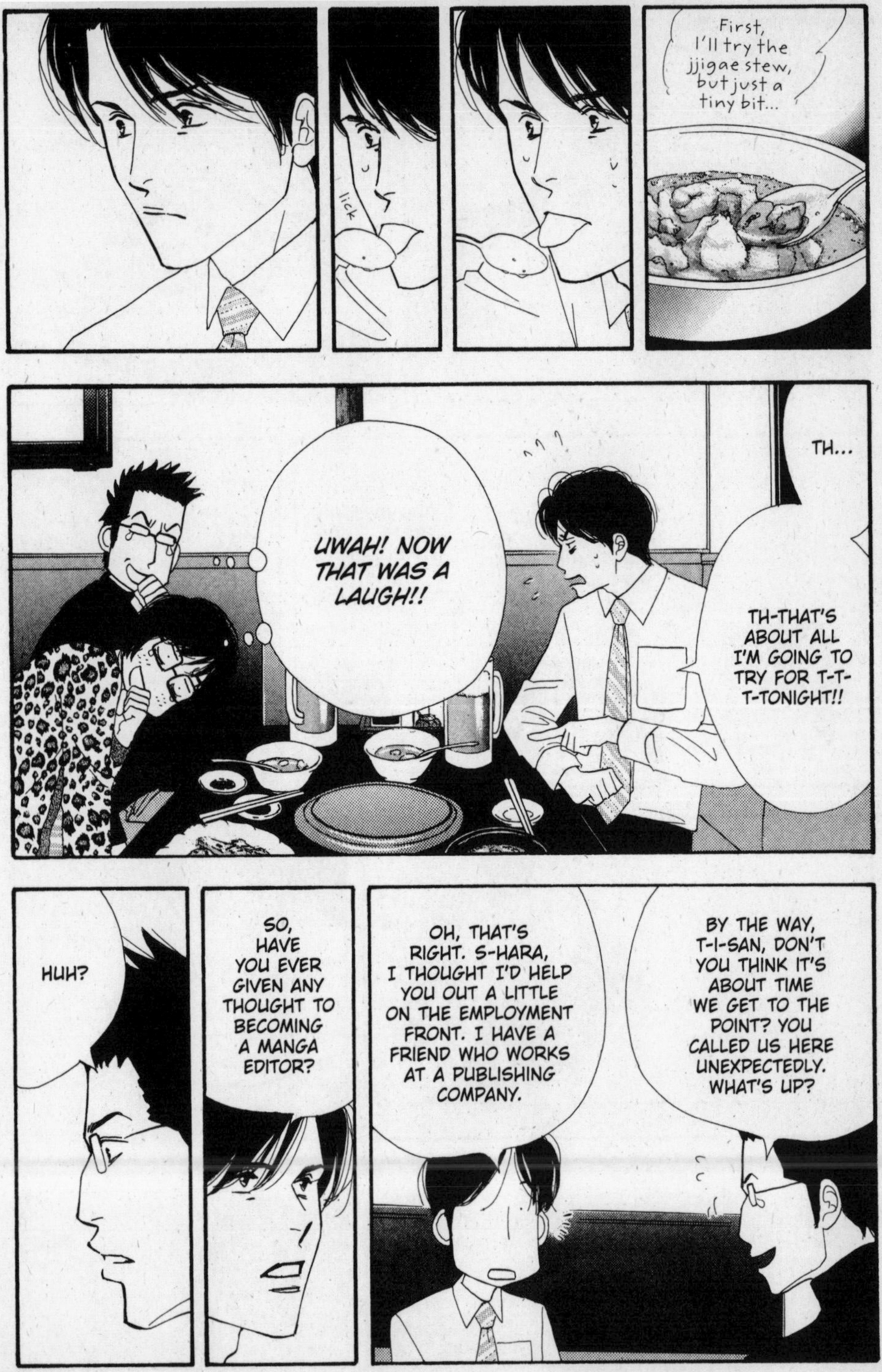
First, I'll try the jjigae stew, but just a tiny bit...
lick
TH...
TH-THAT'S ABOUT ALL I'M GOING TO TRY FOR T-T-T-TONIGHT!!
UWAH! NOW THAT WAS A LAUGH!!
BY THE WAY, T-I-SAN, DON'T YOU THINK IT'S ABOUT TIME WE GET TO THE POINT? YOU CALLED US HERE UNEXPECTEDLY. WHAT'S UP?
OH, THAT'S RIGHT. S-HARA, I THOUGHT I'D HELP YOU OUT A LITTLE ON THE EMPLOYMENT FRONT. I HAVE A FRIEND WHO WORKS AT A PUBLISHING COMPANY.
SO, HAVE YOU EVER GIVEN ANY THOUGHT TO BECOMING A MANGA EDITOR?
HUH?

Tejonya

[Address] Tanaka Building, 1F 5-39-10 Narita Higashi, Suginami-ku, Tokyo
[Telephone] 03-3220-5801
[Hours] Daily 5:00 PM - 2:00 AM, Sundays & holidays 5:00 PM - 1:00 AM
[Closed] Never.
[Directions] A five-minute walk from Minami Asagaya Station on the Maru-no-Uchi Line.
[Parking] None.

NAKASUGI DOORI ROAD
SUGINAMI FIRE DEPARTMENT
ESSO
MIZUHO GINKO BANK
SUGINAMI CITY HALL
TO SHIN KOUENJI
SUGINAMI FIRE DEPARTMENT
SUGINAMI BRANCH TAX OFFICE
MARU-NO-UCHI LINE MINAMI ASAGAYA STATION
OME KAIDO DOORI ROAD
HERE!

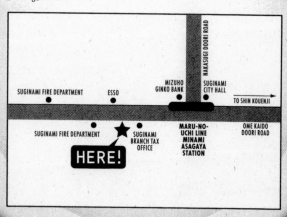

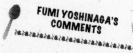

FUMI YOSHINAGA'S COMMENTS

THE BONED RIB SLICES ARE ALSO DELICIOUS. ALL THEIR MEAT IS JUST SUPERB. BUDGET SOMEWHERE PROBABLY AROUND ¥3,500 TO ¥7,000.

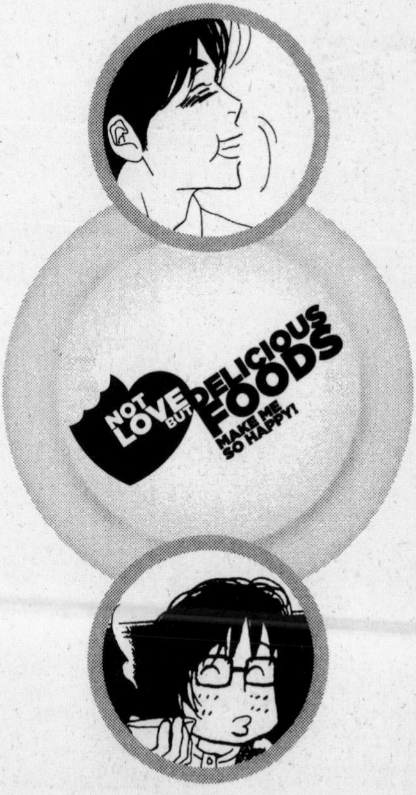
NOT LOVE BUT DELICIOUS FOODS
MAKE ME SO HAPPY!

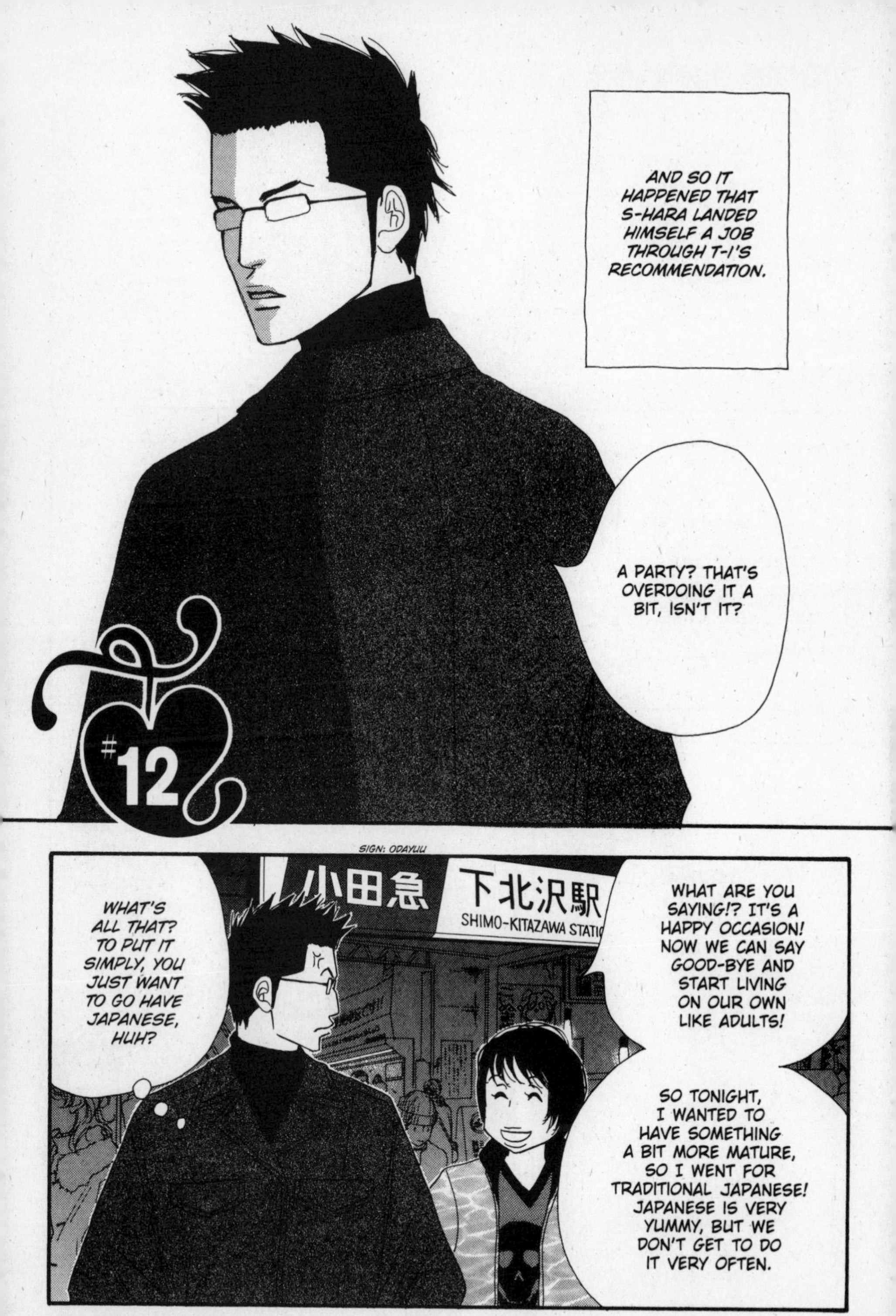
AND SO IT HAPPENED THAT S-HARA LANDED HIMSELF A JOB THROUGH T-I'S RECOMMENDATION.
A PARTY? THAT'S OVERDOING IT A BIT, ISN'T IT?
#12
SIGN: ODAYUU
下北沢駅
SHIMO-KITAZAWA STATIO
小田急
WHAT ARE YOU SAYING!? IT'S A HAPPY OCCASION! NOW WE CAN SAY GOOD-BYE AND START LIVING ON OUR OWN LIKE ADULTS!
SO TONIGHT, I WANTED TO HAVE SOMETHING A BIT MORE MATURE, SO I WENT FOR TRADITIONAL JAPANESE! JAPANESE IS VERY YUMMY, BUT WE DON'T GET TO DO IT VERY OFTEN.
WHAT'S ALL THAT? TO PUT IT SIMPLY, YOU JUST WANT TO GO HAVE JAPANESE, HUH?

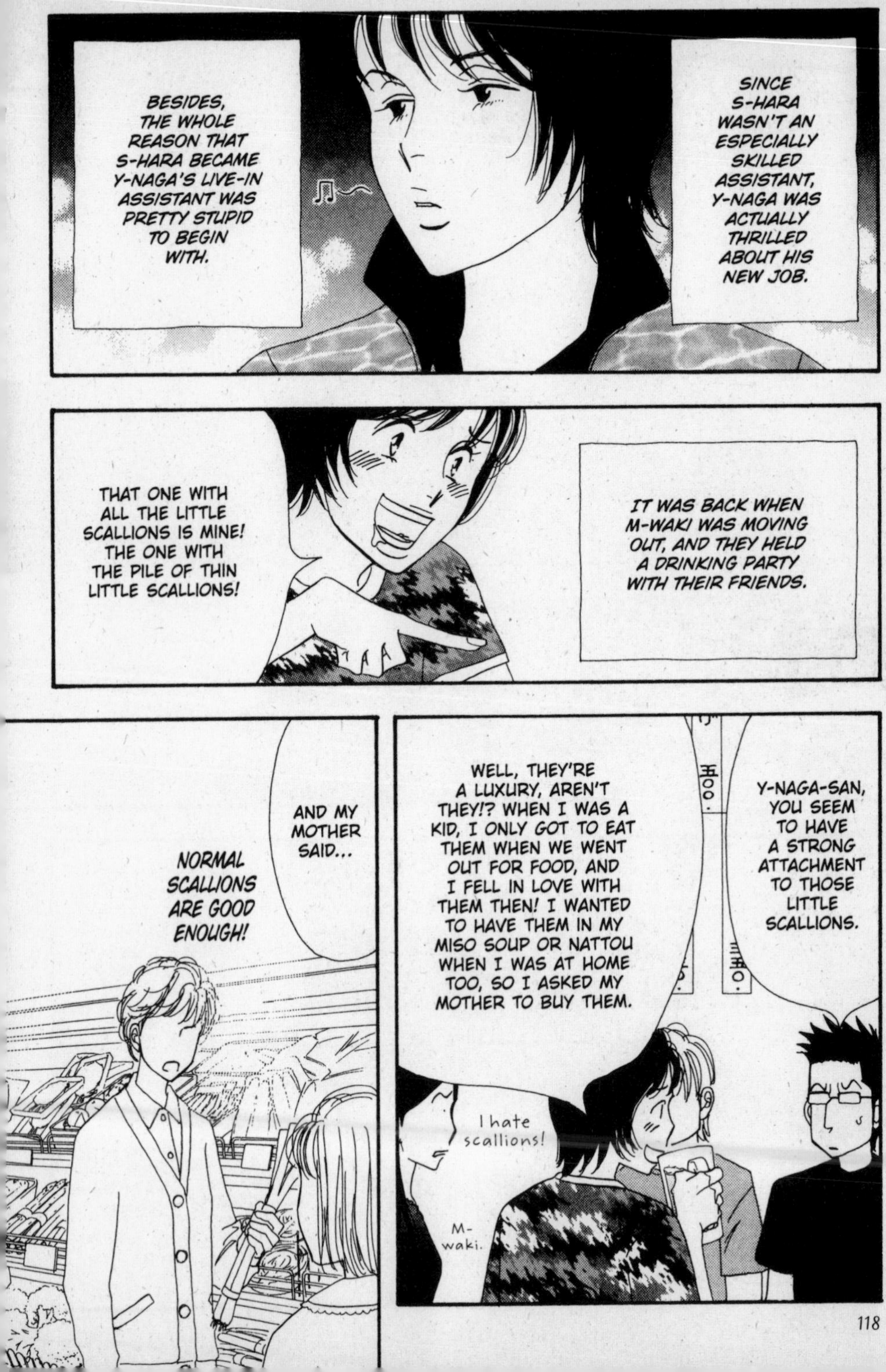
SINCE S-HARA WASN'T AN ESPECIALLY SKILLED ASSISTANT, Y-NAGA WAS ACTUALLY THRILLED ABOUT HIS NEW JOB.
♬~
BESIDES, THE WHOLE REASON THAT S-HARA BECAME Y-NAGA'S LIVE-IN ASSISTANT WAS PRETTY STUPID TO BEGIN WITH.
IT WAS BACK WHEN M-WAKI WAS MOVING OUT, AND THEY HELD A DRINKING PARTY WITH THEIR FRIENDS.
THAT ONE WITH ALL THE LITTLE SCALLIONS IS MINE! THE ONE WITH THE PILE OF THIN LITTLE SCALLIONS!
Y-NAGA-SAN, YOU SEEM TO HAVE A STRONG ATTACHMENT TO THOSE LITTLE SCALLIONS.
WELL, THEY'RE A LUXURY, AREN'T THEY!? WHEN I WAS A KID, I ONLY GOT TO EAT THEM WHEN WE WENT OUT FOR FOOD, AND I FELL IN LOVE WITH THEM THEN! I WANTED TO HAVE THEM IN MY MISO SOUP OR NATTOU WHEN I WAS AT HOME TOO, SO I ASKED MY MOTHER TO BUY THEM.
I hate scallions!
M-waki.
AND MY MOTHER SAID...
NORMAL SCALLIONS ARE GOOD ENOUGH!

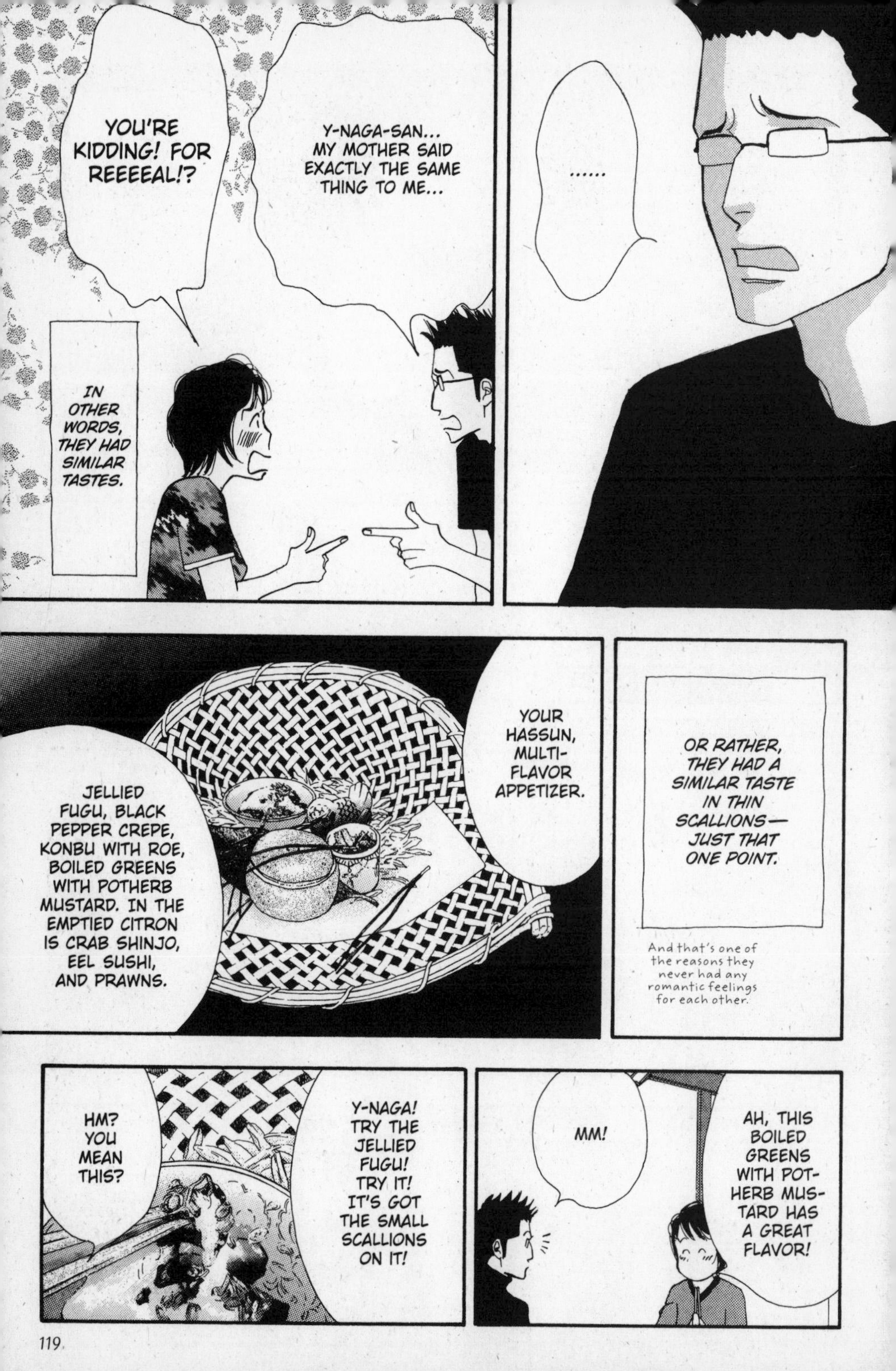
......
Y-NAGA-SAN... MY MOTHER SAID EXACTLY THE SAME THING TO ME...
YOU'RE KIDDING! FOR REEEEAL!?
IN OTHER WORDS, THEY HAD SIMILAR TASTES.
OR RATHER, THEY HAD A SIMILAR TASTE IN THIN SCALLIONS— JUST THAT ONE POINT.
And that's one of the reasons they never had any romantic feelings for each other.
YOUR HASSUN, MULTI-FLAVOR APPETIZER.
JELLIED FUGU, BLACK PEPPER CREPE, KONBU WITH ROE, BOILED GREENS WITH POTHERB MUSTARD. IN THE EMPTIED CITRON IS CRAB SHINJO, EEL SUSHI, AND PRAWNS.
AH, THIS BOILED GREENS WITH POT-HERB MUS-TARD HAS A GREAT FLAVOR!
MM!
Y-NAGA! TRY THE JELLIED FUGU! TRY IT! IT'S GOT THE SMALL SCALLIONS ON IT!
HM? YOU MEAN THIS?

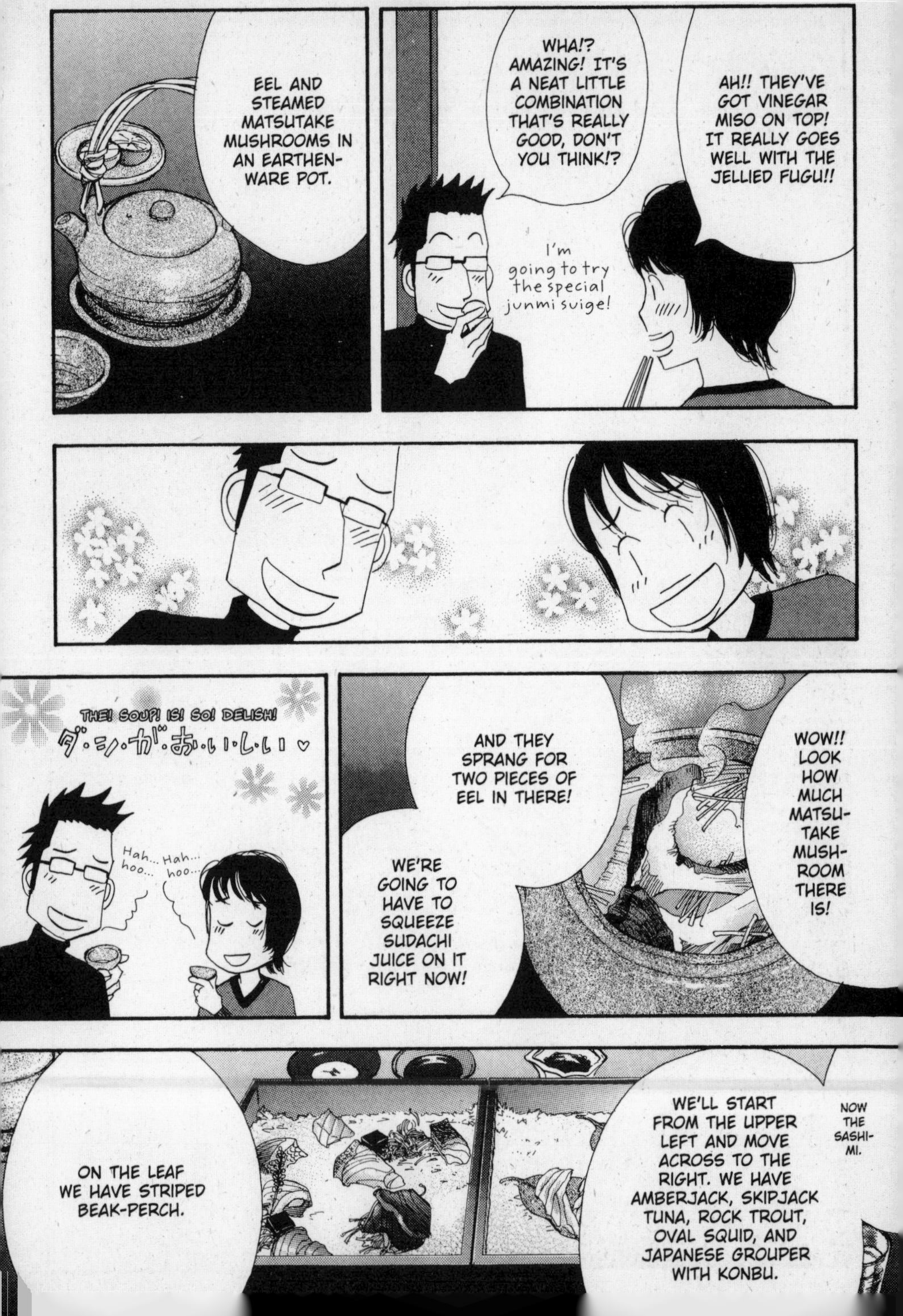
AH!! THEY'VE GOT VINEGAR MISO ON TOP! IT REALLY GOES WELL WITH THE JELLIED FUGU!!
WHA!? AMAZING! IT'S A NEAT LITTLE COMBINATION THAT'S REALLY GOOD, DON'T YOU THINK!?
I'm going to try the special junmi suige!
EEL AND STEAMED MATSUTAKE MUSHROOMS IN AN EARTHENWARE POT.
WOW!! LOOK HOW MUCH MATSUTAKE MUSHROOM THERE IS!
AND THEY SPRANG FOR TWO PIECES OF EEL IN THERE!
WE'RE GOING TO HAVE TO SQUEEZE SUDACHI JUICE ON IT RIGHT NOW!
THE! SOUP! IS! SO! DELISH!
ダ・シ・が・お・い・し・い♡
Hah... hoo...
Hah... hoo...
NOW THE SASHIMI.
WE'LL START FROM THE UPPER LEFT AND MOVE ACROSS TO THE RIGHT. WE HAVE AMBERJACK, SKIPJACK TUNA, ROCK TROUT, OVAL SQUID, AND JAPANESE GROUPER WITH KONBU.
ON THE LEAF WE HAVE STRIPED BEAK-PERCH.

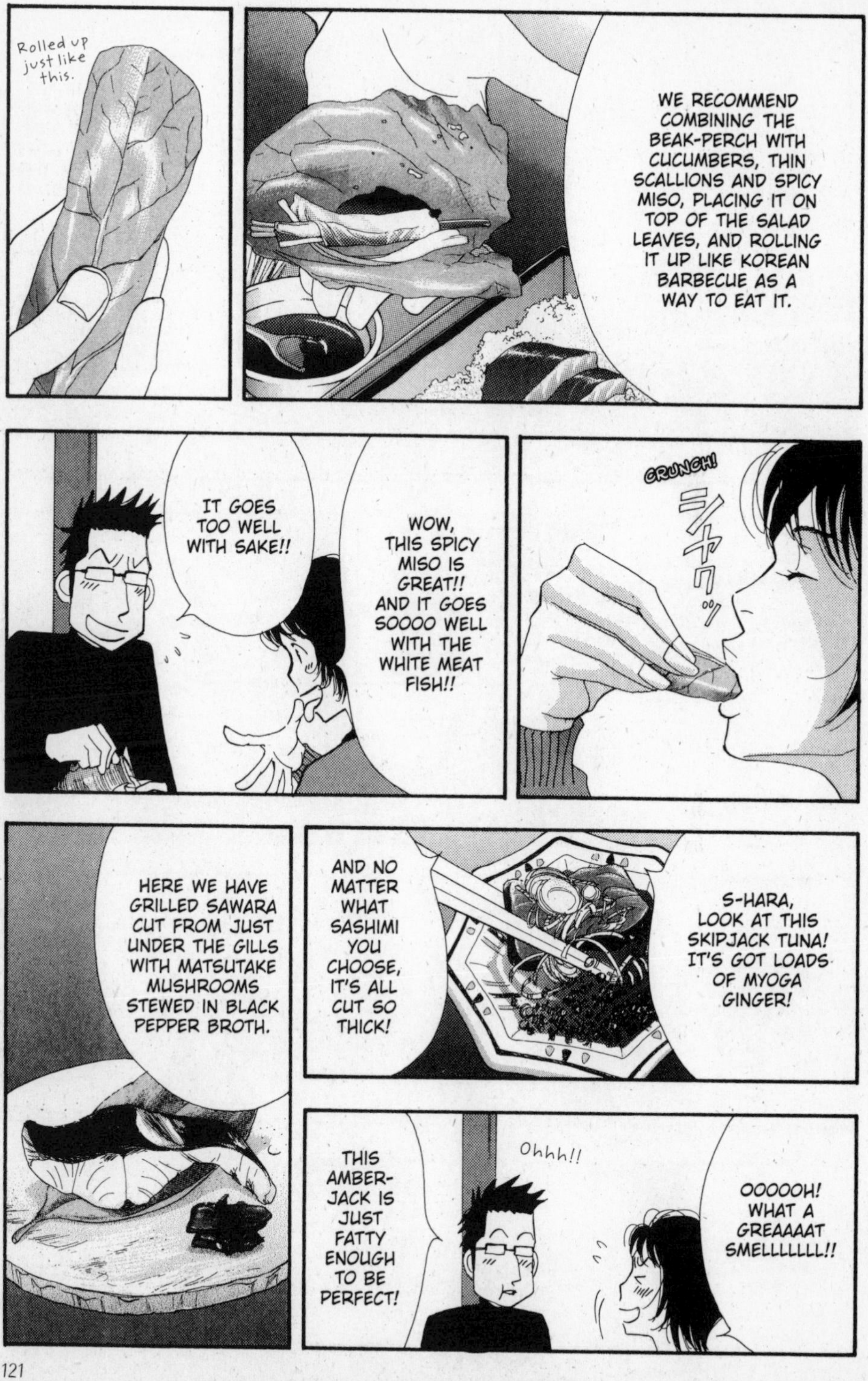

WE RECOMMEND COMBINING THE BEAK-PERCH WITH CUCUMBERS, THIN SCALLIONS AND SPICY MISO, PLACING IT ON TOP OF THE SALAD LEAVES, AND ROLLING IT UP LIKE KOREAN BARBECUE AS A WAY TO EAT IT.
Rolled up just like this.
CRUNCH!
シャクッ
WOW, THIS SPICY MISO IS GREAT!! AND IT GOES SOOOO WELL WITH THE WHITE MEAT FISH!!
IT GOES TOO WELL WITH SAKE!!
S-HARA, LOOK AT THIS SKIPJACK TUNA! IT'S GOT LOADS OF MYOGA GINGER!
AND NO MATTER WHAT SASHIMI YOU CHOOSE, IT'S ALL CUT SO THICK!
OOOOOH! WHAT A GREAAAAT SMELLLLLLLL!!
Ohhh!!
THIS AMBER-JACK IS JUST FATTY ENOUGH TO BE PERFECT!
HERE WE HAVE GRILLED SAWARA CUT FROM JUST UNDER THE GILLS WITH MATSUTAKE MUSHROOMS STEWED IN BLACK PEPPER BROTH.

EH!? IT'S GRILLED, SO WHY IS IT STILL SO JUICY? IT ISN'T DRY AT ALL!
AHHHH... THE USE OF SALT IS JUST PERFECT! THIS IS REALLY GOOD!
プロのお仕事!
PROS AT WORK!
YOUR SEA BREAM AND KING OYSTER STEAMED WITH KONBU.
IT IS BEST WHEN DIPPED IN A SAUCE OF PONZU AND MOMIJI-OROSHI.
fssshh...
THIS STUFF IS EXQUISITE! A MASTERPIECE!!
UUUH... OHHH! THE LUSCIOUS TASTE OF THE KONBU RUNS ALL THE WAY THROUGH THE MEAT OF THE FISH!
It's so soft and absurdly juicy!
YOUR LILY-BULB MANJU.
IT'S MANJU STUFFED WITH WILD DUCK AND LILY BULB WITH SUGAR AND SOY SAUCE SOUP.
I DON'T KNOW WHAT TO DO! THIS IS MARVELOUS TOO! THE SHREDDED LILY BULB IS SO SOFT AND SWEET!
MM! THE SAUCE IS DELICIOUS TOO!

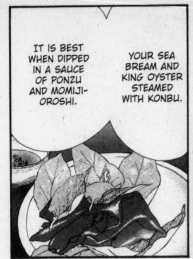

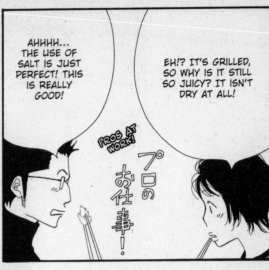

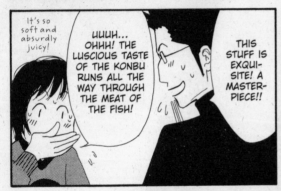

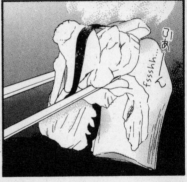

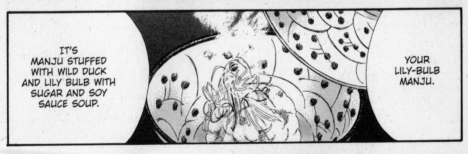

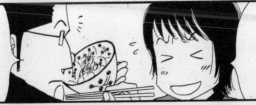

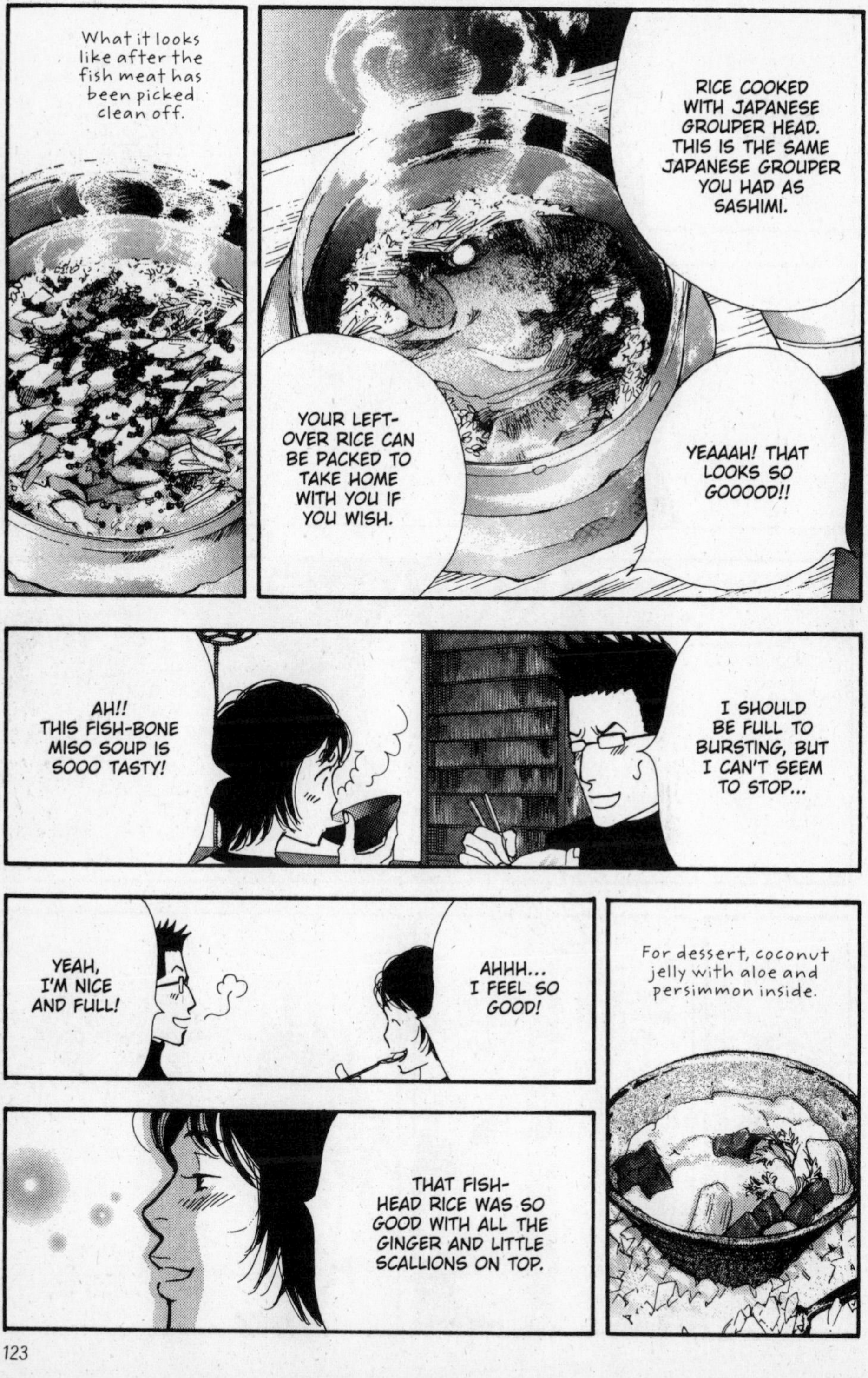
RICE COOKED WITH JAPANESE GROUPER HEAD. THIS IS THE SAME JAPANESE GROUPER YOU HAD AS SASHIMI.
YOUR LEFT-OVER RICE CAN BE PACKED TO TAKE HOME WITH YOU IF YOU WISH.
YEAAAH! THAT LOOKS SO GOOOOD!!
What it looks like after the fish meat has been picked clean off.
I SHOULD BE FULL TO BURSTING, BUT I CAN'T SEEM TO STOP...
AH!! THIS FISH-BONE MISO SOUP IS SOOO TASTY!
For dessert, coconut jelly with aloe and persimmon inside.
AHHH... I FEEL SO GOOD!
YEAH, I'M NICE AND FULL!
THAT FISH-HEAD RICE WAS SO GOOD WITH ALL THE GINGER AND LITTLE SCALLIONS ON TOP.

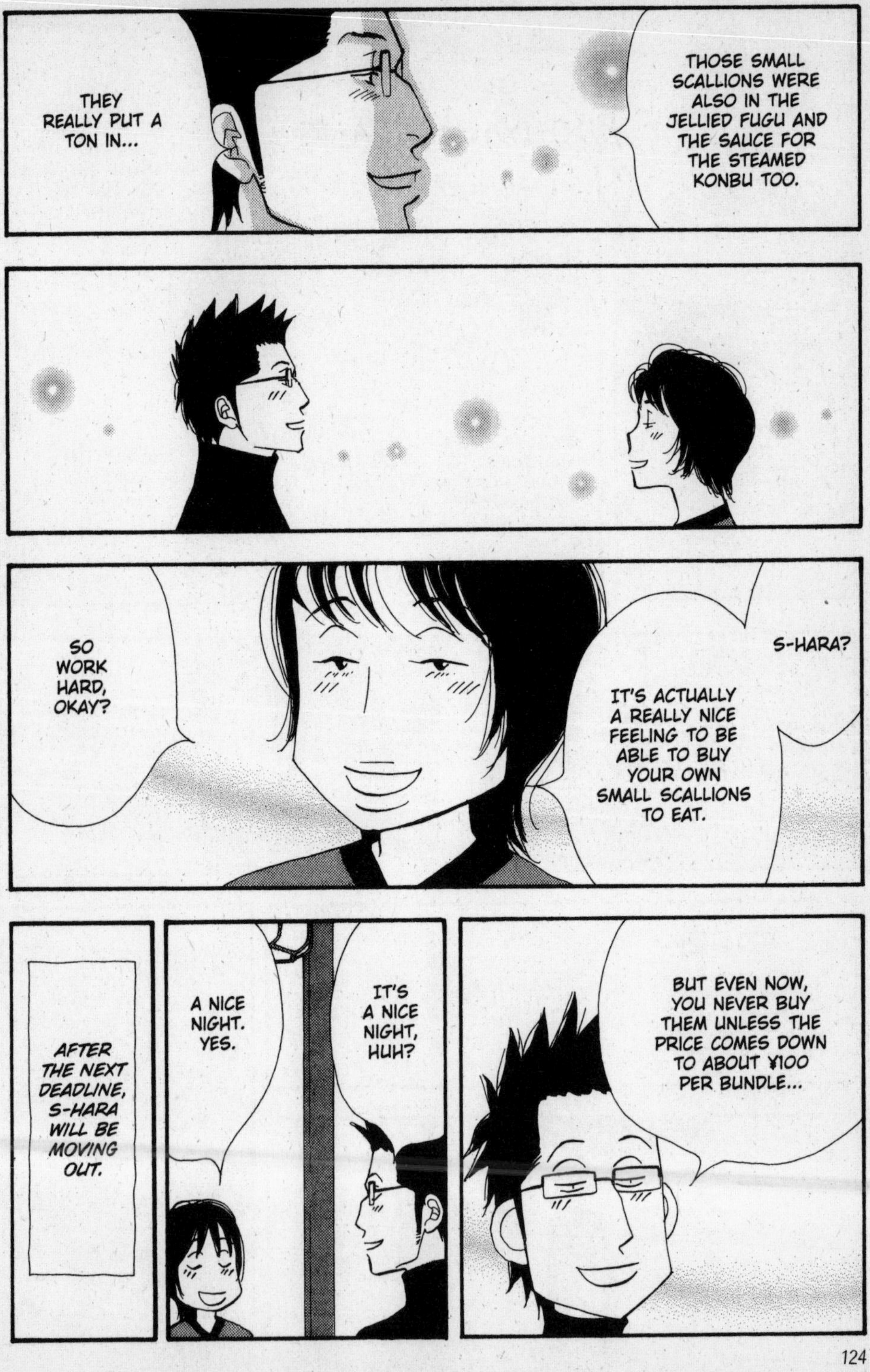
THOSE SMALL SCALLIONS WERE ALSO IN THE JELLIED FUGU AND THE SAUCE FOR THE STEAMED KONBU TOO.
THEY REALLY PUT A TON IN...
S-HARA?
IT'S ACTUALLY A REALLY NICE FEELING TO BE ABLE TO BUY YOUR OWN SMALL SCALLIONS TO EAT.
SO WORK HARD, OKAY?
BUT EVEN NOW, YOU NEVER BUY THEM UNLESS THE PRICE COMES DOWN TO ABOUT ¥100 PER BUNDLE...
IT'S A NICE NIGHT, HUH?
A NICE NIGHT. YES.
AFTER THE NEXT DEADLINE, S-HARA WILL BE MOVING OUT.

Ajidonya Asuka
(Shimo-Kitazawa)

[Address]
Eighth Matsuya Building, 1F
2-20-2 Shimo-Kitazawa,
Setagaya-ku, Tokyo
[Telephone]
03-3410-3443
[Hours]
Monday - Saturday
11:30 AM (last order 2:00 PM)
5:00 PM (last order 10:00 PM)
Sunday
11:30 AM (last order 10:00 PM)
[Closed]
Never.
[Directions]
A two-minute walk
from the south exit of the
Shimo-Kitagawa station
on the Odakyuu line.
[Parking]
None.

TOUOU I-NO-KASHIRA LINE
SHIMO-KITAGAWA STATION
TO SHINJUKU
HONDA THEATER
DOUTOR COFFEE
TO SHIBUYA
ODAKYUU LINE
McDONALD'S
GOURMET CITY
HERE!
MINAMIGUCHI SHOPPING STREET
MITSUI SUMITOMO GINKO BANK
MISTER DONUTS

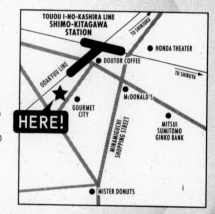

FUMI YOSHINAGA'S COMMENTS

THE EVENING DINNER COURSES ARE ¥7,000, ¥9,000, AND ¥12,000 RESPECTIVELY. THEY ALL FEATURE A LOT OF FOOD, AND ALL OF IT IS DELICIOUS. LUNCH IS ONLY ¥3,500, SO YOU CAN GO JUST TO TRY IT OUT. AND THE VERY POPULAR LILY BULB MANJU (AMONG OTHER THINGS) IS ALWAYS SERVED AT LUNCH.

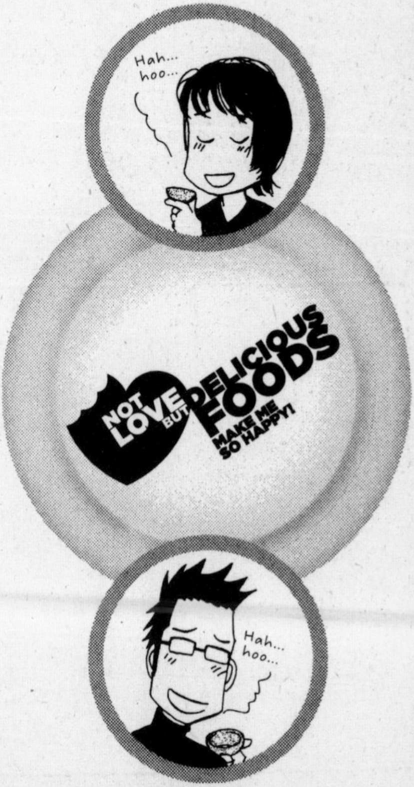
Hah... hoo...
NOT LOVE BUT DELICIOUS FOODS MAKE ME SO HAPPY!
Hah... hoo...

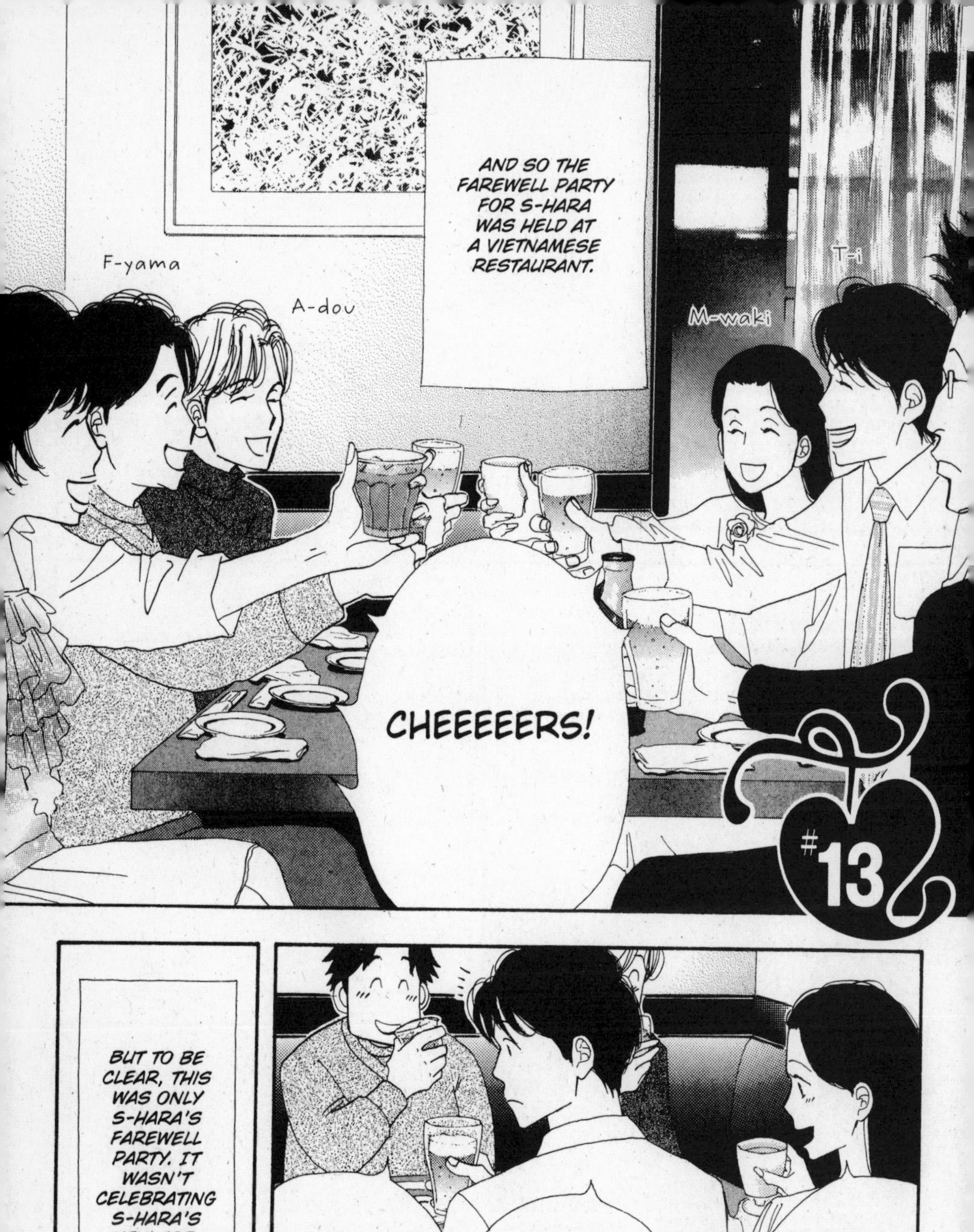
AND SO THE FAREWELL PARTY FOR S-HARA WAS HELD AT A VIETNAMESE RESTAURANT.
T-i
M-waki
A-dou
F-yama
CHEEEEERS!
#13
THIS IS MY FIRST TIME EVER TASTING VIETNAMESE TEA!
OH. BABABA BEER IS LIGHT-TASTING, LIKE BUD.
WOW! THIS LUA MOI AND GUAVA COCKTAIL IS REALLY GOOD!
BUT TO BE CLEAR, THIS WAS ONLY S-HARA'S FAREWELL PARTY. IT WASN'T CELEBRATING S-HARA'S NEW JOB.

Lua Moi: Vietnamese 45-proof liquor.

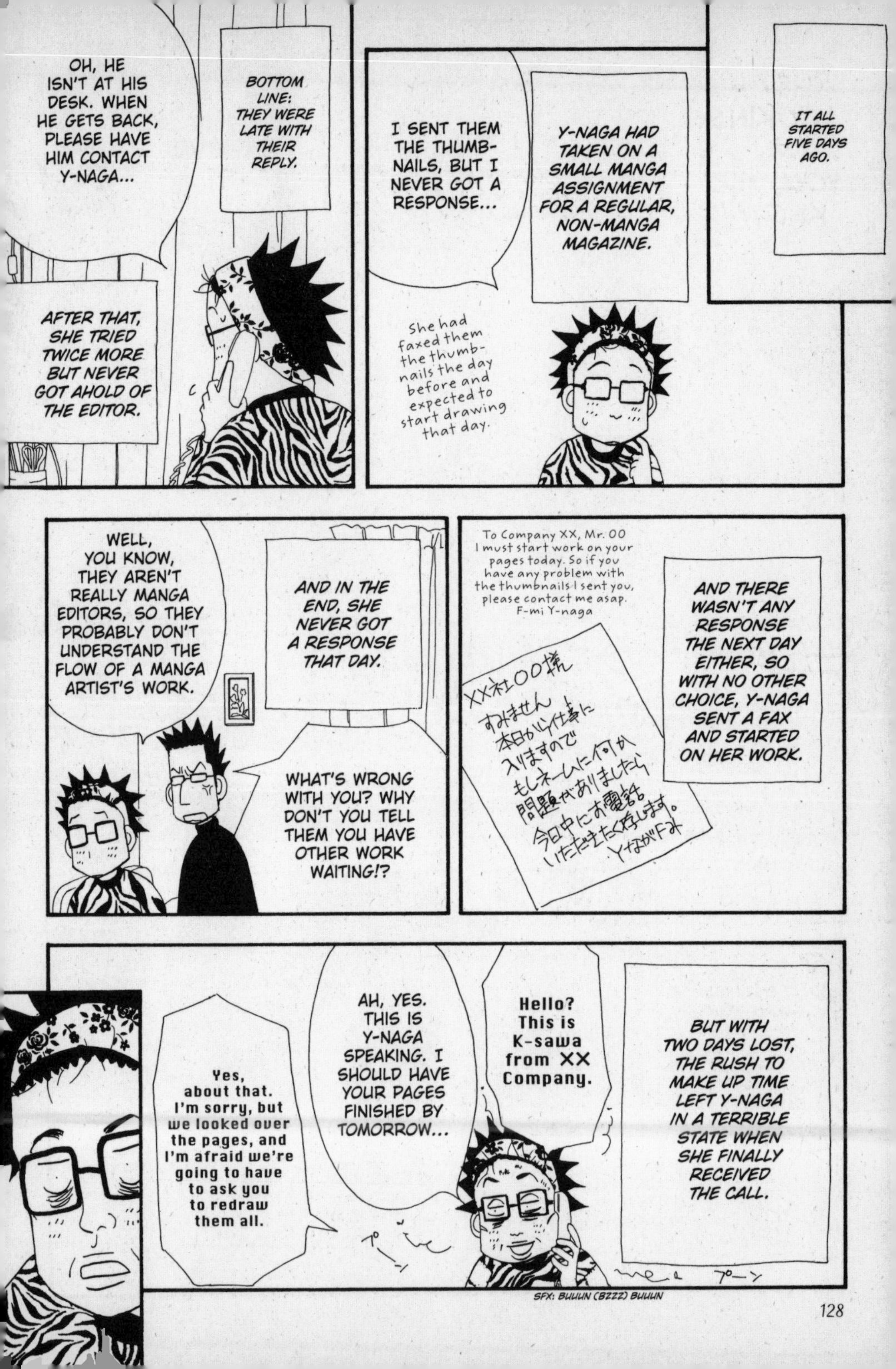
IT ALL STARTED FIVE DAYS AGO.
Y-NAGA HAD TAKEN ON A SMALL MANGA ASSIGNMENT FOR A REGULAR, NON-MANGA MAGAZINE.
I SENT THEM THE THUMB-NAILS, BUT I NEVER GOT A RESPONSE...
She had faxed them the thumb-nails the day before and expected to start drawing that day.
BOTTOM LINE: THEY WERE LATE WITH THEIR REPLY.
OH, HE ISN'T AT HIS DESK. WHEN HE GETS BACK, PLEASE HAVE HIM CONTACT Y-NAGA...
AFTER THAT, SHE TRIED TWICE MORE BUT NEVER GOT AHOLD OF THE EDITOR.
AND THERE WASN'T ANY RESPONSE THE NEXT DAY EITHER, SO WITH NO OTHER CHOICE, Y-NAGA SENT A FAX AND STARTED ON HER WORK.
To Company XX, Mr. OO I must start work on your pages today. So if you have any problem with the thumbnails I sent you, please contact me asap. F-mi Y-naga
XX社OO様
すみません！本日から仕事に入りますので もしネームに何か問題がありましたら 今日中にお電話いただきたく存じます。
YながFみ
AND IN THE END, SHE NEVER GOT A RESPONSE THAT DAY.
WELL, YOU KNOW, THEY AREN'T REALLY MANGA EDITORS, SO THEY PROBABLY DON'T UNDERSTAND THE FLOW OF A MANGA ARTIST'S WORK.
WHAT'S WRONG WITH YOU? WHY DON'T YOU TELL THEM YOU HAVE OTHER WORK WAITING!?
BUT WITH TWO DAYS LOST, THE RUSH TO MAKE UP TIME LEFT Y-NAGA IN A TERRIBLE STATE WHEN SHE FINALLY RECEIVED THE CALL.
Hello? This is K-sawa from XX Company.
AH, YES. THIS IS Y-NAGA SPEAKING. I SHOULD HAVE YOUR PAGES FINISHED BY TOMORROW...
Yes, about that. I'm sorry, but we looked over the pages, and I'm afraid we're going to have to ask you to redraw them all.

SFX: BUUUN (BZZZ) BUUUN

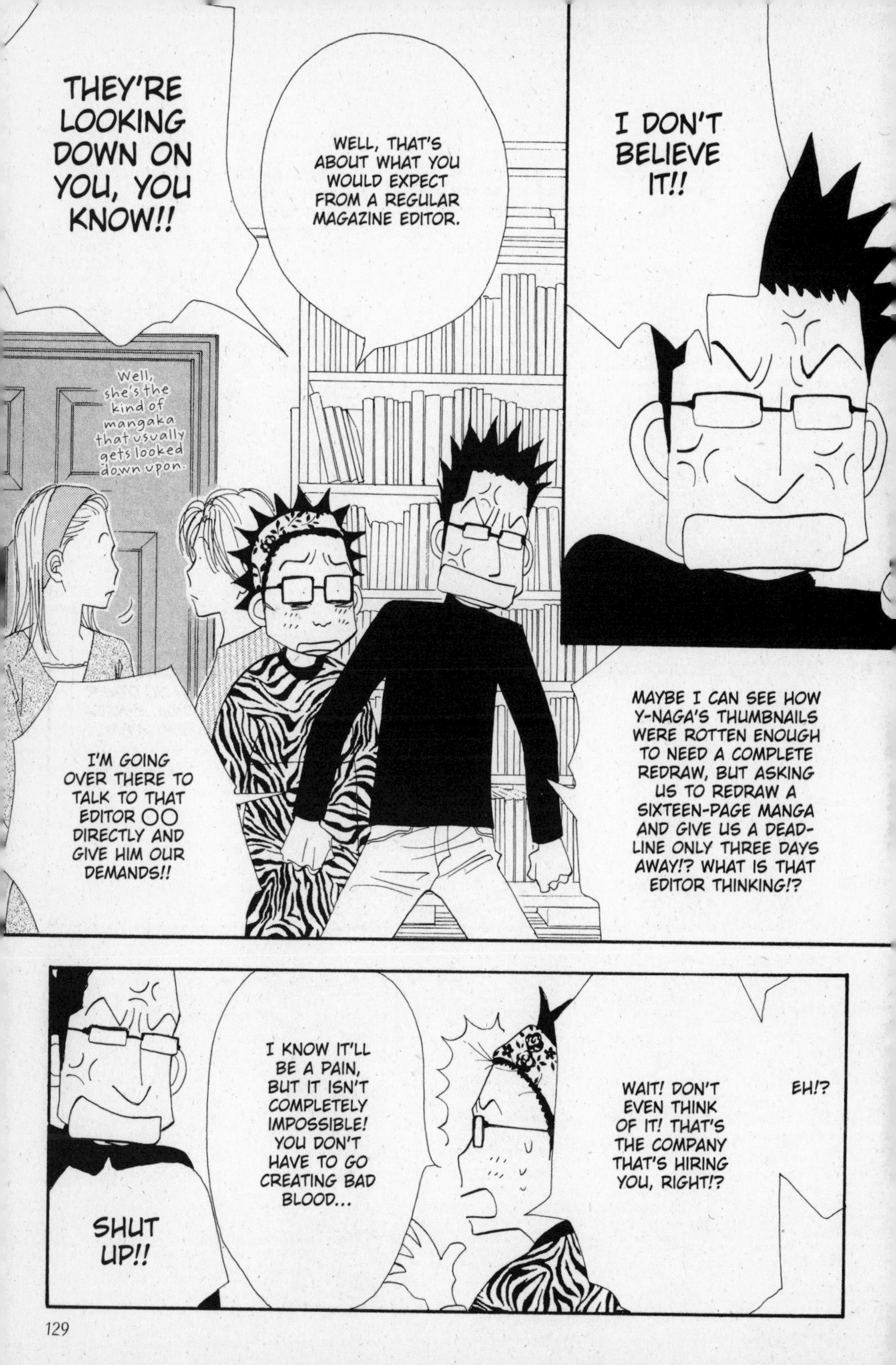

I DON'T BELIEVE IT!!
MAYBE I CAN SEE HOW Y-NAGA'S THUMBNAILS WERE ROTTEN ENOUGH TO NEED A COMPLETE REDRAW, BUT ASKING US TO REDRAW A SIXTEEN-PAGE MANGA AND GIVE US A DEAD-LINE ONLY THREE DAYS AWAY!? WHAT IS THAT EDITOR THINKING!?
I'M GOING OVER THERE TO TALK TO THAT EDITOR ○○ DIRECTLY AND GIVE HIM OUR DEMANDS!!
THEY'RE LOOKING DOWN ON YOU, YOU KNOW!!
WELL, THAT'S ABOUT WHAT YOU WOULD EXPECT FROM A REGULAR MAGAZINE EDITOR.
Well, she's the kind of mangaka that usually gets looked down upon.
EH!?
WAIT! DON'T EVEN THINK OF IT! THAT'S THE COMPANY THAT'S HIRING YOU, RIGHT!?
I KNOW IT'LL BE A PAIN, BUT IT ISN'T COMPLETELY IMPOSSIBLE! YOU DON'T HAVE TO GO CREATING BAD BLOOD...
SHUT UP!!

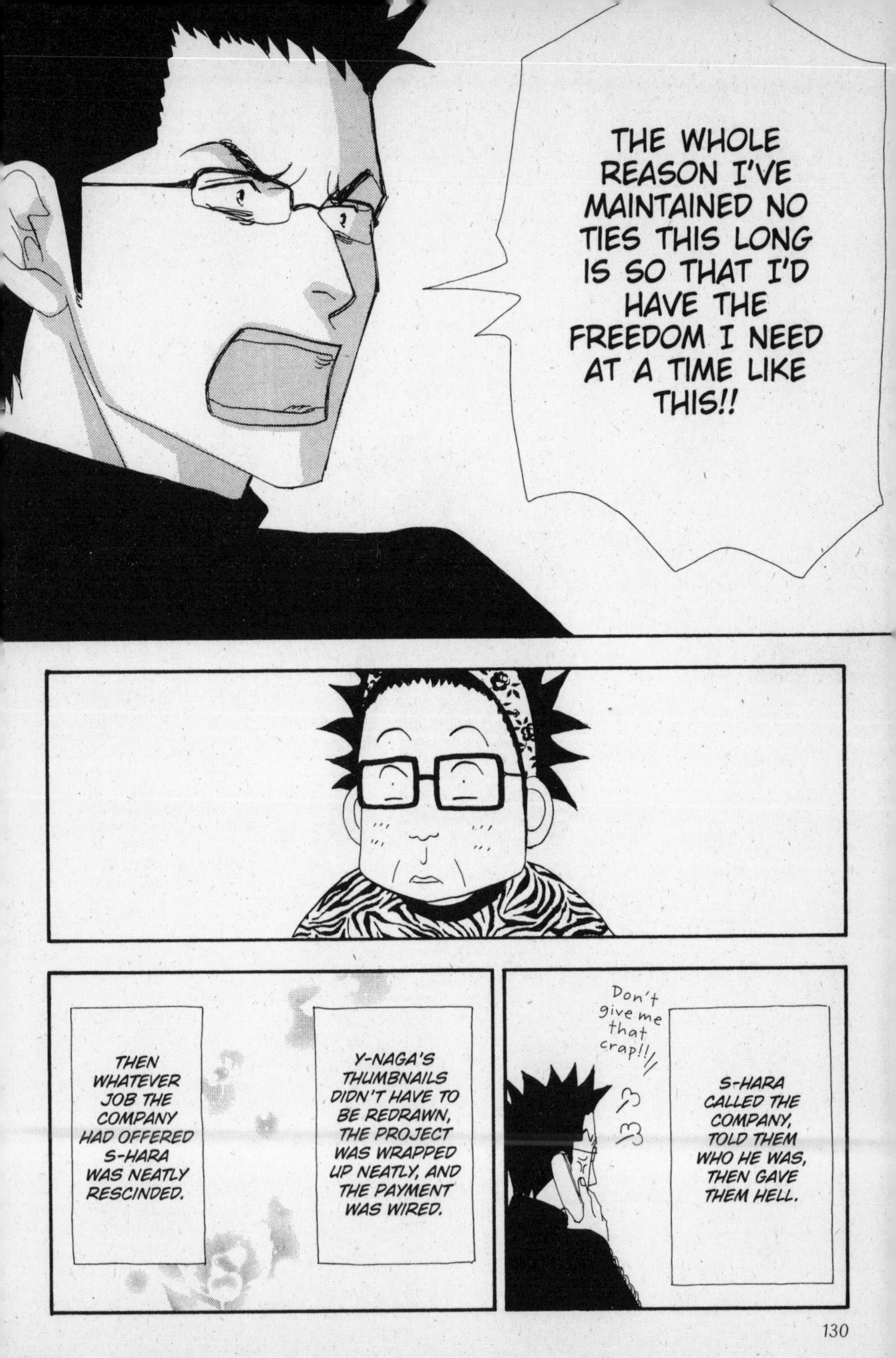
THE WHOLE REASON I'VE MAINTAINED NO TIES THIS LONG IS SO THAT I'D HAVE THE FREEDOM I NEED AT A TIME LIKE THIS!!
S-HARA CALLED THE COMPANY, TOLD THEM WHO HE WAS, THEN GAVE THEM HELL.
Don't give me that crap!!
Y-NAGA'S THUMBNAILS DIDN'T HAVE TO BE REDRAWN, THE PROJECT WAS WRAPPED UP NEATLY, AND THE PAYMENT WAS WIRED.
THEN WHATEVER JOB THE COMPANY HAD OFFERED S-HARA WAS NEATLY RESCINDED.

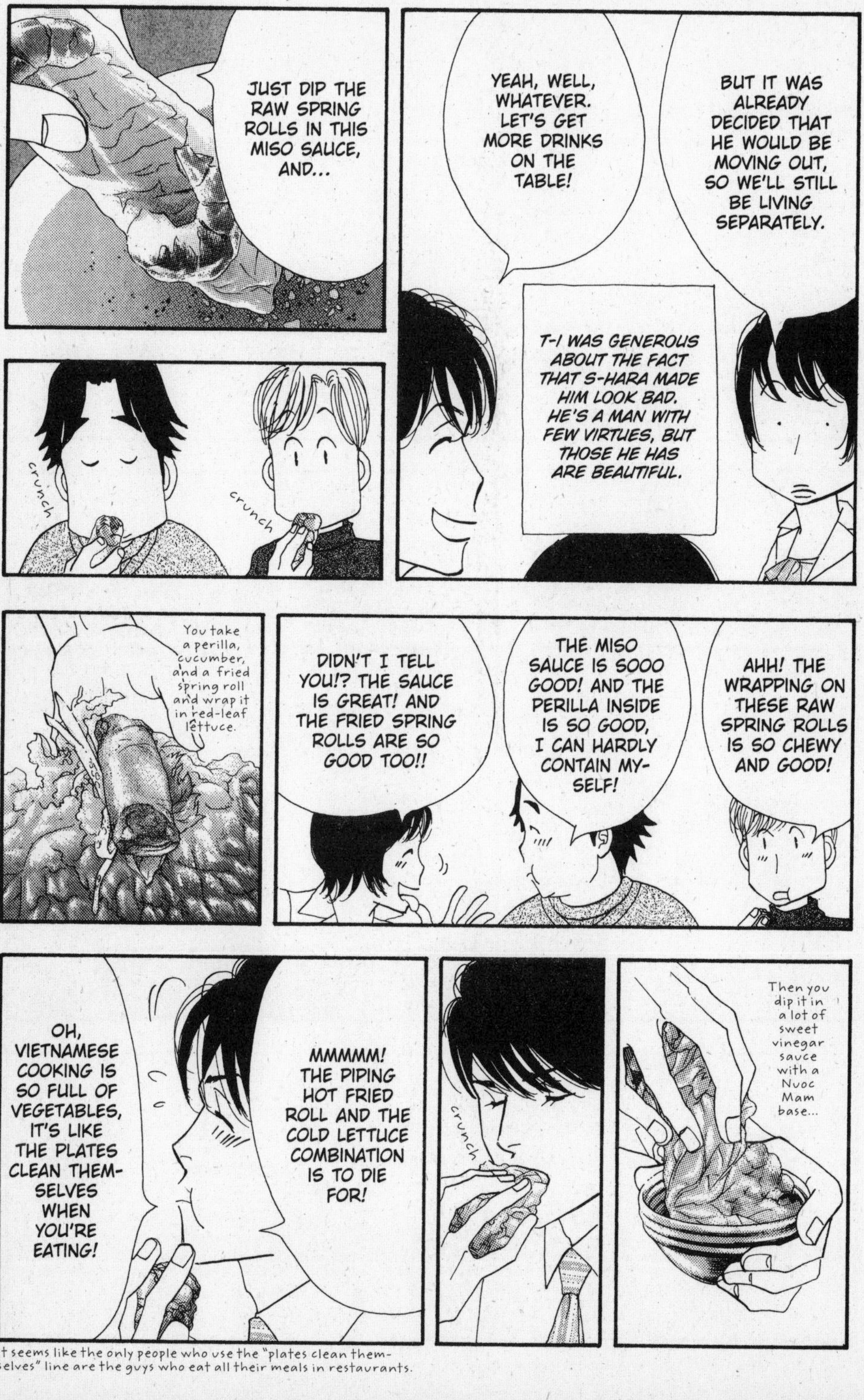
BUT IT WAS ALREADY DECIDED THAT HE WOULD BE MOVING OUT, SO WE'LL STILL BE LIVING SEPARATELY.
YEAH, WELL, WHATEVER. LET'S GET MORE DRINKS ON THE TABLE!
T-I WAS GENEROUS ABOUT THE FACT THAT S-HARA MADE HIM LOOK BAD. HE'S A MAN WITH FEW VIRTUES, BUT THOSE HE HAS ARE BEAUTIFUL.
JUST DIP THE RAW SPRING ROLLS IN THIS MISO SAUCE, AND...
crunch
crunch
AHH! THE WRAPPING ON THESE RAW SPRING ROLLS IS SO CHEWY AND GOOD!
THE MISO SAUCE IS SOOO GOOD! AND THE PERILLA INSIDE IS SO GOOD, I CAN HARDLY CONTAIN MY-SELF!
DIDN'T I TELL YOU!? THE SAUCE IS GREAT! AND THE FRIED SPRING ROLLS ARE SO GOOD TOO!!
You take a perilla, cucumber, and a fried spring roll and wrap it in red-leaf lettuce.
Then you dip it in a lot of sweet vinegar sauce with a Nuoc Mam base...
crunch
MMMMM! THE PIPING HOT FRIED ROLL AND THE COLD LETTUCE COMBINATION IS TO DIE FOR!
OH, VIETNAMESE COOKING IS SO FULL OF VEGETABLES, IT'S LIKE THE PLATES CLEAN THEM-SELVES WHEN YOU'RE EATING!

It seems like the only people who use the "plates clean them-selves" line are the guys who eat all their meals in restaurants.

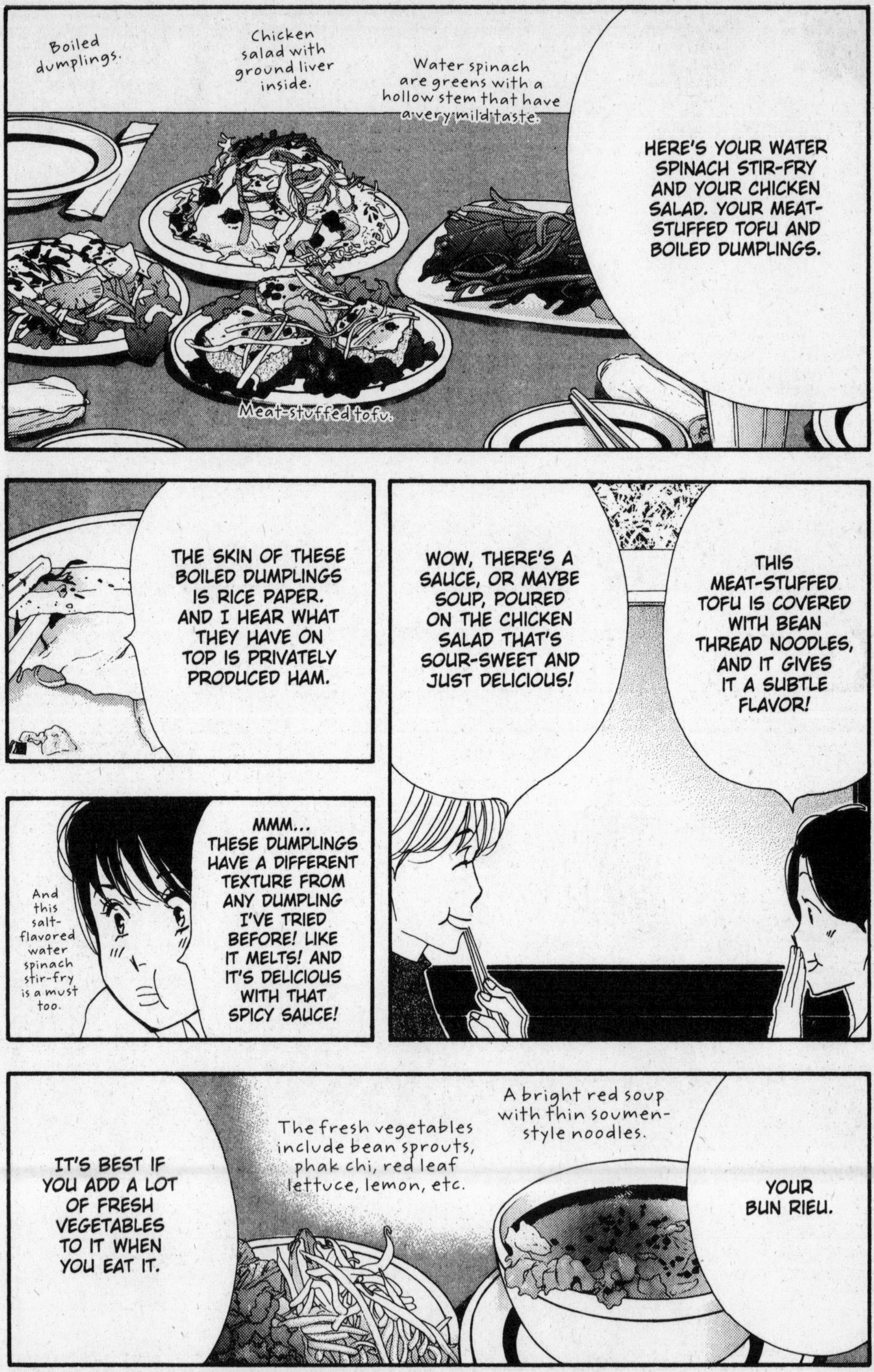
HERE'S YOUR WATER SPINACH STIR-FRY AND YOUR CHICKEN SALAD. YOUR MEAT-STUFFED TOFU AND BOILED DUMPLINGS.
Water spinach are greens with a hollow stem that have a very mild taste.
Chicken salad with ground liver inside.
Boiled dumplings.
Meat-stuffed tofu.
THIS MEAT-STUFFED TOFU IS COVERED WITH BEAN THREAD NOODLES, AND IT GIVES IT A SUBTLE FLAVOR!
WOW, THERE'S A SAUCE, OR MAYBE SOUP, POURED ON THE CHICKEN SALAD THAT'S SOUR-SWEET AND JUST DELICIOUS!
THE SKIN OF THESE BOILED DUMPLINGS IS RICE PAPER. AND I HEAR WHAT THEY HAVE ON TOP IS PRIVATELY PRODUCED HAM.
MMM... THESE DUMPLINGS HAVE A DIFFERENT TEXTURE FROM ANY DUMPLING I'VE TRIED BEFORE! LIKE IT MELTS! AND IT'S DELICIOUS WITH THAT SPICY SAUCE!
And this salt-flavored water spinach stir-fry is a must too.
YOUR BUN RIEU.
A bright red soup with thin soumen-style noodles.
The fresh vegetables include bean sprouts, phak chi, red leaf lettuce, lemon, etc.
IT'S BEST IF YOU ADD A LOT OF FRESH VEGETABLES TO IT WHEN YOU EAT IT.

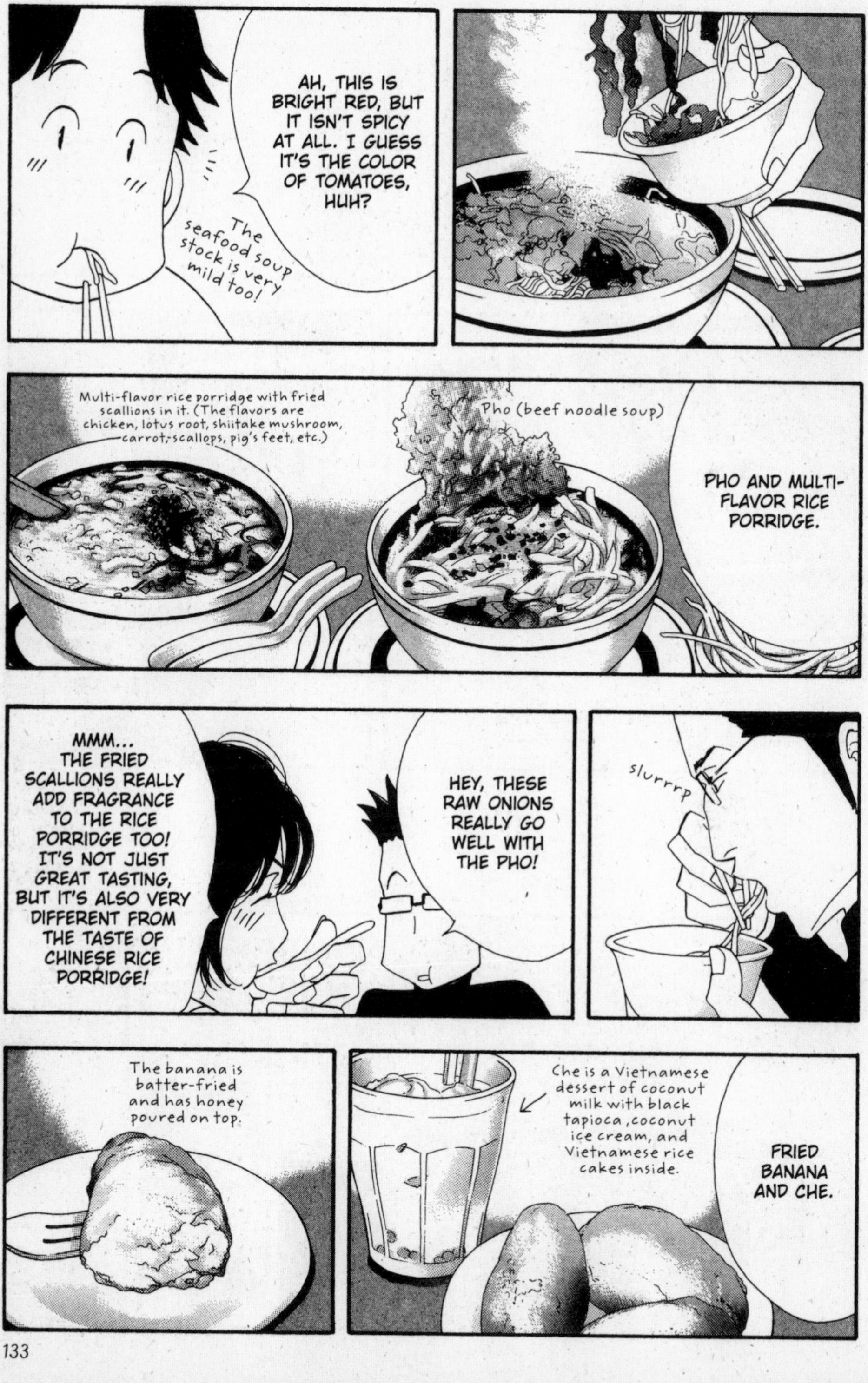
AH, THIS IS BRIGHT RED, BUT IT ISN'T SPICY AT ALL. I GUESS IT'S THE COLOR OF TOMATOES, HUH?
The seafood soup stock is very mild too!
PHO AND MULTI-FLAVOR RICE PORRIDGE.
Pho (beef noodle soup)
Multi-flavor rice porridge with fried scallions in it. (The flavors are chicken, lotus root, shiitake mushroom, carrot, scallops, pig's feet, etc.)
slurrrp
HEY, THESE RAW ONIONS REALLY GO WELL WITH THE PHO!
MMM... THE FRIED SCALLIONS REALLY ADD FRAGRANCE TO THE RICE PORRIDGE TOO! IT'S NOT JUST GREAT TASTING, BUT IT'S ALSO VERY DIFFERENT FROM THE TASTE OF CHINESE RICE PORRIDGE!
FRIED BANANA AND CHE.
Che is a Vietnamese dessert of coconut milk with black tapioca, coconut ice cream, and Vietnamese rice cakes inside.
The banana is batter-fried and has honey poured on top.

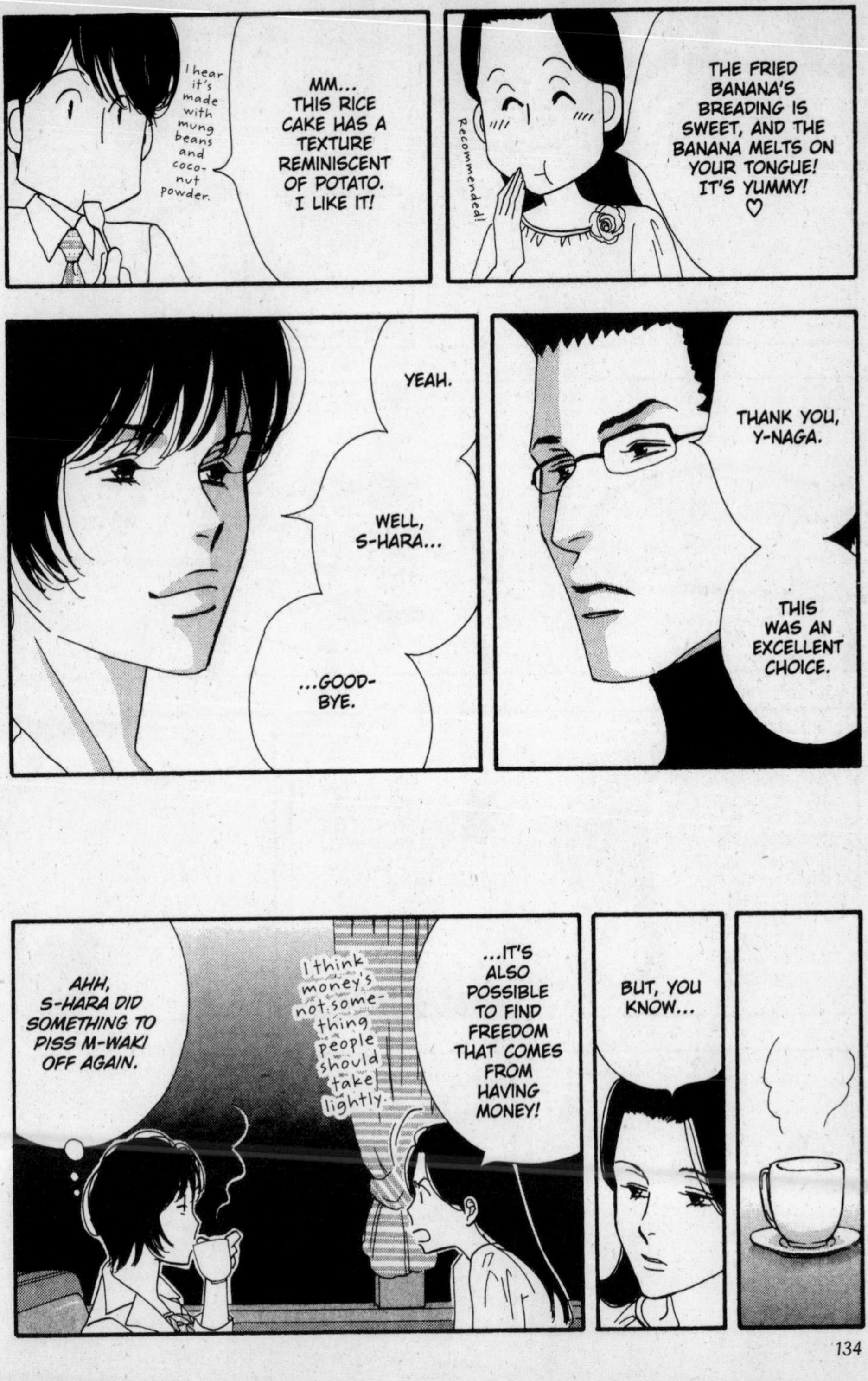
THE FRIED BANANA'S BREADING IS SWEET, AND THE BANANA MELTS ON YOUR TONGUE! IT'S YUMMY! ♡
Recommended!
MM... THIS RICE CAKE HAS A TEXTURE REMINISCENT OF POTATO. I LIKE IT!
I hear it's made with mung beans and coconut powder.
THANK YOU, Y-NAGA.
THIS WAS AN EXCELLENT CHOICE.
YEAH.
WELL, S-HARA...
...GOOD-BYE.
BUT, YOU KNOW...
...IT'S ALSO POSSIBLE TO FIND FREEDOM THAT COMES FROM HAVING MONEY!
I think money's not something people should take lightly.
AHH, S-HARA DID SOMETHING TO PISS M-WAKI OFF AGAIN.

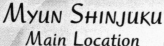

MYUN SHINJUKU
Main Location

[Address]
YKB Shinjuku Gyoen Building, 1F
1-3-8 Shinjuku, Shinjuku-ku, Tokyo
[Telephone]
03-3358-9951
[Hours]
11:00 AM - 3:00 PM,
5:00 PM - 9:50 PM
[Closed]
Never.
[Directions]
A one-minute walk from
the Shinjuku Gyoenmae
Station on the
Maru-no-Uchi Line.
[Parking]
None. (Paid parking is
available in the rear.)

← TO SHINJUKU
MITSUI SUMITOMO GINKO BANK
FIRST KITCHEN
SHINJUKU DOORI ROAD
MARU-NO-UCHI LINE
SHINJUKU GYOUENMAE STATION
OKIDO GATE EXIT
FLORIST
HERE!
SHINJUKU GYOUEN PARK

FUMI YOSHINAGA'S COMMENTS

FOR AN EVENING MEAL, BUDGET AROUND ¥2,500 TO ¥4,000. THERE IS NO PHAK CHI (CORIANDER) IN EITHER THE RAW SPRING ROLLS OR THE FRIED SPRING ROLLS, SO I'M SURE PEOPLE WHO DON'T LIKE PHAK CHI CAN FIND A LOT OF THINGS ON THE MENU TO EAT.

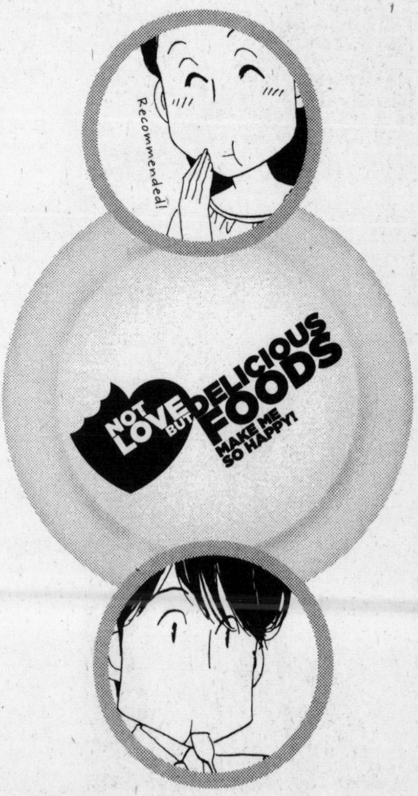
Recommended!
NOT LOVE BUT DELICIOUS FOODS MAKE ME SO HAPPY!

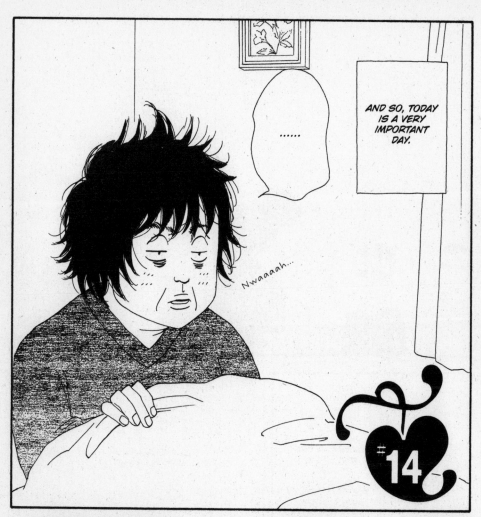

......

Nwaaaah...

AND SO, TODAY IS A VERY IMPORTANT DAY.

#14

creep

H-HELLO...

THE LOCATION SEEMS RIGHT FOR ONE OF THOSE HIDDEN JAPANESE FOOD PLACES, BUT IT'S ACTUALLY A CHINESE FOOD PLACE.

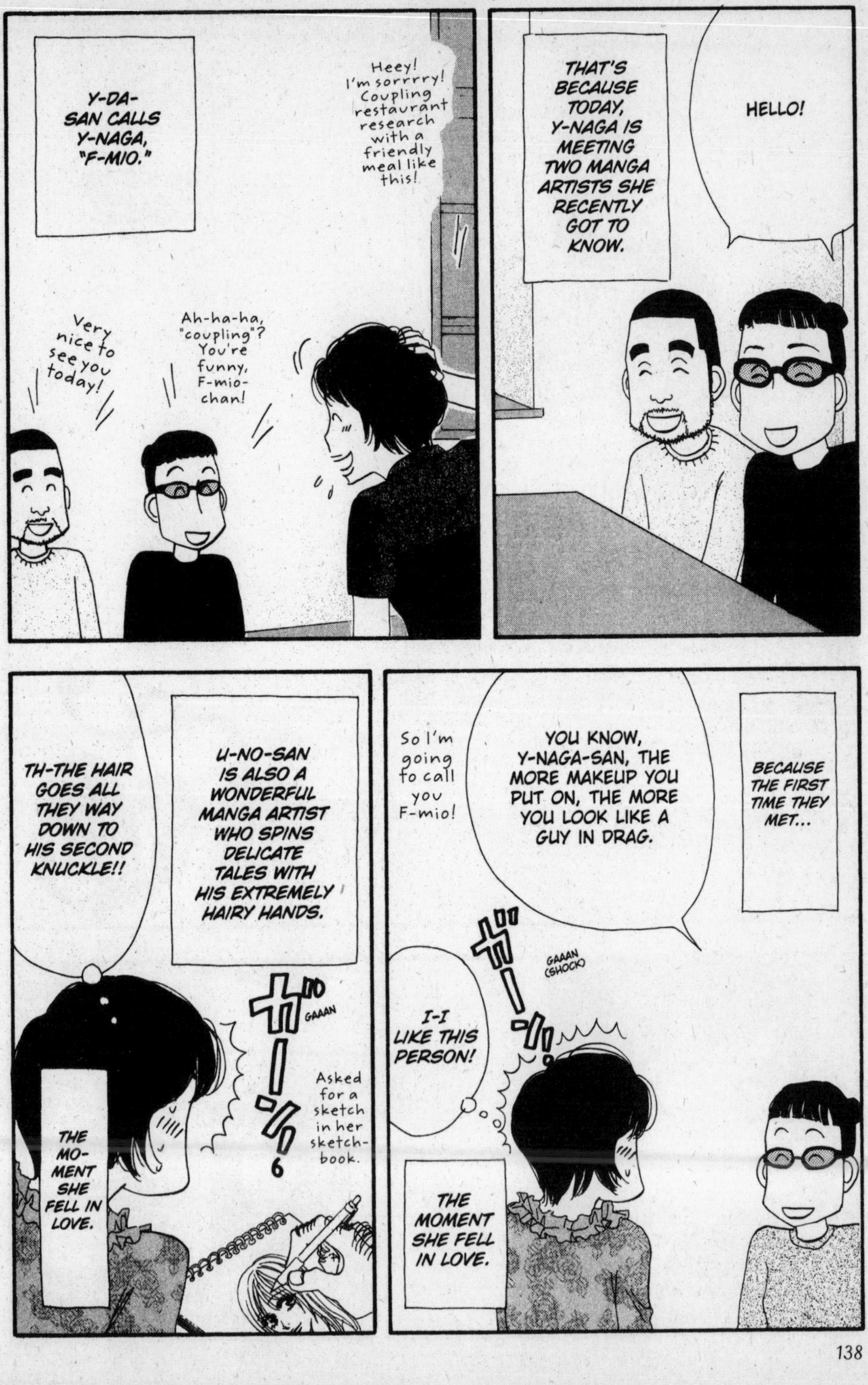
THAT'S BECAUSE TODAY, Y-NAGA IS MEETING TWO MANGA ARTISTS SHE RECENTLY GOT TO KNOW.
HELLO!
Y-DA-SAN CALLS Y-NAGA, "F-MIO."
Heey! I'm sorrrry! Coupling restaurant research with a friendly meal like this!
Ah-ha-ha, "coupling"? You're funny, F-mio-chan!
Very nice to see you today!
BECAUSE THE FIRST TIME THEY MET...
YOU KNOW, Y-NAGA-SAN, THE MORE MAKEUP YOU PUT ON, THE MORE YOU LOOK LIKE A GUY IN DRAG.
So I'm going to call you F-mio!
GAAAN (SHOCK)
I-I LIKE THIS PERSON!
THE MOMENT SHE FELL IN LOVE.
U-NO-SAN IS ALSO A WONDERFUL MANGA ARTIST WHO SPINS DELICATE TALES WITH HIS EXTREMELY HAIRY HANDS.
TH-THE HAIR GOES ALL THEY WAY DOWN TO HIS SECOND KNUCKLE!!
GAAAN
Asked for a sketch in her sketch-book.
THE MOMENT SHE FELL IN LOVE.

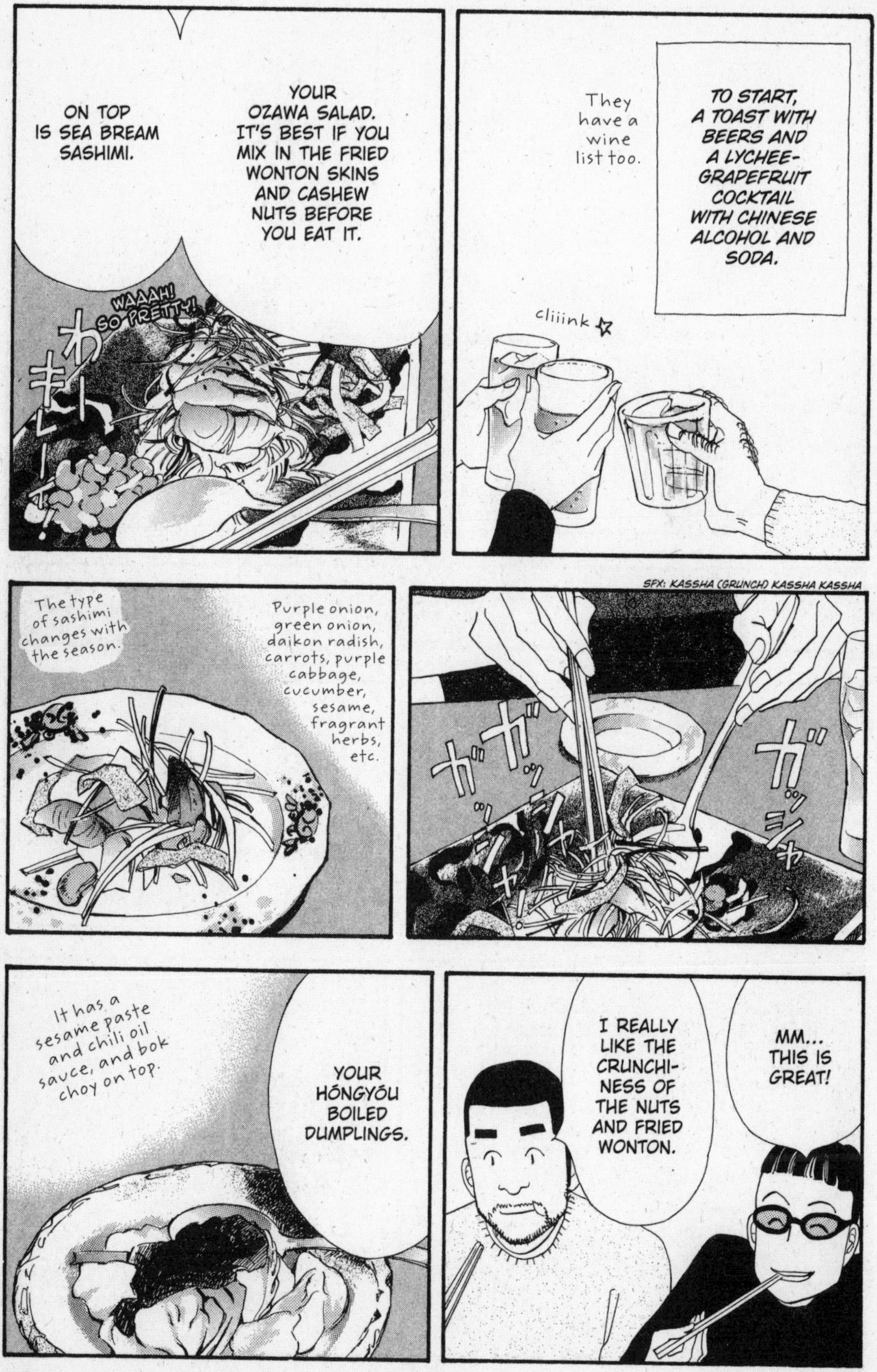
TO START, A TOAST WITH BEERS AND A LYCHEE-GRAPEFRUIT COCKTAIL WITH CHINESE ALCOHOL AND SODA.
They have a wine list too.
cliiink ☆
YOUR OZAWA SALAD. IT'S BEST IF YOU MIX IN THE FRIED WONTON SKINS AND CASHEW NUTS BEFORE YOU EAT IT.
ON TOP IS SEA BREAM SASHIMI.
WAAAH! SO PRETTY!
SFX: KASSHA (GRUNCH) KASSHA KASSHA
Purple onion, green onion, daikon radish, carrots, purple cabbage, cucumber, sesame, fragrant herbs, etc.
The type of sashimi changes with the season.
MM... THIS IS GREAT!
I REALLY LIKE THE CRUNCHINESS OF THE NUTS AND FRIED WONTON.
YOUR HÓNGYÓU BOILED DUMPLINGS.
It has a sesame paste and chili oil sauce, and bok choy on top.

You order this dish for your table, with one prawn for each person.

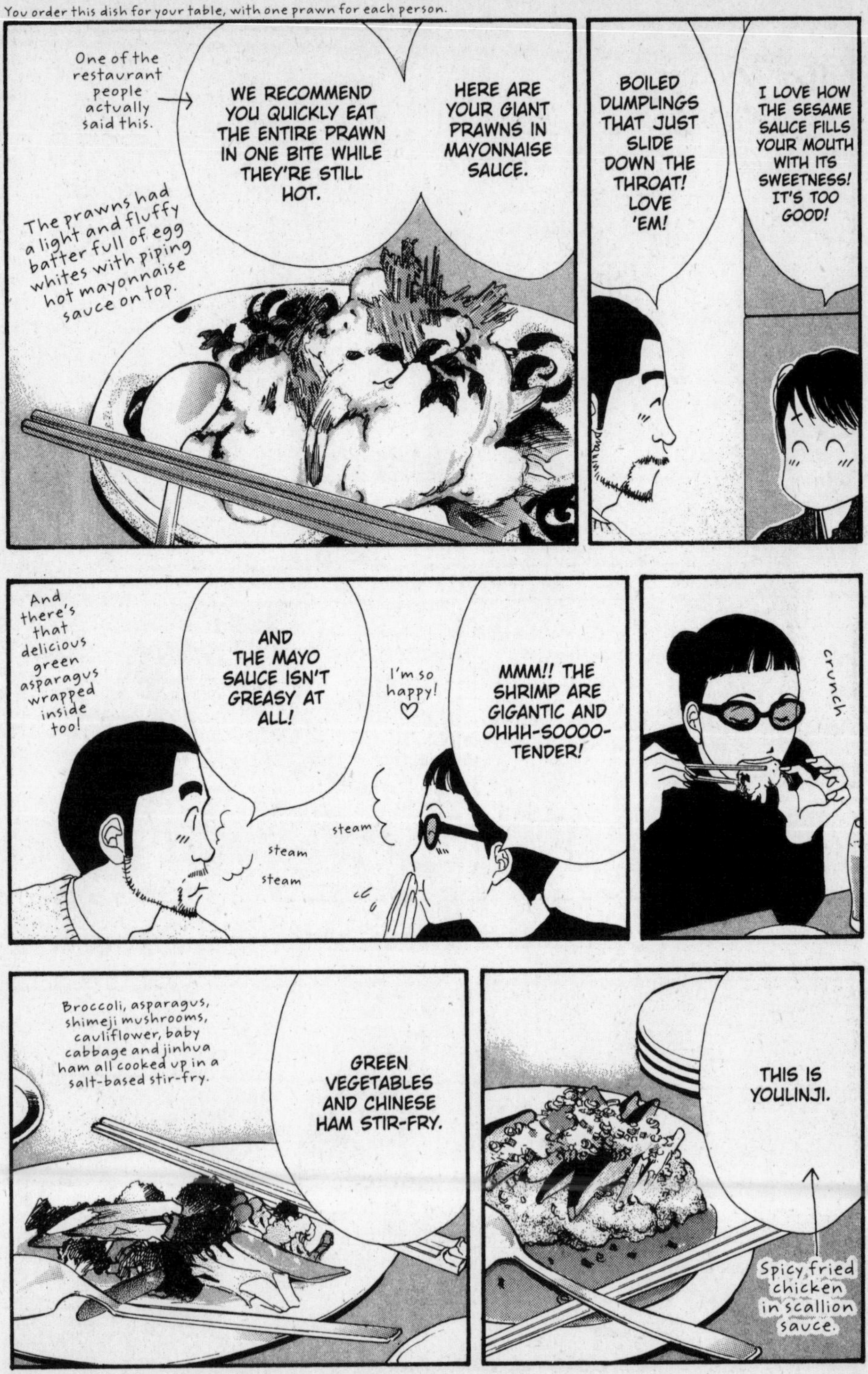

I LOVE HOW THE SESAME SAUCE FILLS YOUR MOUTH WITH ITS SWEETNESS! IT'S TOO GOOD!
BOILED DUMPLINGS THAT JUST SLIDE DOWN THE THROAT! LOVE 'EM!
HERE ARE YOUR GIANT PRAWNS IN MAYONNAISE SAUCE.
WE RECOMMEND YOU QUICKLY EAT THE ENTIRE PRAWN IN ONE BITE WHILE THEY'RE STILL HOT.
One of the restaurant people actually said this.
The prawns had a light and fluffy batter full of egg whites with piping hot mayonnaise sauce on top.
crunch
MMM!! THE SHRIMP ARE GIGANTIC AND OHHH-SOOOO-TENDER!
I'm so happy! ♡
AND THE MAYO SAUCE ISN'T GREASY AT ALL!
And there's that delicious green asparagus wrapped inside too!
steam
steam
steam
THIS IS YOULINJI.
Spicy fried chicken in scallion sauce.
GREEN VEGETABLES AND CHINESE HAM STIR-FRY.
Broccoli, asparagus, shimeji mushrooms, cauliflower, baby cabbage and jinhua ham all cooked up in a salt-based stir-fry.

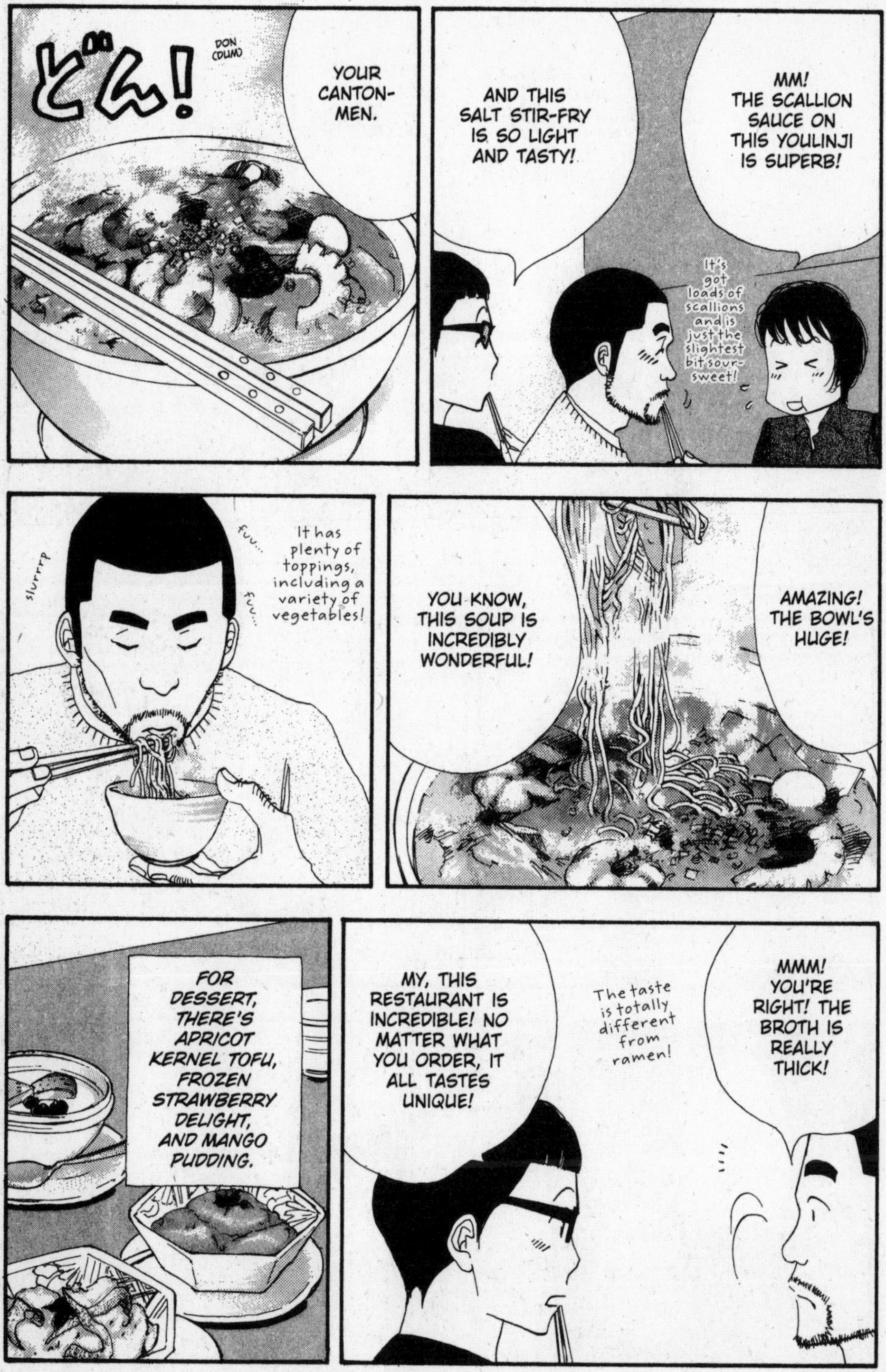
MM! THE SCALLION SAUCE ON THIS YOULINJI IS SUPERB!
It's got loads of scallions and is just the slightest bit sour-sweet!
AND THIS SALT STIR-FRY IS SO LIGHT AND TASTY!
YOUR CANTON-MEN.
DON (DUM)
どん!
AMAZING! THE BOWL'S HUGE!
YOU KNOW, THIS SOUP IS INCREDIBLY WONDERFUL!
It has plenty of toppings, including a variety of vegetables!
fuu... fuu...
slurrrp
MMM! YOU'RE RIGHT! THE BROTH IS REALLY THICK!
The taste is totally different from ramen!
MY, THIS RESTAURANT IS INCREDIBLE! NO MATTER WHAT YOU ORDER, IT ALL TASTES UNIQUE!
FOR DESSERT, THERE'S APRICOT KERNEL TOFU, FROZEN STRAWBERRY DELIGHT, AND MANGO PUDDING.

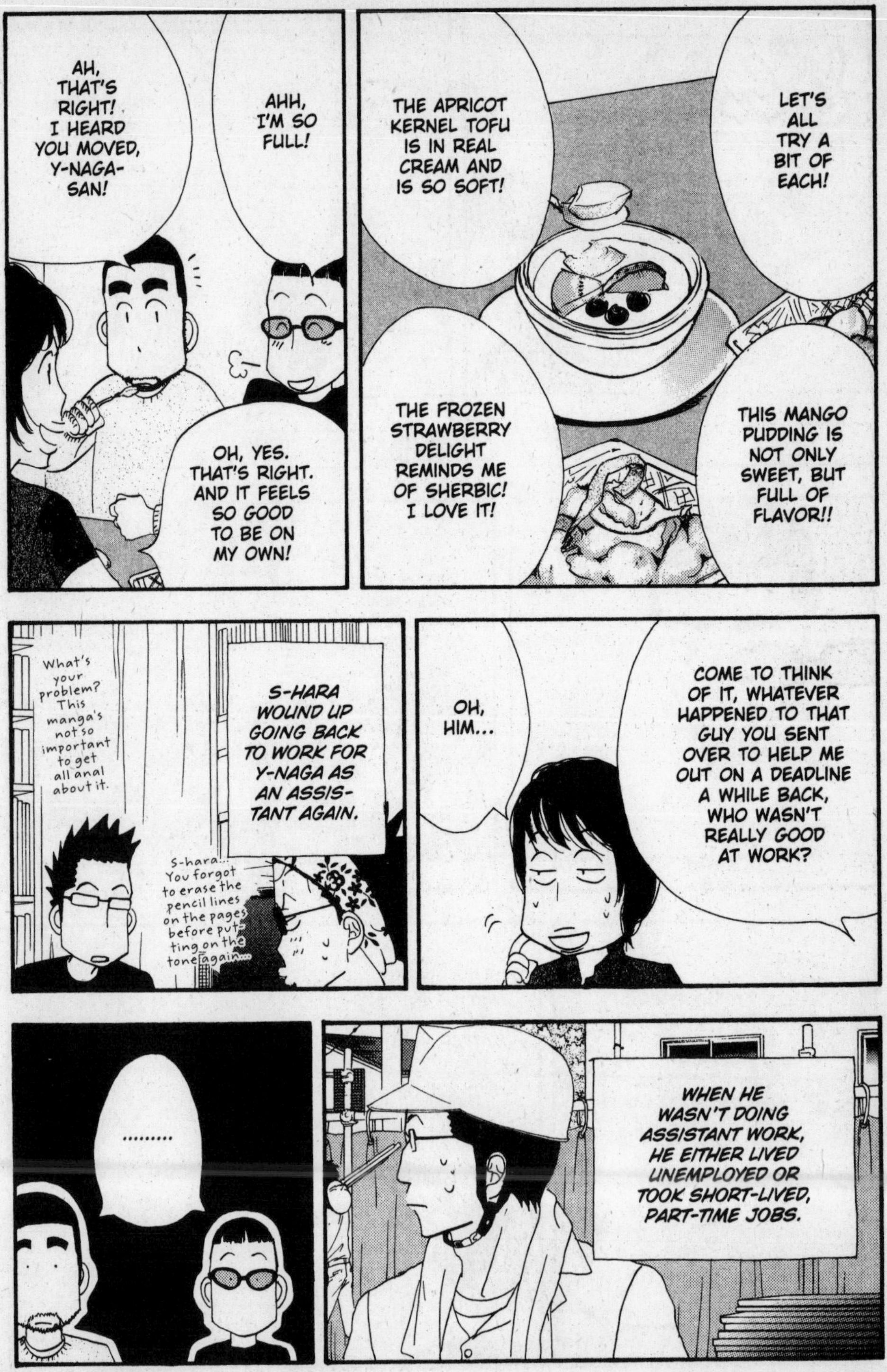
LET'S ALL TRY A BIT OF EACH!
THE APRICOT KERNEL TOFU IS IN REAL CREAM AND IS SO SOFT!
THIS MANGO PUDDING IS NOT ONLY SWEET, BUT FULL OF FLAVOR!!
THE FROZEN STRAWBERRY DELIGHT REMINDS ME OF SHERBIC! I LOVE IT!
AHH, I'M SO FULL!
AH, THAT'S RIGHT! I HEARD YOU MOVED, Y-NAGA-SAN!
OH, YES. THAT'S RIGHT. AND IT FEELS SO GOOD TO BE ON MY OWN!
COME TO THINK OF IT, WHATEVER HAPPENED TO THAT GUY YOU SENT OVER TO HELP ME OUT ON A DEADLINE A WHILE BACK, WHO WASN'T REALLY GOOD AT WORK?
OH, HIM...
S-HARA WOUND UP GOING BACK TO WORK FOR Y-NAGA AS AN ASSISTANT AGAIN.
What's your problem? This manga's not so important to get all anal about it.
S-hara... You forgot to erase the pencil lines on the pages before putting on the tone again...
WHEN HE WASN'T DOING ASSISTANT WORK, HE EITHER LIVED UNEMPLOYED OR TOOK SHORT-LIVED, PART-TIME JOBS.
....

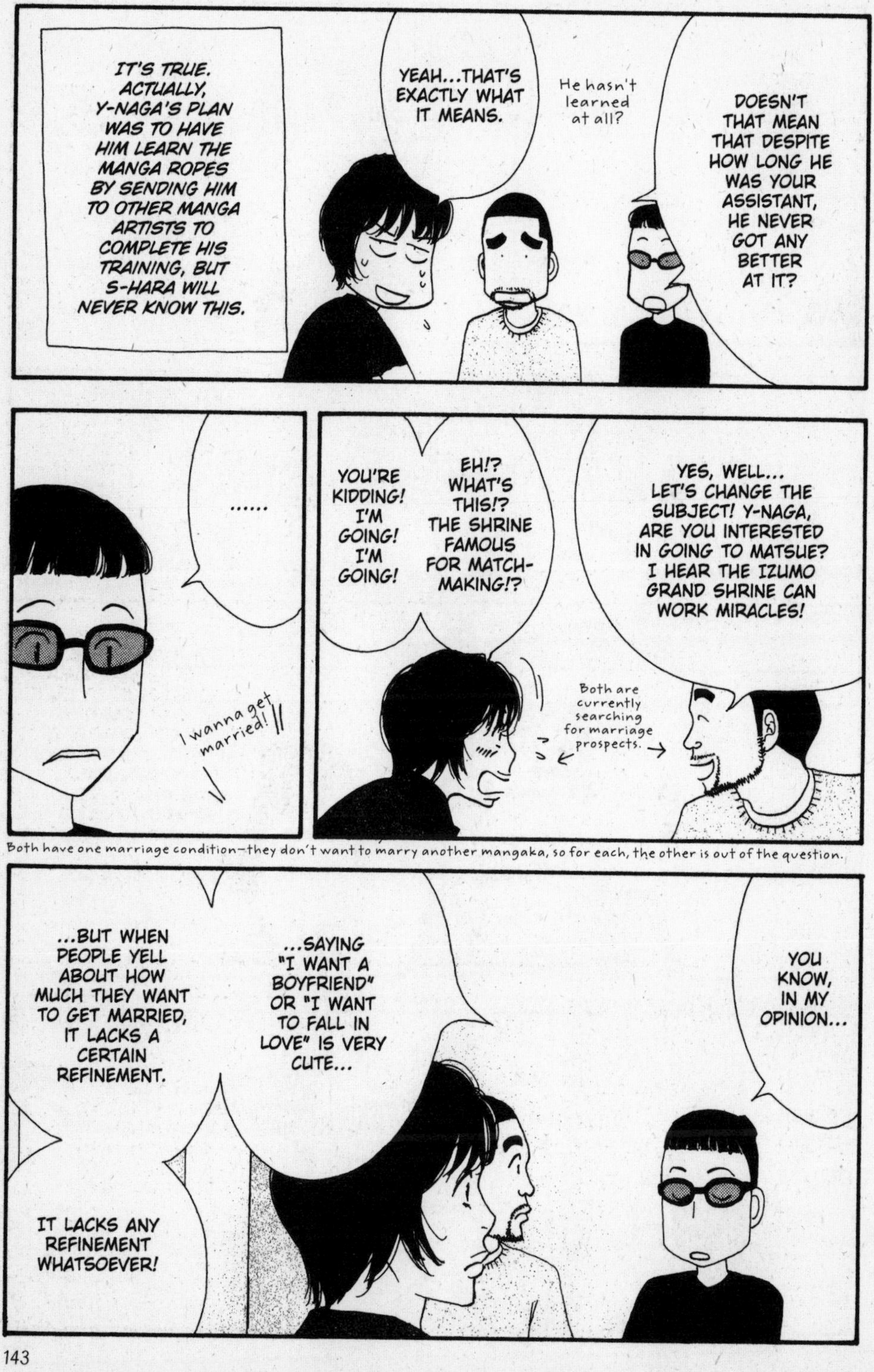
DOESN'T THAT MEAN THAT DESPITE HOW LONG HE WAS YOUR ASSISTANT, HE NEVER GOT ANY BETTER AT IT?
He hasn't learned at all?
YEAH...THAT'S EXACTLY WHAT IT MEANS.
IT'S TRUE. ACTUALLY, Y-NAGA'S PLAN WAS TO HAVE HIM LEARN THE MANGA ROPES BY SENDING HIM TO OTHER MANGA ARTISTS TO COMPLETE HIS TRAINING, BUT S-HARA WILL NEVER KNOW THIS.
YES, WELL... LET'S CHANGE THE SUBJECT! Y-NAGA, ARE YOU INTERESTED IN GOING TO MATSUE? I HEAR THE IZUMO GRAND SHRINE CAN WORK MIRACLES!
EH!? WHAT'S THIS!? THE SHRINE FAMOUS FOR MATCH-MAKING!?
YOU'RE KIDDING! I'M GOING! I'M GOING!
Both are currently searching for marriage prospects.
......
I wanna get married!
Both have one marriage condition—they don't want to marry another mangaka, so for each, the other is out of the question.
YOU KNOW, IN MY OPINION...
...SAYING "I WANT A BOYFRIEND" OR "I WANT TO FALL IN LOVE" IS VERY CUTE...
...BUT WHEN PEOPLE YELL ABOUT HOW MUCH THEY WANT TO GET MARRIED, IT LACKS A CERTAIN REFINEMENT.
IT LACKS ANY REFINEMENT WHATSOEVER!

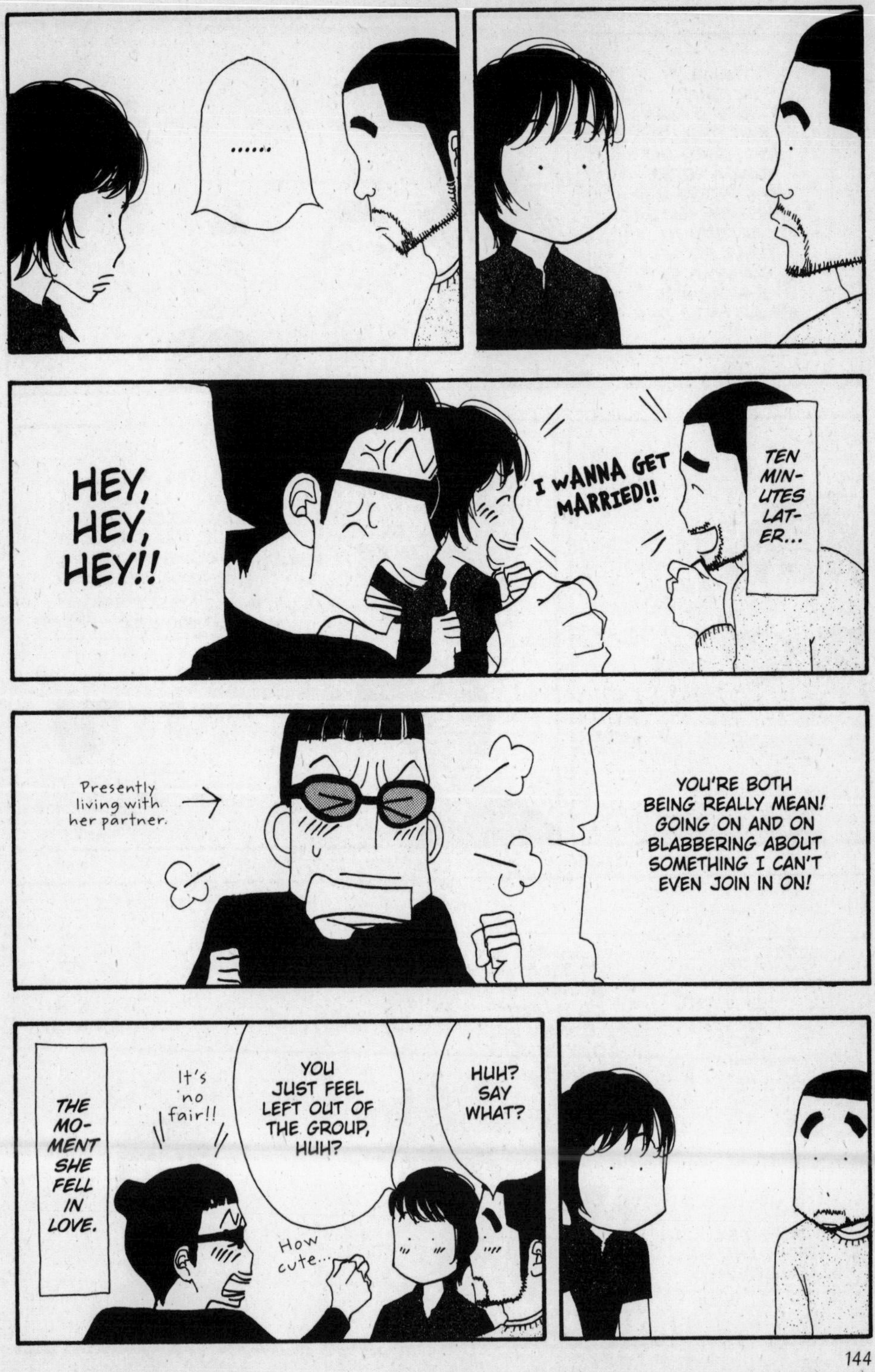
......
TEN MINUTES LATER...
I WANNA GET MARRIED!!
HEY, HEY, HEY!!
YOU'RE BOTH BEING REALLY MEAN! GOING ON AND ON BLABBERING ABOUT SOMETHING I CAN'T EVEN JOIN IN ON!
Presently living with her partner.
HUH? SAY WHAT?
YOU JUST FEEL LEFT OUT OF THE GROUP, HUH?
It's no fair!!
THE MOMENT SHE FELL IN LOVE.
How cute...

Kisurin Ozawa

[Address]
3-32 Asagaya Minami
Suginami-ku, Tokyo
[Telephone]
03-3391-4138
[Hours]
11:00 AM - 3:00 PM
5:00 PM - 11:00 PM
[Closed]
Never.
[Directions]
A five-minute walk from the South Exit of the JR Asagaya Station.
[Parking]
None. (There are paid parking lots nearby.)

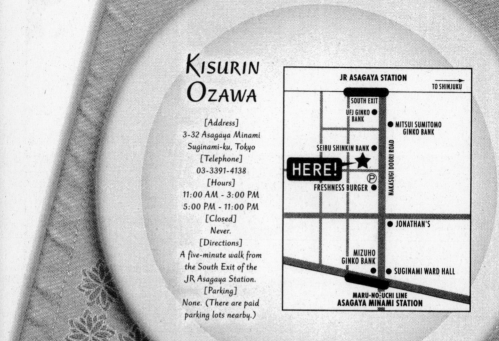

JR ASAGAYA STATION
TO SHINJUKU
SOUTH EXIT
UFJ GINKO BANK
MITSUI SUMITOMO GINKO BANK
SEIBU SHINKIN BANK
HERE!
P
FRESHNESS BURGER
NAKASUGI DOORI ROAD
JONATHAN'S
MIZUHO GINKO BANK
SUGINAMI WARD HALL
MARU-NO-UCHI LINE
ASAGAYA MINAMI STATION

FUMI YOSHINAGA'S COMMENTS

TO HAVE THE SAME KIND OF MEAL AS IN THE MANGA, ACTUALLY YOU NEED ABOUT FOUR OR FIVE PEOPLE IN YOUR GROUP. FOR EVENING MEALS, BUDGET AROUND ¥3,500 TO ¥6,000. ELDERLY COUPLES OR FAMILIES OFTEN COME, AND SO THE RESTAURANT IS LOVED BY A WIDE RANGE OF CUSTOMERS.

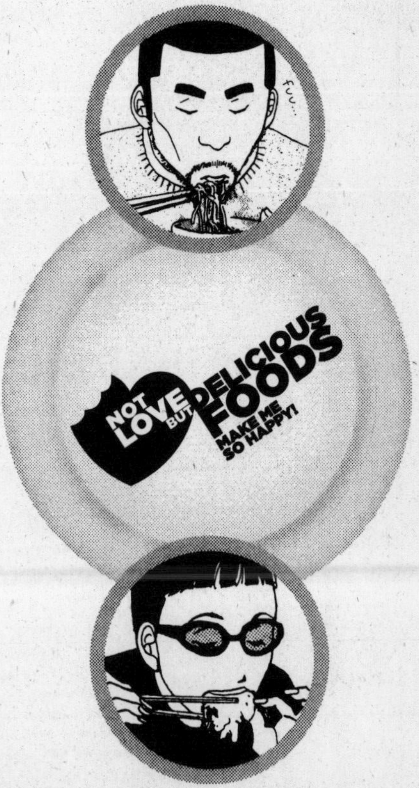
fuu...
NOT LOVE BUT DELICIOUS FOODS
MAKE ME SO HAPPY!

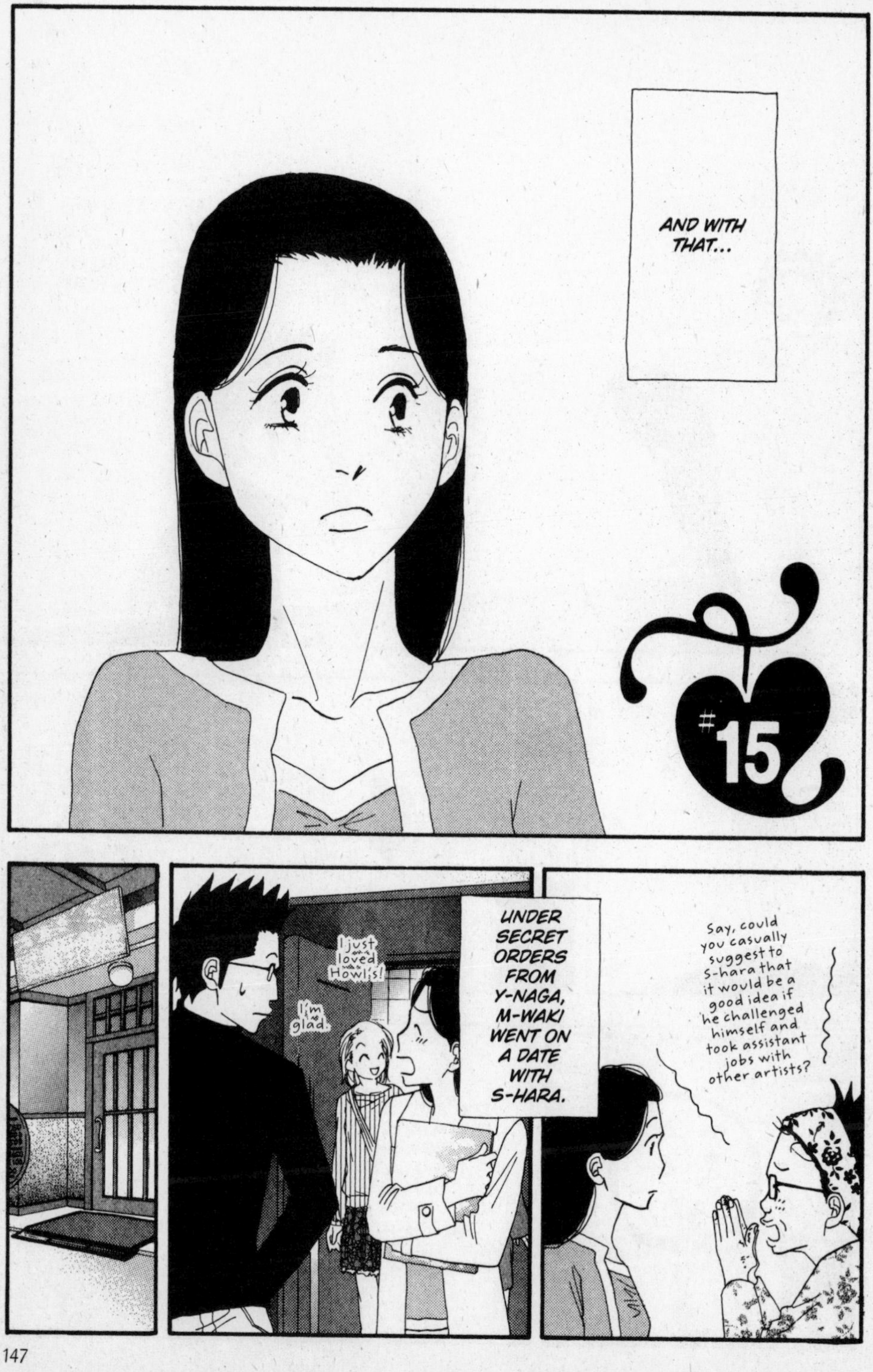
AND WITH THAT...
#15
Say, could you casually suggest to S-hara that it would be a good idea if he challenged himself and took assistant jobs with other artists?
UNDER SECRET ORDERS FROM Y-NAGA, M-WAKI WENT ON A DATE WITH S-HARA.
I just loved Howl's!
I'm glad.

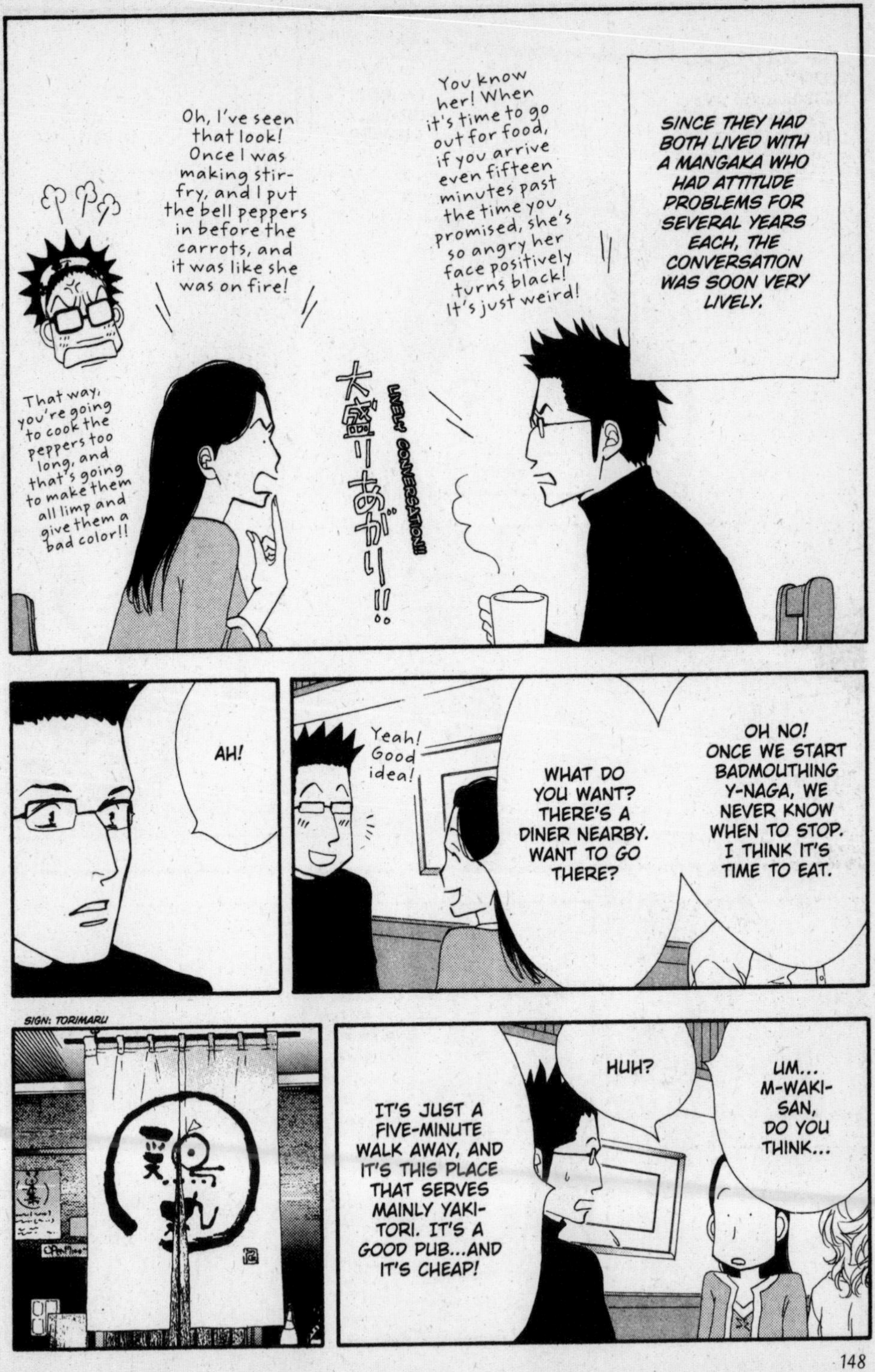
SINCE THEY HAD BOTH LIVED WITH A MANGAKA WHO HAD ATTITUDE PROBLEMS FOR SEVERAL YEARS EACH, THE CONVERSATION WAS SOON VERY LIVELY.
You know her! When it's time to go out for food, if you arrive even fifteen minutes past the time you promised, she's so angry her face positively turns black! It's just weird!
Oh, I've seen that look! Once I was making stir-fry, and I put the bell peppers in before the carrots, and it was like she was on fire!
大盛りあがり!!
LIVELY CONVERSATION!!
That way, you're going to cook the peppers too long, and that's going to make them all limp and give them a bad color!!
OH NO! ONCE WE START BADMOUTHING Y-NAGA, WE NEVER KNOW WHEN TO STOP. I THINK IT'S TIME TO EAT.
WHAT DO YOU WANT? THERE'S A DINER NEARBY. WANT TO GO THERE?
Yeah! Good idea!
AH!
UM... M-WAKI-SAN, DO YOU THINK...
HUH?
IT'S JUST A FIVE-MINUTE WALK AWAY, AND IT'S THIS PLACE THAT SERVES MAINLY YAKI-TORI. IT'S A GOOD PUB...AND IT'S CHEAP!
SIGN: TORIMARU

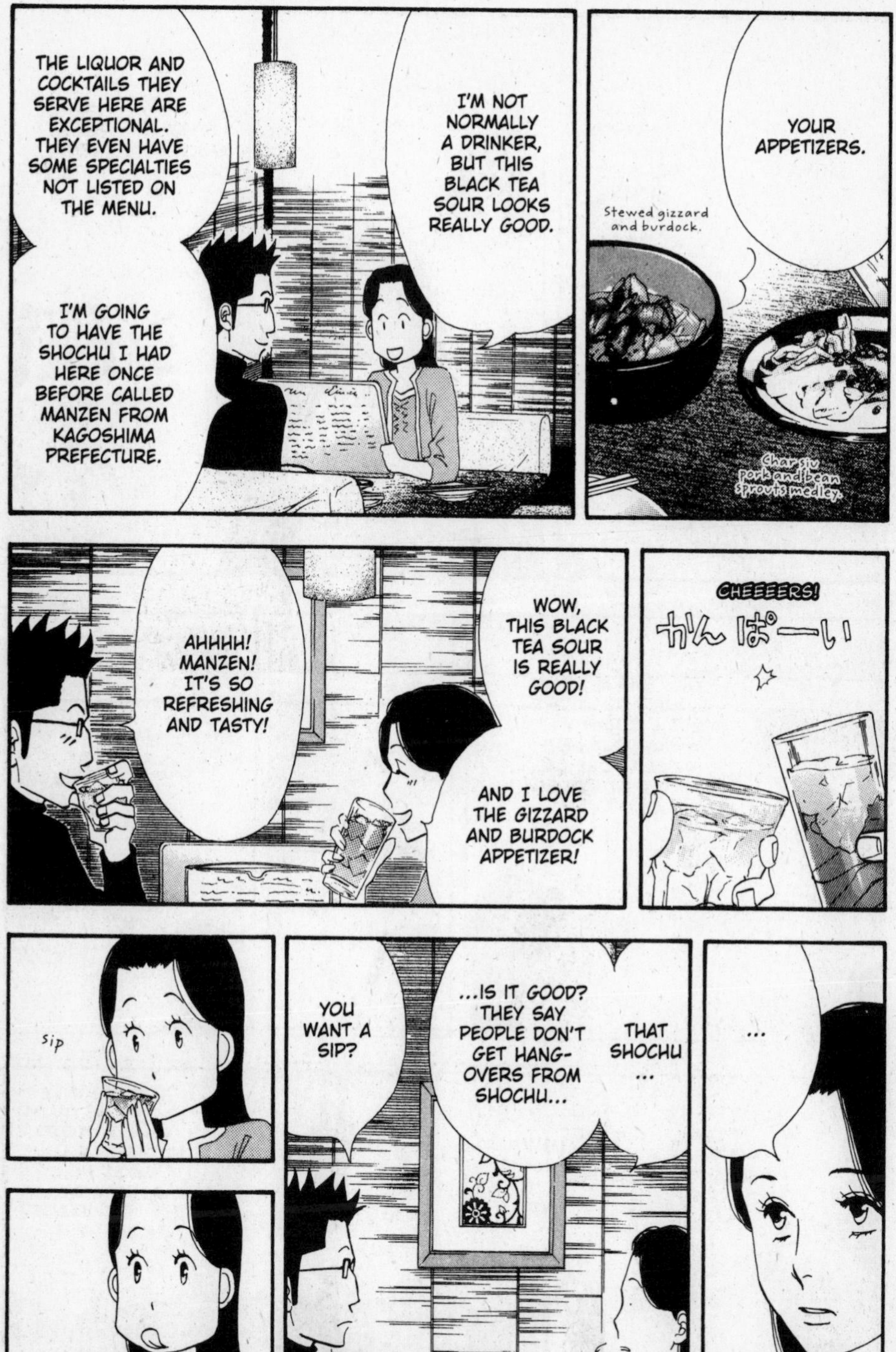
YOUR APPETIZERS.
Stewed gizzard and burdock.
Char siu pork and bean sprouts medley.
I'M NOT NORMALLY A DRINKER, BUT THIS BLACK TEA SOUR LOOKS REALLY GOOD.
THE LIQUOR AND COCKTAILS THEY SERVE HERE ARE EXCEPTIONAL. THEY EVEN HAVE SOME SPECIALTIES NOT LISTED ON THE MENU.
I'M GOING TO HAVE THE SHOCHU I HAD HERE ONCE BEFORE CALLED MANZEN FROM KAGOSHIMA PREFECTURE.
CHEEEERS!
かんぱーい
WOW, THIS BLACK TEA SOUR IS REALLY GOOD!
AHHHH! MANZEN! IT'S SO REFRESHING AND TASTY!
AND I LOVE THE GIZZARD AND BURDOCK APPETIZER!
...
THAT SHOCHU ...
...IS IT GOOD? THEY SAY PEOPLE DON'T GET HANG-OVERS FROM SHOCHU...
YOU WANT A SIP?
sip

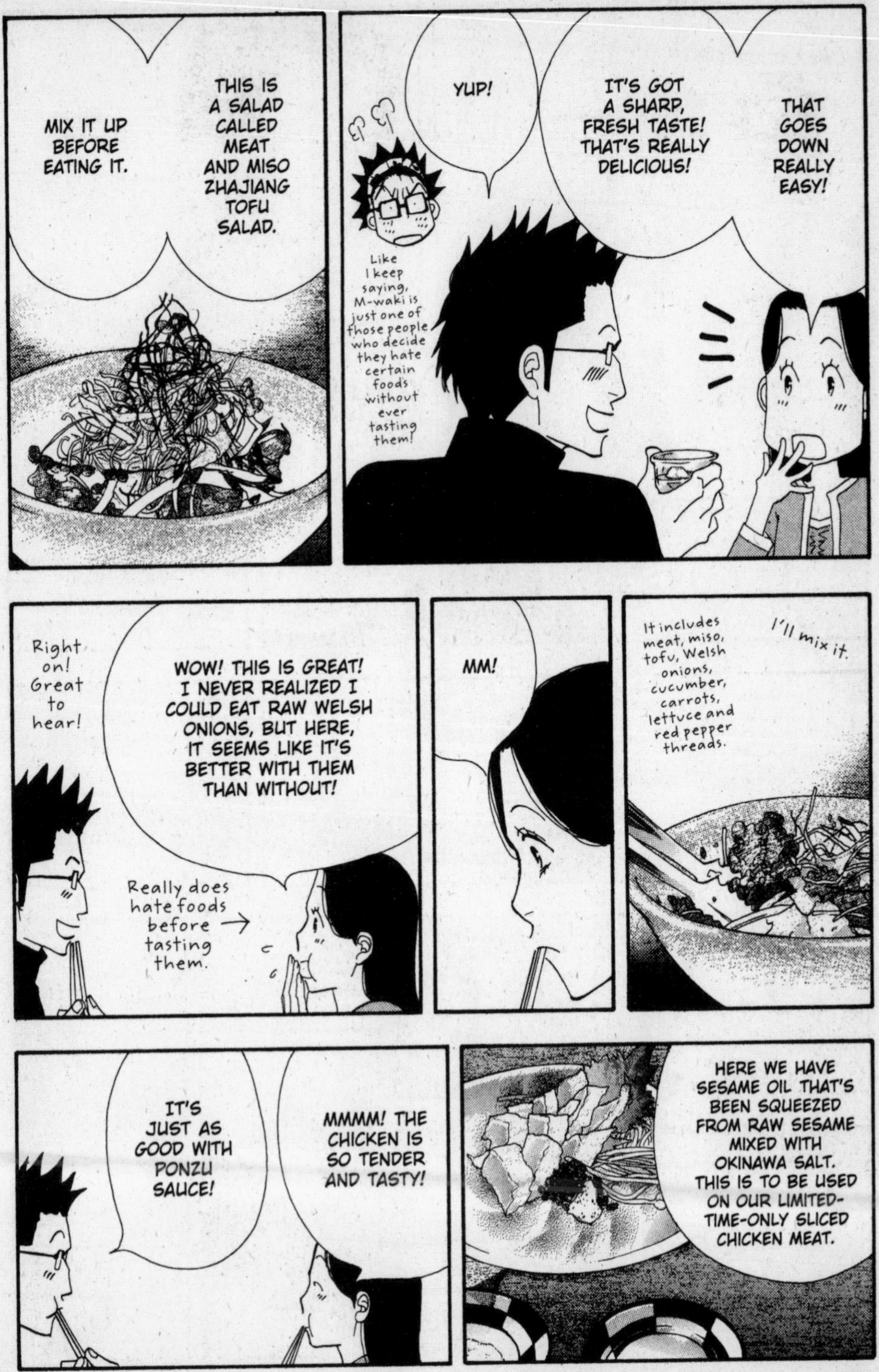
THAT GOES DOWN REALLY EASY!
IT'S GOT A SHARP, FRESH TASTE! THAT'S REALLY DELICIOUS!
YUP!
Like I keep saying, M-waki is just one of those people who decide they hate certain foods without ever tasting them!
THIS IS A SALAD CALLED MEAT AND MISO ZHAJIANG TOFU SALAD.
MIX IT UP BEFORE EATING IT.
I'll mix it.
It includes meat, miso, tofu, Welsh onions, cucumber, carrots, lettuce and red pepper threads.
MM!
WOW! THIS IS GREAT! I NEVER REALIZED I COULD EAT RAW WELSH ONIONS, BUT HERE, IT SEEMS LIKE IT'S BETTER WITH THEM THAN WITHOUT!
Right on! Great to hear!
Really does hate foods before tasting them.
HERE WE HAVE SESAME OIL THAT'S BEEN SQUEEZED FROM RAW SESAME MIXED WITH OKINAWA SALT. THIS IS TO BE USED ON OUR LIMITED-TIME-ONLY SLICED CHICKEN MEAT.
MMMM! THE CHICKEN IS SO TENDER AND TASTY!
IT'S JUST AS GOOD WITH PONZU SAUCE!

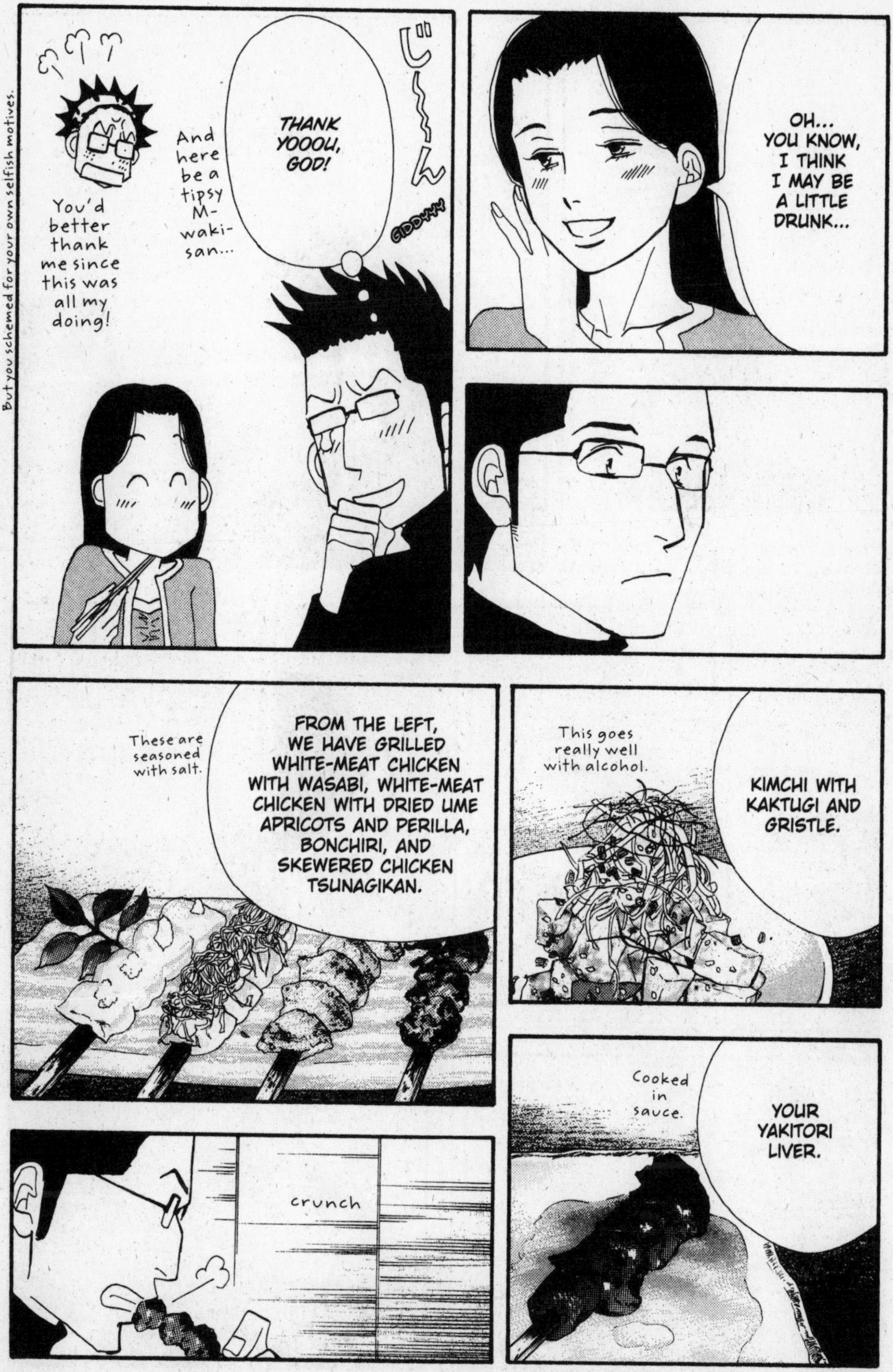
OH... YOU KNOW, I THINK I MAY BE A LITTLE DRUNK...
THANK YOOOU, GOD!
じ〜ん
GIDDYYY
And here be a tipsy M-waki-san...
You'd better thank me since this was all my doing!
But you schemed for your own selfish motives.
KIMCHI WITH KAKTUGI AND GRISTLE.
This goes really well with alcohol.
FROM THE LEFT, WE HAVE GRILLED WHITE-MEAT CHICKEN WITH WASABI, WHITE-MEAT CHICKEN WITH DRIED UME APRICOTS AND PERILLA, BONCHIRI, AND SKEWERED CHICKEN TSUNAGIKAN.
These are seasoned with salt.
YOUR YAKITORI LIVER.
Cooked in sauce.
crunch

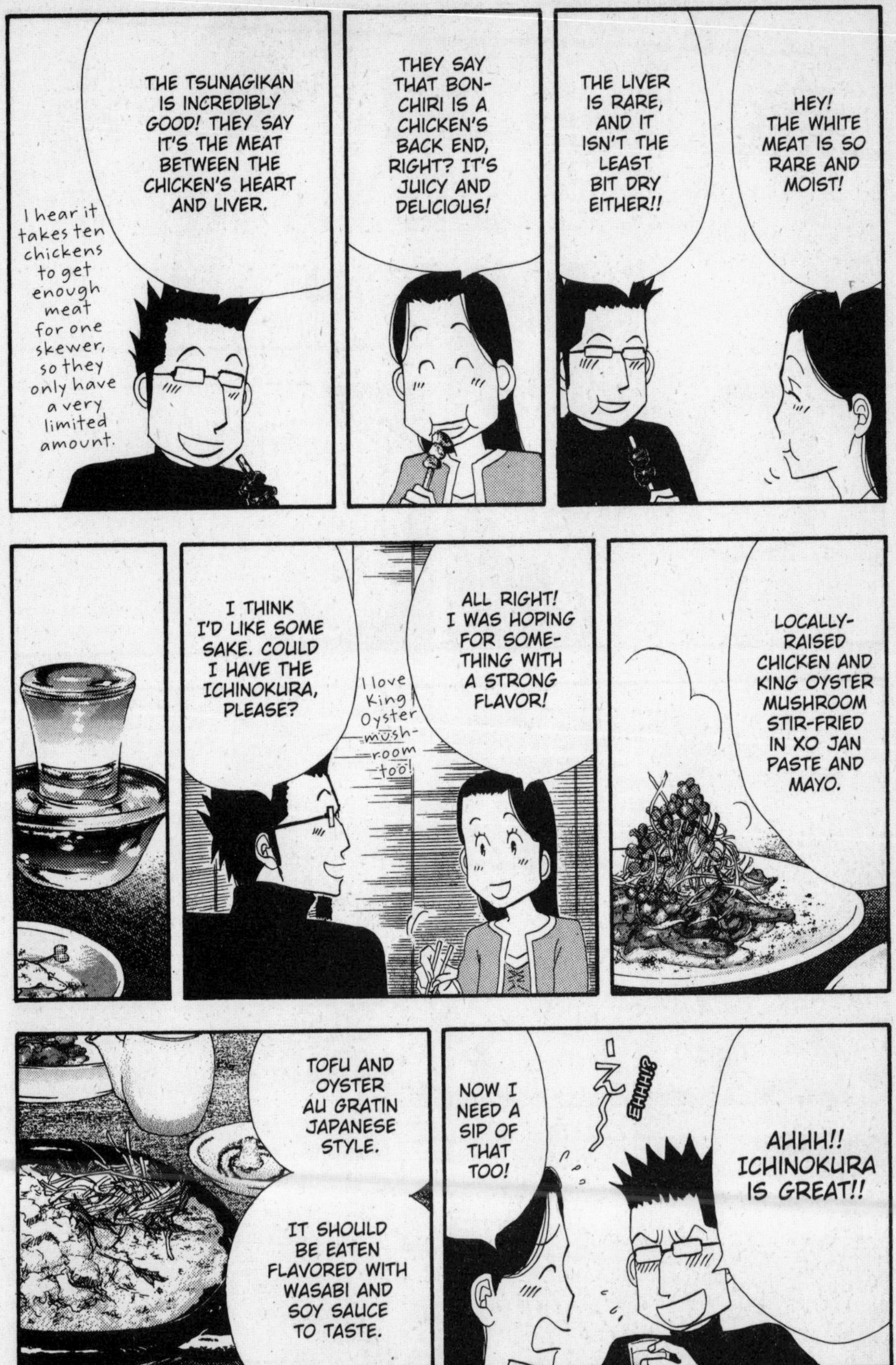
HEY! THE WHITE MEAT IS SO RARE AND MOIST!
THE LIVER IS RARE, AND IT ISN'T THE LEAST BIT DRY EITHER!!
THEY SAY THAT BON-CHIRI IS A CHICKEN'S BACK END, RIGHT? IT'S JUICY AND DELICIOUS!
THE TSUNAGIKAN IS INCREDIBLY GOOD! THEY SAY IT'S THE MEAT BETWEEN THE CHICKEN'S HEART AND LIVER.
I hear it takes ten chickens to get enough meat for one skewer, so they only have a very limited amount.
LOCALLY-RAISED CHICKEN AND KING OYSTER MUSHROOM STIR-FRIED IN XO JAN PASTE AND MAYO.
ALL RIGHT! I WAS HOPING FOR SOME-THING WITH A STRONG FLAVOR!
I love King Oyster mush-room too!
I THINK I'D LIKE SOME SAKE. COULD I HAVE THE ICHINOKURA, PLEASE?
AHHH!! ICHINOKURA IS GREAT!!
EHHH!?
NOW I NEED A SIP OF THAT TOO!
TOFU AND OYSTER AU GRATIN JAPANESE STYLE.
IT SHOULD BE EATEN FLAVORED WITH WASABI AND SOY SAUCE TO TASTE.

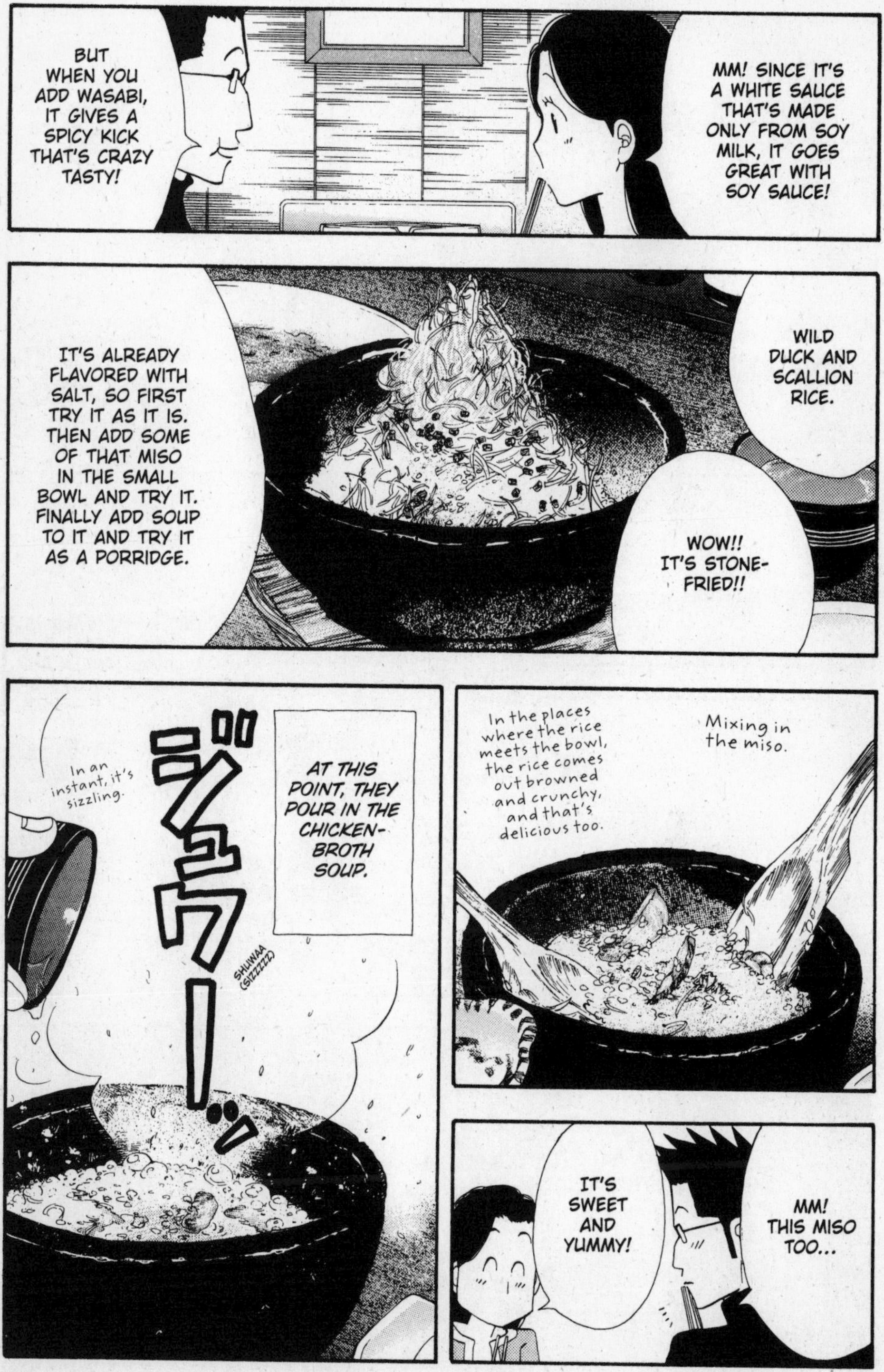
MM! SINCE IT'S A WHITE SAUCE THAT'S MADE ONLY FROM SOY MILK, IT GOES GREAT WITH SOY SAUCE!
BUT WHEN YOU ADD WASABI, IT GIVES A SPICY KICK THAT'S CRAZY TASTY!
WILD DUCK AND SCALLION RICE.
WOW!! IT'S STONE-FRIED!!
IT'S ALREADY FLAVORED WITH SALT, SO FIRST TRY IT AS IT IS. THEN ADD SOME OF THAT MISO IN THE SMALL BOWL AND TRY IT. FINALLY ADD SOUP TO IT AND TRY IT AS A PORRIDGE.
Mixing in the miso.
In the places where the rice meets the bowl, the rice comes out browned and crunchy, and that's delicious too.
MM! THIS MISO TOO...
IT'S SWEET AND YUMMY!
AT THIS POINT, THEY POUR IN THE CHICKEN-BROTH SOUP.
ジュウー
SHUWAA (SIZZZZZ)
In an instant, it's sizzling.

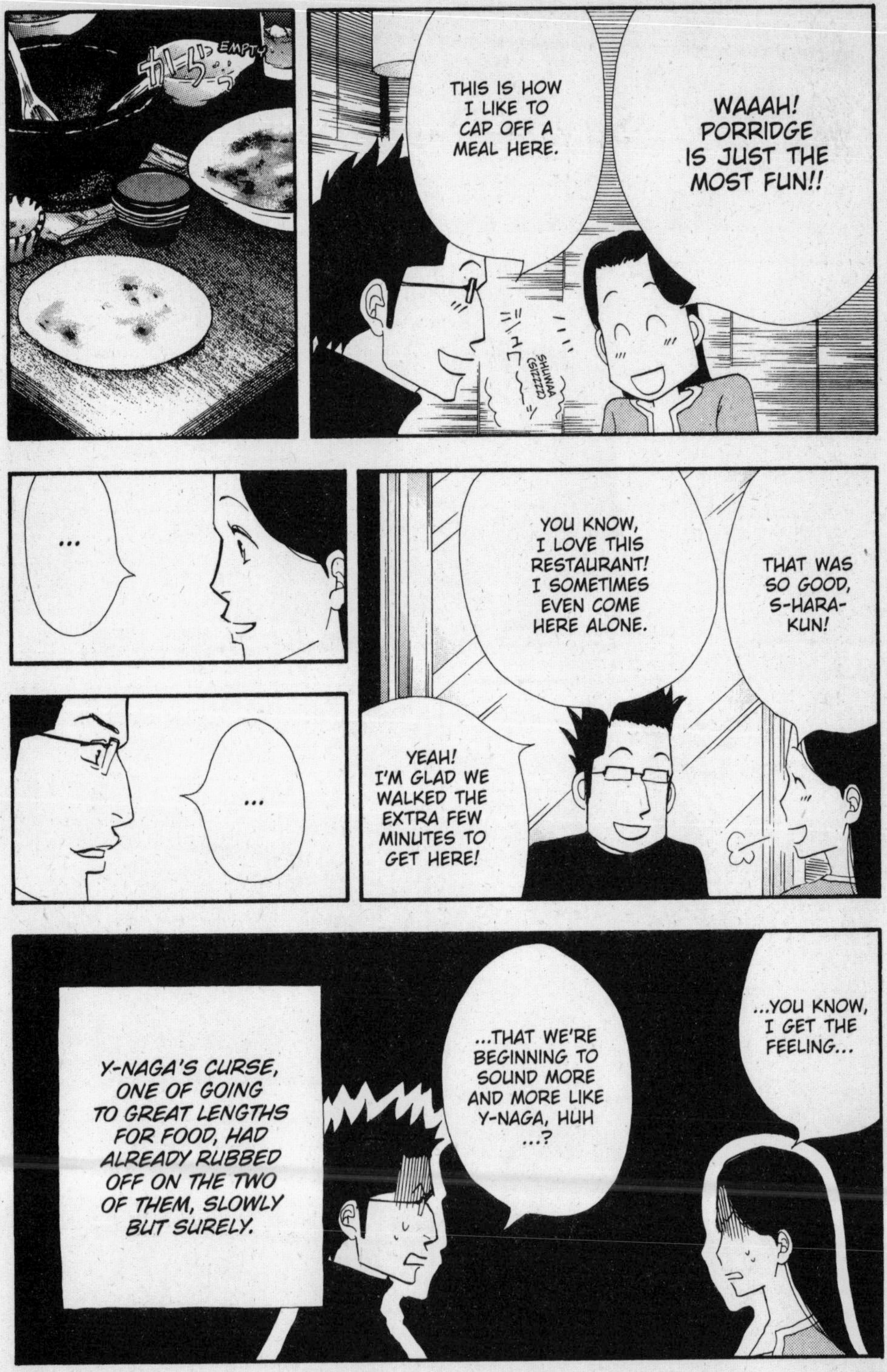
WAAAH! PORRIDGE IS JUST THE MOST FUN!!
THIS IS HOW I LIKE TO CAP OFF A MEAL HERE.
SHUWAA (SIZZZZ)
EMPTY
THAT WAS SO GOOD, S-HARA-KUN!
YOU KNOW, I LOVE THIS RESTAURANT! I SOMETIMES EVEN COME HERE ALONE.
YEAH! I'M GLAD WE WALKED THE EXTRA FEW MINUTES TO GET HERE!
...
...
...YOU KNOW, I GET THE FEELING...
...THAT WE'RE BEGINNING TO SOUND MORE AND MORE LIKE Y-NAGA, HUH ...?
Y-NAGA'S CURSE, ONE OF GOING TO GREAT LENGTHS FOR FOOD, HAD ALREADY RUBBED OFF ON THE TWO OF THEM, SLOWLY BUT SURELY.

Sumibi-Daidokoro Torimaru

[Address] 7th Shimura Building, 1F, 1-9-6 Asagaya Minami, Suginami-ku, Tokyo
[Telephone] 03-5306-0505
[Hours] 5:00 PM - 1:00 AM
[Closed] Thursdays
[Directions] A five-minute walk from the South Exit of the JR Asagaya Station on the JR Chuuou Line. A three-minute walk from Minami Asagaya Station on the Maru-no-Uchi Line.
[Parking] None. (There are paid parking lots nearby.)

NAKASUGI DOORI ROAD
SUZURAN DOORI ROAD
HERE!
NARITA HIGASHI 4
MIZUHO GINKO BANK
SUGINAMI WARD HALL
OME KAIDO ROAD
TO KOUENJI
MARU-NO-UCHI LINE ASAGAYA MINAMI STATION
SUGINAMI NEWSPAPER
7-11
SUGINAMI KEISATSU-SHO MAE

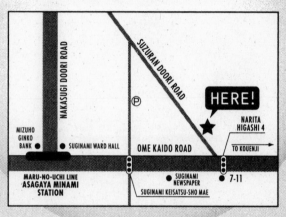

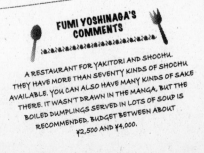

FUMI YOSHINAGA'S COMMENTS

A RESTAURANT FOR YAKITORI AND SHOCHU. THEY HAVE MORE THAN SEVENTY KINDS OF SHOCHU AVAILABLE. YOU CAN ALSO HAVE MANY KINDS OF SAKE THERE. IT WASN'T DRAWN IN THE MANGA, BUT THE BOILED DUMPLINGS SERVED IN LOTS OF SOUP IS RECOMMENDED. BUDGET BETWEEN ABOUT ¥2,500 AND ¥4,000.

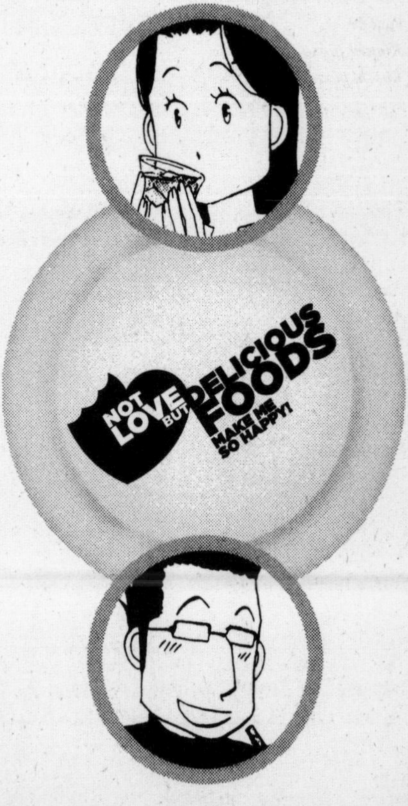
NOT LOVE BUT DELICIOUS FOODS
MAKE ME SO HAPPY!

I would like to express my appreciation to all the restaurants who helped provide material for this book. Thank you so much!

TRANSLATION NOTES

COMMON HONORIFICS

-san: The Japanese equivalent of Mr./Mrs./Miss. If a situation calls for politeness, this is the fail-safe honorific.

-kun: Used most often when referring to boys, this indicates affection or familiarity. Occasionally used by older men among their peers, but it may also be used by anyone referring to a person of lower standing.

-chan: An affectionate honorific indicating familiarity used mostly in reference to girls; also used in reference to cute persons or animals of either gender.

senpai and *kouhai*: Senpai is used to address upperclassmen or more experienced coworkers, kouhai is used in reference to underclassmen or junior coworkers.

no honorific: Indicates familiarity or closeness; if used without permission or reason, addressing someone in this manner would constitute an insult. Although it would be understandable if Y-naga referred to her assistant by name without honorifics (though artists more often use -kun, -chan or -san for assistants), it would be very unusual for S-hara to refer to his boss and senpai without any honorific attached. On the other hand, roommates are generally intimate enough to dispense with the honorifics between themselves. So it's possible that Y-naga and S-hara separate their business from their roommate relationship.

Prices throughout this book are given in Japanese yen. An easy conversion into US dollars is 100 yen per one USD.

Page 7
S-hara, Y-naga F-mi
The Japanese employs a common method of adapting the name of a real person for anonymity's sake. This method uses the initial letter of the first character of the name and attaches a full spelling of the second Chinese character of the name. (As a "random" example, "Y-naga" could refer to the common family name, "Yoshinaga.")

Page 19
Kimchi jjigae
Kimchi jjigae is a Korean-style stew made with kimchi, or fermented vegetables. It is one of the most common Korean dishes, and most of the time it is very thick and spicy.

Page 25
Sukiyaki
A meat dish served in a Japanese hot pot that is slowly cooked at the table. The meat is simmered with a variety of vegetables in a mixture of soy sauce, sugar, and mirin (a sweet sake).

Page 29
Akinoshima
Katsumi Akinoshima was a sumo wrestler known as the "giant killer" for defeating more top-ranked wrestlers than any other wrestler in his class in the history of sumo. His professional career lasted from 1984 to 2003.

Page 33
Peter Barakan
An English actor and long-time Japanese resident who is a popular personality on NHK (public network) radio.

Page 40
Konbujime
A sushi technique in which the raw fish is wrapped in konbu seaweed to infuse the meat with the flavor of the seaweed.

Page 41
Tare
While the word itself is a general term for "sauce" in Japanese, when not specified it generally refers to a sweet soy sauce — a soy sauce base with sugar added — that is usually used for grilled meat, something like teriyaki sauce in the U.S.

Page 42
Edomae
A style of sushi. As the name indicates ("edomae" literally means "Tokyo Bay") it used to refer to sushi made from fish caught in the Tokyo Bay. Nowadays the term has come to mean the general style of sushi served in Tokyo that focuses on the flavor of one ingredient at a time.

Egg Sushi
Egg sushi is the traditional "end of the sushi meal" sushi.

Page 70
Motsunabe
"Motsu" is the Japanese word for animal gizzard. "Nabe," which is the Japanese word for an earthenware pot, is also the name of a dish of boiled meats and vegetables, usually taken from a communal pot in the center of the table, dipped in a sauce, and eaten.

Page 78
Melon-pan, Curry-pan, Yakisoba-pan
"Pan" is the Japanese word for "bread," but it has come to mean any bread-based product like sandwiches or rolls with filling. Melon-pan is a sweetbread that looks vaguely like a cantaloupe melon which may or may not have a very subtle melon flavor. Curry-pan is usually a fried bun that is filled with curry sauce for a sweet/spicy treat. Yakisoba-pan is usually a hot-dog bun-like roll split down the top and filled with yakisoba noodles. All of these breads can be found in any bakery, and buying them at a bakery with many different types of breads is rather like ordering vanilla ice cream at a 31-Flavors-style specialty ice-cream shop.

Page 83
Bakery French Toast
It may sound strange to see this syrupy breakfast-style treat sold at a carry-out bakery, but they have managed to make a French Toast that does not run or drip.

Page 87
Goukon
These meetings of multiple (usually three to six) unmarried men with an equal number of unmarried women have become very popular in Japan in the past decade or so. Generally at these meetings, couples pair off for a while, then switch partners so that each man/woman combination has at least a little bit of face time to make an impression.

Page 92
Augusta
I-ta's guess is right. Augusta is the name of the agency that represents the two singers he mentioned. In Japan, it often happens that one agency represents a certain style of entertainer. For example, Johnny's is famous for representing pretty-boy entertainers and Yoshimoto is famous for representing comedians who got their start in Osaka. So identifying singers by their agency is not an unusual occurence.

Page 97
I-ta-pyon
There are many variations on the honorific "-chan." One of the odder ones is "-pyon," which is also used for a bunny hopping.

Page 104
Gatsunto Mikan
Gatsunto Mikan is a popular frozen treat in Japan. It is as if a can of mikan oranges has been frozen and put on a stick, something like an orange popsicle. Because no cream is added, the flavor is simple and crisp, like that of shaved ice.

Page 119
Crab Shinjo
Steamed crab-meatballs.

Page 120
Sudachi
A lemon-like citrus fruit.

Page 122
Ponzu Sauce and *Momiji-oroshi*
Ponzu sauce is a citrus-based sauce popular in Japan, and *momiji-oroshi* is shredded daikon radish mixed with either chili or carrots, giving it a reddish look that is a little like the red Japanese maple leaves for which it is named.

Page 138
F-mio
Names ending in a vowel the "*o*" (Hideo, Yoshio, etc.) sound like "male" names in the same way that names ending in "*ko*" sound like female names.

Page 149
Sake, *shochu*
The biggest difference between these two Japanese alcohols is that sake (or, more correctly, *nihonshu*) is brewed, while *shochu* is a distilled liquor.

Page 152
Rare chicken
Rare chicken sounds like a health hazard, but remember that there is such a thing as chicken sashimi (sliced raw chicken). Most likely, this restaurant uses sashimi-style chicken for its rare chicken dishes.

NOT LOVE BUT DELICIOUS FOODS MAKE ME SO HAPPY

FUMI YOSHINAGA

Translation: William Flanagan

AI GA NAKUTEMO KUTTE YUKEMASU © Fumi Yoshinaga 2005. All rights reserved. First published in Japan in 2005 by Ohta Publishing Co., Tokyo. English translation rights arranged with Ohta Publishing Co., Tokyo through Tuttle-Mori Agency, Inc., Tokyo.

Translation © 2010 by Hachette Book Group, Inc.

Yen Press
Hachette Book Group
237 Park Avenue, New York, NY 10017

www.HachetteBookGroup.com
www.YenPress.com

Yen Press is an imprint of Hachette Book Group, Inc.
The Yen Press name and logo are trademarks of Hachette Book Group, Inc.

First Yen Press Edition: November 2010

ISBN: 978-0-7595-3187-1

10 9 8 7 6 5 4 3 2 1

BVG

Printed in the United States of America

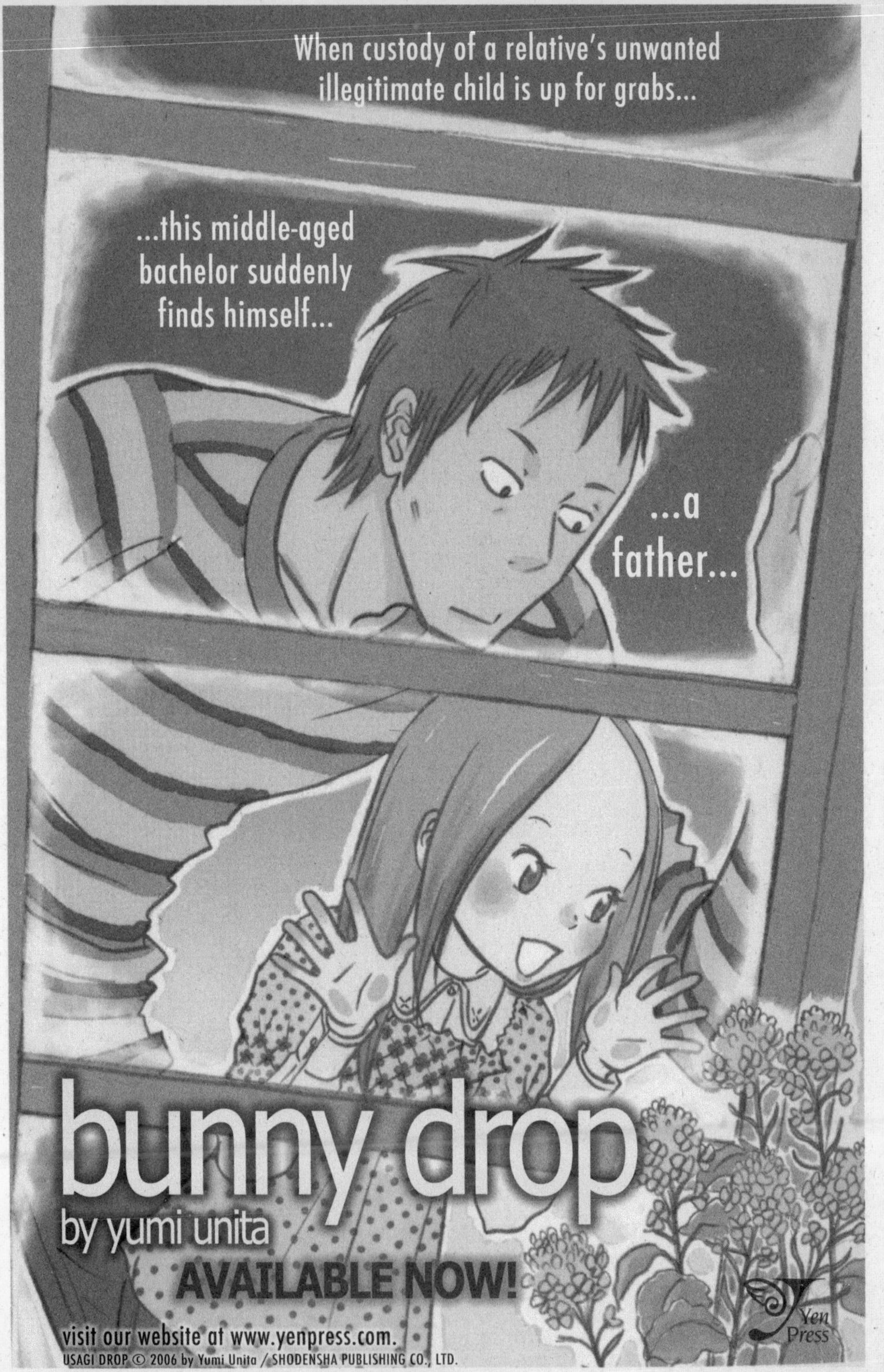
When custody of a relative's unwanted illegitimate child is up for grabs...
...this middle-aged bachelor suddenly finds himself...
...a father...
bunny drop
by yumi unita
AVAILABLE NOW!
visit our website at www.yenpress.com.
USAGI DROP © 2006 by Yumi Unita / SHODENSHA PUBLISHING CO., LTD.
Yen Press